Ben J. Catanzaro

Editor

D1556471

The SPARC
Technical Papers

Springer-Verlag
New York   Berlin   Heidelberg   London   Paris
Tokyo   Hong Kong   Barcelona   Budapest

Ben J. Catanzaro
Sun Microsystems, Inc.
Mountain View, CA 94043

© 1991 by Sun Microsystems, Inc.

Library of Congress Cataloging-in-Publication Data
The SPARC technical papers / Ben J. Catanzaro, editor.
    p. cm. -- (Sun technical reference library)
  Includes bibliographical references and index.
  ISBN 0-387-97634-5 (acid free paper)
  1. Computer architecture. 2. System design. I. Catanzaro, Ben
J. II. Series.
QA76.9.A73S65 1991   91-21275
621.39--dc20

Sun Microsystems, Inc. has reviewed the contents of this book prior to final publication. The book does not necessarily represent the views, opinions, or product strategies of Sun or its subsidiaries. Neither Sun nor Springer-Verlag are responsible for its contents or its accuracy, and therefore make no representations or warranties with respect to it. Sun believes, however, that it presents accurate and valuable information to the interested reader, as of the time of publication.

Sun Microsystems and the Sun logo are registered trademarks of Sun Microsystems, Inc. Catalyst, DVMA, NDE, NETdisk, NeWS, NFS, NSE, ONC, OpenFonts, Open Systems Network, OpenWindows, PC-NFS, Pixrect, SPE, STTYTOOL, Sun-2, Sun-3, Sun-4, Sun386i, SunCGI, Sun Common Lisp, SunGuide, SunGKS, SunIPC, SunLink, SunNet, SunOS, SunPro, SunPHIGS, SunServer, SunTechnology, SunView, SunWindows, TAAC-1, Sun Workstation ®, as well as the word "Sun" followed by a numerical suffix and XView are trademarks of Sun Microsystems, Inc. SPARC is a registered trademark of SPARC International, Inc. SPARCstation, SPARCserver, SPARCengine, SPARCsim, SPARCmon, and SPARCware are trademarks of SPARC International, Inc., licensed exclusively to Sun Microsystems, Inc. Products bearing the SPARC trademark are based on an architecture developed by Sun Microsystems, Inc. AT&T ® is a registered trademark of American Telephone and Telegraph. UNIX ® and UNIX System V ® are registered trademarks of UNIX System Laboratories, Inc. OPEN LOOK is a trademark of AT&T. VAX and VMS are trademarks of Digital Equipment Corporation. System/370 is a trademark of International Business Machines Corporation. MS-DOS is a registered trademark of Microsoft Corporation. Ada ® is a registered trademark of U.S. Government, Ada Joint Program Office. Ethernet is a trademark of Xerox Corporation. All other products or services mentioned in this document are identified by the trademarks or service marks of their respective companies or organizations. The use of general descriptive names, trademarks, etc., in this publication, even if the former are not especially identified, is not to be taken as a sign that such names, as understood by the Trademarks and Merchandise Act, may accordingly be used freely by anyone. The Network Information Service (NIS) was formerly known as Sun Yellow Pages. The functionality of the two remains the same, only the name has changed. The name Yellow Pages is a registered trademark in the United Kingdom of British Telecommunications plc and may not be used without permission.

Typeset by TCSystems, Inc., Shippensburg, PA.
Printed and bound by R.R. Donnelley & Sons, Harrisonburg, VA.
Printed in the United States of America

9 8 7 6 5 4 3 2 1 Printed on acid-free paper.

ISBN 0-387-97634-5 Springer-Verlag New York Berlin Heidelberg
ISBN 3-540-97634-5 Springer-Verlag Berlin Heidelberg New York

SUN TECHNICAL REFERENCE LIBRARY

James Gosling, David S. H. Rosenthal, and Michelle J. Arden
*The NeWS Book: An Introduction to the Network/extensible
Window System*

Mark Hall and John Barry (eds.)
The Sun Technology Papers

Michael Russo
A New User's Guide to the Sun Workstation

John R. Corbin
*The Art of Distributed Applications: Programming Techniques for
Remote Procedure Calls*

George Becker and Kathy Slattery
A System Administrator's Guide to Sun Workstations

Ben J. Catanzaro (ed.)
The SPARC Technical Papers

Preface

With the SPARC (Scalable Processor ARChitecture) architecture and system software as the underlying foundation, Sun Microsystems is delivering a new model of computing—easy workgroup computing—to enhance the way people work, automating processes across groups, departments, and teams locally and globally.

Sun and a large and growing number of companies in the computer industry have embarked on a new approach to meet the needs of computer users and system developers in the 1990s. Originated by Sun, the approach targets users who need a range of compatible computer systems with a variety of application software and want the option to buy those systems from a choice of vendors. The approach also meets the needs of system developers to be part of a broad, growing market of compatible systems and software—developers who need to design products quickly and cost-effectively.

The SPARC approach ensures that computer systems can be easy to use for all classes of users and members of the workgroup, end users, system administrators, and software developers. For the end user, the SPARC technologies facilitate system set-up and the daily use of various applications. For the system administrator supporting the computer installation, setting up and monitoring the network are easier. For the software developer, there are advanced development tools and support. Furthermore, the features of the SPARC hardware and software technologies ensure that SPARC systems and applications play an important role in the years to come.

The SPARC Evolution

To oversee and guide the SPARC evolution, SPARC International, an independent, non-profit corporation, was founded in 1989. Its members are software, hardware, and microprocessor vendors, distributors and users who are committed to the SPARC architecture and want to influence its evolution as an open standard.

SPARC International's charter is to direct the evolution of the SPARC architecture, ensure binary compatibility among all SPARC system implementations, support the compatibility of application software for SPARC systems, and serve the technical and information needs of the SPARC community.

To ensure that SPARC products are binary compatible, SPARC International's Compatibility and Compliance Committee established the SPARC Compliance Definition (SCD), a specification of common interfaces. By developing systems and software that conform to the SCD, SPARC system vendors and application developers ensure that their products are binary compatible and interoperable; they are "SPARC-compliant." The interfaces specified in the SCD are the common elements of a network-wide software environment, which includes the operating system, window system, network services, graphics libraries, and toolkits. The SPARC Compliance Definition 2.0 is a formal definition of SPARC system and software requirements for compatibility with SVR4 and the SVR4/SPARC microprocessor-specific Application Binary Interface (ABI).

Included with SPARC International's program is the formation of the P1754 working group. Established by the IEEE Computer Society Microprocessor Standards Committee, P1754 is to sponsor a microprocessor standard based on the SPARC microprocessor architecture.

SPARC Technology

Since the 1989 introduction of the SPARCstation 1 by Sun Microsystems, the SPARC architecture has demonstrated its importance in the evolution of desktop computing. Before the SPARCstation, SPARC technology was used in high-end servers and engineering workstations. The power of a personal mainframe was available only for those professionals in highly specialized fields, such as electronic design and securities trading.

The advent of the low-cost SPARCstation product family

eliminated the price distinction that had previously barred work-stations from the mass market. Users previously limited to PCs because of cost could take advantage of the high-level of performance and associated productivity increases that the SPARC-station afforded.

With the success of the SPARCstation came the beginning of a mass market for RISC computers. SPARC desktop computers have become the third most popular desktop solution behind the IBM PC-compatible and Apple Macintosh platforms. Recognizing that SPARC systems make up a new class of computing, application software developers began delivering a wide-range of applications for the SPARC desktop and server systems.

In particular, popular personal productivity application software, traditionally supported only on PC-compatibles, moved to the SPARCstation. Applications such as Lotus 1-2-3 and Informix Wingz in spreadsheets, WordPerfect in word processing, Ashton-Tate dBase IV in database management, and Ventura Publisher in publishing are among the popular personal productivity applications for SPARC systems. These packages are part of a list of technical and commercial applications from vendors such as SAS, Mentor Graphics, and Interleaf.

Furthering the migration of software to SPARC systems is the assurance from SPARC International's "SPARC-compliant" designation for products that run unchanged on all SPARC-compliant systems, regardless of size, vendor, or configuration. Similar to the development of shrinkwrap (or "off-the'shelf") software for the PC-compatible industry, the SPARC-compliant market will see the volume distribution of compatible software applications for SVR4/SPARC systems.

The SPARC Architecture

The SPARC architecture, designed by Sun, is the cornerstone of this approach to network computing for the 1990s. Based on RISC (reduced instruction set computer) technology, the SPARC architecture and system software are the underlying building blocks for a range of compatible computer systems from laptop computers to supercomputers. These building block technologies are all openly available to system developers, who can use them to bring to market competitive products that address specific customer needs without sacrificing compatibility.

Three characteristics of the SPARC architecture and system software are of particular significance to the continuing success of this approach to computing.

1. The SPARC building block technologies are open: the essential pieces are available to system vendors from multiple sources. These building block technologies include the SPARC architecture and a comprehensive operating environment made up of: SunOS, a version of the UNIX operating system; OpenWindows, windowing environment, based on the icon-based OPEN LOOK℠ graphical user interface, the X11/NeWS window system, OpenFonts, and ONC/NFS, the de facto distributing computing standard.

   Because the SPARC architecture is open, multiple semiconductor vendors and system vendors can simultaneously design SPARC products. With most RISC and CISC (complex instruction set computer) architectures, one company controls the design, rate of innovation and price of the microprocessor. System developers using such architectures are tied to the innovation rate and price offered by that one company.

   The SPARC approach encourages multiple semiconductor vendors—with multiple areas of expertise—to accelerate the rate of innovation and offer different implementations and competitively priced SPARC chips.

   System developers can take advantage of a variety of SPARC chip suppliers and SPARC software and hardware technology to implement a broad range of compatible systems. They can reduce development costs and shorten time to market by leveraging existing SPARC hardware and software technologies.

2. The SPARC building block technologies are scalable: the SPARC architecture in particular is scalable across a range of semiconductor technologies, SPARC chip implementations, and system configurations. It is the combination of

semiconductor scalability and architectural scalability that permits SPARC system vendors to design laptop computers, desktop computers, high-end multiprocessor systems and supercomputers that all run the same software applications.

Semiconductor vendors have designed SPARC chips using a variety of technologies (refer to the SPARC implementations section), including CMOS, BiCMOS, ECL and gallium arsenide. SPARC implementations have scaled from 10 MIPS (millions of instructions per second) in the first SPARC implementation designed in 1987 to the current 29-MIPS CMOS and 65-MIPS ECL implementations. Under development are SPARC CMOS processor implementations that will offer 50–60 MIPS and gallium arsenide implementations offering up to 250 MIPS within the next two years.

3. The SPARC building block technologies are standard: SPARC-computer systems have been shipped in volume. System shipments to date place the SPARC architecture as the number three volume desktop architecture behind the IBM PC-compatible and Apple Macintosh platforms.

Since its introduction in 1987, the SPARC architecture has become the dominant RISC architecture in the industry, and it is the only RISC processor to date with established volume system shipments. By late 1990, Sun alone had shipped more than 160,000 SPARC systems. Sun estimates that it will have shipped more than 500,000 SPARC systems by late 1991. Growing volumes are expected as other SPARC system developers bring their products to market in 1991 and 1992.

This market momentum is similar in part to the development of the IBM PC-compatible market, in which the availability of applications drove increasing system volumes, which in turn attracted more applications. However, the SPARC market differs from the PC-compatible market because SPARC technology is scalable and openly available. In addition, the binary compatibility of SPARC systems is ensured through several programs sponsored by

SPARC International. As a result, the SPARC market will meet the needs of a broader range of users than the PC-compatible market by delivering a wider range of price/performance options and software. Applications that run on a SPARC laptop also run on SPARC desktop computers, SPARC deskside systems, to supercomputers and on up the performance scale.

The SPARC Technical Papers

This book offers the most comprehensive technical assessment available of the SPARC state-of-the-art. Each paper is written by the expert(s) in the area covered. The book is divided into six sections. Section I covers the system architecture, discussing everything from an overview of scalable architecture to why RISC "has won" over CISC technology.

Section II provides detail on the SPARC implementations that have been developed to date. Everything from custom CMOS products to ECL implementations are covered in detail. In Section III SPARC development tools are presented. Compilers, real-time environments, and embedded system tools are discussed by the leading developers inside and outside of Sun.

Section IV offers a formal look at the system software that gives SPARC its reference point to the outside world. Key developers, S. Kleiman and D. Williams, present their views and two SPARC International White Papers are included. Section V discusses the SPARC system configuration, including the SBus and MBus.

Section VI is unique for a technical book, but it is vital for understanding the significance of SPARC. Here, the SPARC licensing policy is presented. Combined with the technical information in the previous sections, a SPARC developer or a would-be developer will grasp the full implications that SPARC means for the future of the computer industry.

Ben Catanzaro
Palo Alto, California
June 1991

Contents

Contributors

F. Abu Nofal
Anant Agrawal
Christopher Aoki
Kenji B. Armstrong
Max Baron
S. Barton
Andreas Bechtolsheim
Douglas Boyle
Fayé Briggs
Emil W. Brown
D. Carmean
Brian Case
Ben J. Catanzaro
R. Chandramouli
Y. Chang
Robert F. Cmelik
Trevor Creary
David R. Ditzel
Dave Evans
Jerry Fiddler
Robert B. Garner
Vida Ghodssi
J. Goforth
Michael Helft
David Hough
W. Hsu
Jen-Hsun Huang
Kim Ingram

Mark Insley
R. Iwamoto
Donald C. Jackson
Bill Joy
Edmund J. Kelly
Kevin M. Kitagawa
Steve R. Kleiman
Michael F. Klein
Shing I. Kong
Meng Lee
Raymond M. Leong
Jim Ludemann
Steven S. Muchnick
Dave Murata
C. Murphy
Masood Namjoo
U. Naot
M. Parkin
Dave Patterson
Joan Pendleton
James R. Peterson
Joseph Petolino
C. Porter
Mike L. Powell
L. Quach
Sri Rajeer
J. Reaves
R. Reddy

D. Shan

D. Stein

Eric Stromberg

G. Swan

D. Tinker

P. Tong

Richard Tuck

Bill Tuthill

David Weaver

M. Weeks

Tom Westberg

D. Williams

David N. Wilner

Alexander Wu

L. Yang

The SPARC Architecture

The Scalable Processor Architecture (SPARC)

1

Robert B. Garner

Introduction

SPARC is a computer architecture derived from the reduced instruction set computer (RISC) lineage. As an architecture, SPARC is not a particular chip or implementation. Rather, SPARC allows for a spectrum of possible price/performance implementations, ranging from microcomputers to supercomputers.

The SPARC architecture has been licensed to multiple semiconductor companies that market their own implementations. This "open," competitive strategy encourages the evolution of faster and/or cheaper SPARC chips and systems and an expanding installed base for software.

SPARC-compiled application programs behave identically on different SPARC systems executing operating systems that support the architecture. Although such systems will run these programs at different rates, they will all generate the same results.

So that binary versions of user application programs can correctly run on a variety of SPARC systems using a future version of the UNIX System V operating system, there is under development an ABI (Application Binary Interface) standard that describes the formats and contents of SPARC-ABI binaries.

SPARC defines general-purpose integer, floating-point, and coprocessor registers, processor state and status registers, and 69 basic instructions. It assumes a linear, 32-bit virtual address space for user-application programs. SPARC does not define system components visible only to the operating system and unseen at the user-application level, such as I/O registers, caches, and MMUs. (However, Sun has defined a "reference" memory management unit that future SPARC chips will use.)

Reprinted from Sun Technology Journal.

RISC Performance

This section characterizes traits common to SPARC and other RISCs that allow for their high performance levels. For a more complete introduction to RISCs, see [Patterson85].

RISCs are designed to achieve better performance for average programs written in high-level languages. Representative program domains include software engineering, electronic/ mechanical CAD/CAM, business/office systems, AI-based systems, realtime control systems, and operating systems.

The amount of time required to execute a program includes not only the time to execute the program's instructions, but also time lost to I/O and swapping the processor between multiple tasks (context switching). The amount of time consumed by these overheads can significantly affect performance. For example, an infinitely fast processor can speed up a program that spends 33% of its time waiting for I/O by only a factor of 3. RISC-based systems should balance the throughput capabilities of the I/O sub-system and the compute power of the CPU. Also, systems should ideally limit context switching overhead to little more than the saving and restoring of processor state. (Note that an I/O system and MMU can be tailored to the requirements of a particular system since these are not part of SPARC.)

A large, compute-bound program is much larger than a processor's cache(s) and does not spend an inordinate time context switching or waiting for I/O to complete. The execution time for such a program, P, can be expressed as the product of three terms:

$$\text{program time} = I_p \times C_p \times T,$$

where

> I_p = number of Instructions executed by program,
> C_p = average number of Cycles per instruction (CPI) executed by program,
> T = Time per cycle, typically the reciprocal of a chip's clock frequency, F.

Since a processor's MIPS_p (million instructions per second) rate, equals $1 \div (C_p \times T)$, where T is in microseconds, and also equals $F \div C_p$, where F is in megahertz, this relationship is normally expressed, assuming I_p in millions, as

$$\text{program time} = \frac{I_P}{\text{MIPS}_P}.$$

RISCs achieve high levels of performance by minimizing I_p, C_p, and T, or, equivalently, by minimizing I_p and maximizing MIPS_p.

The C_p value for a processor is a function of the compiler and the benchmark program itself but, more important, is a function of a chip's microarchitecture and the size and speed of the cache/memory system attached to the chip. The standard way to compute C_p is to run the target program on chip and cache simulators, and then divide the total number of cycles reported by the simulators by the number of instructions executed. Small values of C_p are achieved when the most frequently executed instructions are executed in the least number of cycles.

Cache organization can influence performance to the same extent as the chip's microarchitecture. A small percentage of the time, the processor attempts to access data and/or instructions that are absent from the cache. During such cache "misses," a cache controller must first fetch the required instructions(s) and/or data from main memory. This naturally increases the execution time of instructions or data accesses that miss, raising the average C_p value. The cache miss rate is very dependent on the nature of the program, the amount of context switching, and the size and organization of the cache.

The number of instructions, I_p, depends on the benchmark, the efficiency or quality of the instruction set, and the quality of the code generated by the compiler. It is also a function of the number and organization of registers defined by the architecture.

The clock frequency, F, depends primarily on the chip technology, projected cost, development time, and the risk designers are willing to take before a completed system is shipped to the market place.

How RISCs Minimize C_p, I_p, and T

- C_p: RISCs achieve small C_p values, generally between 1.5 and 2.0, by defining simple instructions and, in an implementation, interfacing with large, low-miss-rate caches. Ignoring cycles lost to cache misses, processor-only C_p values are now generally between 1.0 and 1.5, and, by having several functional units, future chips will probably be capable of achieving values between 0.5 and 1.0.

RISCs generally have only two categories of instructions: computational instructions that operate on processor-internal registers and load/store instructions that move operands between registers and memory. For example, RISCs typically do not have "add-to-memory" instructions.

Simple instructions imply chip microarchitectures that "pipeline" instruction execution; that is, issue one instruction per cycle even though a given instruction may require multiple cycles to complete. Pipelines can also be designed to execute multiple instructions per cycle. In particular, RISC pipelines efficiently execute control-transfer (branch or jump) instructions and minimize time lose to incorrectly predicted conditional branches. This reduces C_p because control transfers are common in general-purpose program (about 20% of instructions being control transfers and 50% of these being conditional). RISCs also make visible to the compiler certain pipelines "breaks," where the pipeline can be idle waiting for an instruction to complete. The compiler fills these breaks with useful instructions, and consequently the pipe-breaking instructions effectively execute in fewer cycles. Pipe-breaking instructions include conditional branch and load instructions.

RISCs generally have at least two types of pipe-breaking instructions: delayed branches and delayed loads. With a delayed branch, the instruction following a branch, in the so-called delay slot, is executed irrespective of the outcome of the conditional branch. With a delayed load, the instruction that follows the load cannot use the loaded value. A special case is the interlocked delayed load, where, if the instruction after the load uses the loaded value, the load instruction slows down by an amount that depends on the implementation. SPARC defines delayed branches and interlocked delayed loads.

- I_p: By having a large number of registers (more than 16), a RISC compiler can generate code that attempts to keep variables, constants, and return addresses in registers and not in the slower memory. This arrangement reduces the number of executed load and store instructions, thereby reducing I_p.

  RISCs, with their register structures, have taken two different approaches to reducing the number of load and store instructions: either a non-structured, fixed sized register file—typically 32 registers—or a large number of registers organized into "windows"—typically greater than 120 registers. SPARC adopted register windows, which are described in detail below. A software technique which reduces the number of executed loads and stores, particularly utilized in the case of an unstructured register file, is known as "interprocedural register allocation" (IRA) [Chow84, Wall 86]. This approach, used by compilers and linkers, allocates variables to the same registers when it is know that the associated procedures cannot be active at the same time; that is, when one procedure is not a descendant or ancestor of another.

  Another important way that RISCs reduce I_p is by carefully defining the conditional branching mechanism. In particular, if the architecture has condition codes (like SPARC), they are not modified by every instruction, thereby not limiting a compiler's ability to rearrange code.

  One might expect that a RISC requires significantly more instructions than a complex instruction set computer (CISC), since more complicated instructions must be assembled out of simpler RISC instructions, but this has not been borne out in practice. For large C programs, SPARC executes about 20% more instructions that the MC68020 microprocessor does.

- T: The clock period or cycle time (T) of a RISC implementation depends primarily on the design of the cache and the processor pipeline. Because a RISC strives to execute at least an instruction per cycle, the cycle-limiting or critical circuit delay can be the cache access path: the processor generates a new cache address, and the corresponding instruction(s) and/or data must return to the chip in a single clock period. RISCs' simple, fixed-width instructions imply fast chip/cache interfaces. The simple formats also generally speed up instruction decoding and operand dependency calculations, which helps shorten the cycle time.

In summary, RISCs generally have higher average native MIPS values than CISCs, but do not require significantly more instructions to accomplish a given, compute-bound task. By minimizing I_p, CPI_p, and T, they execute programs in less time than CISCs require.

In addition to high performance, RISC machines also offer rapid time-to-market schedules. A new switching technology is available first with a relatively small number of transistors per chip. RISCs, implemented in low-density technologies, have a better "MIPS-to-cost ratio" and a shorter "time-to-market" than CISC chips. As semiconductor technologies and their markets mature, the transistor density per chip increases, and the cost required to build a processor and its system components, such as caches and MMUs, decreases.

SPARC Design Goals

Successive implementations of SPARC will achieve better levels of performance via both high- and low-density circuit technologies. Also, measured by performance, cost, and time to market, SPARC should outperform CISCs implemented in similar technologies.

An important goal is high performance floating-point implementations. By defining an architectural queue and register scoreboarding mechanism in the floating-point unit, SPARC allows for concurrent execution of floating-point and integer instructions with precise traps.

The SPARC architecture was designed to match the needs of

high-level programming languages. A goal was to keep compilers relatively simple and to efficiently support exploratory programming languages and environments, such as LISP and Smalltalk. To help meet these goals, Sun selected a "windowed" register model for the integer unit.

SPARC defines a uniprocessor, "Single thread of control" architecture. However, SPARC has some special support instructions for multiprocessor systems. Because programs running on a SPARC execute only a few more instructions than they do on a CISC and have fewer data memory references, SPARC chips are well suited for high-performance, tightly coupled multiprocessor systems.

The Architecture

A SPARC processor logically comprises an integer unit (IU), a floating-point unit (FPU), and an optional, implementation-defined coprocessor (CP), each with its own set of registers. This organization allows maximum concurrency between integer, floating-point, and coprocessor instructions. All of the registers—with the possible exception of the coprocessor's—are 32 bits wide. Instructions operate on single registers, register pairs, or register quads.

The following sections describe the integer, floating-point, and coprocessor architectures and then summarize the instructions. A complete specification of the architecture is available in the SPARC Architecture Manual [SPARC87]. Articles in the 1988 Spring IEEE COMPCON Conference [MuchnickC88, KleimanC88] cover Sun's SPARC compilers and the port of SunOS to the architecture.

Integer Unit Architecture

The IU may contain from 40 to 520 general-purpose 32-bit registers. This range corresponds to a grouping of the registers into 2 to 32 overlapping register "windows," where the actual number of registers and windows depends on the implementation. (The MB86900 has seven windows, and the CY7C601 has eight.) The number of windows in a particular chip is not discernible by a compiler or application program. (Note that a chip with only two windows, or 40 registers, functions as if had *no* windows. In this case, code assuming the availability of more register windows would execute properly, although much more slowly.)

At any one time, a program can address 32 integer registers: the 8 *ins*, 8 *locals*, and 8 *outs* of the active window and the 8 *globals* that are addressable from any window. The 8 *outs* of one window are also the 8 *ins* of the adjacent window (see Figure 1.1.). Although an instruction can address 24 windowed registers, a single window actually comprises 16 registers—8 *ins* and 8 *locals*. Note that global register 0 is always zero, making the most frequently used constant easily available at all times.

The active window is identified by the 5-bit Current Window Pointer (CWP) in the Processor Status Register (PSR), and is invisible to the user. The save instruction decrements the CWP, making the next window become active and, due to the overlapping, making the *outs* of the old window addressable as the *ins* of the new window. Likewise, incrementing the CWP with the restore instruction makes the previous window active.

A save is typically executed during procedure call and a restore during procedure return. In some cases, such as leaf procedure or IRA optimizations (described above), the allocation of a new window on procedure can be avoided. save and restore also perform a register-to-register add and are used to update both the CWP and the memory stack pointer indivisibly with respect to traps.

Programs nearly always use more windows than a particular chip provides. An overflow trap to the operating system occurs if all the windows are full before a save or an underflow trap occurs if they are empty before a restore. The overflow (underflow) trap handler moves the 16 registers of a window into (from) memory. In SunOS, windows are saved in the memory stack. (Note that hardware—not in current chips—could minimize the probability of window traps by saving and restoring windows in the background.)

Although the overlap of adjacent *ins* and *outs* provides an efficient way to pass parameters, the principal benefit of windows is their cache-like behavior. As a program calls and returns procedures, control moves up and down the execution stack, but gener-

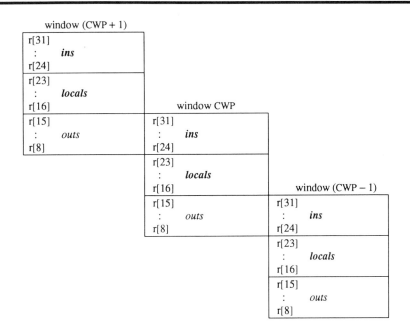

FIGURE 1.1. *SPARC register model. Each box represents eight general-purpose integer registers. A vertical pair of ins and locals is one window. The number of windows is implementation-dependent.*

ally fluctuates around particular levels in the execution stack. The register windows are effective when the average size of these fluctuations is less than the number of windows.

Register windows have several advantages over a fixed set of registers. By acting like a cache, they reduce the number of load and store instructions issued by a compiler, because register-allocated locals and return address need not be explicitly saved to and restored from the memory stack across procedure calls. A consequence is a decrease in the chip/cache and cache/memory operand bandwidth; that is, fewer loads and stores and fewer data cache misses. This benefits chips with multi-cycle load or store instructions/by executing fewer of them—and tightly coupled, cache-consistent multiprocessors—by reducing the memory bus traffic.

Windows perform well in incremental complication environments such as LISP and in object-oriented languages such as Smalltalk. In the later case, IRA is impractical since procedure linking is done dynamically at run time. In general, register windows are better than a fixed register set architecture with static, IRA-based compilers and linkers since windows respond dynamically to the runtime behavior of programs [Steenkiste87].

SPARC does not preclude IRA or related optimizations because the call and return (jmpl) instructions are distinct from the instructions that advance and retract the window pointer (save and restore). With applicable languages, a compiler and linker can perform IRA-type optimizations above the window register hardware, reducing even further the number of window overflows and underflows and the load/store bandwidth.

Dynamic trace data for large C programs based on current compilers, which do not perform IRA or related optimizations, show that about 20% of executed SPARC instructions are loads and stores, including the window overflow/underflow processing overhead. This compares to about 30% of executed instructions for RISCs without register windows when executing programs compiled with IRA and to about 50% of executed instructions for CISC designs with small (less than 16) register sets without IRA. The load/store memory traffic is reduced by around 30% and 60%, respectively.

Trace data for the same programs and compilers show that, on the average, 4% of the saves trap to the window overflow handler. Because 16 registers are saved per overflow trap, this is equivalent to 2/3 of a register write to memory per save instruction.

Register window overflow and underflow are detected by a IU state register, the Window Invalid Mask (WIM), that is invisible to the user. The operating system uses the WIM to mark any window or window group so that an overflow or underflow trap occurs whenever a save or restore would cause the CWP to point to a marked window. To implement the usual LIFO stack of overlapping windows, when window traps occur, the operating system sets a single WIM bit to identify the boundary between the oldest and newest window in the register file.

Note that on process switches, only the windows that contain valid data are saved into memory, not all the windows. On average, this is about half the number of implemented windows—minus one for the reserved trap window (see below). For the 16.67-MHz Sun-4/200 running SunOS, time spent during a context switch saving the average three windows is about 15 microseconds.

The register windows can be managed by the operating system to accommodate very fast trap handling. When a trap or interrupt occurs, the IU disables traps and decrements the CWP by 1, allocating the next window for the trap handler (see Figure 1.2.). Assuming that the trap handler saves the next window into memory before reenabling traps, or is short enough that it is not necessary to re-enable traps, interrupt latency can be limited to only a few cycles. (Note that a trap handler can use only 5 of the 24 registers of the trap window. Two of the eight *locals* are used by the IU trap hardware to save the program counters, and one is used to hold the PSR. The *outs* and *ins* of the new window are not usable because the *in* are the valid *outs* of the procedure that trapped, and the *outs* could be valid *ins* of an earlier procedure if all the windows were in use.)

In specialized hardware applications that may require extremely rapid context switching, such as dedicated I/O controllers or realtime systems, the register windows can be managed differently from the standard arrangement described above. One such scheme is to partition the windows into disjoint pairs, with one pair reserved for each process. One way to accomplish this scheme is to mark ever other window invalid in the WIM, thus protecting each process's registers from the other processes. With this arrangement, a process switch between window pairs would require only a few cycles. (Processes would not use the standard window model but would assume a complier that supported 24 private registers, 8 *globals,* and 8 traps registers. The current SunOS and compilers do not support this scheme).

In addition to the windowed registers and the WIM, the IU

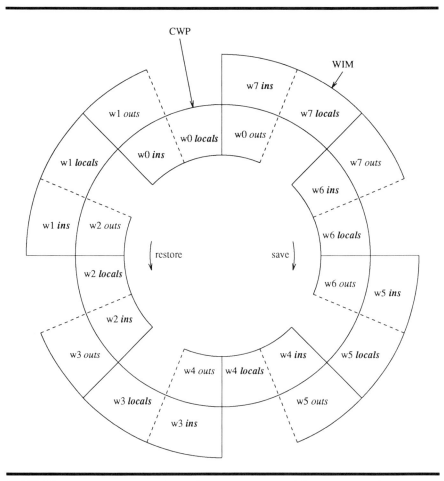

FIGURE 1.2. *SPARC register windows. This representation of the register windows assumes eight windows. Assume W7 is the oldest window, and W0 is the newest and corresponds to a procedure that attempted to execute a save instruction and generated a window-overflow trap. The trap handler cannot use W7s ins or W1s outs, but it is always guranteed W0s locals.*

has several other state registers. The PSR holds a user/supervisor bit, MC68000-compatible integer condition codes (negative, zero, overflow, and carry), the 4-bit processor interrupt level (PIL), FPU and CP disable bits, the CWP, and an 8-bit version/

implementation number. The Trap Base Register (TBR) holds a programmable base address for the trap table and an 8-bit field that identifies the type of the current trap. Like the WIM, the PSR and TBR are only accessible by the operating system.

Floating-Point Unit Architecture

The FPU has thirty-two 32-bit registers. Double-precision values occupy an even-odd pair of registers, and extended-precision values occupy and aligned group of four registers. The floating-point registers can hold a maximum of either 32 single, 16 double, or 8 extended-precision values. The FPU's registers are accessed externally only via memory load and store instructions; there is no direct path between the IU and the FPU. Floating-point load and store double instructions improve the performance of double-precision programs.

Although the user-level floating-point architecture conforms to ANSI/IEEE 754-1985, some nuances of the standard, such as gradual underflow, may be handled by software. An implementation indicates that it cannot produce a correct ANSI/IEEE 754-1985 result by generating a floating-point unfinished or unimplemented trap. System software then simulates the missing functions. The operating system must also emulate the entire FPU if it is not present in a particular system.

SPARC allows floating-point arithmetic operations, such as multiply and add, to execute concurrently with each other and with integer instructions and floating-point loads and stores. For example, it is possible to preload a floating-point value while executing a floating-point multiply and a floating-point add. The degree of concurrency is implementation-dependent, for example, an FPU can have several multipliers and adders. In all current system implementations, floating-point arithmetic instructions occur in parallel with cache misses.

The FPU performs all the required register interlocks, such as not beginning another floating-point instruction until all its operands have been computed, so concurrency is hidden from the user. Programs generate the same results—including the order of floating-point traps—as if all instructions ran sequentially. The interlocks can be implemented by a register "scoreboard," which is a bit per register that indicates when a register is waiting for a result value.

Because of the aforementioned concurrency, the IU's program counters can advance one or more instructions beyond a floating-point instruction that has generated a floating-point trap. In general, if a floating-point arithmetic instruction traps, the IU's program counter may not point to it. To handle traps properly, the FPU maintains a floating-point queue (FQ). The first-in, first-out queue records all pending floating-point arithmetic instructions and their memory addresses at the time of a floating-point trap. (Floating-point loads and stores are ot entered into the FQ.) The head of the queue contains the unfinished instruction that caused the trap. The remaining instructions were not executed. In the SunOS, software emulates all the instructions found in the queue at the time of a floating-point trap. The depth of the queue depends on the FPU microarchitecture.

The user-accessible Floating-point State Register (FSR) contains mode and status information; in particular, there are trap-enable control bits, current-exeception, and accrued-exception status bits for the five ANSI/IEEE 754-1985 trap types. The inexact-trap-enable bit must always be present in all implementations since inexact traps can be common. The floating-point condition codes, floating-point trap type, and the "floating-point queue not empty" bit are also in the FSR. (After a floating-point trap, the operating system retrieves entries from the FQ unti empty, as indicated by this bit. An application program sees a valid FSR at all times.)

Coprocessor Architecture

SPARC supports one, implementation-defined coprocessor. Like the FPU, the coprocessor has its own set of registers, executes instructions concurrently with the IU and FPU, and can be disabled by a state bit in the PSR. Like the FPU's support for precise trapping, the CP includes a coprocessor queue (CQ) that records all pending coprocessor instructions and their addresses at the time of a coprocessor exception.

The Instruction Set

Having introduced the IU, FPU, and CP register architectures, this article goes onto summarize the SPARC instruction set. The instructions are partitioned into memory load/store (including multiprocessor support), integer and floating-point computational, control-transfer, and coprocessor instructions. The article then discusses the instruction formats, traps, changes to the Berkeley RISCs, system issues, and current SPARC performance.

Load/Store Instructions

The load and store instructions move bytes (8 bits), halfwords (16 bits), words (32 bits), and doublewords (64 bits) between the memory and either the IU, FPU, or CP. These are the only instructions that access main memory, which, to user-application programs, is a byte-addressable, 32-bit (4-gigabyte) memory space. Because the CP is implementation-dependent, it can load/store data of other sizes, such as quadwords.

For the floating-point and coprocessor loads and stores, the IU generates the memory address and the FPU or CP sources or sinks the data. I/O device registers are accessed via load/store instructions.

As with most RISCs, the load and store halfword, word, and doubleword instructions trap if the addressed data are not aligned on corresponding boundaries. For example, a load or store word instruction traps if the low-order two address bits are not 0. If necessary, the operating system can emulate unaligned accesses.

The load and store instructions assume "big-endian" Motorola 68000 and IBM 370 compatible byte ordering: Byte 0 is the most significant byte, and byte 3 is the least significant byte in a datum. To preclude possible incompatibilities between SPARC application binaries that can access common data, only one byte ordering has been defined. (Note that portable, high-level-language application programs typically deal with byte and alignment issues in a machine-independent way.)

Two general addressing modes are defined for loads and stores: "$reg_1 + reg_2$" or "reg + signed_13-bit_constant", where "reg" refers to an *in, local, out,* or *global* register. It is possible to obtain register-indirect and absolute addressing modes by using global register 0.

SPARC defines interlocked delayed loads: The instruction that immediately follows a load may use the loaded data, but if it does, the load may slow down, depending on the implementation. (The MB86900 and CY7C601 load interlock cost is one cycle.)

Special load and store alternate instructions, usable only by the operating system, allow access to a number of 32-bit address spaces defined by a particular hardware system. An 8-bit address space identifier (ASI) is supplied by the load/store alternate instructions to the memory, along with the 32-bit data address. The architecture specifies 4 alternate spaces—user instruction, user data, supervisor instruction, and supervisor data— and leaves the remainder to be defined by the external hardware system. These ASIs can be used to access system resources that are invisible to the user, such as the MMU itself. (The IU also specifies one of the four predefined spaces for every instruction fetch and ordinary load or store access, so that an MMU can check access protections.)

Multiprocessor Instructions

Two special instructions support tightly coupled multi-processors: swap and "atomic load and store unsighed byte" (ldstub).

The swap instruction exchanges the contents of an IU register with a word from memory while preventing other memory accesses from intervening on the memory or I/O bus. It can be used in conjunction with a memory-mapped coprocessor to implement other synchronizing instructions, such as the nonblocking "fetch and add" instruction, which fetches a word and then adds to it a value supplied by the processor.

The ldstub instruction reads a byte from memory into an IU register and then rewrites the same byte in memory to all 1's, also while precluding intervening accesses on the memory or I/O bus. ldstub can be used to construct semaphores [Dubois88]. It had byte, rather than word, addressing because word-wide registers may not be aligned at word addresses in general-purpose I/O buses.

Integer Computational Instructions

The integer computational instructions perform an arithmetic or logical operation on two source operands and write the result into a destination register, where a register is an *in, local, out,* or *global.* One of the source operands can be a 13-bit, sign-extended constant. Generally, for every instruction that sets the integer condition codes, a corresponding one does not. The "subtract and set condition codes" instruction, subcc, with *global 0* as its destination is the generic compare instruction. This is usually followed by a branch on condition codes instruction.

The shift instructions shift left or right by a distance specified in either a register or an immediate value in the instruction. The "multiply step" instruction, mulscc, can be used to generate the signed or unsigned 64-bit product of two 32-bit integers. It shifts by 1 bit the 64-bit product formed by concatenating a general-purpose IU register with the 32-bit Y register. At each step, the least significant bit of the Y register determines whether the multiplicand—another IU register—is added to the product or not. In current implementations, a $32 \times N$ signed multiply can execute in $N+4$ cycles, if the compiler knows N in advance. The compiler translates integer multiplications by constants into shifts and adds, so that the average time to perform a multiplication can be small.

Note that SPARC has no special support for division. The general-purpose division algorithm, described in the SPARC Architecture Manuel [SPARC87], requires about 9 cycles per bit of generated quotient on current implementations, although compilers can also speed up divisions by constants.

sethi is a special instruction that can be used in combination with a standard arithmetic instruction to construct a 32-bit constant in two instructions. It loads a 22-bit immediate value into the high 22 bits of a register and clears the low 10 bits. Another instruction is used to load the low 10 bits. Because the arithmetic instructions have a 13-bit signed immediate value, the 22-bit sethi value implies on overlap of 2 bits in the result. In combination with a load or store instruction, sethi can also be used to construct a 32-bit load/store address. (Note that a *global* register can also be used to point to a table of 32-bit constant values.)

Tagged Instructions

The tagged arithmetic instructions can be used by languages, such as LISP, Smalltalk, and Prolog, that benefit from tags. Tagged add, taddcc, and subtract, tsubcc, set the overflow bit if either of the operands has a nonzero tag or if a normal arithmetic overflow occurs.

The tag bits are the least significant two bits of an operand, so that integers are assumed to be 30 bits wide and left-justified in a word with a zero tag. The tsubcc instruction with *global* 0 as its destination is the tagged compare instruction.

Normally, a tagged add/subtract instruction is followed by a conditional branch which, if the overflow bit has been set, transfers control to code that further deciphers the operand types. Two variants, taddcctv and tsubcctv, trap when the overflow bit has been set. These trapping versions can be used for error checking when the compiler knows the operand types. (Similarly, load/store word instructions can check for pointer types because they trap if the low-order two bits are nonzero.)

Floating-Point Computational Instructions

The floating-point computational instructions compute a single-, double-, or extended-precision result that is a function of two source operands in FPU registers and write the result into FPU registers. The floating-point compare instructions write the FSR's floating-point condition codes, which can be tested subsequently by the IU's "branch on floating-point condition codes" instruction. Because there are no mixed-precision instructions, instructions are provided to convert between the formats, including 32-bit integers.

As mentioned above, the floating-point computational instructions can execute concurrently with floating-point loads and stores and with integer instructions. The store FSR instruction, however, causes the FPU to wait for all outstanding floating-point operations to complete.

Control-Transfer Instructions

The program counter can be changed by a PC-relative call, a PC-relative conditional branch, a register-indirect jump (jmpl), or an integer conditioned trap instruction (ticc). call saves the program counter into *out* register 7 and jmpl saves it into an arbitrary integer register. There are three distinct conditional branch instructions for the integer, floating-point, and coprocessor condition codes. They cause a transfer of control if the condition codes match the conditions encoded by the branch instruction.

Most of the control transfers are delayed by one instruction: they take effect after the instruction that follows the control transfer is executed. Although branches have no explicit branch-prediction field, SPARC assumes that if an implementation does not have equal-speed taken and untaken branches, then a chip's pipeline will execute taken branches more rapidly than untaken branches. Because the architecture specifies a symmetric set of condition codes, a knowledgeable compiler can generate code to make the taken branch paths more likely.

There are three types of control transfers that are not delayed: annulling conditional branches, annulling unconditional branches, and conditional traps:

• The conditional branch instructions contain a 1-bit annul field. If the annul bit is set, the delay instruction is not executed if the branch is not taken. The annul bit allows compilers to fill delay slots more frequently than would otherwise be possible.

• If the annul bit is set in the unconditional "branch always" instruction, ba, the delay instruction is not executed. Besides saving code space, ba can emulate unimplemented instructions efficiently at runtime by replacing the unimplemented instruction by an "annulling branch always" to the emulation code.

• The ticc conditional trap instruction, depending on the integer condition codes, transfers control to one of 128 software trap locations given by the instruction. This instruction is used for kernel calls and runtime bounds checking.

Coprocessor Instructions

The architecture defines a set of coprocessor instructions that mirror the floating-point ones: load/store coprocessor, branch on coprocessor condition codes, and a class of coprocessor computational instructions. The definition of the computational instructions is a function of the coprocessor.

Instruction Formats

SPARC defines 55 basic integer instructions, 14 floating-point instructions, and two coprocessor computational formats. All instructions are 32 bits wide. Figure 1.3. summarizes the instruction set, and Figure 1.4. shows all the instruction formats. A few key points:

- Format 1 has a 30-bit word displacement for the call instruction. Thus, a call or branch can be made to an arbitrarily distant location in a single instruction.
- Format 2 defines two instruction types: sethi and branch. The 22-bit word displacement defines a ±8-Mbyte distance for the PC-relative conditional branch instruction.
- Format 3, which has specifiers for two source registers and a destination register, encodes the remaining instructions. As in the Berkeley RISC and SOAR architectures, when $i = 1$, a sign-extended 13-bit immediate value substitutes for the second register specifier. For the load/store instructions, the upper 8 bits of this field are used as the "address space identifier" and, along with the i bit, as an opcode extension field for the floating-point and coprocessor instructions.
- Unused opcode space is reserved for future expansion. Unimplemented instructions trap, and reserved fields must be 0.

Traps

The operating system establishes a trap-table address in the Trap Base Register. When a trap occurs, control vectors into the table at an offset specified by a trap number. The table allows for 128 hardware-defined and 128 software-defined traps. SPARC defines three kinds of traps: asynchronous, synchronous, and floating-point/coprocessor:

- An asynchronous trap is recognized when traps are enabled, and the external interrupt request level is greater than the

DATA TRANSFER:

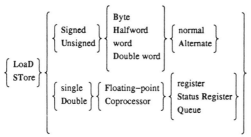

Atomic SWAP word   Atomic Load–Store Unsigned Byte

INTEGER COMPUTATIONAL:

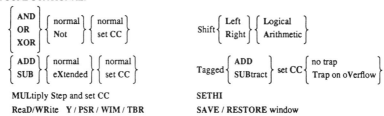

MULtiply Step and set CC   SETHI

ReaD/WRite   Y / PSR / WIM / TBR   SAVE / RESTORE window

FLOATING-POINT COMPUTATIONAL:

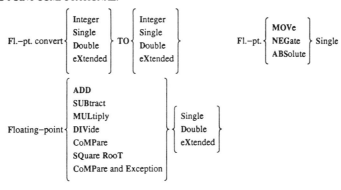

CONTROL TRANSFER:

$$\text{Branch} \left\{ \begin{array}{l} \text{Integer CC} \\ \text{Floating–point CC} \\ \text{Coprocessor CC} \end{array} \right\} \left\{ \begin{array}{l} \text{execute dly–instr} \\ \text{annul dly–instr} \end{array} \right\}$$

CALL   JuMP and Link

Trap Integer CC   RETurn from Trap

FIGURE 1.3. *SPARC instruction-set summary. The figure implies several non-SPARC instructions, such as "store signed" and "shift left arithmetic."*

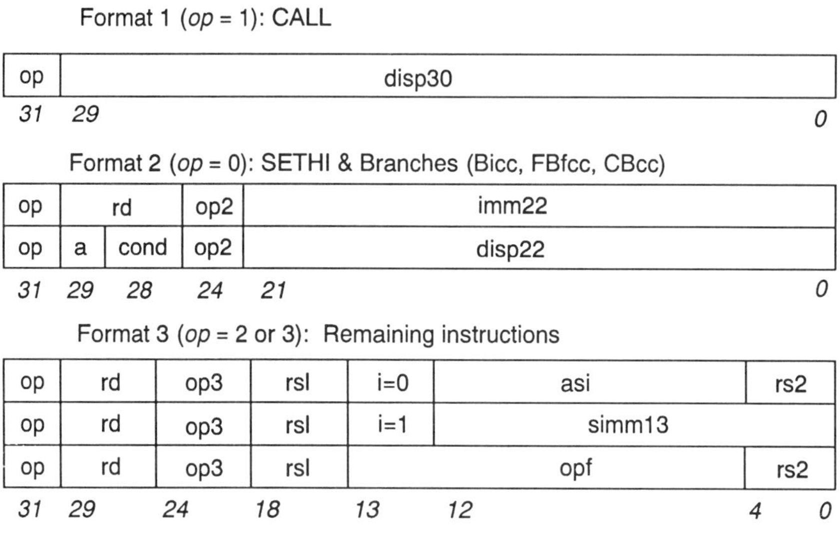

Format 1 (*op* = 1): CALL

op	disp30

31   29   0

Format 2 (*op* = 0): SETHI & Branches (Bicc, FBfcc, CBcc)

op	rd		op2	imm22
op	a	cond	op2	disp22

31 29   28   24   21   0

Format 3 (*op* = 2 or 3): Remaining instructions

op	rd	op3	rsl	i=0	asi	rs2
op	rd	op3	rsl	i=1	simm13	
op	rd	op3	rsl		opf	rs2

31 29   24   18   13   12   4   0

FIGURE 1.4. *SPARC instruction formats.*

PSR's processor interrupt level (or is the highest level). Asynchronous traps are not related to any particular instruction and logically occur between executed instructions.

- A synchronous trap is caused by a particular instruction and is taken before the instruction changes any processor system state visible to the user.

- A floating-point/coprocessor trap is caused by a particular floating-point (coprocessor) instruction. The trapped instruction does not change any system or FPU (CP) state. However, because the IU can execute instructions in parallel with the FPU (CP), the IU's program counter can advance beyond the particular floating-point (coprocessor) instruction that caused the exception. The FPU (CP) signals the exception asynchronously, and the IU does not take the trap until it encounters a floating-point (coprocessor) instruction in the instruction stream. Thus, even though floating-point (coprocessor) traps can be asynchronous, their occurrence can be controlled in a synchronous fashion.

The IU takes only the highest priority trap at any given time, so asynchronous interrupts must persist until they are acknowledged. Interrupt acknowledgement takes place when a program stores into a device's memory-mapped interrupt control register.

The PSR's trap-enable bit must be set for traps to occur normally. If a synchronous trap occurs while traps are disabled, the IU generates a nonmaskable reset trap, thus detecting a probable operating system error.

Comparison to the Berkeley RISC and SOAR Architectures

SPARC retains the register windows found in the Berkeley architectures, although unlike SOAR's [Pendleton86], its windowed registers do not have main memory addresses. The instruction formats are nearly identical to those of RISC I and II (Berkeley81, PattSeq81, Katevenis83] and SOAR [Ungar84]. Other window schemes were considered, as were compare-and-branch instructions, and SOAR's word-addressed memory and absolute branch addresses. Gate-count limitations in the MB86900 gate-array had a positive influence by encouraging simplicity.

We added the following to the Berkeley instruction sets: floating-point and coprocessor architectures, atomic load/store for multiprocessors, load/store alternate, multiply step, the branch annul bit (similar to the nullification bit in HP's Precision Architecture [Mahon86]), the window invalid mask (WIM), the save and restore instructions, the processor interrupt level (PIL), and instructions for all 16 functions of two logical variables (such as "and not"). Although SOAR, "Smalltalk on a RISC," supports conditional trapping and tags, SPARC defines them differently.

System Architecture

SPARC does not specify an I/O interface, a cache/memory architecture, or an MMU. Although the instruction set has no intrinsic bias favoring either virtual- or real-addressed caches, most systems are currently based on virtual-addressed caches in order to minimize the cycle time.

SPARC does not specify an MMU for the following reasons: An MMU definition is best established by the requirements of particular hardware and operating systems: is not visible to application-level programs; and is not a performance bottleneck with virtual-addressed caches because it is not in series between the processor and the cache. Sun has defined a "reference" MMU, however, that future SPARC chips will use.

Current SPARC Performance

This section compares the performance of two current Sun SPARC-based systems against two MC68020-based systems with current compilers and operating systems. An analysis is done in terms of the performance model introduced above.

SPARC system performance depends on many interrelated parameters. A system's compute-bound performance is inversely proportional to the execution time of a program being run, which as shown above, equals the number of instructions executed, I_p, divided by the average instruction execution rate, $MIPS_p$.

To determine the relative performance of a compute-bound program for two processors executing in systems a and b, we take the ratio of the program times for the two systems:

$$\text{rel performance } P_{a \text{ vs. } b} = \frac{\text{program time } P_b}{\text{program time } P_a} = \frac{I_b/MIPS_b}{I_a/MIPS_a} = \frac{I_b}{I_a} = \frac{MIPS_a}{MIPS_b}.$$

The I_b/I_a term is a relative efficiency factor that depends only on the quality of the code generated by the compiler and the quality of the instruction sets. Based on trace data from large C programs, Sun's compilers currently show a I_{68020}/I_{SPARC} value of .80; or, in other words, execute about 25% more instructions than the MC68020 does.

The native MIPS rate is a function of an implementation's cycle time, average memory access time, and microarchitecture. Given a Sun-4/200 large-integer-C-program execution rate of 10.0 SPARC MIPS (16.67 MHz/1.67 CPI) and a Sun-3/200 rate of 3.8 MC68020 MIPS (25 MHz/6.6 CPI), this equation implies that a Sun-4/200 is about twice the speed of a Sun-3/200:

$$\text{rel integer performance}_{\text{Sun}-4/200 \text{ vs. Sun}-3/200} =$$
$$.80 \times \frac{10.0 \text{ MIPS}_{\text{Sun}-4/200}}{3.8 \text{ MIPS}_{\text{Sun}-3/200}} = 2.1.$$

It is also interesting to compare the CPU-bound, integer performance of the single-board Sun-3/60 against the contemporaneous Sun-4/110. Given a Sun-4/110 large-integer-C-program execution rate of 7.3 SPARC MIPS (14.3-MHz/1.96 CPI) and a Sun-3/60 rate of 2.8 MC68020 MIPS (20-MHz/7.1 CPI), this equation also implies that a Sun-4/110 is about twice the speed of a Sun-3/60:

$$\text{rel integer performance}_{\text{Sun}-4/110 \text{ vs. Sun}-3/60} =$$
$$.80 \times \frac{7.3 \text{ MIPS}_{\text{Sun}-4/110}}{2.8 \text{ MIPS}_{\text{Sun}-3/60}} = 2.1.$$

Floating-point performance depends to a larger extent on the details of the FPU implementation, such as the degree of pipelining, the partitioning of the FPU into one or more chips, and the number and width of data buses. Floating-point performance in the first Sun-4/200 machines is limited by the performance of the Weitek 1164/65 data-path chips, so the performance relative to the Sun-3/200 series is about 1.6 times the Sun-3/200+FPA (which, with its optional, full-board Floating-Point Accelerator, uses the same Weitek chips as the MB86910).

Bassed on times reported by the operating system, integer program benchmarks—compilers, document processors, queue simulators, gate-level simulators, Dhrystone, Stanford integer— run at a geometric average of 3 times a Sun-3/200 and 11 times a Micro VAX II. Floating-point programs—Spice, DoDuc, Linpack, Whetstone, Livermore Loops, Digital Review, Stanford floating-point—run at an average of 8.5 times a Micro VAX II.

Conclusion

The SPARC architecture allows for high-performance processor and system implementations, including multiprocessors, at a variety of price/performance technology points. The simple instruction set makes possible chips with very high MIPS and MFLOPS rates and short time-to-market cycles. Because the architecture has been licensed to several semiconductor companies, it will be implemented in a variety of technologies.

The architecture is simple and powerful enough that its integer portion was the first 32-bit microprocessor implemented in a single gate-array chip. Combined with a large hardware cache, a tuned operating system, and optimizing compilers, it exceeds the performance of contemporaneous CISC-based systems by factors of 2 to 10. With implementations using both emerging and mature circuit technologies, we expect performance and cost to rapidly improve over time.

Acknowledgments

Many people at Sun contributed to the definition of the SPARC architecture, including: Anant Agrawal, Fayé Briggs, Will Brown, John Gilmore, Dave Goldberg, David Hough, Don Jackson, Bill Joy, Steve Kleiman, Tom Lyon, Steven Muchnick, Masood Namjoo, Dave Patterson (consultant from UC Berkeley), Joan Pendleton, Wayne Rosing, K.G. Tan, Richard Tuck, Dave Weaver, Alex Wu, and the author, who was chairman of the SPARC Architecture Committee.

The logic design of the MB86900 [NamjooC88, QuachC88] was done by Anant Agrawal and Masood Namjoo. The MB86910 logic was done by Don Jackson with assistance from Rick Iwamoto and Larry Yang. The Cypress 7C601 and BIT ECL chips were designed with larger engineering teams [NamjCyprC88, AgrawalC88].

Will Brown wrote an architectural and machine-cycle simulator, SAS. Ed Kelly and the author designed the Sun-4/200 processor board. K.G. Tan and Wayne Rosing managed the gate-array and architecture projects, and Jim Slager managed the full custom CMOS chips.

Thanks to Steve Muchnick, David Weaver, Dave Ditzel, Dave Patterson, Anant Agrawal, Ed Kelly, and Joe Petolino for their suggestions in improving this article.

A version of this paper first appeared in the Summer 1988 issue of SunTechnology on pp.42–55 and was reprinted in **The SunTechnology Papers**, published by Springer-Verlag in 1990.

SPARC History

The SPARC architecture was defined at Sun between 1984 and 1987 and is derived from the RISC work done at the University of California at Berkeley from 1980 through 1982. Enhancements to the Berkeley chips, including new floating-point and coprocessor architectures, multiprocessor support, and a fundamental change to a portion of the register architecture,[1] were made by a team of

---

[1] The decoupling of the instructions that advance and retract the register file window pointer (save and restore) from the instructions that call to and return from subroutines (call and jmpl). This significantly expands on the number of ways that compilers can allocate variables to windowed registers.

Sun engineers having operating system, compiler, and hardware experience.

Rapid time to market with a SPARC workstation was an important goal, so a gate array technology was selected for the first SPARC implementation. In late 1985, three Sun engineers designed the logic for the first SPARC processor using a new 20K-gate, 1.5-micron, 255-pin CMOS gate array family offered by Fujitsu Microelectronics.

Fujitsu verified the integer unit design in January 1986 and delivered the first working chips (MB86900) to Sun in April 1986. The floating-point unit (MB86910), which controls two Weitek WTL1164/65 data-path chips, was delivered in July 1986. The MB86900 was the first 32-bit microprocessor built on a single gate-array chip. The peak execution rate is one instruction per 60-nanosecond (16.67 MHz) cycle.

The second SPARC implementation is the Cypress Semiconductor 7C600 family. The CY7C601 integer unit is a full-custom, 1.2-micron, 207-pin CMOS chip designed by a combined Sun and Cypress engineering team. The first working CY7C601 was delivered in May 1988. The peak execution rate is one instruction per 30-nanosecond (33 MHz) cycle. The CY7C608 floating-point control chip, designed by two Sun engineers, is a 25K-gate, 1.5-micron, 280-pin CMOS gate array manufactured by LSI Logic. It controls a 74ACT8847 floating-point chip from Texas Instruments.

The first SPARC system, the Sun-4/200 family, uses the 16.67-MHz gate arrays on a board designed in mid 1985 that includes a virtual address, direct-mapped, 128K-byte-cache—as large as practical for the time. Since minimizing the design, debug, test, and manufacture cycle was important, the Sun-4/200 employed exactly the same backplan, memory system, and I/O architecture used in the Sun-3/200 family. A stable SunOS was running on a prototype system in June 1986, two months after the first IU arrived. First customer ship (FCS) was in August 1987, although earlier Sun had delivered Sun-4/200s internally and to alpha customers.

On July 8, 1987, Sun announced not only the open SPARC architecture, but also the Sun-4/200 system, a large set of vendor application software and three licensees of the new architecture.

The lower-cost Sun-4/110, also based on the Fujitsu gate arrays, was announced on February 8, 1988. (See/tech note.)

To this date, SPARC has been licensed to four semiconductor companies: Fujitsu Microelectronics markets the MB86900 family and is working on standard cell and a full-custom CMOS implementations; Cypress Semiconductor markets the 7C600 family; Bipolar Integrated Technology (BIT) is designing a custom ECL chip set; and LSI Logic is designing a standard-cell integer unit, including a standard ASIC macro.

References

[AgrawalC88] A. Agrawal, E.W. Brown, J. Petolino, D. Russel, J. Peterson, "Design Considerations for a Bipolar Implementation of SPARC," *33rd Annual IEEE Computer Conference (COMPCON'88)*, March 1–3, San Francisco, CA.

[Berkeley81) D.T. Fitzpatrick, J.K. Foderaro, M. Katevenis, H.A. Landman, D. Patterson, J.B. Peek, Z. Peshkess, C. Sequin, R. Sherburne, & K. Van Dyke, "VLSI Implementations of a Reduced Instruction Set Computer," *Proceedings of the CMU Conference on VLSI Systems and Computations*, October, 1981, Pittsburgh, Pennsylvania.

[Chow84] F.C. Chow & J. Hennessy, "Register Allocation by Priority-based Coloring," Proceedings of the SIGPLAN '86 Symposium on Compiler Construction, Montreal, Canada, June, 1984.

[Dubois88] M. Dubois, C. Scheurich, & F. Briggs, "Synchronization, Coherence and Ordering of Events in Multiprocessors," to appear in *IEEE Com.*,March 1988.

[GarnerC88] R.B. Garner, A. Agrawal, F. Briggs, E.W. Brown, D. Hough, W.N. Joy, S. Kleiman, S. Muchnick, M. Namjoo, D. Patterson, J. Pendleton, K.G. Tan, & R. Tuck, "The Scalable Processor Architecture (SPARC)," *33rd Annual IEEE Computer Conference (COMPCON '88)*, March 1–3, San Francisco, CA.

[Katevenis83] M. Katevenis, *Reduced Instruction Set Computer Architectures for VLSI*, Ph.D. dissertation, Computer Science Div., Univ. of California, Berkeley, 1983. Also published by M.I.T. Press, Cambridge, MA, 1985.

[KleimanC88] S. Kleiman & D. Williams, "SunOS on SPARC," *33rd Annual IEEE Computer Conference (COMPCON '88)*, March 1–3, San Francisco, CA.

[Mahon86] M. Mahon, R.B. Lee, T.C. Miller, J.C. Huck, & W.R. Bryg, "Hewlett-Packard Precision Architecture: The Processor" *HP J.*, vol. 37, no. 8, Aug. 1986.

[MuchnickC88] S. Muchnick, C. Aoki, V. Ghodssi, M. Helft, M. Lee, R. Tuck, D.Weaver & A. Wu, "Optimizing Compilers for the SPARC Architecture: An Overview," *33rd Annual IEEE Computer Conference (COMPCON '88)*, March 1–3, San Francisco, CA.

[NamjooC88] M. Namjoo, A. Agrawal, D. Jackson, Le Quach, "CMOS Gate Array Implementation of the SPARC Architecture," *33rd Annual IEEE Computer Conference (COMPCON '88)*, March 1–3, San Franscisco, CA.

[NamjCyprC88] M. Namjoo, et. al., "CMOS Custom Implementation of the SPARC Architecture," *33rd Annual IEEE Computer Conference (COMPCON '88)*, March 1–3, San Francisco, CA.

[Patterson85] D. Patterson, "Reduced Instruction Set Computers," *CACM*, vol. 28, no. 1, Jan. 1985.

[PattSeq81] D. Patterson & C. Sequin, "RISC I: A Reduced Instruction Set VLSI Computer," *Proc. of 8th Annual Int'l. Symp. on Comp. Arch.*, May 1981.

[Pendleton86] J. Pendleton, S. Kong, E.W. Brown, F. Dunlap, C. Marino, D. Ungar, D. Patterson, & D. Hodges, "A 32-bit Microprocessor for Smalltalk," *IEEE J. of Solid-State Circuits*, vol. SC-21, no. 5, Oct. 1986.

.[QuachC88] L. Quach & R. Chueh, "CMOS Gate Array Implementation of the SPARC Architecture," *33rd Annual IEEE Computer Conference (COMPCON '88)*, March 1–3, San Francisco, CA.

[SPARC87] *The SPARC™ Architecture Manual*, Sun Microsystems, Inc., Mountain View, CA, Part No. 800-1399-07. Also published by Fujitsu Microelectronics, Inc., 3320 Scott Blvd., Santa Clara, CA 95054.

[Steenkiste 87] P. Steenkiste, *LISP on a Reduced-Instruction-Set Processor: Characterization and Optimization*, Ph.D. dissertation, Computer Systems Laboratory, Stanford University, 1987. Technical Report CSL-TR-87-324.

[Ungar84] D. Ungar, R. Blau, P. Foley, A Samples & D. Patterson, "Architecture of SOAR: Smalltalk on a RISC," *Proc. of 11th Annual Int. Symp. on Comp. Arch.*, June 1984.

[Wall86] D. Wall, "Global Register Allocation at Link Time," Proceedings of the SIGPLAN '86 Symposium on Compiler Construction, Palo Alto, CA, June, 1986.

The Scalable Processor Architecture (SPARC)

Robert B. Garner • Anant Agrawal • Fayé Briggs •
Emil W. Brown • David Hough • Bill Joy •
Steve R. Kleiman • Steven S. Muchnick • Masood Namjoo •
Dave Patterson • Joan Pendleton • Richard Tuck

2

Abstract

Sun Microsystems' SPARC architecture, based on the RISCs and SOAR architectures developed at UC Berkeley, was designed for easily pipelined, cost-effective, high-performance, multi-technology implementations. The goal is that the cost/performance ratio of successive implementations should scale with, or track, improvements in circuit technology while remaining ahead of CISC-based systems. The simple instruction set, well-matched to compiler technology, allows for implementations with very high MIPS rates and short development cycles.

The combined integer and floating-point architecture includes multi-processor, coprocessor, and tagged arithmetic support. System functions, such as an MMU, are not integrated into the architecture.

Sun Microsystems is encouraging other companies to implement SPARC. Its first implementation is a pair of 20K-gate CMOS gate arrays plus two float chips; higher-performance custom CMOS and ECL are under development.

Introduction

The Scalable Processor Architecture (SPARC™) defines a general-purpose, 32-bit integer, IEEE-standard floating-point, 32-bit byte-addressed processor architecture. The design goal was that successive SPARC implementations should achieve increasingly higher levels of performance via faster and possibly less dense circuit technologies. The simple nature of the architecture enables

1988 IEEE Reprinted with Permission, from Proceedings of COMPCON '88, March 1-3, San Francisco, CA.

easily pipelined, cost-effective, high-performance implementations across a range of device integration levels and technologies.

SPARC was defined at Sun Microsystems over the period 1984 to 1987. The genesis of the architecture was the Berkeley RISC and SOAR designs [PattSeq81, Katevenis83, Ungar84, Pendleton86]. Changes, including extensions for multiprocessors, floating-point and tightly coupled coprocessors, were made with the guidance of an operating system/compiler/hardware team.

We implemented the first SPARC processor with a pair of Fujitsu 20K-gate, 1.5-micron CMOS gate arrays, a pair of floating-point accelerator chips, and a 128-Kbyte cache giving a 60 ns (16.67 MHz) instruction cycle time. The first SPARC-based workstations and servers, the Sun-4/200™ series, were announced concurrently with the architecture and a large set of vendor application software on July 8, 1987.

Unlike other existing commercial CPU architectures, Sun Microsystems is encouraging companies to design and market implementations of the architecture. In addition to the project with Fujitsu Microelectronics, Sun is working with Cypress Semiconductor to develop a custom 0.8-micron CMOS implementation and with Bipolar Integrated Technology on a custom ECL implementation. Sun and AT&T are also defining an Application Binary Interface (ABI) for third-party software vendors to be supported by a future version of UNIX® System V. SPARC conforms to the DARPA and Software Engineering Institute "Core Set of Assembly Language Instructions." [Core87]

This paper introduces the SPARC architecture and its more interesting features. A complete, implementation-independent specification is available elsewhere [SPARC87]. We also describe the differences from the Berkeley RISC/SOAR designs. Companion papers cover compilers [Muchnick88], how Sun's operating system uses the architecture [Kleiman88], and the Fujitsu [Namjoo88, Quach88], Cypress [NamjCypr88], and BIT implementations [Agrawal88]. An introduction to RISCs is in [Patterson85].

Registers

A SPARC processor is divided into two parts: an Integer Unit (IU) and a Floating-Point Unit (FPU). An optional coprocessor (CP) can also be present. Each of these units contains its own set of registers, and all registers are 32 bits wide.

Window Registers

The IU may contain from 40 to 520 registers, depending on the implementation.[1] These are partitioned into 2 to 32 overlapping register windows plus 8 *global* registers. (The *global* register g0 always delivers the value zero.) At any one time, a program can address 32 general-purpose registers: the 8 *ins*, 8 *locals*, and 8 *outs* of the active window and the 8 *globals*. The *outs* of a given window correspond to the *ins* of the next window and each window has its own set of *locals*. The active window is identified by the 5-bit Current Window Pointer (CWP). Decrementing the CWP at procedure entry causes the next window to become active and incrementing the CWP at procedure exit causes the previous window to become active. The accompanying compiler paper explains how windowed registers can be used [Muchnick88].

Register windows have several advantages over a fixed set of registers. Their principal advantage is a reduction in the number of load and store instructions required to execute a program. As a consequence, there is also a decrease in the number of data cache misses. The reduced number of loads and stores is also beneficial in implementations that have multi-cycle load or store instructions and in tightly coupled multiprocessors.

For large C programs, dynamic trace data show that about 20% of executed SPARC instructions are loads and stores, including the window overflow/underflow processing overhead. This compares to about 30% to 40% of executed instructions for RISCs without register windows.

Register windows also work well in incremental compilation environments such as LISP and in object-oriented programming environments such as Smalltalk, where interprocedural register allocation is impractical. Even though these exploratory programming languages benefit from register windows, SPARC does not

---

[1] A minimal, 40-register, two-window implementation comprises 8 *ins*, 8 *locals*, 8 *outs*, 8 *globals*, and 8 trap handler *locals*. An implementation with 40 registers functions as if there were no windows, although window-based code would execute properly, though less efficiently.

preclude interprocedural register allocation optimizations since the subroutine call and return instructions are distinct from the instructions that advance and retract the window pointer.

Register window overflow and underflow conditions are handled in software by a kernel trap handler. An IU state register, the Window Invalid Mask (WIM), can tag any window (or set of windows) so that an overflow or underflow trap is generated whenever the CWP is about to point to a tagged window. To implement the usual LIFO stack of overlapping windows, one of the WIM bits is set to identify the boundary between the oldest and the newest window. Note that on process switches only the active windows are saved, not the entire set of windows.[2] See the accompanying system paper for a more detailed description of window overflow/underflow handling.

In specialized systems, the register windows can be managed in a variety of different ways. For example, in device controller applications that require context switching, the windows can be partitioned into non-overlapping pairs, with one pair allocated per process. Each process would have—not including the 8 *globals*—24 private registers plus a set of 8 registers for trap handling. The WIM would protect each process's registers from the other processes.

The register windows also allow for fast trap handling. When a trap or interrupt occurs, the CWP is decremented—as for a procedure call—making available to the trap handler six of the *local* registers of the next window. (Two of the *locals* are written with the IU's two Program Counters.) Thus, the interrupt latency to a simple handler can be as small as a few cycles.

Floating-Point Registers

The FPU has thirty-two 32-bit-wide registers. Double-precision values occupy an even-odd pair and extended-precision values occupy an aligned group of four registers. The FPU's registers are accessed externally only via load and store instructions; there is no direct path between the IU and the FPU. The instruc-

---

[2] The cost of saving or restoring a window is not large: on the Sun-4/200, it approximates the overhead of 7 cache misses.

tion set defines doubleword (64-bit) floating-point loads and stores to boost double-precision performance. Also, in order to decrease context switch time, the FPU can be disabled so that its registers need not be saved when switching from a process that does not use floating-point.

SPARC allows floating-point operations, such as multiply and add, to execute concurrently with each other, with floating-point loads and stores, and with integer instructions. This concurrency is hidden from the programmer: a program generates the same results—including traps—as if all instructions were executed sequentially.

Because of this concurrency, the IU's Program Counters can advance beyond floating-point instructions in the instruction stream. There is a special group of registers, the Floating-point Queue (FQ), that records the floating-point instructions (and their addresses) that were pending completion at the time of a floating-point trap. The queue's head contains the unfinished instruction (and its address) that caused the floating-point trap.

Instructions

SPARC defines 55 basic integer and 13 floating-point instructions. Figure 2.1 illustrates the instruction formats and Figure 2.2 summarizes the instruction set.

Instruction Formats

All instructions are 32 bits wide. The first format holds a 30-bit word displacement for the PC-relative CALL instruction. Thus a PC-relative call or an unconditional branch can be made to an arbitrarily distant location in a single instruction. (Note that there is also a register-indirect call encoded via a format 3 instruction.) The return address of the CALL is stored into *out* register 7.

Format 2 defines two instruction types: SETHI and branches. SETHI loads the 22-bit immediate value into the high 22 bits of the destination IU register and clears its low 10 bits. SETHI, in conjunction with a format 3 instruction, is used to create 32-bit constants. (Note that the immediate fields of formats 2 and 3 overlap by three bits.) Format 2's 22-bit word displacement defines the

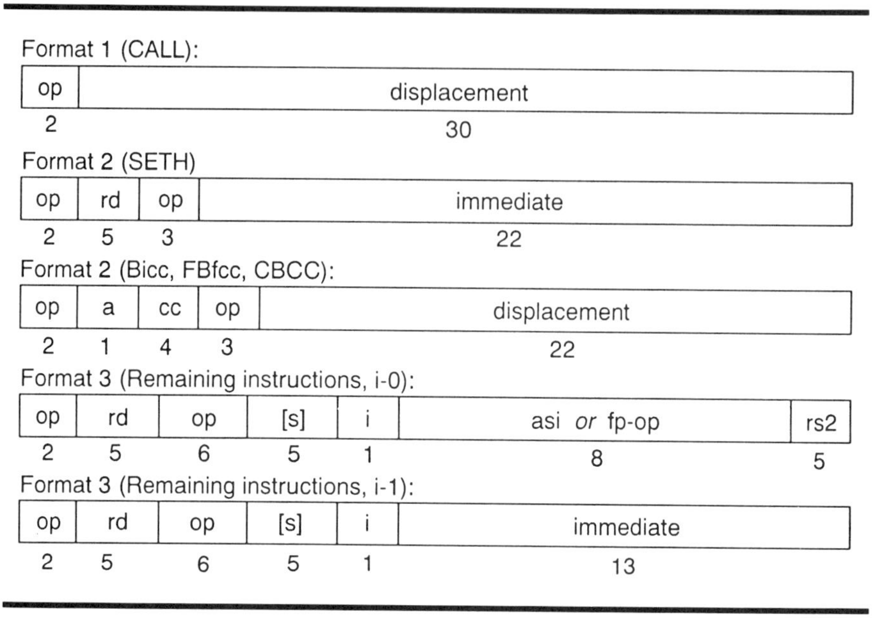

Format 1 (CALL):

op	displacement
2	30

Format 2 (SETH)

op	rd	op	immediate
2	5	3	22

Format 2 (Bicc, FBfcc, CBCC):

op	a	cc	op	displacement
2	1	4	3	22

Format 3 (Remaining instructions, i-0):

op	rd	op	[s]	i	asi *or* fp-op	rs2
2	5	6	5	1	8	5

Format 3 (Remaining instructions, i-1):

op	rd	op	[s]	i	immediate
2	5	6	5	1	13

FIGURE 2.1. *SPARC instruction formats.*

± 8-Mbyte displacement for PC-relative conditional branch instructions.

Format 3, which has specifiers for two source registers and a destination register, encodes the remaining instructions. Like Berkeley's RISC and SOAR, if the *i* bit is set, a sign-extended 13-bit immediate substitutes for the second register specifier. The upper 8 bits of this field are used as an opcode extension field for the floating-point instructions and as an "address space identifier" for the load/store instructions (see section on Load/Store Instructions).

Load/Store Instructions

Only the load/store instructions access memory. For the floating-point and coprocessor load/stores, the IU generates the memory address and the FPU or coprocessor sources or sinks the data. The load/store halfword (16-bit), word (32-bit), and doubleword (64-bit) instructions trap if the data are not aligned on halfword, word, and doubleword boundaries, respectively. The

DATA TRANSFER:

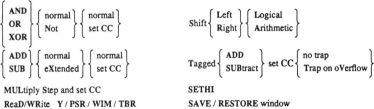

Atomic SWAP word   Atomic Load–Store Unsigned Byte

INTEGER COMPUTATIONAL:

$$\begin{Bmatrix} AND \\ OR \\ XOR \end{Bmatrix} \begin{Bmatrix} normal \\ Not \end{Bmatrix} \begin{Bmatrix} normal \\ set\ CC \end{Bmatrix} \qquad Shift \begin{Bmatrix} Left \\ Right \end{Bmatrix} \begin{Bmatrix} Logical \\ Arithmetic \end{Bmatrix}$$

$$\begin{Bmatrix} ADD \\ SUB \end{Bmatrix} \begin{Bmatrix} normal \\ eXtended \end{Bmatrix} \begin{Bmatrix} normal \\ set\ CC \end{Bmatrix} \qquad Tagged \begin{Bmatrix} ADD \\ SUBtract \end{Bmatrix} set\ CC \begin{Bmatrix} no\ trap \\ Trap\ on\ oVerflow \end{Bmatrix}$$

MULtiply Step and set CC   SETHI

ReaD/WRite Y / PSR / WIM / TBR   SAVE / RESTORE window

FLOATING-POINT COMPUTATIONAL:

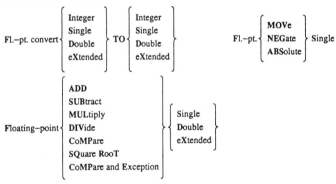

CONTROL TRANSFER:

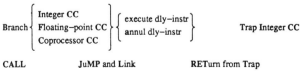

CALL   JuMP and Link   RETurn from Trap

FIGURE 2.2. *SPARC instruction set summary. (This summary implies several nonexistent instructions: e.g., STore Signed, Shift Left Arithmetic, and FL-pt. convert self to self.)*

aligned doubleword constraint allows for faster load/store double instructions in implementations with 64-bit data buses.

The load/store instructions assume "big-endian," Motorola 68000-compatible byte ordering: byte 0 is the most significant and byte 3 is the least significant byte in a word. We chose one arrangement without an option for the other to preclude incompatibility problems between binaries that access sharable data records.

Two memory addressing modes are supported via the 3rd format: "$reg_1 + reg_2$" or "reg + signed_13-bit_constant". Register indirect and absolute addressing modes are implied when g0 is specified. The two addressing modes are defined for both load and store instructions.[3]

Unlike some other RISCs that implement "delayed" loads, the instruction that immediately follows a load may use the load data. This feature simplifies the scheduling of instructions by compilers. In some SPARC implementations there may be a performance advantage if the instruction placed after a load does not specify the register being loaded.

For all instruction and normal data fetches from the uniform 32-bit memory address space, the IU indicates a user or supervisor reference by sending to the memory system the user/supervisor bit from the Processor Status Register (PSR). This, in conjunction with a data/instruction indicator define an Address Space Identifier (ASI) that can be matched against protection bits in a system's Memory Management Unit (MMU).

The privileged load/store integer "alternate" instructions define a mechanism that allows the supervisor to access an arbitrary, or alternate, ASI. Either the user instruction or user data spaces or up to 252 other system-dependent, 32-bit address spaces can be specified by an constant from the instruction. The MMU itself, for example, might be mapped into an alternate space.

There are two special instructions for tightly coupled multiprocessor support: SWAP and load-store unsigned byte (LDSTUB). SWAP atomically exchanges the contents of an IU register with a word from memory. It can be used in conjunction

---

[3] The "$reg_1 + reg_2$" mode does not significantly affect the performance of store instructions since most caches require more than one cycle, on the average, to accept both the data and the address.

with a memory-mapped coprocessor to implement other synchro-nizing instructions, such as the non-blocking "fetch and add" in-struction [GottKrus81]. The second instruction, LDSTUB, atomi-cally reads a byte from memory into an IU register and then rewrites the same byte in memory to all ones. It is the atomic instruction necessary for the blocking synchronization schemes, such as semaphores [Dubois88]. Since word-wide registers are not necessarily aligned in general-purpose I/O buses, LDSTUB reads and writes bytes to preclude the occurrence of processor align-ment errors.

Integer Computational Instructions

Format 3 integer instructions compute a two's complement result that is a function of two source operands, and either write the result into a destination IU register or discard it. Most have two versions: one that modifies the integer condition codes and one that does not. The "subtract and set condition codes" instruction (SUBcc) with a destination of g0 is the generic compare in-struction.

The shift instructions shift left or right by a distance specified in a register or an immediate value in the instruction. The "multi-ply step" instruction (MULScc) is used to generate the 64-bit product of two signed or unsigned words. It shifts by one bit the 64-bit product formed by concatenating a general-purpose IU reg-ister with the 32-bit Y register. At each step, the LSB of the Y register determines whether the multiplicand—another IU register—is added to the product. A 32×32 signed multiply re-quires 36 cycles. As mentioned in the companion compiler paper, higher-level language multiplications execute in an average of 6 cycles.

There are four special instructions for languages that can ben-efit from operand tags, such as LISP and Smalltalk. The "tagged add/subtract" instructions (TADDcc, TSUBcc) set the overflow condition code bit if either of the operands has a nonzero (or a normal arithmetic overflow occurs), where the tag is the least significant two bits of a word. (Thus, these instructions assume left-justified, 30-bit signed integers.) Normally, a tagged add/ subtract is followed by a conditional branch instruction (BVS), which, if the overflow bit has been set, transfers control to code that further deciphers the operand types. There are also two variants, TADDccTV and TSUBccTV, that trap if the overflow bit has been set and can be used to detect operand type errors.

There are two special instructions used to adjust the Current Window Pointer: SAVE and RESTORE which respectively decrement and increment the CWP, or trap if the adjustment would cause a window overflow or underflow. They also operate like an ordinary ADD instruction and thus can be used to atomically adjust both the CWP and a program stack pointer.

Control Transfer Instructions

Most control transfers, such as "branch on integer condition codes" (Bicc) and "jump and link" (JMPL) are delayed by one instruction: they take effect after the instruction that follows the control transfer is executed. This "delay" instruction is usually executed irrespective of the outcome of the branch. However, three kinds of control transfers are not delayed:

1. The conditional branch instructions, in addition to the condition specifier, have a special "annul" bit. If the annul bit is set, the delay instruction—normally executed—is not executed if the conditional branch is not taken. This feature can shorten execution time by allowing compilers to move an instruction from within a loop into the delay slot of a loop-terminating branch, or move an instruction from one arm of an IF-THEN-ELSE statement into the other. By use of the annul bit, compiled code contains less than 5% NOPs.

2. A special interpretation of the annul bit is made by the "branch always" (BA) instruction. If a BA with the annul bit set is executed, its delay instruction is not executed. This unique instruction is like the traditional, non-delayed branch. It can be used to efficiently emulate unimplemented instructions if, at runtime, the unimplemented instruction is replaced with an annulling BA whose target is the emulation code.

3. The "trap on integer condition codes" (Ticc) instruction, without a delay, conditionally transfers control to one of 128 software trap locations. Ticc's are used for kernel calls and compiler run-time checking. The Trap Base Register (TBR) holds the location of the software/hardware trap table. The low bits of this register are set to the trap type when a trap is taken.

Floating-Point Computational Instructions

The "floating-point operate" instructions (FPop) compute a single, double, or extended-precision result that is a function of two source operands in FPU registers and write the result into FPU registers. The floating-point compare instructions write a 2-bit condition code in the FPU's Floating-point Status Register (FSR) that can be tested by the "branch on floating-point condition codes" (FBfcc) instruction. The operands and results for all FPops are of the same precision so there are instructions that convert between all formats, including integers. The FPop's are encoded via the 9-bit "opf" field of two format 3 instructions.

As mentioned previously, the floating-point computational instructions can execute concurrently with floating-point loads and stores and with integer instructions. In all implementations, they also execute concurrently with cache misses. If a floating-point store attempts to write a result whose computation has not yet finished, the IU stalls until the floating-point operation is complete. A "store FSR" instruction also causes the FPU to wait for outstanding floating-point operations to finish.

In general, a user program sees a complete ANSI/IEEE 754-1985 implementation, even though the hardware may not implement every nuance of the standard, such as gradual underflow. Software emulates missing hardware functionality via FPU-generated traps.

Coprocessor Instructions

SPARC has instruction support for a single coprocessor (in addition to the floating-point unit). The coprocessor instructions mirror the floating-point instructions: load/store coprocessor, "branch on coprocessor condition codes", and "coprocessor operate" (CPop). Coprocessor operate instructions can execute concurrently with integer instructions.

Comparison to Berkeley RISC and SOAR

We adopted Berkeley's register windows for SPARC, although unlike SOAR [Pendleton86], windowed registers do not have main memory addresses. Because it is a condition-code and three-register-address based instruction set, the instruction formats are nearly identical to RISC I/II [PattSeq81, Katevenis83] and SOAR [Ungar84]. Seriously considered as alternatives were different windowing schemes, "compare-and-branch" instructions, and SOAR's word-addressed memory and absolute branch addresses. Gate count limitations of the architecture's first implementation had a positive effect by encouraging simplicity. Opcode space has been reserved for future expansion. Unimplemented instructions trap and reserved fields are zero.

We added these features to the Berkeley instruction sets: a floating-point and coprocessor architecture, atomic load/store for multiprocessors, load/store alternate, multiply step, the branch annul bit (similar to the nullification bit in HP's Precision Architecture [Mahon86]), the Window Invalid Mask, SAVE,RESTORE, and single instructions for all 16 functions of two binary variables (e.g., and_not, nor). Although SOAR supports conditional trapping and tags, these are defined differently in SPARC.

System Architecture

SPARC does not specify I/O interfaces, cache/memory architectures, or memory management units (MMUs). Although the instruction set has no intrinsic bias favoring either virtual or real address caches, in order to minimize cycle time, many system implementations are based on virtual caches. Since the architecture of an MMU is best established by the particular requirements of the system hardware/software designers, and is not a performance bottleneck in virtual address caches, SPARC does not define an MMU. System issues are discussed further in the operating system paper [Kleiman88].

Performance

SPARC's performance depends on many interrelated parameters. In general, a processor's ability to execute a compute-bound task is proportional to the product of the average number of instructions executed per second (MIPS) and the number of instructions required to execute the program.

The number of instructions depends on the quality of the code generated by compilers and the efficiency of the instruction set. Based on data from C and Fortran programs, SPARC machines execute from 0 to 25% more instructions than CISCs (e.g., VAX®, Motorola 68000). The companion compiler paper includes data on static code expansion.

The native MIPS rate is a function of an implementation's cycle time, average memory access time, and microarchitecture. It is influenced by the available circuit technologies and the system's cost, performance, and time-to-market goals. SPARC's simple instruction set allows for implementations with very high MIPS rates and short product development cycles.

Conclusion

The SPARC instruction set allows for high-performance processor and system implementations at a variety of price/performance technology points. The architecture is simple and powerful enough that we could implement its integer portion in a single CMOS gate array that executes instructions from a 128-Kbyte cache at a peak rate of 15 MIPS and yet far exceeds the performance of existing CISC-based systems [Schafir87, Chu87].

Acknowledgments

In addition to the authors, many people at Sun Microsystems contributed to the definition of the architecture, including K.G. Tan, Wayne Rosing, Don Jackson, Dave Weaver, Dave Goldberg, Tom Lyon, Alex Wu, and John Gilmore. The gate-array IU (Fujitsu MB86900) was designed by Anant Agrawal and Masood Namjoo and the FPC (Fujitsu MB86910), which interfaces with the Weitek WTL1164/65 floating-point chips, was designed by Don Jackson with help from Rick Iwamoto and Larry Yang. Will Brown wrote an architectural and machine cycle simulator. Ed Kelly and Robert Garner designed the Sun-4/200 processor board. K.G. Tan and Wayne Rosing managed the gate-array and architecture projects.

Thanks to Dave Ditzel, Dave Weaver, Ed Kelly, and Joe Petolino for their useful suggestions in improving this paper.

UNIX is a trademark of AT&T Bell Laboratories. SPARC and Sun-4 are trademarks of Sun Microsystem, Inc. VAX is a trademark of Digital Equipment Corp.

References

[Agrawal88] A. Agrawal, E.W. Brown, J. Petolino, D. Russel, J. Peterson, "Design Considerations for a Bipolar Implementation of SPARC," this proceedings.

[Chu87] N. Chu, L. Poltrack, J. Bartlett, J. Friedland, A. MacRae, *Sun Performance*, Sun Microsystems, Inc., Mountain View, CA.

[Core87] *Core Set of Assembly Language Instructions for MIPS-based Microprocessors*, Software Engineering Institute, Pittsburgh, PA.

[Dubois88] M. Dubois, C. Scheurich, & F. Briggs, "Synchronization, Coherence and Ordering of Events in Multiprocessors," to appear in *IEEE Com.*, March 1988.

[GottKrus81] A. Gottlieb & C. Kruskal, "Coordinating parallel processors: A Partial unification," *Comp. Arch. News*, vol. 9, no. 6, Oct. 1981.

[Katevenis83] M. Katevenis, *Reduced Instruction Set Computer Architectures for VLSI*, Ph.D. dissertation, Computer Science Div., Univ. of California, Berkeley, 1983. Also published by M.I.T. Press, Cambridge, MA.

[Kleiman88] S. Kleiman & D. Williams, "SunOS and SPARC," this proceedings.

[Mahon86] M. Mahon, R.B. Lee, T.C. Miller, J.C. Huck, & W.R. Bryg, "Hewlett-Packard Precision Architecture: The Processor," *HP J.*, vol. 37, no. 8, Aug. 1986

[Muchnick88] S. Muchnick, C. Aoki, V. Ghodssi, M. Helft, M. Lee, R. Tuck, D. Weaver, & A. Wu, "Optimizing Compilers for the SPARC Architecture: An Overview," this proceedings.

[Namjoo88] M. Namjoo, A. Agrawal, D. Jackson, Le Quach, "CMOS Gate Array Implementation of the SPARC Architecture," this proceedings.

[NamjCypr88] M. Namjoo, et al., "CMOS Custom Implementation of the SPARC Architecture," this proceedings.

[Patterson85] D. Patterson, "Reduced Instruction Set Computers," *CACM*, vol. 28, no. 1, Jan. 1985.

[PattSeq81] D. Patterson & C. Sequin, "RISC I: A Reduced Instruction Set VLSI Computer," *Proc. of 8th Annual Intl. Symp. on Comp. Arch.*, May 1981.

[Pendleton86] J. Pendleton, S. Kong, E.W. Brown, F. Dunlap, C. Marino, D. Ungar, D. Patterson, & D. Hodges, "A 32-bit Microprocessor for Smalltalk," *IEEE J. of Solid-State Circuits*, vol. SC-21, no. 5, Oct. 1986.

[Quach88] L. Quach & R. Chueh, "CMOS Gate Array Implementation of the SPARC Architecture," this proceedings.

[Schafir87] M. Schafir & A. Nguyen, *Sun-4/200 Benchmarks*, Sun Microsystems, Inc., Mountain View, CA.

[SPARC87] *The SPARC™ Architecture Manual*, Sun Microsystems, Inc., Mountain View, CA. Also published by Fujitsu Microelectronics, Inc. 3320 Scott Blvd., Santa Clara, CA 95054.

[Ungar84] D. Ungar, R. Blau, P. Foley, A. Samples, & D. Patterson, "Architecture of SOAR: Smalltalk on a RISC," *Proc. of 11th Annual Intl. Symp. on Comp. Arch.*, June 1984.

A RISC Tutorial

BILL TUTHILL • RICHARD TUCK

3

Introduction

Sun Microsystems® has designed a RISC architecture, called Scalable Processor ARChitecture (SPARC™), and has implemented that architecture with the Sun-4™ family of supercomputing workstations and servers. SPARC stands for, emphasizing its applicability to large as well as small machines. SPARC systems have an open computer architecture—the design specification is published, and other vendors are producing microprocessors implementing the design. As with the Network File System (NFS™), we hope that the intelligent and aggressive nature of the SPARC design will become an industry standard.

The term "scalable" refers to the size of the smallest lines on a chip. As lines become smaller, chips get faster. However, some chip designs do not shrink well—they do not scale properly—because the architecture is too complicated. Because of its simplicity, SPARC scales well. Consequently, SPARC systems will get faster as better chip-making techniques are perfected.

Although this document is neither detailed nor highly technical, it assumes that you are acquainted with the vocabulary of a computer architecture. (An *architecture* is an abstract structure with a fixed set of machine instructions.) The first section defines RISC and it's benefits. The second section gives an overview of the SPARC architecture. The third section compares the SPARC design with other RISC architectures, pinpointing the advantages of Sun's design.

What is RISC?

RISC, an acronym for Reduced Instruction Set Computer, is a style of computer architecture emphasizing simplicity and efficiency. RISC designs begin with a necessary and sufficient instruction set.

Typically, a few simple operations account for almost all computations—these operations must execute rapidly. RISC is an outgrowth of a school of system design whose motto is "small is beautiful." This school follows Von Neumann's advice on instruction set design:

> The really decisive consideration in selecting an instruction set is *'simplicity of the equipment demanded by the [instruction set], and the clarity of its application to the actually important problems, together with [its speed] handling those problems.'*

Simpler hardware, by itself, would seem of marginal benefit to the user. The advantage of a RISC architecture is the inherent speed of a simple design and the ease of implementing and debugging this simple design. Currently, RISC machines are about two to five times faster than machines with comparable traditional architectures,† and are easier to implement, resulting in shorter design cycles.

RISC architecture can be thought of as a delayed reaction to the evolution from assembly language to high-level languages. Assembly language programs occasionally employ elaborate machine instructions, whereas high-level language compilers generally do not. For example, Sun's C compiler uses only about 30% of the available Motorola 68020 instructions. Studies show that approximately 80% of the computations for a typical program requires only about 20% of a processor's instruction set.

RISC is to hardware what the UNIX® operating system is to software. The UNIX system proves that operating systems can be both simple and useful. Hardware studies suggest the same conclusion. As technology reduces the cost of processing and memory, overly complex instruction sets become a performance liability. The designers of RISC machines strive for hardware simplicity, with close cooperation between machine architecture and compiler design. At each step, computer architects must ask: to what extent does a feature improve or degrade performance and is it worth the cost of implementation? Each additional feature, no

---

† By comparable we mean architectures that cost about the same to implement. A Cray-2 supercomputer is not comparable to an IBM® PC in this sense.

matter how useful it is in an isolated instance, makes all others perform more slowly by its mere presence.

The goal of RISC architecture is to maximize the effective speed of a design by performing infrequent functions in software, including hardware-only features that yield a net performance gain. Performance gains are measured by conducting detailed studies of large high-level language programs. RISC improves performance by providing the building blocks from which high-level functions can be synthesized without the overhead of general yet complex instructions.

The UNIX system was simpler than other operating systems because its developers, Thompson and Ritchie, found that they could build a successful timesharing system with no records, special access method,s or file types. Likewise, as a result of extensive studies, RISC architectures eliminate complicated instructions requiring microcode support, such as elaborate subroutine calls and text-editing functions. Just as UNIX retained the important hierarchical filesystem, recent RISC architectures retain floating-point functions because these functions are performed more efficiently in hardware than in software.

Portability is the real key to the commercial success of UNIX, and the same is true for RISC architectures. At the mere cost of recompilation, programs that run on VAX® computers or systems that use the various 68000 CPUs will run faster on RISC machines. RISC architectures are more portable than traditional architectures because they are easier to implement, allowing rapid integration of new technologies as they become available. Users benefit because architectural portability allows more rapid improvements in the price/performance of computing.

For computer architects, the word technology refers to how chips are made—how lines are drawn, how wide these lines are, and the chemical process involved. The use of gallium arsenide in fabrication, which creates faster chips, is an example of a recent development in chip technology.

RISC Architecture

The following characteristics are typical of RISC architectures. Although none of these are required for an architecture to be called

RISC, this list describes the most current RISC architectures, including the SPARC design.

- Single-cycle execution. Most instructions are executed in a single machine cycle.
- Hardwired control with little or no microcode. Microcode adds a level of complexity and raises the number of cycles per instruction.
- Load/Store, register-to-register design. All computational instructions involve registers. Memory accesses are made with only load and store instructions.
- Simple fixed-format instructions with few addressing modes. All instructions are the same length (typically 32 bits) and have just a few ways to address memory.
- Pipelining. The instruction set design allows for the processing of several instructions at the same time.
- High-performance memory. RISC machines have at least 32 general-purpose registers and large cache memories.
- Migration of functions to software. Only those features that measurably improve performance are implemented in hardware. Software contains sequences of simple instructions for executing complex functions rather than complex instructions themselves, which improves system efficiency.
- More concurrency is visible to software. For example, branches take effect *after* execution of the following instruction, permitting a fetch of the next instruction during execution of the current instruction.
- The real keys to enhanced performance are single-cycle execution and keeping the cycle time as short as possible. Many characteristics of RISC architectures, such as load/store and register-to-register design, facilitate single-cycle execution. Simple fixed-format instructions, on the other hand, permit shorter cycles by reducing decoding time.
- Note that some of these features, particularly pipelining and high-performance memories, have been used in super-computer designs for many years. The difference is that in

RISC architectures these ideas are integrated into a processor with a simple instruction set and no microcode.

• Moving functionality from runtime to compile time also enhances performance—functions calculated at compile time do not require further calculating each time the program runs. Furthermore, optimizing compilers can rearrange pipelined instruction sequences and arrange register-to-register operations to reuse computational results.

Earlier Architectures

The IBM System/360, introduced in 1964, was the first computer to have an *architecture* (an abstract structure with a fixed set of machine instructions) separate from a hardware *implementation* (how computer designers actually built that structure). The IBM 360 architecture is still used today; IBM has brought out many computers implementing this architecture (or extension of it) in various ways. Sometimes instructions are performed in hardware; other times in microcode.

Microcode is composed of low-level hardware instructions that implement higher-level instructions required by an architecture. At first, microcode was programmed by an elite group of engineers and then burned into ROM (read-only memory) where it could only be changed by replacing the ROM. In the early 1970s, ROM was already quite dense—8192 bits of ROM took up the same space as 8 bits of register.

The biggest problem was that the microcode was never bug-free and replacing ROMs became prohibitively expensive. So microcode was placed in read-write memory chips called control-store RAMs (random-access memory). In the mid-1970s, RAM chips offered a good solution, because RAM was faster, although more expensive, than the ferrite-core memory used in many computers. Thus, microcode ran faster than programs loaded into core memory.

Given the slow speed and small size of ferrite-core memory, complicated instruction sets were the best solutions for reducing program size and therefore, increasing program efficiency. Instruction set design placed great emphasis on increasing the functionality and reducing the size of instructions. Almost all computer designers believed that rich instruction sets would simplify compiler design, help alleviate the software crisis, and improve the quality of computer architectures.

Because of the scarcity of programmers and the intractability of assembly language, software costs in the 1960s rose as quickly as hardware costs dropped. This led the trade press to make dire predictions of an impending software crisis. The software crisis was somewhat diminished in the commercial sector by the development of high-level languages, the packaging of standard software products, and increases in CPU speed and memory size that allowed programmers to use medium-level languages. Clearly, complicated instruction sets did nothing to alleviate the software crisis.

The improvement of the integrated circuit in the 1970s make microcode memory even cheaper and faster, encouraging the growth of microprograms. The IBM 370/168 and the VAX 11/780 each have more than 400,000 bits of microcode. Because microcode allowed machines to do more, enhanced functionality became a selling point.

However, not all computer designers held these opinions. Seymour Cray, for one, believed that complexity was bad, and continued to build the fastest computers in the world by using simple, register-oriented instruction sets. The CDC 6600 and the Cray-I supercomputer were the precursors of modern RISC architectures. In 1975 Cray made the following remarks about his computer designs:

> [Registers] made the instructions very simple. That is somewhat unique. Most machines have rather elaborate instruction sets involving many more memory references in the instructions than the machines I have designed. Simplicity, I guess, is a way of saying it. I am all for simplicity. If it's very complicated, I can't understand it.

Many computer designers of the late 1970s did not grasp the implications of various technological changes. At that time, semiconductor memory began to replace ferrite-core memory; integrated circuits were becoming cheaper and performing 10 times faster than core memory. Also, the invention of cache memories substantially improved the speed of non-microcoded programs.

Finally, compiler technology had progressed rapidly; optimizing compilers generated code that used only a small subset of most instruction sets. All of this meant that architectural assumptions made earlier in the decade were no longer valid.

A new set of simplified design criteria emerged:

- Instructions should be simple unless there is a good reason for complexity. To be worthwhile, a new instruction that increases cycle time by 10% must reduce the total number of cycles executed by at least 10%.

- Microcode is generally no faster than sequences of hardwired instructions. Moving software into microcode does not make it better, it just makes it harder to modify.

- Fixed-format instructions and pipelined execution are more important than program size. As memory gets cheaper and faster, the space/time tradeoff resolves in favor of time—reducing space no longer decreases time.

- Compiler technology should simplify instructions, rather than generate more complex instructions. Instead of substituting a complicated microcoded instruction for several simple instructions, which compilers did in the 1970s, optimizing compilers can form sequences of simple, fast instructions out of complex high-level code. Operands can be kept in registers to increase speed even further.

Early RISC Machines

In the mid-1970s, some computer architects observed that even complex computers execute mostly simple instructions. This observation led to work on the IBM 801—the first intentional RISC machine (although the term RISC had yet to be coined). Built from off-the-shelf ECL (emitter-coupled logic) and completed in 1979, the IBM 801 was a 32-bit minicomputer with simple single-cycle instructions, 32 registers, separate cache memories for instructions and data, and delayed branch instructions. The 801 was the predecessor of the chip now used as the CPU for the IBM PC/RT™ computer, introduced early in 1986.

The term RISC was coined as part of David Peterson's 1980 course in microprocessor design at the University of California at Berkeley. The RISC-I chip design was completed in 1982, and the RISC-II chip design was completed in 1984. The RISC-II was a 32-bit microprocessor with 138 registers, and a 330-ns cycle time (for the 3-micron version). Even then, without the aid of elaborate compiler technology, the RISC-II chip outperformed the VAX 11/780 at computer integer arithmetic.

The MIPS project began at Stanford a short time later, with a group under the direction of John Hennessy. Hennessy's group declared that the acronym MIPS stood for Microprocessor without Interlocked Pipeline Stages; however, it has come to mean Millions of Instructions Per Second. This group entrusted the compiler with pipeline management. The main goal of their design was high performance, perhaps at the expense of simplicity. The Stanford MIPS device was a 32-bit microprocessor with 16 registers, and a 500-ns cycle time. The commercial processor marketed by MIPS computer company is an outgrowth of the Stanford MIPS architecture.

Several other companies have announced RISC-type machines, including Ridge, Pyramid, and Hewlett-Packard with the Precision Architecture (Spectrum). Figure 3.1. whows how these various RISC architectures are related.

Using any given benchmark, the performance, P, of a particular computer is inversely proportional to the product of the benchmark's instruction count, I, the average number of clock cycles per instruction, C, and the inverse of the clock speed, S:

$$P = \frac{1}{I \cdot C \cdot \frac{1}{S}}$$

Let's assume that a RISC machine runs at the same clock speed as a corresponding traditional machine; S is identical. The number of clock cycles per instruction, C, is between 1.3 to 1.7 for RISC machines, but betwccn 4 and 10 for traditional machines. This would make the instruction execution rate of RISC machines about 3 to 6 times faster than traditional machines. But, because traditional machines have more powerful instructions, RISC machines must execute more instructions for the same program, typi-

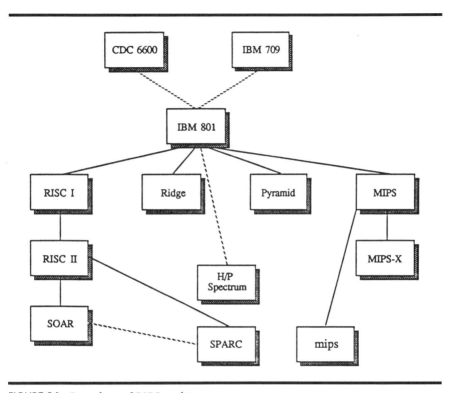

FIGURE 3.1. *Genealogy of RISC architecture.*

cally about 20% to 40% more. Since RISC machines execute 20% to 40% more instructions 3 to 6 times more quickly, they are about 2 to 5 times faster than traditional machines for executing typical large programs.

Compiled programs on RISC machines are larger than compiled programs on traditional machines, partly because several simple instructions replace one complex instruction and partly because of decreased code density. All RISC instructions are 32 bits wide, whereas some instructions on traditional machines are narrower. But the number of instructions actually executed may not be as great as the increased program size would indicate. Global registers, for example, often simplify call/return sequences so that context switches become less expensive.

Designers of RISC machines dramatically reduce the clock cycles per instruction while slightly increasing the instruction count per program, resulting in an overall performance increase. Moreover, RISC architectures scale better to new technology than more complicated architectures. Sometimes architectural cleverness backfires—because of complicated design, the performance of a machine will not improve at the same rate as technology advances. Simple RISC architectures, by contrast, will scale upward as cycle times decrease and memory sizes increase.

SPARC Architecture

An architecture, or abstract design, often spans several hardware implementations. This section introduces the SPARC architecture, without going into specifics about particular implementations.

The SPARC CPU is composed of an Integer Unit (IU) that performs basic processing and a Floating-Point Unit (FPU) that performs floating-point calculations. According to the architecture, the IU and the FPU may or may not be implemented on the same chip. Although not a formal part of the architecture, SPARC system-based computers from Sun Microsystems have a memory management unit (MMU), a large virtual-address cache for instructions and data, and are organized around a 32-bit data and instruction bus. (See Figure 3.2.)

The integer and floating-point units operate concurrently.

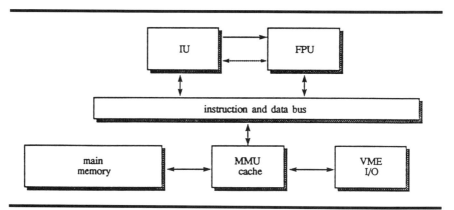

FIGURE 3.2. *Sample SPARC implementation.*

The IU extracts floating-point operations from the instruction stream and places them in a queue for the FPU. The FPU performs floating-point calculations with a set number of floating-point arithmetic units (the number is implementation-dependent). The SPARC architecture also specifies an interface for the connection of an additional coprocessor.

Instruction Categories

The SPARC architecture has about 50 integer instructions, a few more than earlier RISC designs, but less than half the number of Motorola 68000 integer instructions. SPARC instructions fall into five basic categories:

1. Load and store instructions (the only way to access memory). These instructions use two registers or a register and a constant to calculate the memory address involved. Half-word accesses must be aligned on 2-byte boundaries, word accesses on 4-byte boundaries, and double-word accesses on 8-byte boundaries. These alignment restrictions greatly speed up memory access.

2. Arithmetic/logical/shift instructions. These instructions compute a result that is a function of two source operands and then place the result in a register. They perform arithmetic, tagged arithmetic, logical, or shift operations. Tagged arithmetic is useful for implementing artificial intelligence (AI) languages.

3. Coprocessor operations. These include floating-point calculations, operations on floating-point registers, and instructions involving the optional coprocessor. Floating-point operations execute concurrently with IU instructions and with other floating-point operations when necessary. This architectural concurrency hides floating-point operations from the applications programmer.

4. Control-transfer instructions. These include jumps, calls, traps, and branches. Control transfers are usually delayed until after execution of the next instruction, so that the

pipeline is not emptied every time a control transfer occurs. Thus, compilers can be optimized for delayed branching.

5. Read/write control register instructions. These include instructions to read and write the contents of various control registers. Generally the source or destination is implied by the instruction.

Register Windows

A unique feature contributing to the high performance of the SPARC design is its overlapping register windows. An analogy can be made comparing the register windows with a rotating, high-performance tire. Some part of the tire's tread is always on the ground. As it rotates, the tire's zigzag tread grips a different portion of the road. The zigzag tread is analogous to the overlap of register windows. Results left in registers become operands for the next operation, obviating the need for extra load and store instructions.

According to the architectural specification, there may be anywhere between 6 and 32 register windows, each window having 24 working registers, plus 8 global registers.† Each register window is logically divided into three groups: 8 *in* registers, 8 *local* registers, and 8 *out* registers. The *out* registers for one window become *in* registers for the next; they are, in fact, the same registers. The current window pointer keeps track of which window is currently active. Figure 3.3. is a diagram of a SPARC implementation with 6 register windows. Note that the first actual SPARC implementation has 7 windows, so in addition to the windows in this diagram, there would also be *w0 in, w0 local,* and *w0 out.*

For a function call, the register windows rotate counterclockwise; for a return from a function call, they rotate clockwise.

The alternative to register windows encompasses slower, more elaborate register allocations performed during compile time. For languages such as C, Pascal, and Modula-2, this strategy is difficult and time consuming. For exploratory programming en-

---

† The first implementation has 7 register windows with 24 registers each (but count only 16 since 8 overlap), plus 8 global registers, for a total of 120 registers.

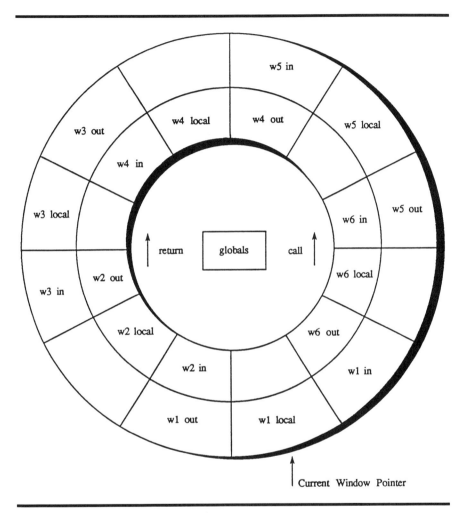

FIGURE 3.3. *Overlapping register windows.*

vironments such as Lisp and Smalltalk, where compiler speed is crucial to improve programmer productivity, users may find slower optimizing compilers unacceptable and not able to achieve the potential performance of RISC machines. Recent research suggests that register windows and tagged arithmetic, found in SPARC systems but not in other commercial RISC machines, are sufficient to provide excellent performance for expert system development requiring AI languages such as Lisp and Smalltalk.†

Traps and Exceptions

The SPARC design supports a full set of traps and interrupts. They are handled by a table that supports 128 hardware and 128 software traps. Even though floating-point instructions can execute concurrently with integer instructions, floating-point traps are precise because the FPU supplies (from the table) the address of the instruction that failed.

Memory Protection

Some SPARC instructions are privileged and can only be executed while the processor is in supervisor mode. This instruction execution protection ensures that user programs cannot accidentally alter the state of the machine with respect to its peripherals and vice versa.

The SPARC design also provides memory protection, which is essential for smooth multiasking operation. Memory protection makes it impossible for user programs that have run amok to trash the system, other user programs, or themselves.

An Open Architecture
Advantages of Open Architecture

The SPARC design is the first open RISC architecture, and one of the few open CPU architectures. An architectural standard would lift the industry out of often useless debates over the merits of various mircoprocessors. Standard products are more beneficial than proprietary ones, because standards allow users to acquire the most cost-effective hardware and software in a competitive multi-vendor marketplace. Integrated circuits would come from chip vendors, while software would be supplied by systems vendors.

---

† D. Ungar, R. Blau, P. Foley, A.D. Samples, D. Patterson, "Architecture of SOAR: Smalltalk on a RISC," in Proceedings of the 11th Annual International Symposium on Computer Architecture, Ann Arbor, 1984.

This advantage is lost when users are limited by a processor with proprietary hardware and software.

RISC architectures, and the SPARC design in particular, are easy to implement because they are relatively simple. Since they have short design cycles, RISC machines can absorb new technologies almost immediately, unlike complicated computer architectures.

The SPARC architecture is an aggressive, forward-thinking design. Even in the first implementation, processor cycle time is very fast—equivalent to the access time of static random-access memory (SRAM) rather than dynamic random-access memory (DRAM). Because registers are used intensively in a load/store architecture, the high cost of fast memory (as with SRAM) can be concentrated where it is used the most—in registers. Because the clock cycles per instruction are kept to a minimum, pipelining is simple and fast, since few restarts are necessary. So the high performance of SPARC systems results from both simple design and technological leverage.

SPARC Design and RISC

Like other RISC architectures, SPARC systems provide:

- Single-cycle execution. All instructions except loads, stores, and floating-point operations can be executed in one machine cycle.

- Simple instruction format. All instructions are 32 bits wide and word-aligned in memory. Op-codes and addresses are always in the same place, so decoding hardware can be simplified.

- Register-intensive architecture. Instructions operate on two registers or on a register and a constant, placing the result in a third register. The only way to access memory is with load and store instructions.

- Large register windows. The processor has access to a large number of registers configured into overlapping sets, so that compilers can automatically cache values and pass parameters in registers.

- Delayed control transfer. The processor fetches the next instruction following a control transfer before completing the transfer. Compilers can rearrange code, placing useful instructions after a delayed control transfer, thus maximizing throughput.

How SPARC Design is Different

SPARC systems were designed to support:

- The C programming language and the UNIX operating system;
- Numerical applications (using FORTRAN); and
- Artificial intelligence and expert system applications using Lisp and Prolog.

Supporting C is relatively easy; most modern hardware architectures are able to do so. The one essential feature is byte addressability. However, numerical applications require fast floating point, and artificial intelligence applications require large address spaces and interchangeability of data types.

The floating-point processor, with pipelined floating-point operation capabilities, achieves the high performance needed for numerical applications. Floating-point coprocessors are generally not part of RISC machines, but they are available for microprocessors such as the Motorola 68020 and the Intel 80386, and for SPARC systems as well.

For artificial intelligence and expert system applications, SPARC systems offer tagged instructions and word alignment. Because languages such as Lisp and Prolog are often interpreted, word alignment makes it easier for interpreters to manipulate and interchange integers and different types of pointers. In the tagged instructions, the two low-order bits of an operand specify the type of operand. If an operand is an integer, most of the time it is added to (or subtracted from) a register. If an operand is a pointer, most of the time a memory reference is involved. Language interpreters can leave operands in the appropriate registers, greatly improving the performance of exploratory programming environments.

The SPARC architecture does not specify a memory management unit (MMU) because we expect the same processor to be used in different types of machines. For example, a single-user machine with embedded applications, such as the Macintosh, does not need an MMU. By contrast, a multitasking machine used for timesharing, such as a traditional UNIX box, needs a paging MMU. Furthermore, a multiprocessor such as a vector machine or hypercube requires specialized memory management facilities. The SPARC architecture can be implemented with a different MMU configuration for each of these purposes, without affecting user programs.

Speed Advantage of SPARC Systems

Recall the equation in the first chapter, where the performance, P, of a processor is inversely proportional to the product of a benchmark's instruction count, I, the average clock cycle per instruction, C, and the inverse of the clock speed:

$$P = \frac{1}{I \cdot C \cdot \frac{1}{S}}$$

Working this equation for SPARC systems and for two popular microprocessors, we come up with the numbers (I indicates millions of instructions so P is in MIPS) in Table 3.1.

Thus, SPARC systems have a considerable theoretical performance advantage over other micrprocessors on the market. The table compares three processors running at the same clock speed; higher clock speeds are possible with all three processors.

Processor Performance				
CPU	I	C	S	P
Motorola 68030	1.0	5.2	16.67	3.21
Intel 80386	1.1	4.4	16.67	3.44
SPARC	1.2	1.3	16.67	10.69

TABLE 3.1 *Processor performance.*

SPARC Machines and Other RISC Machines

The SPARC design has more similarities to Berkeley's RISC-II architecture than to any other RISC architecture. Like the RISC-II architecture, it uses register windows to reduce the number of load/store instructions. The SPARC architecture allows 32 register windows, but the initial implementation has only 7 windows. The tagged instructions are derived from the Smalltalk On A RISC, (SOAR) processor developed at Berkeley after implementing RISC-II.

Until recently, RISC architectures have performed poorly on floating-point calculations. The IBM 801, for example, implemented floating-point operations in software. The Berkeley RISC-I and RISC-II outperformed a VAX 11/780 in integer arithmetic, but not in floating-point arithmetic. This was also true of the Stanford MIPS processor. SPARC systems, on the other hand, are designed for optimal floating-point performance, and support single-, double-, and extended-precision operands and operations, as specified by the ANSI/IEEE 754 floating-point standard.

High floating-point performance results from concurrency of the IU and FPU. The integer unit loads and stores floating-point operands, while the floating-point unit performs calculations. If an error (such as a floating-point exception) occurs, the floating-point unit specifies precisely where the trap took place; execution is expediently resumed at the discretion of the integer unit. Furthermore, the floating-point unit has an internal instruction queue; it can operate while the integer unit is processing unrelated functions.

Conclusion

SPARC systems deliver very high levels of performance. The flexibility of the architecture makes future systems capable of delivering performance many times greater than the performance of the initial implementation. Moreover, the open architecture makes it possible to absorb technological advances almost as soon as they occur.

Why RISC Has Won

Davⁱᵈ R. Ditzel

4

Special to Workstation News

RISC has won. Why is it so clear? After 10 years of arguing the technical merits of complex instructions, these arguments are now rarely heard from CISC proponents. RISC has been able to demonstrate long-term benefits in cost/performance over CISC architectures. However, with RISC architectures so clearly in the ascendancy, a new doublespeak is emerging. Some would like us to believe that CISC can become RISC by adding "RISC techniques." Can something complicated be simplified by adding still more to it? Let's go back and examine the principles behind RISC in order to answer this question.

Basic Principles of RISC

A Reduced Instruction Set Computer (RISC) is really about good engineering design tradeoffs. In the late 1970s, many researchers were shocked to find out that their Complex Instruction Set Computer (CISC) architectures, such as the VAX, MC68000 and Intel 80×86, were spending most of their time performing relatively simple instructions. Attempts to "help" compiler writers with fancy new instructions and addressing modes had largely backfired. Few of these complex instructions were ever used by compilers.

Some say the era of CISC computers ended when the use of compilers took over from assembly language programming. The designers of RISC worked to match the instruction set to advanced compiler technology. They followed various principles, such as: making all instructions of similar complexity, making instructions all of a fixed length and sticking to complete orthogonality with respect to operations and addressing modes. CISC systems had tried to convey power through the instruction set alone, but all too often, these optimizations merely ended up crippling the hardware and compiler.

RISC takes the opposite approach. RISC instructions make possible the creation of simple, high-performance hardware implementations. RISC instructions are simple to decode, are fixed in length, are simple to pipeline and have few side effects. These simple instructions give the compiler more opportunity to apply optimizations that improve the quality of the code. RISC gives compilers room to do their job by including sufficient registers—at least 32 integer registers and 16 floating point registers. A simple load/store memory model greatly simplifies the implementation of traps and interrupts in pipelined computers. RISC has succeeded because it has been an "enabling technology."

Benefits of RISC

By following the basic principles of RISC, a number of benefits are obtained. Pipelining works better, so the average number of clocks needed to execute an instruction is close to one, rather than the ten needed for CISC computers such as the VAX. This translates directly into performance gains. By being simpler to implement, a RISC architecture requires fewer gates for a specific chip. Hence, designs can be completed in a shorter amount of time. By keeping the machine simple, the cycle time can be short and performance can be pushed by increasing the clock rate.

Another key benefit of a simplified microprocessor implementation using RISC is that it allows many different companies to participate in microprocessor design. CISC processors are each typically dominated by a single large company that controls all implementations. RISC processors have made it possible for many different companies to participate in microprocessor design. For example, there are more than a dozen SPARC processor designs delivered or in progress from Bipolar Integrated Technology, Cypress Semiconductor/Ross Technology, Fujitsu Microelectronics, LSI Logic, Matra Semiconductor, Philips/Signetics and Texas Instruments. This increased competition leads directly to an acceleration in the rate of innovation, more variety and reduced pricing due to a non-monopoly environment.

Myths of RISC

Sometimes, people confuse the concepts of RISC with particular characteristics of RISC processors. Because RISC has fewer gates than CISC, it was first able to utilize pipelining as a technique to improve performance. However, using pipelining does not convert a CISC into a RISC.

What RISC is all about is carefully picking instructions that encourage the design of efficient implementations and optimizing compilers. Although many people think that RISC is defined by fewer instructions, whether a RISC design has more or fewer instructions than a CISC is largely irrelevant. Although most RISC processors usually do have fewer instructions, these instructions—by being simpler—are easier to execute than "complex" instructions.

Just because RISC instructions tend to be simpler, that does not mean that more instructions end up being executed. Careful measurements have shown that RISC processors do not execute significantly more instructions than CISC processors. A compiler's ability to optimize RISC instructions and keep more data in larger RISC register sets have evened out any differences between the complexity of RISC and CISC instructions.

A final fallacy is that somehow CISC can catch up to RISC. It is true that CISC processors can use almost any implementation technique as RISC, such as pipelining or on-chip caches. However, what is most often overlooked is that RISC will always be the first to use new techniques because RISC's greater simplicity speeds up design time. CISC always carry the baggage of extra instructions and hence uses up its silicon budget sooner than RISC. The inherent simplicity of RISC means that it is likely to remain a generation or two ahead of CISC in cost/performance.

The Future of RISC

What's next for RISC? Just about the time that CISC processors will start offering techniques such as pipelining and on-chip caches, RISC will be using even more advanced techniques. The next generation of RISC processors will use *super-scalar* execution techniques. This means that they will be capable of executing multiple instructions per cycle. This is already apparent with the IBM RS/6000 workstations. Super-scalar SPARC processors are about to emerge from LSI Logic, Cypress Semiconductor/Ross Technology and Texas Instruments. CISC processors may eventually be able to move to super-scalar execution, though by then RISC will be off to the next technique. CISC can never catch up.

RISC for Workstations

Workstations have broken the stranglehold on the desktop once owned by CISC platforms running MS DOS. Every major manufacturer of workstations now has a RISC offering. Indeed, essentially every industry observer is predicting a much more rapid increase in sales of RISC systems than for CISC computers. In terms of RISC processor volume, SPARC processors seem to have taken the lead. Analysts, such as Alex Brown and Sons, estimate that by the end of 1990, SPARC-based RISC systems would retain their large lead, commanding 71 percent of the RISC market. In second place will be the various systems using the MIPS RISC architecture, with 17 percent, followed by Hewlett-Packard's Precision Architecture, at 4 percent. As with personal computers, the driving force will be the availability of software. SPARC-based systems now have access to more than 2,100 SPARCware solutions.

RISC promises a new era of performance and low cost for computer users. Just as personal computers and workstations have taken over many of the tasks of minicomputers and terminals, RISC represents an evolution in the way computers operate.

SPARC: A Total Solution for RISC

BRIAN CASE

5

What sets SPARC apart from other RISC architectures is that it is not *just* an architecture. It's an entire system solution for high-performance, low-cost RISC computers based on open standards. The complete SPARC environment includes: a range of compatible CPU implementations from different vendors; a licensable, standard UNIX operating system, a window system and graphical user interface; essential file transfer software; optimized buses; an ABI distribution format for application software; and a wealth of compilers and development tools.

Unlike other RISC architectures—which are either proprietary or licensed as a single design to semiconductor houses for fabrication—SPARC was designed from the start to become a standard. Sun Microsystems has followed an open strategy of encouraging multiple semiconductor manufacturers to develop their own SPARC implementations. This fosters a wider variety of SPARC CPUs and offers greater opportunities for competition in various niches. And by providing an entire systems environment that is binary compatible, sun has helped SPARC become the leading RISC architecture, attracting the industry's widest selection of compatible RISC/UNIX software.

Reinventing the PC Model

While SPARC's open, standard concept differs from the traditional approach to 32-bit CPU architectures, there is a historical precedence. The move toward standards can be traced to the rapid acceleration of the personal computer market in the '80s. This market became huge in a short time because it was built around open standards for the processor architecture, the I/O bus architecture and the operating system. These standards drove the expansion of the market because they made possible the high sales volumes needed for low-cost production.

As a further consequence of these standards, a de facto binary format for the distribution of application programs emerged, which created a fourth standard. This standard software distribution format appealed to application developers, while the promise of a growing software base attracted more end users and hardware manufacturers, which led to an even higher production volume.

Realizing that the growth of the UNIX workstation market would require this same kind of standardization and that no standard RISC processor was available. Sun defined the SPARC processor architecture and made it generally available. Since then, Sun has defined and offered as open standards the other technologies that are key to rapid, PC-like growth. These technologies include the MBus processor interconnection bus, the SBus I/O and peripheral bus and the SPARC ABI.

In each case, these technologies have been defined with the future in mind. SPARC itself is a scalable RISC architecture that facilitates implementations in all ranges of cost and performance. MBus is a high-performance processor-to-memory interconnect designed to accommodate next-generation multiprocessor systems. SBus is a simple, yet high-performance I/O bus that allows sophisticated peripherals to be built on small cards. Because very little interface logic is required, SBus cards will be inexpensive. The SPARC ABI includes support for features such as dynamic linking that are important for adding functionality to future systems.

Architectural Similarities

One of the most obvious similarities between SPARC and other RISC architectures is the "size" of the machine. SPARC, like all other existing RISC architectures, is a 32-bit machine because the internal registers naturally hold 32-bit data and because a register can hold a 32-bit linear address. The size of internal or external data and address paths does not affect the classification of a machine. For example, all 68000-family implementations are 32-bit machines despite the fact that the original implementation had buses smaller than 32 bits and the newest implementations have (internal) buses wider than 32 bits. Although some new microprocessor architectures are being called 64-bit machines based on the data paths in their implementations, an architecture may be called a 64-bit machine only if it allows the direct implementation of 64-bit, linear-address pointers.

All RISCs have three-address, register-to-register operations; i.e., each of two source registers and one destination register is specified by separate fields in the instruction format and each field has enough bits to name any of the general registers. This allows an optimizing compiler to generate "non-destructive" computations when the source-register values need to be saved for use in future computations.

SPARC integer instructions allow one source operand to be either a register or a 13-bit constant. Other RISC architectures also have this feature, with the size of the constant allowed by the instruction format depending on other architectural details.

Although the SPARC architecture specification permits an implementation to have a very large register file, up to 520 registers (32 windows, 16 registers/window and eight global registers), the number of registers available at any one time (32 registers) is the same as in most other RISCs. In addition, the SPARC architecture specifies a fixed-size floating-point register file of 32 registers that is separate from the integer register file. Some RISCs, such as the MIPS architecture, have separate integer and FP register files while other architectures, such as the Motorola 88000, specify a combined file. Generally, separate integer and FP registers allow a compiler to keep a greater number of important values in high-speed registers.

Data memory in a RISC machine is accessed only through load-register and store-register instructions. In SPARC, load and store instructions have two basic addressing modes: register-plus-register and register-plus-immediate. The immediate is a 13-bit constant, as in the SPARC arithmetic instructions. Other useful addressing modes can be sythesized by specifying register R0, which in SPARC always reads as zero. This allows simple register indirect and absolute addressing to be performed by load and store instructions. Most other RISC architectures have approximately the same flexibility.

One similarity between SPARC and other RISC architectures is in the basic structure of the integer pipeline. Although this similarity is not actually architectural, it is heavily influenced by architecture. Current SPARC implementations have a four-stage pipeline consisting of instruction fetch, decode and register read, execute (ALU operation) and register-file write back. When other pipelines differ, it is usually by the addition of a fifth data-fetch stage before register write back.

The pipeline similarities are a consequence of the basic RISC constraints:

- Each instruction fetch is one, aligned word
- Instructions have consistent, easily decoded formats
- Each instruction can specify at most one arithmetic operation and one memory reference
- Each instruction can specify at most one destination register.

These constraints lead directly to a four- or five-stage pipeline because each of the constraints implies a separate, concurrently executing piece of hardware.

Architectural Differences: Register Windows

Despite the significant commonality between RISCs, the RISC constraints do allow considerable architectural freedom. As a result, SPARC is unique in some respects.

The most visible architectural difference between SPARC and its peers is in the register file model. SPARC defines a set of overlapping register windows arranged as a circular buffer. When a SAVE instruction is executed, the next window is allocated for use by a new procedure. When a RESTORE instruction is executed, the previous window is made active to restore the context of an old procedure. The overlapping of the windows—eight registers out of 16 are shared between caller and callee—permits very fast parameter passing between procedures.

Most other RISC architectures have a flat space of 32 integer registers. To avoid an excessive number of loads and stores around procedure calls, sophisticated register allocation algorithms must be integrated into compilers for these machines. These algorithms are generally effective for traditional programs, but do not currently handle the needs of dynamic linking as efficiently as register windows.

With the introduction of dynamic linking in AT&T's UNIX System V Release 4, register windows have become increasingly important, since compilers can no longer allocate registers between the main program and library routines. Because some library routines are linked at run time, the compiler may not know about register usage in the library routine.

When algorithms that handle dynamic linking in a flat register file work as well as register windows, SPARC will be able to fully exploit them. This is because the allocation of a new register window on a procedure call is distinct from the procedure call itself. Thus, if desired, SPARC compilers can easily treat the SPARC register file as a single, flat set of 32 integer registers. Thus, from a compiler point of view, register windows are at least no worse than a flat, 32-register file.

Register Windows Good for AI, Realtime

Recent research suggest that register windows and tagged arithmetic, found in the SPARC architecture but not in other commercial RISC machines, can provide significant performance gains for object-oriented languages such as C++, Lisp and Smalltalk. SPARC is also well-suited to many realtime and embedded applications due to its extremely short interrupt latency. When interrupts are enabled, the time from an interrupt to first instruction of the appropriate trap handler is typically only six machine cycles. The SPARC register window mechanism makes this possible since storing processor state in registers is much faster than storing in memory, as most architectures require. In realtime applications with a small number of tasks, the register windows can be partitioned into a few banks of two register windows each so that context switches are very fast. (Two windows are required per context to provide space for the hardware interrupt handler.) No register state need be saved to memory at all between these context switches.

Artificial intelligence applications require large address

spaces and dynamic binding. For AI and expert system applications, SPARC systems offer instructions supporting tagged arithmetic. In a tagged operation, the two low-order bits of each operand specify its type. If both operands are small (up to 30 bits) integers, the operation can be executed in one cycle. If one or both are actually pointers to larger values (as indicated by the tag bits), the tagged operation causes a branch or trap to more elaborate code to handle that case. Since most of the time the operands are both small integers, this can greatly improve performance of applications written in languages with dynamic typing. Franz Inc. reported a 15 percent performance gain in its SPARC Lisp product due to tagged arithmetic.

Annulling Delayed Branches

Another SPARC feature that is not found in all RISCs is annulling delayed branches. These branches are just like the delayed branches found in other RISCs except that the instruction in the delay slot of the branch is not executed under some conditions. SPARC conditional annulling branches execute the delay instruction only if the branch is taken. This behavior is especially appropriate for the conditional branches that close loops.

Using the annulling feature, the first instruction in the loop can be copied into the delay slot of the branch regardless of its function (unless it is itself a branch). This guarantees that the benefit of the delayed branch—one less cycle in the loop—can be realized.

Except for delayed branches, all operations defined by the SPARC architecture are interlocked fully. In particular, a load followed by an instruction that uses the loaded data will cause a SPARC implemenation to stall until the loaded data is available. This situation is called a "load-use interlock."

In contrast, the original MIPS architecture specified a single load delay slot to allow an instruction to be executed while the data-cache access proceeded. The restriction was that the instruction in the load-delay slot, i.e., immediately following the load, must not reference the register being loaded.

It is interesting to note that the MIPS-II architecture, which is implemented in the R6000 ECL chip set, adds an annulling delayed branch to the MIPS-I instruction set and eliminates the load delay slot that is a part of the architecture of the R2000/R3000 chips. Thus, there is some indication that RISC architectures will converge over time and that the differences between architectures will primarily be a matter of instruction encoding.

Conditional-Branch Architecture

Another important difference between SPARC and other RISCs is in the conditional-branch architecture. SPARC defines a tradition set of condition codes to communicate relational information from comparison instructions to conditional branches. In contrast, many other RISCs define compare instructions that create relational information as a piece of data in a register and conditional branches that branch based on the contents of a register.

Historically, the problem with condition codes is that they are set as an uncontrollable side-effect of the execution of arithmetic instructions, not just the instructions that perform the desired comparisons. Generating relational information into registers, as is done by many RISCs, is one way around the problem, but one or more of the general registers must be used to hold the information. SPARC mitigates the side effect problem by allowing each arithmetic and logical instruction to decide whether or not it will modify the condition codes. The modification of the condition codes is determined by a single bit in the instruction encoding.

The SPARC Software Environment

While there are architectural differences between SPARC and other RISCs, an area that sets SPARC apart is its system software, which is broad, available now and based on standards. This not only allows designers to quickly develop a system, but assures a range of compatible machines from other vendors that can share the same software. Sun has defined an ABI for SPARC that will greatly simplify the creation of UNIX software that will run across all SPARC systems, from laptops to supercomputers. In addition, Sun licenses its robust operating system, SunOS™, a merge of UNIX System V and 4.3/4.2 BSD. Products designed around

SunOS can easily be migrated to AT&T's UNIX System V Release 4, today's UNIX standard.

The close connection between SunOS and System V.4 offers particular benefits to software developers. With a large base of compatible systems, they can reduce the costs they would have incurred in creating multiple versions of their application. This gives them more time to concentrate on designing innovative products—which will have a large installed base. Meanwhile, end users are assured that their investment won't become obsolete due to a large, growing market for SPARC hardware and software. And there are reduced training and software maintenance costs.

Sun also licenses its other essential system software. This includes: Open Windows™, made up of the OPEN LOOK™ graphical user interface; the X11/NeWS™ window system and XView™ toolkit; and ONC/NFS™, the de facto networking standard. Another approach is for SPARC system developers to acquire these software elements through Interactive Systems Corporation, the leader in the UNIX systems porting business.

Among the SPARC system software products being offered by Sun are optimizing compilers that allow the development of efficient application software in languages such as C, C++, FORTRAN, Pascal, Lisp and Modula 2. (Sun's C and FORTRAN compilers are also available from Interactive.) There is also a growing list of software companies such as Wind River Systems, JMI, Mizar and Ready Systems that offer products that support SPARC in realtime and embedded markets.

For hardware and software design, Sun offers several useful tools. The SPARC Architectural Simulator (SPARCsim™) eases the development task by allowing designers to simulate an entire SPARC system architecture before building a prototype. Information can be fed into other analysis tools such as the SPARC Trace Analyzer. The SPARC Remote Debugger has full source-code symbolic debugging capabilities for debugging processes on remote SPARC systems. When combined with SPARCmon™ (SPARC target monitor), the remote debugger enables developers to write and debug programs using the robust Sun workstation environment, then transfer the program to the target and perform final debugging as if it were on the development system.

SPARC Buses: MBus, SBus

The SPARC architecture together with the ABI standardizes the compiler interface, the operating system interface and the window system interface. This standardization will be universal in SPARC-based general-purpose computers (as opposed to SPARC-based embedded computers) because application software will depend on the ABI.

Other aspects of the SPARC picture are more optional. MBus, for example, is an extension of the time-honored "pin-compatible" packaging so familiar to those who buy second-source microprocessors. The idea was that a manufacturer could buy a microprocessor from any of the sources and plug it into a standard socket because all the sources built chips with the same pin-out.

In the near future, semiconductor manufacturers will be able to put on a single chip what today takes a few chips to implement. To be able to replace the multi-chip solution with the single chip, a standard "pin-out" at a level higher than actual microprocessor packages is needed. This standard pin-out is MBus.

In addition to providing an upgrade path that can track increasing circuit densities, MBus provides a standard, higher-level protocol for small-scale multiprocessors. Systems with a small number of processors will appear on the desktop sometime during this decade and MBus will be there to support them.

SBus was also created with the needs of the desktop in mind, but will be appropriate for very large systems, such as file and compute servers, as well. SBus is low-overhead, high-throughput synchronous bus for the local attachment of peripheral controllers over a small distance. The bus is designed so that slave devices require a minimum of buffers and control logic. Its small card size—the size of an index card—encourages highly integrated design and low power consumption. SBus is optimized for the technologies that will become dominant in the '90s: CMOS and surface mount.

Unlike the traditional PC plug-in card but like cards for the VME and similar buses, SBus cards can be made wider to accommodate complex peripherals. For example, the monochrome display controller for the SPARCStation™ 1 is contained on a single-wide SBus card while the GX display controller (for Sun's low-cost graphics models) is implemented on a double-wide card.

Large systems, such as file and compute servers, will likely be based on multiprocessors. SBus will serve these systems well because each processor can have at least one local SBus. Thus, as the size of the server is increased with the addition of processors, the available I/O capacity of the system also increases commensurately.

The installed base of SBus machines will continue to grow, since Sun will use SBus as its I/O interconnect for future systems and vendors of other SPARC computers are utilizing SBus. Sun has made SBus an open specification, meaning that system and board developers can implement SBus designs free of any licensing restrictions. In order to simplify development even further, the SBus DMA interface chip is being made available by LSI Logic. It enables SBus card vendors to design intelligent functions such as graphics accelerators and I/O controllers for SBus.

SPARC: The Standard for the '90s

As a total system solution for RISC, SPARC has been very successful. More than 53,000 SPARC systems have been shipped to date, more than any other RISC/UNIX computer. SPARC's rich development environment, fast-growing selection of application software and variety of implementations have helped SPARC become the choice for many system vendors. It delivers high levels of performance for a low cost. The flexibility of the architecture paves the way for future implementations that will offer performance many times greater than today's systems. Moreover, the openness of the architecture encourages multiple vendors to apply their latest technological innovations to the same processor architecture, benefitting all.

The Role of RISC in Advanced Computer Design

DAVID R. DITZEL

6

It has now been a decade since the start of the RISC (Reduced Instruction Set Computer) versus CISC (Complex Instruction Set Computer) debate.† However, it has only been in the last few years that RISC has emerged as the processor architecture of choice for computers aiming for improved performance at a reasonable price. This change has been driven by the recent commercial availability of RISC chips such as SPARC, the Motorola 88000 and the R3000.

Whether RISC is better than CISC is no longer merely a topic of academic debate. CISC architectures such as Digital's VAX, Motorola's 68000 family and Intel's 80×86 now have commercial RISC competitors that are out-performing and out-price/performing them at every turn. RISC is here to stay and the success of RISC will lead to the decline of most CISC architectures.

RISC has succeeded in part because of its simplicity: simple machines run faster and more efficiently. However, RISC also has long-term advantages over CISC architecture that go far beyond simple instructions. RISC architectures are designed to provide a far superior interface between the hardware and the compiler. They are far easier to implement and design and so will be the first to take advantage of new techniques. Given their inherent inefficiences, CISC architectures will never be able to catch up.

Six key technologies are critical to the future evolution of advanced computer design and to the rate at which the technology will be advanced. They are open implementations, new architectures, pin-out standards, new technologies, multiprocessing and compiler technology.

---

† D.R. Ditzel and D.A. Patterson, The Case for the Reduced Instruction Set Computer, *Computer Architecture News*, August 1980.

SPARC Leads the Pack

Today's leading RISC architectures have basic similarities. For arithmetic and logical operations, all RISCs address 32 32-bit integer registers at a time. All have 32-bit-long fixed-length instructions and use 32-bit pointers for a 4-gigabyte virtual address space. And all RISCs have byte addressing of memory and a simple load/store memory model.

Which RISC architecture is the best? That depends on your criteria, but the vote of the marketplace is clear. According to analysts like International Data Corp., Dataquest and Alex Brown & Co., SPARC (Scalable Processor ARChitecture) is the leading RISC architecture. Following SPARC are the R3000 from MIPS and Motorola's 88000.

SPARC was designed to be simple enough for low-end laptops, yet powerful enough for mainframe or supercomputer applications. It is a superset of most current commercial RISC chips. While most RISCs have delayed branch schemes, the SPARC delayed branch instruction can also be "annulled," meaning that the instruction will be cancelled under certain conditions. Annulled branches greatly improve the compiler's ability to schedule instructions and avoids the excessively high number of no-ops that other RISC architectures often execute.

At any particular time, SPARC appears to the programmer as having 32 floating point registers and 32 integer registers. Unlike other RISC architectures, SPARC can use up to 512 registers operating as register windows under program control. When a SAVE instruction is executed, the next window is allocated for use by a new procedure. When a RESTORE instruction is executed, the previous window is made active to restore the context of an old procedure. The overlapping of the windows—eight registers out of 16 are shared between caller and callee—permits very fast parameter-passing between procedures.

Most other RISC architectures have only a flat space of 32 integer registers. To avoid an excessive number of loads and stores around procedure calls, sophisticated register allocation algorithms must be integrated into compilers for these machines. These algorithms are generally effective for traditional programs, but do not currently handle the needs of dynamic linking as efficiently as register windows.

With the introduction of dynamic linking in AT&T's UNIX System V Release 4, register windows have become increasingly important, since compilers can no longer allocate registers between the main program and library routines. Because some library routines are linked at run time, the compiler cannot know about register usage in the dynamically linked library routine and hence cannot perform inter-procedural register allocation. Register windows eliminate this problem.

Recent research suggests that register windows and tagged arithmetic, found in the SPARC architecture but not in other commercial RISC machines, can provide significant performance gains for object-oriented languages such as C++, Lisp and Smalltalk. SPARC is also well-suited to many realtime and embedded applications due to its extremely short interrupt latency. The large number of registers can also be used as banks of registers so that no registers need to be saved during a context switch.

Open Architecture Implementations

One of the most influential factors in the evolution of future processor design is not a technology, but an approach. The rate of innovation in microprocessor design is controlled to a large extent by the number of innovators. With most RISC and CISC architectures, one company is essentially in control of its own proprietary architecture—and the innovation, as well.

What really sets SPARC apart from other RISC and CISC architectures is that is is not *just* an implementation, but an open architecture definition. By allowing many companies to have their own design teams, SPARC lets each team add innovation and accelerate the rate of improvement in microprocessor design. This strategy fosters a wider variety of SPARC CPUs—giving microprocessor users more choices as well as second-source alternatives—and offers greater opportunities for competition in various niches.

The fact that this innovation is occurring with RISC is only due to the fact that no proprietary CISC vendor has been willing to open up its architecture for others to implement. The lack of any such monopoly for SPARC chips will foster competition, which means that SPARC chips will cost less than offerings based on proprietary architectures.

New Architectures: Superscalar Execution

CISC architectures have typically had implementations that need an average of 10 or more clocks cycles to execute every instruction. Most RISC processors have come close to executing one instruction every clock cycle; the next generation of RISC processors will be able to execute more than one instruction per clock cycle. This multiple-instruction-per-clock execution is known as *superscalar* execution.

IBM is already using superscalar execution in its new $S6000 workstation—the successor to the unpopular RT that employs a new CPU architecture. The RS6000/520 is able to achieve 24 MIPS at 20 MHz in a design that is theoretically capable of doing five instructions at a time. Floating-point performance in superscalar designs can also be quite impressive, since loop overhead can be completely hidden.

LSI Logic's Lightning SPARC processor will also be able to execute up to five instructions per clock cycle, for 80 MIPS of sustainable performance. Cypress Semiconductor/Ross Technology is working on a superscalar SPARC design called Pinnacle; Texas Instruments is working on a highly integrated BiCMOS superscalar SPARC design. Three next-generation superscalar SPARC designs will make possible a variety of cost and performance tradeoffs that no individual design could meet.

An interesting alternative to superscalar execution is super-pipelining. This technique increases the pipeline length in attempt to speed up the basic clock rate of a one instruction/cycle processor. If the goal was to make a machine run twice as fast, one might do this either by making the pipeline twice as long, or by doing two instructions in parallel with a superscalar processor. While a superscalar processor might issue four or five instructions in parallel, making a pipeline four or five times longer is impractical. Pipeline breakage, clock skew, memory latency and software incompatibility problems make superpipelining less attractive than superscalar operation for multiple generations of chip implementations. Superpipelining makes most sense for scientific codes in which basic block lengths are large, because it requires special instruction scheduling optimizations to avoid pipeline breakage penalties. Superscalar operation, on the other hand, provides for very high floating point rates, as demonstrated by the IBM RS/6000.

Chip Pin-Out Standards: The MBus

Personal computer and workstation users have for years wished that each new generation of microprocessors would be pin-compatible with the previous generation, which would allow them to upgrade their computers simply by replacing the micro-processor chip. So far, we have all been disappointed. Even within a particular processor architecture controlled by a single manufac-turer, no two generations of chips have been able to stick to a standard pin-out.

All that is about to change. For the first time in the history of the microprocessor industry, a common microprocessor pin-out standard is emerging. Individual manufacturers are already plan-ning multiple generations of processors that conform to this pin-out. Even more revolutionary is the notion that several different semiconductor manufacturers will design SPARC processors to this standard.

The common pin-out is a side effect of RISC architectures, specifically SPARC, becoming an open standard. Systems manu-facturers, led by companies such as Sun Microsystems, ICL and Xerox, need a common pin-out to enable quick upgrades for the ever-increasing variety of SPARC processors.

The SPARC MBus was designed with enough bandwidth to accommodate microprocessors for the next three to five years. The MBus uses a 64-bit transfer operating at a 40-MHz synchronous clock rate to achieve a bandwidth of 320 megabytes per second. The 40-MHz clock rate was selected as the highest speed at which CMOS chips could operate using a bus of only a few inches on standard PC boards.

In addition, the MBus protocols allow the processor to have its own internal cache or even a large second-level cache. Building multiprocessors with MBus-based microprocessors is trivial be-cause all of the cache coherence logic is built into the MBus protocol and associated microprocessor. Multiple chips need only be wired in parallel to build a multiprocessor.

The Cypress/Ross Technology 7C604 SPARC cache controller/MMU and the LSI Logic L64815 SPARC cache controller/MMU are the first chips to appear using the MBus. LSI Logic has announced that its next-generation Lightning SPARC processor will use the same MBus specification. Other implementations of SPARC chips are expected to follow the MBus standard as well.

New Semiconductor Technologies

Most RISC chips today are implemented in CMOS technology. In the last year, we have seen two single-chip RISC processors implemented in ECL: the 80-MHz B5000 SPRAC processor from Bipolar Integrated Technology and a 60-MHz ECL R6000 processor designed by MIPS Computer Systems using the BIT process. We can expect to see RISC microprocessors implemented in GaAs and BiCMOS technologies in the next year or two.

Microprocessor clock rates are primarily determined by the underlying technologies, all of which are making continued improvements. Over the next two years, we should see CMOS processors operating at 40 to 80 MHz, BiCMOS chips at 50 to 100 MHz, ECL at 80 to 150 MHz and GaAs at 150 to 250 MHz.

Multiprocessors Will Improve Processing Power

Because processor clock rates are limited at any particular point in time, other techniques will have to be used to exceed fundamental device scaling. The area that promises the most improvement in processing power is the use of multiple processors in a single system. Multiprocessor systems will become the norm rather than the exception in the future.

Small numbers of processors may be tied together directly using the MBus. Large numbers of processors (such as those that number in the hundreds or thousands) must be tied together using more elaborate interconnection schemes. Most small-scale multiprocessors will use a shared memory paradigm, but shared memory may not be appropriate for the largest multiprocessor systems.

Building the hardware for multiprocessors will be easy. Building the software to make multiprocessors applicable to most of today's programming problems will be exceedingly hard. It is relatively easy to have an operating system run a different process on each processor. However, in order to run a single task on multiple processors the application program must currently be re-written. Within the next three to five years, we will see compiler technology that will be able to automatically de-compose only a small fraction of today's programs to run over multiple processors.

It will be the common availability of multiple processors systems in the early 1990s that will drive us to learn to use them effectively in the latter half of the decade.

Compiler Technology

Advanced compiler technology is commonly associated with RISC technology, though the reasons are often misunderstood. Processor architectures such as SPARC were designed with optimizing compilers in mind. SPARC features such as fixed-length instructions, large register sets, register windows and delayed branches with annulling work well with modern compiler technology.

CISC machines, on the other hand, often cripple the benefit of optimizing compilers due to too-small register sets, non-orthogonal instructions, bizarre addressing modes and the inability to predict the time it will take a series of instructions to execute. It's not that optimizing compilers are essential for RISC: they simply work much better with them.

The future challenge for compiler writers will be to generate code that runs reasonably well on all implementations of the same architecture. Superscalar architectures will be able to run well with existing code and optimizations for these processors generally will not hurt performance on today's RISC processors. Other techniques, such as superpipelining, may require special compiler changes to run well and can end up pessimizing the performance of existing processors.

Conclusion

RISC has become an enabling technology. Its simplicity has allowed it to be non-proprietary and results in entire families of RISC processors such as SPARC. The competition fostered by multiple implementations is, in turn, accelerating new architectural techniques such as superscalar execution.

Newer technologies like ECL and GaAs will be used with RISC first because it requires fewer gates than CISC architectures. Advanced techniques will initially be used on RISC processors and then, with improvements in VLSI technology, these techniques will fit on CISC based chips. This trend is evident today, with CISC processors now claiming to use "RISC techniques." The irony is that there isn't any specific RISC technique. Innovation can occur easiest with RISC; CISC is doomed by its inherent complexity to always lag behind.

Multiprocessor systems will be driven to use RISC to achieve ultimate performance merely because each RISC processor will be far more powerful than the corresponding CISC available at the same time. Finally, because RISC was designed to work with compilers, we will see a trend in which the best compiler optimization will be for RISC processors. Advanced computer design owes RISC a debt of gratitude.

SPARC Implementations

First 32-Bit SPARC-Based Processors Implemented in High-Speed CMOS

7

Masood Namjoo

Abstract

This paper presents an overview of the first two implementations of Sun Microsystem's Scalable Processor ARChitecture (SPARC). The first implementation, MB86900, is designed using a 20,000 gate 1.3 micron CMOS gate-array from Fujitsu. It operates at a clock rate of 16.6 MHz and delivers an average performance of 10 integer MIPS. The second, CY7C601, is a full custom chip designed using Cypress Semiconductor's 0.8 micron CMOS process. It operates at a clock rate of 33 MHz and delivers an average performance of 20 integer MIPS. In this paper we discuss the basic features of these processors, their similarities and differences and the trade-offs used in their design. We also address the issues of design verification, test generation and fault simulation.

Introduction

During the last three years several different RISC-based micro-processors were introduced by different vendors among them were the first implementations of Sun Microsystem's SPARC architecture. The SPARC architecture is based on the UC Berkeley RISC project; it uses a large windowed register file and defines a simple and efficient set of integer and floating-point instructions which can be grouped into the following five major categories.

    a. Arithmetic, Logical and Shift Instructions—These instructions perform a specific operation on two source operands and write the results into a destination register. Most of these instructions have two types: one type does not change the condition code bits and the other type sets the condition code bits based on the computed result.

b. Special Registers Read/Write Instruction—The SPARC architecture defines four special registers. These registers are: Processor Status Register(PSR), Trap Base Register (TBR), Window Invalid Mask (WIM) and Y register used during integer multiplications for generating a 64-bit product. The instructions in this category are used to read the contents or write a new value into these special registers.

c. Memory Reference Instructions—This category is made up of load and store instructions. Integer load and store instructions operate on byte, halfword, word, and double-word operands. Floating-point and coprocessors loads and stores operate on word and double-word operands only. Special instructions are defined for use with multiprocessor applications. These instructions are "atomic" in nature and perform a load from a memory location followed by a store into the same memory location without releasing the processor's bus until the transaction is completed. All integer load and store instructions have alternate versions which can be used to access up to 256 different address spaces in the system.

d. Control Transfer Instructions—This category consists of conditional and unconditional relative branches with 22-bit word displacement, call with 30-bit word displacement and register indirect absolute jumps and returns. Branch instructions use a single delayed instruction. The delayed-branch concept is a simple way to improve the processor's performance by filling up the processor's pipeline with useful instructions while the target of the branch is being calculated. Normally, the target of a branch is not known until later in the processor's pipeline. Instead of waiting for the target calculation, the processor executes the following instruction and then executes the branch itself. The instruction in the delay slot of a branch may be nullified by specifying the annul bit in the instruction. For conditional branches the delay slot instruction is always executed unless the branch is not taken (i.e., when the conditions are false) and the annul bit is set. For unconditional branches, on the other hand, the delay slot instruction is nullified whenever the annul bit is set.

e. Floating-point/Coprocessor Instructions—The SPARC architecture defines single, double, and extended precision formats for most frequent floating-point instructions, conforming to the IEEE-standard. The coprocessor instructions, on the other hand, may be defined by the user. The floating-point and coprocessor instructions are executed by separate units concurrent with the execution of integer instructions.

SPARC instructions have very simple formats and use only two essential addressing modes: register+register and register+signed-immediate. The simplified format of instructions results in faster decoding of instructions and more efficient usage of the processor's data path. The execution unit can be easily optimized for speed allowing shorter cycle time for the entire processor. In the following sections the general features of the first two CMOS implementations of SPARC, their similarities and differences, and the design verification procedures used in the development of these processors are discussed.

Implementations of SPARC

Similar to any RISC-based design, one major goal in the design of SPARC processors has been to reduce the average number of cycles per instruction (CPI). Using present technology, one can design a SPARC processor capable of executing instructions at a rate of one or more instructions per clock cycle. The main bottleneck is the bandwidth to and from the memory for executing load and store instructions. For this reason the usage of a fast cache is necessary in applications where the performance is important. For a given clock rate, the processor-cache bus bandwidth can be doubled by using a 64-bit instead of 32-bit bus. This would increase the number of pins on the processor chip, making it larger and more expensive. Since the initial CMOS implementations of SPARC were targeted for a large variety of applications, a 32-bit bus was adopted, allowing most instructions to be executed in a single cycle with the exception of load and store instructions that use the same bus for fetching instructions as well as data.

Different implementations of the SPARC may have different

number of windows. For an implementation with N windows the total number of general purpose registers is $16 \times N + 8$. The gate-array implementation (MB86900) provides 120 general purpose registers, from which 8 are global registers and the rest are divided into 7 overlapped windows of 24 registers each (N = 7 was chosen due to the available RAM size in the gate-array). The full custom implementation (CY7C601), on the other hands, provides 136 general purpose registers; 8 global registers and 8 overlapped windows of 24 registers each. Since all instructions use 5-bit source and destination fields, only 32 registers corresponding to the current window are accessible to the programmer at any given time. The current window is identified by the value of CWP field in the Processor Status Register (PRS).

External Bus Structure

As mentioned earlier both designs use a single 32-bit data bus ($D<31:0>$) and a single 32-bit address bus ($A<31:0>$) for interface to the cache or memory. In the gate-array version, the low portion of the address bus is sent (unlatched) a cycle earlier than the high portion. In a cache-based system, this would allow the system designer to latch the low address externally and use the output of the latch directly to access the cache data and cache tag RAMs. The high portion of the address is not as critical as the low portion and therefore is latched on the chip before it is sent out. The external latch in this scheme also functions as a buffer for driving the heavily loaded cache address lines. Once the cache tags are read, the high portion of the address is used to compare the tags in that cycle and to send a cache miss/hit signal to the processor. In the custom version, the address generation logic is highly optimized for speed and therefore all address bits are sent unlatched. This would allow the maximum time for cache access and tag comparison.

Almost every cycle on the bus is either an instruction fetch, a data fetch, or a data store cycle. For every cache access the result of cache miss/hit is given to the processor a cycle later. During a cache miss, the cache control logic first stops the processor, then handles the miss and strobes the missed instruction/data to the processor while the processor is stopped. Since the processor normally advances to the next cycle, the missed cache address must be somehow regenerated.

One external difference between the gate-array and custom version is that the custom version has some additional logic for regenerating the missed address during a cache-miss process. This is done simply by asserting a signal which forces the processor to send the old address on the bus. In the gate-array version, the missed address must be saved and regenerated externally during a cache miss.

In both designs, the same $(D<31:0>)$ bus is used for fetching instructions as well as data. This results in two-cycle execution of single-word load and three-cycle execution of double-word load instructions. For the case of stores, the processor uses an extra cycle in order to allow time for tag check (before the write operation) and turning the bus around by the system. Therefore, execution of single-word stores takes three cycles and execution of double-word stores takes four cycles. Observation of large benchmarks on SPARC indicates instruction mixes with approximately 15% loads and 5% stores, minimizing the effect of multicycle loads and stores on the average number of cycles per instruction.

Internal Control Logic

Both designs use a four-stage pipeline. In the basic pipeline operation, the processor fetches an instruction during the fetch-stage (F). The fetched instruction is decoded in the decode-stage (D) and source operands are read from the register file. In the execute-stage (E), the instruction is executed and in the write-stage (W) the results are written into the destination register. The write-stage is aborted if a trap or exception is raised while the instruction is being executed.

The instruction pipeline consists of various fields of instructions corresponding to the decode, execute and write stages of the pipeline and a two-stage instruction buffer. The instruction buffer, continues to prefetch new instructions once the processor encounters an instruction that needs more than one cycle to complete. This buffer is empty during a sequence of single-cycle instructions and is used only when a multi-cycle instruction is decoded. Multi-cycle instructions use one or more internally generated opcodes to complete execution. These internal opcodes, generated using random logic in the gate-array version and a PLA in the custom version, are jammed into the instruction pipeline as needed.

In the gate-array version taken branch instructions execute in one and untaken branches execute in two cycles. The control logic is designed so that all branches are assumed to be taken and the target instruction is fetched immediately. The processor, however, would ignore the target instruction if the condition code evaluation resulted in false condition. In the custom version, on the other hands, all branch instructions (conditional or unconditional) are performed in a single cycle. The single-cycle branch execution results from the early availability of condition codes generated by a highly optimized ALU and condition code evaluation logic.

Floating-Point Coprocessor

In both implementations, the floating-point unit is tightly coupled with the integer unit and integer instructions can execute concurrently with floating-point operations. The interface to the floating-point is however different for the two implementations.

The gate-array version uses a separate 32-bit F bus ($F<31:0>$) for dispatching floating-point instructions to the floating-point unit. Every floating-point instruction uses the F bus for two cycles. In the first cycle the instruction itself and in second cycle the address of the instruction is sent to the floating-point unit. In the custom version, the floating-point unit receives its instructions directly from the data bus and uses additional control logic to synchronize its pipeline with the integer unit's pipeline. As a result, a new floating-point instruction can be fetched every cycle. The gate-array version works with a companion floating-point controller chip and can be interfaced to either W1164/W1165 or TI-8847 arithmetic units capable of delivering 1.1 to 1.8 mega-flops for double-precision linpack benchmark. The custom version works with a different floating-point controller chip which interfaces to the TI8847 floating-point chip capable of delivering approximately 3 times the floating-point performance of the gate-array version. The custom version also supports an additional coprocessor port which can be used to interface to a user defined coprocessor unit.

The floating-point unit and coprocessor have their own set of registers (thirty-two 32-bit registers), a status register (FSR/CSR), a queue for holding the instructions that need to be executed (FQ/CQ), and the logic for handling load/store instructions, dispatching the instructions to the arithmetic units, and checking dependencies between instructions.

Design Verification

In the development of custom and semi-custom VLSI designs, one important issue that needs careful consideration is design correctness and quality of testing. Most of today's VLSI processors have a very short development cycle. Complex chips go through their design phase and get to their first Silicon within a few months rather than years. Due to importance of design quality, extensive logic simulation and timing verification is needed in order to guarantee fully functional parts based on the first Silicon. In both SPARC designs, the gate-level model of the entire processor chip, was simulated in an environment that consisted of a simplified cache/memory model, the floating-point unit and a stimulus generation unit for controlling those synchronous and asynchronous input signals that are not usually exercised during normal program execution.

In this simulation environment, the design is tested using self-test diagnostics written in SPARC assembly language. The procedure for running simulation with a particular diagnostic consists of assembling the program, loading the cache with the object code generated by the assembler, executing all instructions in the program on the simulation model, and comparing instruction/address traces as well as the final state of the processor against a non-pipelined instruction-level SPARC architecture simulator written in C language.

The stimulus generation unit is controlled by programmable seeds which are fetched from a seed memory in parallel with program execution. Associated with every instruction's address is a seed that is generated by the assembler. Using different seeds different external events such as cache-miss bus cycles, memory exception bus cycles and external interrupts are simulated in a controllable and repeatable manner.

From testability point of view, both designs provide controllability and observability of all internal logic blocks and registers through the processor's datapath using normal instructions. The gate-array version uses a fully scannable design which connects all internal registers together as a single scan chain. The fully scannable design of the gate-array reduced the overall effort spent on test pattern generation with the use of ATPG, resulting in a fault coverage above 97%. The custom version, on the other hand, does not use scan design. Fault simulation, therefore, was needed in order to improve the overall fault coverage. Approximately 160,000 vectors were used for functional verification of the chip from which 30,000 vectors were fault simulated resulting in a coverage of greater than 98% for detectable faults.

The gate-array version does not use any PLA's tri-state internal bus, or precharge circuitry. The entire control logic is implemented using random logic gates with less than 1000 equivalent 2-input nand gates. In the custom version, most of the control logic is implemented using PLAs which are automatically generated from truth tables.

Finally, both designs were fully verified using a static timing verifier at the chip-level which traces all internal and external time critical paths and reports the results in the form of short-path and long-path set-up/hold time violations. After full chip timing verification, the worst case cycle time for the gate-array was 60ns and for the full custom version 30ns. With an average CPI of 1.5 this gives a performance of approximately 10 integer MIPS for the gate-array and 20 integer MIPS for the custom version of the SPARC chips.

Conclusions

The first implementations of SPARC architecture in CMOS technology show a major improvement in performance in comparison with non-RISC machines. This level of processor performance, until a few years ago, was achievable only in main-frames. Even higher levels of performance can be reached with future more advanced process and packaging technologies. As processor chips become faster the engineering of systems and boards that use these chips at their highest speed is becoming a new challenge. Therefore, extensive system-level logic simulation and timing verification is necessary for a successful product.

References

1. R. Garner et al., "The Scalable Processor Architecture (SPARC)," *Proceedings of the IEEE Compcon*, Spring 1988, pp. 278–283.

2. S. Muchnick et al., "Optimizing Compilers for the SPARC Architecture: An Overview," *Proceedings of the IEEE Compcon*, Spring 1988, pp. 284–288.

3. S. Kleiman, D. Williams, "UNIX on SPARC," *Proceedings of the IEEE Compcon*, Spring 1988, pp. 289–293.

4. M. Namjoo, A. Agrawal, D.C. Jackson, L. Quach "CMOS Gate Array Implementation of the SPARC Architecture," *Proceedings of the IEEE Compcon*, Spring 1988, pp. 10–13.

5. L. Quach, R. Chuek, "CMOS Gate Array Implementation of SPARC," *Proceedings of the IEEE Compcon*, Spring 1988, pp. 14–17.

6. M. Namjoo et al., "CMOS Custom Implementation of the SPARC Architecture," *Proceedings of the IEEE Compcon*, Spring 1988, pp. 18–20.

7. A. Agrawal, E.W. Brown, J. Petolino, J.R. Peterson, "Design Considerations for a Bipolar Implementation of SPARC," *Proceedsing of the IEEE Compcon*, Spring 1988, pp. 6–9.

SPARC: An ASIC Solution for High-Performance Microprocessors

8

ANANT AGRAWAL • ROBERT B. GARNER • DONALD C. JACKSON

Abstract

Sun Microsystems' Scalable Processor Architecture (SPARC) defines a general purpose 32-bit processor architecture. It was designed to allow cost effective and high performance implementations across a range of technologies. The simple yet efficient nature of the architecture makes it possible to implement it in a short period of time. It also makes SPARC very attractive for implementation in ASIC technologies, without sacrificing high performance. Its first implementation has been done in Fujitsu's C20K gate array, and is the first high performance microprocessor to be designed in an ASIC technology. This paper summarizes the architecture and its gate array implementation.

Sun Microsystems is working towards making SPARC a truly open, multi-vendor processor architecture. It has already been licensed to three semiconductor companies: Fujitsu Microelectronics, Cypress Semiconductor and Bipolar Integrated Technology. A number of system houses including AT&T and Xerox have announced their intent to use SPARC in future products. In addition, the semiconductor licensees have had a number of design wins.

Introduction

SPARC™ defines a 32-bit general-purpose integer, IEEE-standard floating-point processor instruction set. The design goal was to define a very simple yet efficient architecture that could be implemented cost effectively in various technologies, where some of could be faster and possibly less dense.

The simplicity of the architecture enabled us to implement the first SPARC integer unit (IU) in a single Fujitsu 20K-gate, 1.5-micron CMOS gate array. The floating-point unit was implemented using two Weitek chips and a controller chip implemented in the same Fujitsu gate array technology. This, coupled with a 128-Kbyte cache, gave us the first SPARC-based workstations and servers, running at 60 ns (16.67 MHz) cycle time. They were announced concurrently with the architecture and a large set of vendor application software on July 8, 1987.

In addition to the gate array designed with Fujitsu Microelectronics, Sun is currently working with Cypress Semiconductor to develop a custom 0.8-micron CMOS implementation and with Bipolar Integrated Technology on a custom ECL implementation.

This paper introduces the SPARC architecture and its first implementation. Also covered is the suitability of the architecture for realtime applications. A complete architectural specification is available in [SPARC87]. Papers have been written that cover the architecture [Garner88], compilers [Muchnick88], SunOS on SPARC [Kleiman88], and the Fujitsu [Namjoo88, Quach88] and Cypress [NamjCypr88] implementations. [Agrawal88] talks about some of the design consideration for the bipolar ECL implementation of SPARC. An introduction to RISCs is in [Patterson85].

The SPARC allows for a floating-point coprocessor and a second non-dedicated coprocessor with user defined instructions.

Integer Unit

SPARC defines 55 basic integer instructions and their variations. Instructions include a comprehensive set of logical, arithmetic, control transfer, memory reference and multiprocessor instructions. Support for AI languages is provided through tagged arithmetic instructions.

Registers

SPARC is a register intensive architecture where a large bank of registers is divided into sets of overlapping registers known as *windows* [Katevenis83]. The architecture defines up to 32 windows. The actual number may vary across implementations. Thus, the IU may contain from 40 to 520 registers[1]. Each window con-

---

[1] A minimal, 40-register, two-window implementation comprises 8 *ins*, 8 *locals*, 8 *outs*, 8 *globals*, and 8 trap handler *locals*.

sists of 32 registers which are divided into 8 *global* registers (same for all windows), 8 *ins*, 8 *locals* (unique to each window), and 8 *outs*. Adjacent register windows share eight registers (*outs-ins*). Overlapped windows provide an efficient way to pass parameters during procedure calls and returns. The compiler paper [Muchnick88] explains how windowed registers can be used.

The active window is identified by the Current Window Pointer (CWP), a 5-bit pointer, withing the Processor State Register. Decrementing the CWP at procedure entry causes the next window to become active and incrementing the CWP at procedure exit causes the previous window to become active. An IU state register, the Window Invalid Mask (WIM), is used to tag a window (or sets of windows). An overflow or underflow trap occurs if, due to an operation that changes CWP, it is about to point to a tagged window. To implement the usual LIFO stack of overlapping windows, one of the WIM bits is set to identify the boundary between the oldest and the newest window.

Register windows have several advantages over a fixed set of registers. Their principal advantage is a reduction in the number of load and store instructions required to execute a program. As a consequence, there is also a decrease in the number of data cache misses. The reduced number of loads and stores is also beneficial in implementations that have multi-cycle load or store instructions and in tightly coupled multiprocessors.

Register windows also work well in incremental compilation environments such as LISP and in object-oriented programming environments such as Smalltalk, where interprocedural register allocation is impractical. Even though these exploratory programming languages benefit from register windows, SPARC does not preclude interprocedural register allocation optimizations since the subroutine call and return instructions are distinct from the instructions that advance and retract the window pointer.

In addition to the window registers there are a number of other architecturally defined registers in the integer unit. They include the processor state register (PSR), the window invalid mask (WIM), the trap base register (TBR), the program counters (PC and NPC) and the multiply step register (Y). These are described in detail in [SPARC87].

Instructions

All the SPARC instructions are 32-bits wide and are defined by one of the three formats illustrated in Figure 8.1. Special care was taken in encoding instructions to enable the fastest possible implementations.

Format 1 defines a PC-relative CALL instruction with a 30-bit word displacement. Thus a call or an unconditional branch can be made to any arbitrary location in the address space with a single instruction.

SETHI and branch instructions use format 2. This format defines a 22-bit immediate field. For PC-relative branches it provides ± 8-Mbyte of displacement. SETHI loads the immediate value into the high 22 bits of the destination IU register and clears its low 10 bits. SETHI, in conjunction with a format 3 instruction, can be used to create 32-bit constants.

Format 3 encodes the remaining instructions including floating point and co-processor instructions. It specifies a destination register and either two source registers or a source register and a

Format 1 (CALL):

op	displacement
2	30

Format 2 (SETH)

op	rd	op	immediate
2	5	3	22

Format 2 (Bicc, FBfcc, CBCC):

op	a	cc	op	displacement
2	1	4	3	22

Format 3 (Remaining instructions, i-0):

op	rd	op	[s]	i	asi *or* fp-op	rs2
2	5	6	5	1	8	5

Format 3 (Remaining instructions, i-1):

op	rd	op	[s]	i	immediate
2	5	6	5	1	13

FIGURE 8.1. *SPARC instruction formats.*

13-bit sign extended immediate field. Eight bits of the immediate field are used as an opcode extension field for specifying floating-point/co-processor instructions and, as an "address space identifier" for the load/store instructions.

Memory Reference Instructions Memory can be accessed only through load/store instructions. For all such instructions, including floating-point and co-processor load/stores, the IU generates the memory address and the IU, FPU or co-processor sources or sinks the data.

All memory reference instructions use format three, and support both "reg_1, + reg_2" and "reg + signed_13-bit_constant" addressing modes. Register indirect and absolute addressing modes can be emulated using g0. Load/store instructions support signed/unsigned byte, half-word, word and double word transfers. If the data is not aligned at the proper boundary, the instruction traps.

For all instruction fetches and normal data accesses the IU provides a 32-bit virtual address and an 8-bit address identifier (ASI). Data fetches could be either *normal* or *alternate*. For all instructions and *normal* data fetches ASIs indicate a user/supervisor and data/instruction reference. This can be used to provide protection mechanism in a system's memory management units.

Alternate instructions are privileged and can be executed only in supervisor mode. Their format is restricted to "reg_1 + reg_2". They use eight ASI bits to specify either the user instruction or user data spaces, or up to 252 other system-dependent, 32-bit address spaces. The SPARC architecture defines only user/supervisor, instruction/data spaces; the remainder can be defined by the system architecture.

Unlike many other RISC architectures, SPARC does not have "delayed loads". An instruction immediately following a load instruction may use the load data. This simplifies the job of scheduling instructions by compilers. Depending on implementation this case may cause the sequence to take an additional cycle to complete the operation.

Multiprocessor Instructions SWAP and load-store unsigned byte (LDSTUB) instructions provide support for tightly coupled multiprocessors. SWAP exchanges the contents of an IU register with a word from memory. It can be used in conjunction with a memory-mapped co-processor to implement synchronizing instructions, such as the non-blocking "fetch and add" instruction. LDSTUB, reads a byte from memory into an IU register and then rewrites the same byte in memory to all ones. It can be used for the blocking synchronization schemes, such as semaphores [Dubois88]. Both the instructions are atomic.

Arithmetic/Logical Instructions   These format 3 integer instructions perform either a logical or an arithmetic operation on two operands and optionally write the result into a destination register. Arithmetic instructions have two types: ones that update the integer condition codes and ones that do not. There are four condition codes negative (N), zero (Z), overflow (V) and carry (C). They are stored in the Processor State Register.

The "multiply step" instructions (MULScc) are used to generate the 64-bit product of two signed or unsigned words in multiple cycles. Though (MULScc) processes the multiplier one bit at a time, as mentioned in the compiler paper [Muchnick88], higher-level language multiplications execute in an average of 6 cycles.

Tagged Instructions   These instructions provide support for languages that can benefit from operaned tags, such as LISP and Smalltalk. They assume 30-bit left justified signed integers and use the least significant two bits of a word as a tag. The "tagged add/subtract" instructions (TADDcc, TSUBcc) set the overflow condition code bit if either of the operands has a nonzero tag (or if a normal arithmetic overflow occurs). Normally, a tagged add/subtract is followed by a conditional branch instruction, which, if the overflow bit has been set, transfers control to code that further deciphers the operand types. Two variants, TADDccTV and TSUBccTV, trap if the overflow bit has been set and can be used to detect operand type errors.

Special Instructions   These instructions are used to read and write architecturally defined registers. Some of them are privileged and can be executed only in the supervisor mode. SAVE and RE-STORE instructions are used to decrement or increment the Current Window Pointer. They trap if the adjustment would cause a window overflow or underflow. They also operate like an ordinary ADD instruction and thus can also be used to atomically adjust a program stack pointer.

Control Transfer Instructions These instructions consist of call, branch, jump and link and trap on condition code instructions. For efficient execution of these instructions, SPARC uses the concept of delayed branches. For most of these instructions the instruction that follows the control transfer instruction is executed before program control is transferred to the target instruction.

Compilers try to move a useful instruction from a location before the branch into the delayed slot. When this is not possible, a NOP is generally placed in the delay slot. However, in SPARC conditional branches have a special "annul" bit. If the annul bit is set and the conditional branch is not taken, the delay instruction is not executed. This feature allows compilers to move an instruction from the target, or move an instruction from one arm of an IF-THEN-ELSE statement into the other. By use of the annul bit, compiled code contains less than 5% NOPs.

Traditional non-delayed branches can be emulated using the "branch always" (BA) instruction. If a BA with the annul bit set is executed, its delay instruction is not executed. It can also be used to efficiently emulate unimplemented instructions if, at runtime, the unimplemented instruction is replaced with an annulling BA whose target is the emulation code.

The "trap on condition code" (Ticc) instructions do not have a delay slot and they conditionally transfers control to one of 128 software trap locations. Ticc's are used for kernel calls and compiler run-time checking.

Floating-Point Unit

SPARC defines thirteen basic floating-point instructions. IEEE single, double and extended precision data types are supported. The FPU has thirty-two 32-bit-wide registers. Double-precision values occupy an even-odd pair and extended-precision values occupy an aligned group of four registers. Data cannot be transferred directly from IU registers to FPU registers, it has to be done through the memory. The instruction set defines doubleword (64-bit) floating-point loads and stores to boost double-precision performance. Also, in order to decrease context switch time, the FPU can be disabled so that its registers need not be saved when switching from a process that does not use floating-point.

SPARC allows floating-point operations, such as multiply and add, to execute concurrently with each other, with floating-point loads and stores, and with integer instructions. This concurrency is hidden from the programmer: a program generates the same results, including traps, as if all instructions were executed sequentially.

Because of this concurrency, the IU's program counters can advance beyond floating-point instructions in the instruction stream, before the floating-point instruction completes. There is a special group of registers, the Floating-point Queue (FQ), that records the floating-point instructions (and their addresses) that were pending completion at the time of a floating-point trap. The queue's head contains the unfinished instruction (and its address) that caused the floating-point trap.

Floating-point operations can also execute concurrently with cache misses. If a floating-point store attempts to write a result whose computation has not yet finished, the IU stalls until the floating-point operation is complete. A "store FSR" instruction also causes the FPU to wait for outstanding float-point operations to finish.

The "floating-point operate" instructions (FPop) are specified via the 9-bit "opf" field of format 3 instructions. They compute a single, double, or extended-precision result that is a function of two source operands in FPU registers and write the result into FPU registers. The floating-point compare instructions write a 2-bit condition code in the FPU's Floating-point Status Register (FSR) that can be tested by the "branch on floating-point condition codes" (FBfcc) instruction. There are instructions that convert between all formats, including integers.

In general, a user program sees a complete ANSI/IEEE 754-1985 implementation, even though the hardware may not implement every nuance of the standard, such as gradual underflow. Software emulates missing hardware functionality via FPU-generated traps.

Coprocessor

As mentioned earlier, SPARC has instruction support for a single co-processor (in addition to the floating-point unit). The co-processor instructions mirror the floating-point instructions: load/store co-processor, "branch on co-processor condition codes", and "co-processor operate" (CPop). Coprocessor operate instructions, can execute concurrently with integer instructions, and have not been defined as a part of the SPARC architecture.

Real Time Applications

The SPARC allows for fast trap handling which is very useful in real time applications. The register windows in SPARC always provide eight free registers for trap handling, thus allowing for fast entry into trap handlers. When a trap or interrupt occurs, the CWP is decremented—as for a procedure call—making available to the trap handler six of the *local* registers of the next window. (Two of the *locals* are written with the IU's two Program Counters.) For a simple handler it takes about six cycles (in the first implementation) to enter the handler and another six to exit.[2] This assumes no cache misses. For cache misses this number would increase depending on the miss cost. If more registers than allocated for the handler are required then a window save is necessary. This will increase the cost of interrupt handling. Note that on process switches only the active windows are saved, not the entire set of windows.[3]

The register windows can be managed in a variety of different ways for different applications. For applications that require rapid context switching, such as device controllers, the windows can be partitioned into non-overlapping pairs, with one pair allocated per process. At process switch time, pairs of windows could be switched providing each process with 24 private registers plus 8

---

[2] This assumes that handler runs with traps disabled, there are no subroutine calls and only five of the local registers are required.

---

[3] The cost of saving or restoring a window is not larger on the Sun-4/200, it approximates the overhead of 7 cache misses.

global registers and a set of 8 registers for trap handling. With a large register file a number of these contexts can simultaneously reside in the processor and the WIM could be used to protect each process's registers from the other processes.

Gate Array Implementation

This section talks about the MB86900 integer unit (IU), first implementation of the SPARC processor architecture, and briefly describes the MB86910, referred to here as Floating Point Controller (FPC). Covered here are the microarchitecture, the pipeline, external interface, and performance of the IU.

Processor Pipeline

As illustrated in Figure 8.2. the IU has a four-stage pipeline consisting of *Fetch, Decode, Execute* and *Write* stages. There is an additional half cycle required to write results back in the register file. During the *Fetch* stage an instruction is fetched from the external cache (memory system) and latched into the on-chip instruction register. During the *Decode* stage the instruction is decoded, source operands are read from the register file and stored in staging registers. Also, during this stage the next instruction address (in the case of branches and calls, the target address) is generated and put out on the address low bus (see "external interfaces" below). ⁻During the *Execute* stage arithmetic and logical operations are performed on the source operands. The results of the operations are saved in the result register. For branch instructions this stage is used to evaluate the condition codes. Memory reference instructions generate data addresses in this stage. The *Write* stage marks the completion of an instruction. During this stage the results are written into the Write Register and processor state is updated. Traps and exceptions prevent the processor state from changing. Upon successful completion of the write stage contents of the write register are transferred to the register file during the first half of the next cycle.

Microarchitecture

Both the MB86900 IU and the MB86910 FPC are each implemented in a 20,000 gate gate array chip fabricated by Fujitsu, using

1.5 micron (with 10% gate shrink) CMOS triple-layer metal technology. One quarter of the IU gate-array is occupied by a 4 Kbit register file and the other three quarters are used by the data path and control circuitry. The gate arrays has been partitioned hierarchically into blocks, sub-blocks, and sub-sub-blocks allowing easy routing and predictable post-layout wire delays for the entire chip. Both of the chips are fully scannable. Figure 8.3 is a block diagram of the IU chip. It has been divided into the following four functional units:

Register File Unit—This unit consists of a custom designed three ported register file containing 128, 32-bit registers. Of the 32 windows possible in the architecture, the MB86900 IU implements seven.

The register file has two read ports and one write port. The uniform format of instructions allows reading both of the source operands of any instruction and writing the result of a previously fetched instruction into the register file. This entire read/write operation occurs in a single cycle. Internal forwarding in the register file is avoided by performing the write operation before the read. Also, while the write operation is taking place, the two read address are translated from logical address (5-bit window address) to physical (7-bit) address.

Execution Unit—This unit consists of a 32-bit carry-look-ahead ALU (which performs all arithmetic and logical operations), a 32-bit barrel shifter, condition-code-generation logic, load-alignment logic and related pipeline registers required to save the operands and intermediate results. Because of pipeline dependencies, two levels of internal forwarding or bypass are required. As illustrated in Figure 8.2., the first path bypasses the output of the ALU directly to the inputs of the operand registers and is activated when the source operand of an instruction is the same as the destination operand of the instruction right before it. The second path bypasses the output of the result register to the inputs of the operand registers and is used when the source operand of an instruction is same as the destination operand of the instruction prior to the previous one. In a four stage pipeline one might expect another bypass, but it is avoided by performing a write before a read in the register file.

Instruction Fetch Unit—This unit contains the address generation and the PC logic. It is used in the *Decode* stage to generate

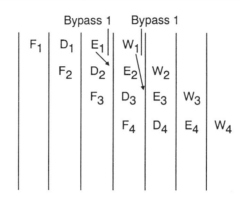

FIGURE 8.2. *Instruction pipeline.*

branch addresses and in the *Execute* stage to generate data addresses. There are four program counters corresponding to the four stages of the instruction pipeline. These Program Counters are used in case of exceptions that may occur as late as the last stage in the processor pipeline. This unit also includes Trap Base register (TBR), Trap Type register (TT), Y register (used by multiply step instruction), and Window Invalid Mask register (WIM).

Control Unit—This Unit contains copies of instruction registers and instruction decoders corresponding to the four stages of the pipeline. Majority of the controls for the IU are generated here and dispatched to the various units. Also included in this unit is the main state machine, the Processor Status Register (PSR) and the exception/trap handling and external interface logic.

Both execution and instruction units took approximately 3800 gates (two input NAND equivalent) and the control unit took 4200 gates to implement. Thus the whole IU is implemented using about 12K gates and 4K bits of 3 ported register file. The number of gates could be further reduced by the use of non-scannable flip flops.

Most instructions in the MB86910 can complete at the rate of one per cycle. However, as illustrated in Table 8.1., there is a subset of instructions that take more than one cycle (this is the feature of this implementation, not the SPARC architecture itself).

Memory reference instructions use the single instruction/data bus (see below in external interfaces) more than once (to transfer instructions as well as data), hence they take more than one cycle to complete. The IU uses a dual-instruction buffer to keep the pipeline full. These buffers are used to hold the pre-fetched instructions during the execution of multi-cycle instructions.

Because of pipeline dependencies, condition codes are evaluated in the execute cycle of conditional branch instructions. However, for a single delayed slot, the target address needs to be sent out in the decode cycle. We first assume that branches are always taken. But, in the next stage if it is determined that the branch should not have been taken the target instruction in the pipeline is replaced with a NOP and the correct next instruction is fetched. This results in an untaken branch costing an extra cycle.

For simplicity of control generation and ease of debugging, multicycle instructions are implemented via *help instructions.* Multiple-cycle instructions are replaced by a sequence of internally generated single cycle help instructions. The *help instructions* make the design and debugging process simple by maintaining a smooth flow in the pipeline.

Figure 8.4. shows a single-word load instruction that takes one extra cycle in the pipeline and, therefore uses one internal *help instructions* to complete. In this case, the EH1 cycle is used to fetch the load operand.

External Interfaces

The IU has three major busses. A 32-bit instruction/data (*I/D-Bus*) bus, a 32-bit floating point bus (*F-bus*) and a 32-bit address bus. The *I/D-Bus* is a bidirectional bus used to transfer instructions and data between the cache and the IU. It is also used to transfer data to and from the FPC (and the co-processor). *F-bus* is used for transferring the floating point instructions and then their address to the FPC in two cycles. The address bus is divided into two groups: AL (low address, bits 17..00) and AH (high-address, bits 31..16). AL is available towards the end of the cycle before the cache access cycle. AL is latched in external registers that can directly drive large banks of RAMs. AH is available during the cache access cycle. In a cache-based system this allows the designer to use latched AL to read the cache. RAMs and cache tags while AH is being sent out of the chip for tag comparison. AL and AH bits are overlapped in bits 16 and 17, allowing direct addressing of a cache with a size from 64K to 256K bytes.

Instruction fetch and load cycles are identical. The same cycle in which a word is fetched, the cache tags are read and checked. In the case of a cache-hit the IU treats the fetched instruction as a correct instruction and continues to fetch the next instruction in the following cycle. However, if the cache is missed, the external cache controller logic must hold the IU operation in the cycle

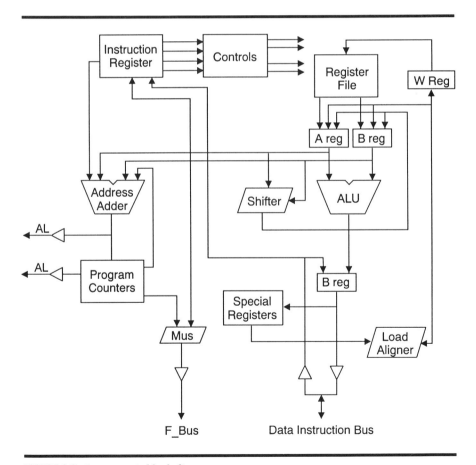

FIGURE 8.3. *Integer unit block diagram.*

following the fetch by asserting one of the HOLD input signals. During this period, the cache controller fills the missed cache line and strobes (using the MDS signal) the correct instruction/data into the IU.

In the MB86900, bus request/grant operations are implemented in a very simple manner: the IU may be forced into a WAIT state in any cycle for any duration of time using an external HOLD signal. For certain instructions that require atomic multicycle bus transactions the IU asserts a LOCK signal. Back to back multicycle instructions do not lock out I/O since the LOCK signal is guaranteed to be deasserted for at least one cycle during the execution of an instruction. Normally a device that needs the bus simply asserts the HOLD signal in the first cycle that it sees the LOCK signal is inactive. Once the IU is in the WAIT state, its output drivers can be turned off.

All I/O devices are memory mapped and normal load/store instructions are used to read from or write into the I/O devices. The 8-bit ASI output signals plus the address determine the mapping of user space, supervisor space, MMU, cache tags, and other I/O devices in the system. A set of alternate load and store instructions is defined that are privileged and can be used to access any Address Space between 0 and 255 in the system.

All floating-point instructions are decoded inside the IU and are dispatched, with their addresses, to the floating-point unit over the F-bus in two consecutive cycles. A few control signals are used

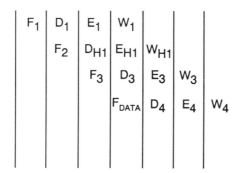

FIGURE 8.4. *Load instruction.*

for synchronization between the two chips. The FPC detects dependencies between various floating-point instructions and signals the IU to wait if necessary. It also detects the floating-point exceptions and signals them to the IU.

Traps and Exceptions

Execution of a given instruction can raise several traps or exceptions. The source of a trap can be internal (synchronous) or external. In both cases the IU handles the traps in a similar manner. All traps raised during the execution of any instructions are deferred to the last stage of the pipeline, at that stage the highest priority trap is taken. Traps are vectored using the *Trap Base Address Register* (TBR) to point to the trap table. When a trap is taken the current window pointer is decremented, further traps are disabled, the two program counters (PC and NPC) are automatically saved and the program continues at the trap vector location. External interrupts are given to the IU using 4-bit interrupt input signals. A non-zero value on these inputs is detected by the IU as an external interrupt request. This value is compared with the processor interrupt level in the PSR and an interrupt is taken if the external interrupt request level is greater than the processor interrupt level. The highest level interrupt (level-15) is defined to be non-maskable, although all traps can be disabled via the Enable Trap Et-so bit in the PSR.

All external interrupts are ignored when traps are disabled. If a synchronous trap is detected while traps are disabled, the IU enters into an Error Mode and remains in that mode until it is reset by external logic. At reset, the IU is initialized and starts execution from address zero.

Floating-point exceptions, in general, occur asynchronously with respect to the IU pipeline since integer instructions are executed concurrently with the floating-point instructions and floating-point instructions take a variable number of cycles to complete their execution or generate an exception. However, in SPARC floating-point exceptions are taken *synchronously*. Floating point exceptions detected during the execution of an instruction are kept pending till another floating point instruction enters the IU pipeline. At that time the floating-point trap is taken (if it is the highest priority).

Performance

The number of instructions executed per second (MIPS) and the number of instructions required to execute the program are good indication of the performance of a processor and its compilers. The number of instructions depends on the quality of the code generated by compilers and the efficiency of the instruction set. Based on data from C and Fortran programs, SPARC machines execute from 0 to 25% more instructions than CISCs (e.g., VAX® Motorola 68000).

The number of instructions executed per cycle is a function of cycle time, average memory access time, and the average number of cycles per instruction. (Note: Nf is the number of cycles needed by the floating-point arithmetic unit to complete a floating-point instruction. This number varies depending on the type of floating-point operation, for example using a Weitek chip set, a double-precision floating-point add takes, 14 cycles and a double precision multiply operation takes 16 cycles).

Based on the above table for cycles required for each instruction, the instruction mix (which varies across benchmarks) and the

Instruction type	Number of cycles
Load (word/halfword/byte)	2
Load (double)	3
Store (word/halfword/byte)	3
Store (double)	4
Atomic load and store	4
Floating-point ops	2 + Nf
Jump and Rett	2
Branch (untaken)	2
Branch (taken)	1
All other instructions	1

TABLE 8.1. *Instruction execution times.*

miss cost (assumed 10 cycles here), the cycles per instruction number, for a CPU-intensive, integer program, may vary from 1.3 to 1.7.

Conclusion

This paper summarized the SPARC architecture and its first implementation. We started the gate level design in July of 1985 and had first fully functional silicon by April 1986. Multiuser UNIX was running in June. With the help of timing verification tools the design was then optimized to meet the cycle time goals. We released a new design to fabrication and had silicon back by December 1986. Running at 60 ns the processor delivers a performance that far exceeds the performance of existing CISC-based systems [Schafir87, Chu87]. This, coupled with the gate array implementation and a short design cycle time, demonstrates the efficiency and the simplicity of the architecture.

MB86900 is the first general purpose 32-bit integer processor implemented in a single gate array. Gate array implementation was a low-risk and low-cost approach that enabled us to bring a product to market much sooner and yet allowed us to achieve an aggressive clock rate of 16.67 MHz. With high density ASICs becoming available, it is possible to design a core cell or a "hard macro" based on the SPARC design. This will open up a number of new application areas particularly for controllers where application-specific glue logic is required. SPARC provides a very cost effective solution for such applications.

Acknowledgments

Many people at Sun Microsystems contributed to the definition of the architecture, including Faye Briggs, Emil W. Brown, David Hough, Bill Joy, Steve Kleiman, Steven Muchnick, Masood Namjoo, Dave Patterson, Joan Pendelton, Richard Tuck, Dave Weaver, Dave Goldberg, Tom Lyon, Alex Wu, and John Gilmore. The gate-array IU (Fujitsu MB86900) was designed by Anant Agrawal and Masood Namjoo. Don Jackson designed the FPC (Fujitsu MB86910) with additional help from Rick Iwamoto and Larry Yang. Le Quach from Fujitsu, Phil Mak, Susan Rohani, Quyen Wu and J.K. Lu provided the CAD tools, simulation and other support. Will Brown wrote an architectural and machine cycle simulator. Ed Kelly and Robert Garner designed the Sun-4/200 processor board. K.G. Tan and Wayne Rosing managed the gate-array and architecture projects.

Thanks to Will Brown, Joe Petolino, and Ed Kelly for their useful suggestions in improving this paper.

UNIX is a trademark of AT&T Bell Laboratories. SPARC and Sun-4 are trademarks of Sun Microsystems, Inc. VAX is a trademark of Digital Equipment Corp.

References

[Agrawal88] A. Agrawal, E.W. Brown, J. Petolino, J. Peterson, "Design Considerations for a Bipolar Implementation of SPARC," IEEE COMPCON 88.

[Chu87] N. Chu, L. Poltrack, J. Bartlett, J. Friedland, A. MacRae, Sun Performance, Sun Microsystems, Inc., Mountain View, CA.

[Dubois88] M. Dubois, C. Scheurich, & F. Briggs, "Synchronization, Coherence and Ordering of Events in Multiprocessors," to appear in *IEEE Com.*, February 1988.

[Garner88] Robert Garner, Anant Agrawal, Faye Briggs, Emil W. Brown, David Hough, Bill Joy, Steve Kleiman, Steven Muchnick, Masood Namjoo, Dave Patterson, Joan Pendelton and Richard Tuck. "The Scalable Processor Architecture" (SPARC) IEEE COMPCON 88.

[Katevenis83] M. Katevenis, *Reduced Instruction Set Computer Architectures for VLSI*, Ph.D. dissertation, Computer Science Div., Univ. of California, Berkeley, 1983. Also published by M.I.T. Press, Cambridge, MA.

[Kleiman88] S. Kleiman & D. Williams, "SunOS on SPARC," IEEE COMPCON 88.

[Muchnick88] S. Muchnick, C. Aoki, V. Ghodssi, M. Helft, M. Lee, R. Tuck, D. Weaver, & A. Wu, "Optimizing Compilers for the SPARC Architecture: An Overview," IEEE COMPCON 88.

[Namjoo88] M. Namjoo, A. Agrawal, D. Jackson, Le Quach, "CMOS Gate Array Implementation of the SPARC Architecture," IEEE COMPCON 88.

[NamjCypr88] M. Namjoo, et al., "CMOS Custom Implementation of the SPARC Architecture," IEEE COMPCON 88.

[Patterson85] D. Patterson, "Reduced Instruction Set Computers," *CACM*, vol. 28, no. 1, Jan. 1985.

[Quach88] L. Quach & R. Chueh, "CMOS Gate Array Implementation of the SPARC Architecture," IEEE COMPCON 88.

[Schafir87] M. Schafir & A. Nguyen, *Sun-4/200 Benchmarks*, Sun Microsystems, Inc., Mountain View, CA.

[SPARC87] *The SPARC Architecture Manual*, Sun Microsystems, Inc., Mountain View, CA. Also published by Fujitsu Microelectronics, Inc., 3320 Scott Blvd., Santa Clara, CA 95054.

SPARC Implementations: ASIC vs. Custom Design

9

MASOOD NAMJOO

Abstract

The first two implementations of the SPARC architecture, MB86900 and CY7C601 were designed using high speed CMOS technology with processor clock speed in the range of 16.6 MHz to 33 MHz. In a system with a reasonable size external cache, these processors execute integer operations at a rate of approximately 1.5 clock cycles per instruction resulting in a sustained performance in the range of 10 to 20 MIPS. MB86900 design uses a single 20,000 gate 1.3 micron CMOS gate-array from Fujitsu and operates at a cycle time of 60ns. CY7C601, on the other hand, is a full custom chip designed using Cypress Semiconductor's 0.8 micron CMOS process and operates at a cycle time of 30ns. In this paper we discuss the basic features of these processors, their similarities and differences and the trade-offs used in their design. We also address the issues of design verification, test generation and fault simulation.

Introduction

The SPARC architecture is based on the UC Berkeley RISC project; it uses a large windowed register file and defines a simple and efficient set of integer and floating-point instructions which can be grouped into the following five major categories.

    a) Arithmetic, Logical and Shift Instructions—These instructions perform a specific operation on two source operands and write the results into a destination register. Most of these instructions have two types: one type does not change the condition code bits and the other type sets the condition code bits based on the computed result.

    b) Special Registers Read/Write Instructions—The SPARC architecture defines four special registers. These registers are: Processor Status Register(PSR), Trap Base Register (TBR), Window Invalid Mask (WIM), and Y register used during integer multiplications for generating a 64-bit product. The instructions in this category are used to read the contents or write a new value into these special registers.

c) Memory Reference Instructions—This category is made up of load and store instructions. Integer load and store instructions operate on byte, halfword, and word, and double-word operands. Floating-point and coprocessor loads and stores operate on word and double-word operands only. Special instructions are defined for use with multiprocessor applications. These instructions are "atomic" in nature and perform a load from a memory location followed by a store into the same memory location without releasing the processor's bus until the transaction is completed. All integer load and store instructions have alternate versions which can be used to access up to 256 different address spaces in the system.

d) Control Transfer Instructions—This category consists of conditional and unconditional relative branches with 22-bit word displacement, call with 30-bit word displacement and register indirect absolute jumps and returns. Branch instructions use a single delayed instruction. The delayed-branch concept is a simple way to improve the processor's performance by filling up the processor's pipeline with useful instructions while the target of the branch is being calculated. Normally, the target of a branch is not known until later in the processor's pipeline. Instead of waiting for the target calculation, the processor executes the following instruction and then executes the branch itself. The instruction in the delay slot of a branch may be nullified by specifying the annul bit in the instruction. For conditional branches the delay slot instruction is always executed unless the branch is not taken (i.e., when the conditions are false) and the annul bit is set. For unconditional branches, on the other hand, the delay slot instruction is nullified whenever the annul bit is set.

e) Floating-point/Coprocessor Instructions—The SPARC architecture defines single, double, and extended precision formats for most frequent floating-point instructions, conforming to the IEEE-standard. The coprocessor instructions, on the other hand, may be defined by the user. The floating-point and coprocessor instructions are executed by separate units concurrent with the execution of integer instructions.

SPARC instructions have very simple formats and use only two essential addressing modes: register+register and register+signed-immediate. The simplified format of instructions results in faster decoding of instructions and more efficient usage of the processor's data path. The execution unit can be easily optimized for speed allowing shorter cycle time for the entire processor. The following sections describe the general features of these SPARC implementations and outline the procedures used for their design verification.

Implementations of SPARC

Since the initial CMOS implementations of SPARC were targeted for a large variety of applications, a 32-bit bus was adopted, allowing most instructions to be executed in a single cycle with the exception of load and store instructions that use the same bus for fetching instructions as well as data and therefore take more than one cycle to complete.

In order to reach the highest performance in these processors, the memory subsystem must be capable of feeding the processor with a new instruction in every cycle. For this reason an external cache is needed. For higher levels of processor performance the bandwidth of the bus between the processor and cache needs to be increased (e.g., 64-bit instead of 32-bit bus). Using a 64-bit bus, the processor can be designed to fetch and execute multiple instructions or data in a single cycle.

The SPARC architecture allows different implementations to have different number of windows. For an implementation with N windows the total number of general purpose registers is $16 \times N + 8$. The gate-array implementation (MB86900) provides 120 general purpose registers, from which 8 are global registers and the rest are divided into 7 overlapped windows of 24 registers each (N=7 was chosen due to the available RAM size in the gate-array). The full custom implementation (CY7C601), on the other hand, provides 136 general purpose registers; 8 global registers and 8 overlapped windows of 24 registers each. Since all instructions use 5-bit source and destination fields, only 32 registers corresponding to the current window are accessible to the programmer at any given time. The current window is identified by the value of CWP field in the Processor Status Register (PSR).

External Bus Structure

As mentioned earlier both designs use a single 32-bit data bus ($D<31:0>$) and a single 32-bit address bus ($A<30>$) for interface to the cache or memory. In the gate-array version, the low portion of the address bus is sent (unlatched) a cycle earlier than the high portion. In a cache-based system, this would allow the system designer to latch the low address externally and use the output of the latch directly to access the cache data and cache tag RAMs. The high portion of the address is not as critical as the low portion and therefore is latched on the chip before it is sent out. The external latch in this scheme also functions as a buffer for driving the heavily loaded cache address lines. Once the cache tags are read, the high portion of the address is used to compare the tags in that cycle and to send a cache miss/hit signal to the processor. In the custom version, the address generation logic is highly optimized for speed and therefore all address bits are sent unlatched. This would allow the maximum time for cache access and tag comparison.

Almost every cycle on the bus is either an instruction fetch, a data fetch, or a data store cycle. For every cache access the result of cache miss/hit is given to the processor a cycle later. During a cache miss, the cache crowd logic first stops the processor, then handles the miss and strobes the missed instruction/data to the processor while the processor is stopped. Since the processor normally advances to the next cycle, the missed cache address must be somehow regenerated.

One external difference between the gate-array and custom version is that the custom version has some additional logic for regenerating the missed address during a cache-miss process. This is done simply by asserting a signal which forces the processor to send the old address on the bus. In the gate-array version, the missed address must be saved and regenerated externally during a cache miss.

In both designs, the same $D<31:0>$ bus is used for fetching instructions as well as data. This results in two-cycle execution of single-word load and three-cycle execution of double-word load instructions. For the case of stores, the processor uses an extra cycle in order to allow time for tag check (before the write operation) and turning the bus around by the system. Therefore, execution of single-word stores takes three cycles and execution of double-word stores takes four cycles. Observation of large benchmarks on SPARC indicates instruction mixes with approximately 15% loads and 5% stores, minimizing the effect of multi-cycle loads and stores on the average number of cycles per instruction.

Microarchitecture and Internal Control Logic

Both designs use a four-stage pipeline. In the basic pipeline operation, the processor fetches an instruction during the fetch-stage (F). The fetched instruction is decoded in the decode-stage (D) and source operands are read from the register file. In the execute-stage (E), the instruction is executed and in the write-stage (W) the results are written into the destination register. The write-stage is aborted if a trap or exception is raised while the instruction is being executed.

The instruction pipeline consists of various fields of instructions corresponding to the decode, execute and write stages of the pipeline and a two-stage instruction buffer. The instruction buffer, continues to prefetch new instructions once the processor encounters an instruction that needs more than one cycle to complete. This buffer is empty during a sequence of single-cycle instructions and is used only when a multi-cycle instruction is decoded. Multi-cycle instructions use one or more internally generated opcodes to complete execution. These internal opcodes, generated using random logic in the gate-array version and a PLA in the custom version, are jammed into the instruction pipeline as needed.

In the gate-array version taken branch instructions execute in one and untaken branches execute in two cycles. The control logic is designed so that all branches are assumed to be taken and the target instruction is fetched immediately. The processor, however, would ignore the target instruction if the condition code evaluation resulted in false condition. In the custom version, on the other hand, all branch instructions (conditional or unconditional) are performed in a single cycle. The single-cycle branch execution results from the early availability of condition codes generated by a highly optimized ALU and condition code evaluation logic.

Support for Floating-Point/Coprocessor

In both implementations, the floating-point unit is tightly coupled with the integer unit and integer instructions can execute concurrently with floating-point operations. The interface to the floating-point is however different for the two implementations.

The gate-array version uses a separate 32-bit F bus ($F<31:0>$) for dispatching floating-point instructions to the floating-point unit. Every floating-point instruction uses the F bus for two cycles. In the first cycle the instruction itself and in second cycle the address of the instruction is sent to the floating-point unit. In the custom version, the floating-point unit receives its instructions directly from the data bus and uses additional control logic to synchronize its pipeline with the integer unit's pipeline. As a result, a new floating-point instruction can be fetched every cycle. The gate-array version works with a companion floating-point controller chip and can be interfaced to either W1164/W1165 or T18847 arithmetic units capable of delivering 1.1 to 1.8 mega-flops for double-precision linpack benchmark. The custom version works with a different floating-point controller chip which interfaces to the T18847 floating-point chip capable of delivering approximately 3 times the floating-point performance of the gate-array version. The custom version also supports an additional coprocessor port which can be used to interface to a user defined coprocessor unit.

The floating-point unit and coprocessor have their own set of registers (thirty-two 32-bit registers), a status register (FSR/CSR), a queue for holding the instructions that need to be executed (FQ/CQ), and the logic for handling load/store instructions, dispatching the instructions to the arithmetic units, and checking dependencies between instructions.

Design Verification

In the development of custom and semi-custom VLSI designs, one important issue that needs careful consideration is design correctness and quality of testing. Most of today's VLSI processors have a very short development cycle. Complex chips go through their design phase and get to their first Silicon within a few months rather than years. Due to importance of design quality, extensive logic simulation and timing verification is needed in order to guarantee fully functional parts based on the first Silicon. In both SPARC designs, the gate-level model of the entire processor chip, was simulated in an environment that consisted of a simplified cache/memory model, the floating-point unit and a stimulus generation unit for controlling those synchronous and asynchronous input signals that are not usually exercised during normal program execution.

In this simulation environment, the design is tested using self-test diagnostics written in SPARC assembly language. The procedure for running simulation with a particular diagnostic consists of assembling the program, loading the cache with the object code generated by the assembler, executing all instructions in the program on the simulation model, and comparing instruction/ address traces as well as the final state of the processor against a non-pipelined instruction-level SPARC architecture simulator written in C language.

The stimulus generation unit is controlled by programmable seeds which are fetched from a seed memory in parallel with program execution. Associated with every instruction's address is a seed that is generated by the assembler. Using different seeds different external events such as cache-miss bus cycles, memory exception bus cycles and external interrupts are simulated in a controllable and repeatable manner.

From testability point of view, both designs provide controllability and observability of all internal logic blocks and registers through the processor's datapath using normal instructions. The gate-array version uses a fully scannable design which connects all internal registers together as a single scan chain. The fully scannable design of the gate-array reduced the overall effort spent on test pattern generation with the use of ATPG, resulting in a fault coverage above 97%. The custom version, on the other hand, does not use scan design. Fault simulation, therefore, was needed in order to improve the overall fault coverage. Approximately 160,000 vectors were used for functional verification of the chip from which 30,000 vectors were fault simulated resulting in a coverage of greater than 98% for detectable faults.

The gate-array version does not use any PLA's, tri-state internal bus, or precharge circuitry. The entire control logic is implemented using random logic gates with less than 1000 equivalent 2-input nand gates. In the custom version, most of the control logic is implemented using PLA's which are automatically generated from truth tables.

Finally, both designs were fully verified using a static timing verifier at the chip-level which traces all internal and external time critical paths and reports the results in the form of short-path and long-path set-up/hold time violations. After full chip timing verification, the worst case cycle time for the gate-array was 60ns and for the full custom version 30ns. With an average CPI of 1.5 this gives a performance of approximately 10 integer MIPS for the gate-array and 20 integer MIPS for the custom version of the SPARC chips.

Summary and Conclusions

The first implementations of SPARC architecture in CMOS technology show a major improvement in performance in comparison with non-RISC machines. This level of processor performance, until a few years ago, was achievable only in main-frames. Even higher levels of performance can be reached with future more advanced process and packaging technologies. As processor chips become faster the engineering of systems and boards that use these chips at their highest speed is becoming a new challenge. Therefore, extensive system-level logic simulation and timing verification is necessary for a successful product.

References

1. R. Garner et al., "The Scalable Processor Architecture (SPARC)," *Proceedings of the IEEE Compcon*, Spring 1988, pp. 278–283.

2. S. Muchnick et al., "Optimizing Compilers for the SPARC Architecture: An Overview," *Proceedings of the IEEE Compcon*, Spring 1988, pp. 284–288.

3. S. Kleiman, D. Williams, "UNIX on SPARC," *Proceedings of the IEEE Compson*, Spring 1988, pp. 289–293.

4. M. Namjoo, A. Agrawal, D.C. Jackson, L. Quach "CMOS Gate Array Implementation of the SPARC Architecture," *Proceedings of the IEEE Compcon*, Spring 1988, pp. 10–13.

5. L. Quach, R. Chueh, "CMOS Gate Array Implementation of SPARC," *Proceedings of the IEEE Compcon*, Spring 1988, pp. 14–17.

6. M. Namjoo et al., "CMOS Custom Implementation of the SPARC Architecture," *Proceedings of the IEEE Compcon*, Spring 1988, pp. 18–20.

7. A. Agrawal, E.W. Brown, J. Petolino, J.R. Peterson, "Design Considerations for a Bipolar Implementation of SPARC," *Proceedings of the IEEE Compcon*, Spring 1988, pp. 6–9.

Sunrise: A High-Performance 32-Bit Microprocessor

MASOOD NAMJOO • ANANT AGRAWAL

10

Abstract

This article describes Sunrise processor which is the first implementation of the SPARC architecture, Sun Microsystems' new 32-bit RISC architecture. Sunrise is a high-performance microprocessor designed by Sun Microsystems using Fujitsu's high-speed CMOS gate-array technology. With a typical cycle time of 50ns, the sustained performance of Sunrise processor exceeds 10 MIPS when executing instructions from a reasonable size cache. In a typical system the Sunrise processor works with a floating-point controller chip, also designed by Sun Microsystems, and two commercial floating-point arithmetic processors, such as Weitek W1164 and W1165, and a high speed cache. The cache is an important factor in the performance of the Sunrise processor and must be capable of delivering one instruction to the processor in every cycle. For this reason, the pipeline and control are optimized for a cache-based system.

Sunrise has a reduced-instruction-set-computer architecture. The architecture defines a simple, yet efficient set of instructions. Most of these instructions execute in a single cycle and as a result of this the average number of cycles per instruction (CPI) is very low. Those instructions that cannot complete in a single cycle (such as loads and stores) use a minimum number of additional cycles to complete execution.

The processor has a total of 120 general purpose registers from which eight are global registers and the rest are configured as a set of overlapped windows of 24 registers each. As shown in Figure 10.1 each two adjacent windows are overlapped in 8 registers. A field in the processor status register determines the current window used by the program. Overlaped windows provide an efficient way for passing parameters during procedure calls and returns. Normally, during a procedure call the "caller" puts its parameters in those registers which are overlapped with the window used by "callee" (next window). After the execution of the call the window is changed to the next window in which the parameters are directly accessible by the callee.

The large on-chip register file reduces the overhead of load and stores operations considerably allowing a peek execution rate of approximately 1 cycle per instruction when all operands are kept inside the processor's register file.

Most instructions use only two different formats. In the first format two registers (rs1 and rs2) are used as the source operands and a third register (rd) is used as the destination operand. In the second format a register (rs1) and an immediate value are used as the source operand and a second register (rd) is used as the destination operand. This simplified format of instructions allows the source operands be read from the register file in a very short time without any delay due to decoding of instructions and as a result of this, the cycle time, which is a major factor in the processor's performance, is decreased.

Branch instructions use a single delayed instruction. Delayed branch concept is a simple way to improve the performance by filling up the processor's pipeline with useful instructions while the target of the branch is being calculated. Normally, the target of a branch is not known until later in the processor's pipeline. Instead of waiting for the target calculation the processor executes the following instruction and then it executes the branch itself. For conditional branches the delayed instruction is always executed when the branch is taken (i.e., when the conditions are true). The architecture provide a simple mechanism to nullify the effect of the delayed instruction if the branch is not taken.

A few special instructions are defined for supporting multiprocessor applications. These instructions are "atomic" in nature and perform a load from a memory location followed by a store into the same memory location without releasing the processor's bus to other processors until the transaction is completed.

A rich set of single precision and double precision floating-point instructions are implemented which are fully IEEE compatible. These instructions are executed by the floating-point unit which consists of a special floating-point controller chip and two Weitek floating-point arithmetic units (W1164 and W1165). There are 32 floating-point register on the controller chip. These registers can be directly loaded from the memory or stored into the memory in the same number of cycles that is needed to load or store an interger register.

Unlike other coprocessors, the Sunrise processor and its floating-point unit are tightly synchronized maximizing the performance of the system. All floating-point instructions are decoded inside the processor and are dispatched to the floating-point unit using a dedicated 32-bit bus and a set of control signals used for synchronization of the two chips. Integer instructions and floating

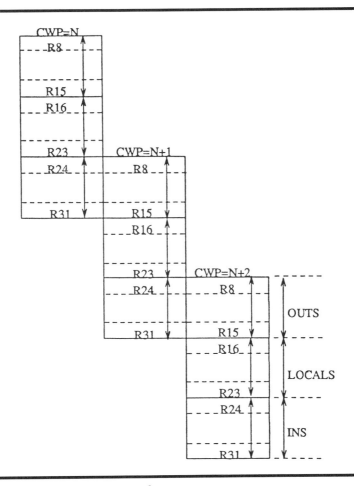

FIGURE 10.1. *Overlapped register windows.*

point instructions may be executed concurrently provided that there is no dependencies between these instructions. The floating-point controller chip has a two-entry deep instruction queue which is used to improve the concurrent operation of the two units.

The entire Sunrise processor is implemented in a single 20,000-gate gate-array chip fabricated by Fujitsu; using 1.5 micron technology with a typical gate delay of 1.2 ns. One quarter of this gate-array is occupied by a very large register file defined by the processor architecture and the other three quarters are used by the data path and control circuitry. The design has been carefully partitioned in a hierarchical manner into blocks, sub-blocks and sub-sub-blocks allowing easy routability and predictable post-layout wire delays for the entire chip. The processor chip has a total of 156 I/O signals and uses a 256 pin PGA (Pin Grid Array) package.

System Design Using Sunrise Processor

Figure 10.2. shows a typical system configuration using the chip-set consisting of the Sunrise processor chip, Sunrise floating-point controller chip. Weitek 1164 multiplier chip and Weitek 1165 ALU chip. These four chips are the core of any system designed around Sunrise processor.

Two separate 32-bit buses are used for address and data to access the storage. The cache is an essential part of the system and must be capable of delivering one instruction to the processor in every cycle. The processor bus cycles and the timing of I/O signals are optimized for cache-based systems. For example, the address bits are divided into two groups: low-address bits and high-address bits. The low-address bits (bits 17..00) are available earlier than the high-address bits (bits 31..16). In a cache-based system this allows the designer to use the lower address bits to read the cache RAMs and cache tags, and the higher address bits to compare the tags later. The low order and high order bits of the address are overlapped in bits 16 and 17, allowing direct addressing of a virtual cache with a size up to 256K bytes.

From a hardware point of view, the higher 16-bits of the address bus are taken directly from an on-chip Memory Address

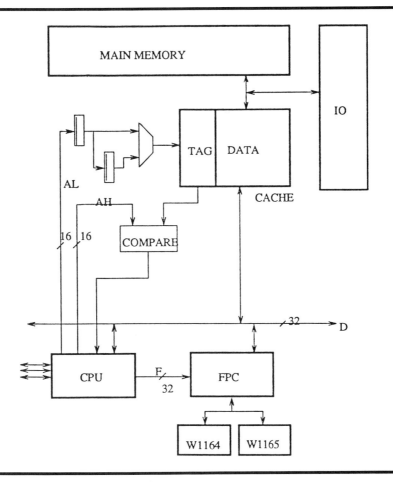

FIGURE 10.2. *A typical system configuration.*

Register that holds the address of the instruction or data to be fetched in that cycle. The lower 18-bits of the address are 'un-latched' and sent a cycle earlier. These bits must be latched in an external Memory Address Register before they are used. The processor provides necessary control signals that are used to synchronize the internal and external Memory Address Registers. The processor also sends out an 8-bit Address Space Identifier (ASI) field for the instruction or data. Normally, these 8-bits carry information such as processor mode (user/superuser) and the type of fetch (instruction/data). During the execution of alternate load and store instructions, these bits carry the ASI for load or store data.

Every processor cycle in this system is either an instruction fetch cycle, a load cycle or a store cycle. When the processor sends out an instruction address, the cache is accessed and the instruction is fetched into the processor in the same cycle. This instruction may or may not be the correct instruction depending on whether or not the instruction actually existed in the cache. Within the same cycle the cache tags are read and checked. In the case of a cache-hit the processor treats the fetched instruction as a correct instruction and continues to fetch the next instruction in the following cycle. However, if the cache is missed, the external cache controller logic must hold the processor operation in the cycle following the cycle in which the instruction is fetched. This can be done by asserting one of the MHOLD input signals. Assertion of MHOLD signal forces the processor pipeline into a WAIT state for the duration of the time that the signal is asserted. During this period, the cache controller fills the missed cache line and strobes (using MDS signal) the missed instruction into the processor's instruction register when ready. The processor, in this case, ignores the previous instruction and uses the new instruction as the correct instruction to be executed.

Since a new instruction address is sent every cycle before the tag comparison result for the previous address is ready, the cache address must be saved by the external circuitry for one extra cycle. This delayed address will be needed by the cache in the case of a cache-miss; otherwise it is ignored.

In Sunrise processor, bus request/grant operations are implemented in very simple manner. Basically, the processor may be forced into a WAIT state in any cycle for any duration of time using BHOLD signal. A LOCK signal is provided and is asserted when the processor is in the middle of a multi-cycle bus transaction that should not be aborted. Normally, a device that needs the bus simply asserts the BHOLD signal in the first cycle that it sees the LOCK signal is inactive. Once the processor is in the WAIT state, AOE and DOE control signals may be used to turn off the output drivers of the chip during the bus grant period.

All IO devices are memory mapped and normal load/store

instructions are used to read from or write into the IO devices. The 8-bit ASI output signals determine the mapping of user space, super-user space, MMU, cache tags and other IO devices in the system. A set of alternate load and store instructions are defined which are privileged and can be used to access any Address Space between 0 and 256 in the system.

Interrupts are vectored. An on chip trap base address register is used to point to the interrupt table. External interrupts are given to the processor using four interrupt input signals. Any logic level other than zero on these four inputs is detected by the processor as an external interrupt request. This value is compared with the current processor interrupt level which can be set in the processor status register and the interrupt is taken if the external interrupt request level is greater than the processor interrupt level. The highest level interrupt (level-15) is defined to be non-maskable.

Bus Transactions

The Sunrise processor is designed so that the maximum bandwidth of the data bus is utilized. For non-load/store instructions every processor cycle is an instruction fetch cycle. Load and store instructions use extra cycles for operand access. Figure 10.3. shows the activities on the processor bus when a load or a store instruction is being executed.

Processor Microarchitecture

A block diagram of the processor chip is shown in Figure 10.4. The chip consists of four major units described below.

1. *Register File Unit*—The Register File Unit contains a total of 120 32-bit general purpose registers, from which eight registers are global and the rest are divided into seven overlapped frames (windows) of 24 registers each. Although the Sunrise processor implements only seven windows, the actual number of windows is implementation dependent and future implementations may provide more windows. A pointer in the Processor Status Register, called

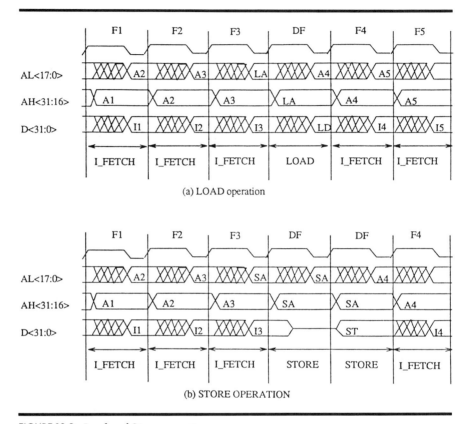

FIGURE 10.3. *Load and Store operations.*

Current Window Pointer (CWP), is used to point to the current window in the register file.

The register file has two read ports and a single write port. The uniform format of instructions allows reading both source operands of any instruction and writing the result of a previously fetched instruction into the register file, through the write port, all in a single cycle.

2. *Execution Unit*—The processor's Execution Unit consists of a fast 32-bit carry-look-ahead ALU (which performs all arithmetic and logic operations), a 32-bit barrell shifter, condition code generation logic, load and store alignment logic, and related pipeline registers required to save the

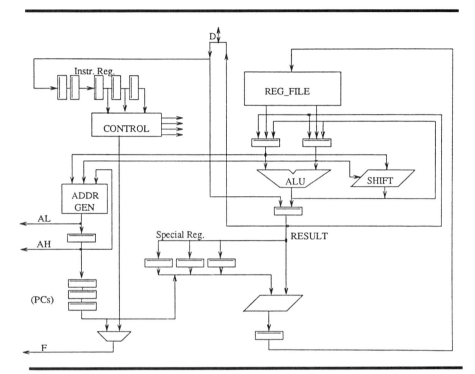

FIGURE 10.4. *Block diagram of the processor chip.*

operands and intermediate results. All arithmetic and logic instructions use the Execution Unit for a single cycle to complete their execution. This is true even if there are dependencies between the operands and results of consecutive instructions. For this to work properly, the data path in the Execution Unit incorporates two bypass paths. The first bypass path feeds the output of the ALU directly to the input of the operand registers. This bypass is activated when a source operand of an instruction depends on the results of its previous instruction. The second bypass path feeds the output of the result register to the input of the operand registers. It is activated when a source operand of an instruction depends on the result of the instruction prior to the previous instruction in the pipeline.

3. *Instruction Fetch Unit*—The Instruction Fetch Unit consists of the processor's Program Counters and instruction/data address generation circuitry. There are four Program Counters corresponding to the four stages of the instruction pipeline (see section on processor pipeline). These Program Counters are necessary and are used in the case of exceptions that may occur as late as the last stage in the processor pipeline. This unit also includes the circuitry for special registers, such as Trap Base register (TBR), Trap Type register (TT), Y register (used by multiply step instruction), and Window Invalid Mask register (WIM).

4. *Control Unit*—The control core of the processor is the Control Unit. It implements the main state machine, instruction pipeline, instruction decoder, Processor Status Register (PSR), circuitry for exception/trap handling, and the interface to the cache and floating-point unit. The Control Unit maintains a copy of the instructions that execute in different stages of the pipeline. The majority of the control signals for other units are generated in this unit and are dispatched to their destination units.

Processor Pipeline

The processor has a four-stage deep pipeline. Each stage of the processor pipeline performs a subset of operations that are needed to complete the execution of an instruction. All operations performed in a given pipeline stage occur in one full clock cycle. A brief description of each pipeline stage follows:

1. Fetch Stage—In this stage of the pipeline, the address of an instruction is sent out. Once the instruction is fetched, it enters the processor's pipeline at the completion of this stage.

2. Decode Stage—In the Decode stage of the pipeline the instruction is decoded and source operands are read from the register file. The source operands read during the Decode stage of the pipeline are passed to both the Execution

Unit and the Instruction Fetch Unit for execution of the instruction in later stages. The Decode stage of the pipeline is also used to generate the next instruction address (and in the case of branches, the branch target address). More precisely, while instruction i(n) is being decoded in the Decode stage, the address for instruction i(n+2) is being calculated by the Instruction Fetch Unit.

3. Execute Stage—While the instruction is in the Execution stage, the Execution Unit performs arithmetic and logic operations if the instruction uses the arithmetic and logic unit. The results of the operations in the Execution stage are saved in temporary registers before they are actually written into the register file. The decision to write the results into the register file is made during the last stage of the processor's pipeline.

4. Write Stage—In the Write stage of the pipeline a decision is made whether to write the results into the register file, which means the instruction has completed successfully, or to prohibit any changes in the state of the processor. The Write stage will abort if an exception is raised during the execution of that instruction.

As shown in Figure 10.5. four instructions can execute simultaneously in the processor pipeline. While instruction i(n) is being fetched, instruction i(n−1) is being decoded in the Decode stage, instruction i(n−2) is being executed in the Execution stage, and instruction i(n−3) is writing its results into the register file. A given instruction may raise several exceptions (traps) during the course of its execution. When multiple traps are raised simultaneously, the trap handling logic guarantees that the highest priority trap is taken by the processor.

In this processor since branch instructions are delayed by one instruction, all taken PC-relative branches execute in a single cycle. This is done by fetching the target instruction before the condition codes are ready. If after evaluation of the condition codes it was determined that the branch was untaken, the processor ignores the target instruction and continues to fetch the next instruction in the sequence.

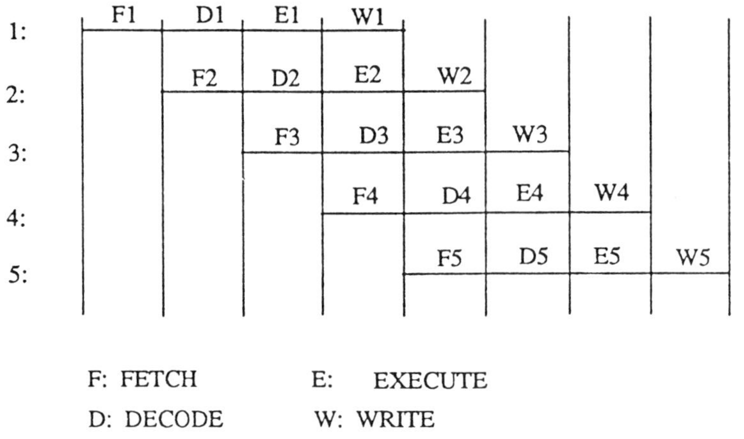

FIGURE 10.5. *Four stage instruction pipeline.*

Instruction Buffer

The Sunrise processor uses a dual-instruction buffer in order to keep the pipeline full at all times. These buffers are used to prefetch instructions during the execution of multiple-cycle instructions and to speed up the execution by utilizing the data bus more efficiently. The buffer is empty when the processor is executing a sequence of single-cycle instructions in a row. When a multiple-cycle instruction enters into the pipeline, its following instructions are prefetched into the buffer untill the multiple-cycle instruction is complete.

Internal Instructions

In the Sunrise processor all control circuitry has been implemented using random logic. For single-cycle instructions this is a straight-forward task. The control for multiple-cycle instructions has been designed so that from the pipeline point of view each multiple-cycle instruction behaves like several consecutive single-cycle instructions. This is accomplished using so called "internal instructions". Internal instructions are generated automatically by the processor and are injected into the processor's pipeline as they are needed. Load and store instructions are examples of instructions that need more than one cycle to complete. Figure 10.6. shows a single-word load instruction which takes one extra cycle in the pipeline and therefore it uses one internal instruction to complete. In this case the EH1 cycle is used to fetch the load operand, Figure 10.7. shows a single-word store instruction which takes two extra cycles in the pipeline and therefore it uses two internal instructions to complete. In this case the store address is sent during the EH11 cycle and the data is sent during the EH21. After the completion of a multiple-cycle instruction the processor first executes all instructions in the instruction buffer and then continues its normal operation by fetching instructions from the external cache.

Traps and Interrupts

Execution of a given instruction may raise several traps or exceptions. Traps may be synchronous (generated by the processor) or asynchronous such as external interrupts. When a trap is detected the following actions are taken by the processor.

1. The Program Counters corresponding to the trapped instruction and the instruction following the trapped instruction are saved in the register file.

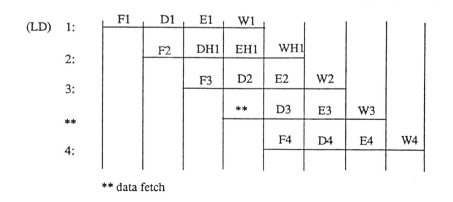

** data fetch

FIGURE 10.6. *Execution of a LOAD in the pipeline.*

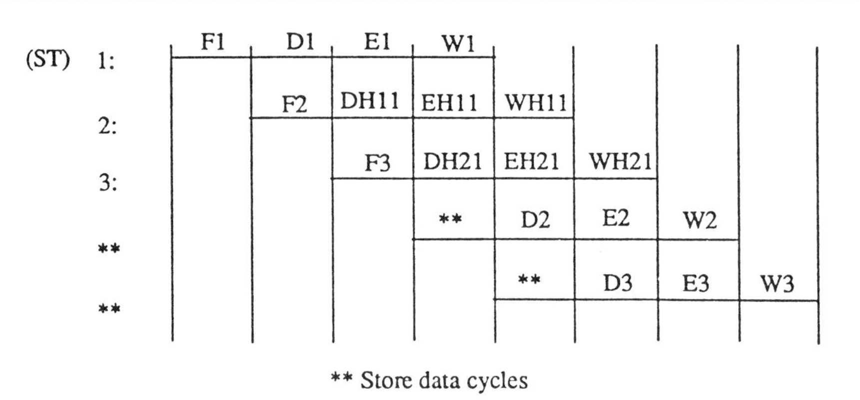

(ST) 1:	F1	D1	E1	W1				
2:		F2	DH11	EH11	WH11			
3:			F3	DH21	EH21	WH21		
**				**	D2	E2	W2	
**					**	D3	E3	W3

** Store data cycles

FIGURE 10.7. *Execution of a STORE in the pipeline.*

2. Execution of the trapped instruction is aborted and all fetched but unfinished instructions are flushed out of the processor's pipeline.

3. All traps are disabled. The processor's mode is set to the superuser mode and the Current Window Pointer is set to point to the next window.

4. The trap address is computed based on the content of the Trap Base Register and the Trap Type of the highest priority trap and is loaded into the Program Counter.

5. Execution is restarted from the new trap address.

The Sunrise processor provides 15 External Interrupt Levels that are maskable (with the exception of Level-15) by a 4-bit Processor Interrupt Level. All external interrupts are ignored when traps are disabled. If a synchronous trap is detected while traps are disabled, the processor enters into an Error Mode and remains in that mode until it is reset externally. At reset the processor enters into an initial state and starts execution from address zero.

Floating-Point Unit Interface

The Sunrise processor is designed so that it can execute integer instructions concurrently with the floating-point instructions.

When a floating-point instruction is encountered, it is sent to an external floating-point controller through a dedicated 32-bit bus. The floating-point controller consists of 32 32-bit floating-point registers, the Floating-Point Status Register (FSR) and the Floating-Point Queue (FQ). The Floating-Point Queue maintains information related to the instructions that have been dispatched to the floating-point controller but have not yet completed their execution. Each entry of the queue consists of two pieces of information: the floating-point instruction and its address. The following is a summary of the functions performed by the floating-point controller chip.

1. Maintaining the Floating-Point Status Register and Floating-Point Queue.

2. Decoding floating-point instructions and generating proper control signals for the floating-point arithmetic units.

3. Detecting dependencies between floating-point instructions and signaling the processor to wait if necessary.

4. Executing floating-point load and store instructions (the memory address is computed in the processor).

5. Detecting floating-point exceptions and signalling the processor.

Floating-Point Loads/Stores

The Sunrise processor supports both single-word and double-word floating point load/store operations. From the pipeline point of view, floating-point load/stores behave exactly the same as integer loads and stores. Similar to the integer loads and stores, the memory address is computed by the processor. The only difference is that the floating-point controller either receives the data from the data bus (in the case of load) or puts the data on the data bus (in the case of stores). Any exception raised during the execution of floating-point loads and stores is detected and handled by the processor. The floating-point controller would hold the processor when there is a dependency between the operands of load/store and the operands of previous instructions in the floating-point queue.

Branch on Floating-Point Conditions

Branch on floating-point condition instructions behave very similar to the branch on integer condition instructions. The only difference is that the condition code bits for these instructions are generated by the floating-point controller. The processor enters into a wait state whenever it needs the floating-point conditions and these condition bits are not ready.

Floating Point Operations

Once the processor encounters a floating-point instruction, the instruction and its address are sent to the external floating-point controller chip. The floating-point controller chip decodes the instruction and takes one of the following actions:

1. It holds the processor if a situation arises so that the floating-point controller must wait, for example, when the floating-point queue is full.

2. It accepts the new instruction and enters the instruction and its address into the floating-point queue for later execution. In this case the processor will advance to the next instruction without waiting as if the floating-point instruction was completed immediately.

Floating-Point Exceptions

Floating-point exceptions, in general, occur asynchronously with respect to the processor's pipeline. The reasons are (1) integer instructions are executed concurrently with the floating-point instructions and (2) different floating-point instructions take a different number of cycles to complete their execution or generate an exception. In the Sunrise processor, floating-point exceptions are taken in a synchronous manner. When a floating-point exception is raised two situations may happen.

1. If the current instruction being executed in the integer unit is a floating-point instruction, the floating-point exception is taken by the processor only if there are no higher priority traps pending.

2. If the current instruction being executed in the integer unit is not a floating-point instruction the floating-point exception is kept pending until the next floating-point instruction begins.

Sunrise Performance

Three major factors affecting the performance of a processor are: the cycle time, the average number of cycles per instruction, and the relative code density, which is a measure of instruction set effectiveness.

Cycle Time

The entire design of the Sunrise processor was analyzed carefully in order to identify the longest delay paths in the design. The goal was to reach a typical cycle time of 50ns or less. This goal was achieved using an iterative approach in which all internal or external paths that had a delay longer than 50ns were either improved or in some cases redesigned. The worse case cycle time for the Sunrise processor is approximately 62ns allowing design of a system with 16MHz clock rate.

Number of Cycles per Instructions

In Sunrise processor most instructions complete their execution in a single cycle. A small subset of instructions take more than one cycle to complete. These multiple-cycle instruction, as was explained earlier, use one or more internal instructions to complete their execution. Table 10.1 gives a summary of instruction execution times. (Note: Cf is the number of cycles needed by the floating-point arithmetic unit to complete a floating-point instruction. This number varies depending on the type of floating-point operation.)

Based on the above table and a conservative instruction mix ratio (15% loads, 5% stores, 15% taken branches and 5% untaken branches) the average number of cycles per instruction (CPI), excluding cache miss penalty, would be about 1.3. Using a 64K-

Instruction type	Number of cycles	Number of internal instructions
Load (word/halfword/byte)	2	1
Load (double)	3	2
Store (word/halfword/byte)	3	2
Store (double)	4	3
Atomic Load and Store	4	3
Floating-point ops	2 + Cf	1
Jump and Rett	2	1
Branch (untaken)	2	0
Branch (taken)	1	0
All Other instructions	1	0

TABLE 10.1.

byte cache the miss ratio would be approximately 1%, and if we assume a 10 cycle cache miss penalty then the CPI would be:

$$CPI = 1.3 + [0.01 * (1 + 0.15 + 0.05) * 10] = 1.42$$

With a cycle time of 62ns the above CPI translates into a 11.36 native MIPS machine.

Conclusions

In this article we presented Sunrise processor, the first implementation of SPARC architecture, on a single 20,000-gate gate-array. The performance of this gate-array exceeds most existing commercial 32-bit microprocessors. This proves the effectiveness of SPARC and in general RISC-based architectures and paves the way to the design of future higher performance implementations of this architecture. In order to achive such a high performance the entire control logic was implemented using random logic with as few as possible number of levels of logic. The Sunrise processor was fully simulated using a simulation model that consists of gate level models of the Sunrise processor chip, the floating-point controller chip, a high level model of the cache and Weitek floating-point arithmetic chips (W1164 multiplier and W1165 adder). A large number of functional test cases were written by the designers (in assembly language) in order to verify the correctness of the design. These test cases check the processor's data path and control logic using a large variety of instruction sequences and data patterns. The simulation model was also used to generate pin-test vectors for testing the ICs at the manufacturing stage. The extensive amount of simulation paid off eventually once the first silicon of Sunrise run multi-user Unix in a prototype system.

CMOS Custom Implementation of the SPARC Architecture

11

M. Namjoo • F. Abu-Nofal • D. Carmean •
R. Chandramouli • Y. Chang • J. Goforth • W. Hsu •
R. Iwamoto • C. Murphy • U. Naot • M. Parkin •
J. Pendleton • C. Porter • J. Reaves • R. Reddy •
G. Swan • D. Tinker • P. Tong • L. Yang

Introduction

Using custom circuitry, a higher level of performance is achieved for a new implementation of the SPARC™ architecture. CYC601 processor (integer unit), running at a clock rate of 25–33 MHz, implements the complete set of SPARC instructions in a 0.8 micron CMOS technology. This paper gives an overview of the processor chip and its interface to the external cache, floating-point unit, and a generic coprocessor. Companion papers provide more information on the SPARC architecture and software tools.

Processor Microarchitecture

Figure 11.1. shows a block diagram of the processor chip. The major components are: (1) a 4-stage instruction pipeline with a dual instruction buffer which is used to maximize its throughput, (2) a three port register file with 136 32-bit general purpose registers, configured as eight overlapped windows (each with twenty-four registers) and eight global registers, (3) a fast precharged arithmetic and logic unit, (4) a separate 32-bit adder for branch

1988 IEEE. Reprinted with Permission, from Proceedings of COMPCON '88, March 1–3, San Francisco, CA.

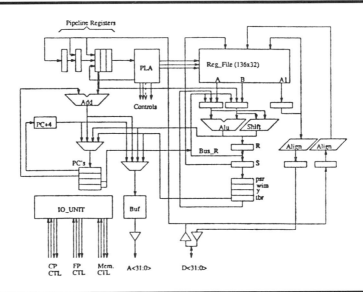

FIGURE 11.1. *Chip block diagram.*

target calculation, and (5) the circuitry for load/store alignment and special registers (PSR, TBR, WIM, and Y).

In the basic pipeline operation, the processor fetches an instruction during the fetch-stage (F). The fetched instruction is decoded in the decode-stage (D) and source operands are read from the register file. In the execute-stage (E), the instruction is executed and in the write-stage (W) the results are written into the destination register. The write-stage is aborted if a trap or exception is raised while the instruction is being executed.

All instructions with the exception of loads/stores and jump/return execute in a single cycle. Execution of load and store instructions take more than one cycle because they use the same bus for accessing instructions as well as operands from the memory. Jump/return instructions take one extra cycle because they use register-indirect operands and the processor must read the operands from the register file before calculating the target address. All Conditional branch instructions, however, are performed in a single cycle. The single-cycle branch execution, which applies to both taken and untaken branches, results from the early availability of the condition codes generated by a highly optimized ALU and condition code evaluation logic.

The instruction pipeline consists of various fields of instructions corresponding to the decode, execute and write stages of the pipeline and a two-stage instruction buffer. The instruction buffer, shown in Figure 11.2., continues to prefetch new instructions once the processor encounters an instruction that needs more than one cycle to complete. This buffer is empty during a sequence of single-cycle instructions and is used only when a multi-cycle instruction is decoded. Multi-cycle instructions use one or more internally generated opcodes to complete execution. These internal opcodes are generated using a small on-chip PLA and are jammed into the pipeline as needed. Figure 11.3. shows the execution of a single-word load instruction that uses an extra cycle in the pipeline to complete.

External Interface

The processor provides a simple interface to the cache, the floating-point unit, and a generic coprocessor. Almost all output signals of the processor are sent unlatched and are available a cycle before the cycle in which they are needed. In a typical system these signals should be latched externally before they are used.

Cache/Memory Interface

The chip uses two major buses for accessing the cache: a 32-bit address-bus ($A<31:0>$) and a 32-bit bi-directional data-bus

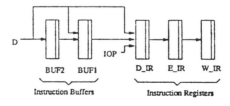

FIGURE 11.2. *Instruction buffer.*

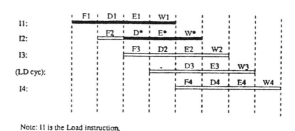

Note: I1 is the Load instruction.

FIGURE 11.3. *Execution of a single-word load instruction.*

($D<31:0>$). In addition, the chip generates an 8-bit address-space-identifier ($ASI<7:0>$) which carry information such as processor mode (user/super-user) and memory access type (instruction/data). Figure 11.4. shows the processor bus cycles during load and store operations.

In a typical cache-based system, the latched value of the address is used to access the cache data as well as cache tags. During the same cycle the cache tags are checked and depending on the result (miss or hit) the cache controller either stops the processor chip to handle the cache-miss or continues as normal in the case of

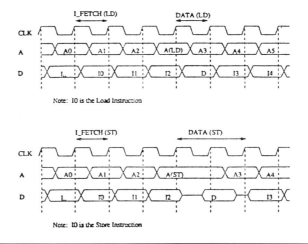

FIGURE 11.4. *Load/Store bus cycles.*

a cache-hit. Figure 11.5. shows a timing diagram in which instruction 10 causes a cache-miss. In this case the cache controller stops the processor chip (using MHOLD signal) in the cycle following the fetch cycle and starts the cache-fill sequence. Once the cache is ready, it asserts the MAO (missed-address-output select) signal that forces the processor to put the address and controls for the missed instruction on the bus. The missed instruction is then strobed into the processor's instruction register using the MDS (memory-data-strobe) signal.

Floating-Point/Coprocessor Interface

The processor chip supports two identical coprocessor ports. One of these ports is used for interface to the floating-point unit (FP) and the other port may be used for interface to a generic user-defined coprocessor (CP). In this interface, as shown in Figure 11.6., the coprocessors are connected directly to the address and data bus. For every instruction fetch, both FP and CP capture the instruction and its address from the data-bus and address-bus respectively. These instructions are entered into the pipeline registers of both floating-point and coprocessor units. The integer chip provides all necessary control signals for synchronizing its pipeline with the pipeline in FP and CP. When a floating-point/coprocessor instruction is decoded by the integer chip, it signals the FP/CP to start executing it immediately. Note that this decision has to be made by the integer chip because instructions may

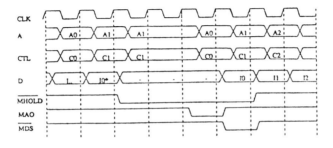

FIGURE 11.5. *Cache miss on instruction fetch.*

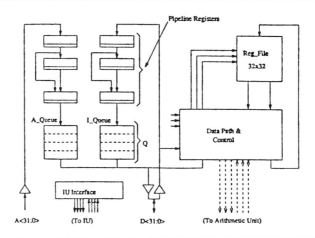

FIGURE 11.6. *Generic floating-point/coprocessor block diagram.*

be flushed from the pipeline due to traps and nullification which are known only by the integer chip. All floating-point and co-processor instructions take only one cycle in the integer chip. Therefore, a new floating-point or coprocessor instruction can be started in every cycle.

The coprocessors have their own set of registers (thirty-two 32-bit registers each), a status register, a queue for holding the instructions that need to be executed, and the logic for decoding instructions, checking dependencies between instructions, dispatching instructions to the arithmetic units, and performing load/ store operations from or to the cache.

I/O and Interrupts

I/O derives are memory mapped and accessed using basic load and store operations. The architecture defines a set of alternate load and store instructions that allow the user to select different I/O devices using different ASI values.

Internal traps (synchronous) and external traps (asynchronous) are handled in the same manner. Basically, once the processor detects a trap condition, it enters into a trap sequence, saves the necessary state, flushes the instructions in the pipeline and then resumes execution from the address defined by the trap base address (TBR) and the trap-type value.

External interrupts are given to the processor chip using four input signals. Any level other than "0" on these pins is detected as a valid interrupt level. An on-chip synchronizer is used to synchronize the interrupts and prevent spurious interrupts.

Summary and Concluding Remarks

CYC601 with a cycle time in the range of 30 to 40 ns can perform integer instructions at a peak rate of 25 to 33 MIPS. The average number of cycles per instruction (CPI) for this processor is approximately 1.54. This assumes an instruction mix with 15% loads (which take one extra cycle), 5% stores (which take two extra cycles), 20% branches (which execute in a single cycle—no penalty), and additional cycles lost due to load interlocks, jump/returns, nullification of delay-slot instruction in branches, and penalty for a 128 Kbyte cache-miss on instructions as well as data.

Acknowledgments

This project was jointly developed by Sun Microsystems, Inc., under the supervision of Jim Slager and Cypress Semiconductor, Inc., under the supervision of Uday Kapoor and Chris Porter. Many others contributed to this project including Al Marston in the area of circuit design, Ken Okin, Chien Nguyen, Larry Goss in the area of external pin specification, Chuck Tucker, Gary Formica, Matt Clayson, Bob Davidson, and Debbie Weed in layout design, Joe Sirott, Mike Klein, Rajiv Kane, David Cooke in CAD development, and Chris Christensen, Mike Russo, and Joseph Yang in CAD support.

References

1. R. Garner et al., "The Scalable Processor Architecture (SPARC)," *this proceedings.*

2. S. Kleiman, D. Williams, "UNIX on SPARC," *this proceedings.*

3. S. Muchnick, C. Aoki, V. Ghodssi, M. Helft, M. Lee, R. Tuck, D. Weaver, A. Wu, "Optimizing Compilers for the SPARC Architecture: An Overview," *this proceedings.*

4. M. Namjoo, A. Agrawal, D.C. Jackson, L. Quach "CMOS Gate Array Implementation of the SPARC Architecture," *this proceedings.*

CMOS Gate-Array Implementation of the SPARC Architecture

Masood Namjoo • Anant Agrawal • Donald C. Jackson • L. Quach

Introduction

This article describes MB86900 processor, the first implementation of the SPARC architecture. MB86900, referred to here as the Integer Unit (IU), is a high-performance microprocessor designed with Fujitsu's high-speed CMOS gate-array technology. In a typical system the MB86900 IU works with a companion floating-point controller chip, MB86910, two commercial floating-point arithmetic processors, and a cache which is an essential component of the system.

The MB86900 has a reduced-instruction-set-computer (RISC) architecture. The architecture defines a simple, yet efficient set of instructions. Most of these instructions execute in a single cycle, resulting in a very low average number of cycles per instruction (CPI). Instructions that cannot finish in a single cycle, such as loads and stores, use a minimum number of additional cycles.

The simplified format of instructions allows the source operands to be read immediately from the register file without any delay caused by the decoding of instructions. This significantly decreases the cycle time, contributing to the processor's speed. The processor has a large on-chip register file that reduces the overhead of load and store operations considerably, allowing a peak execution rate of approximately 1 cycle per instruction when all operands are kept inside the processor's register file. More

1988 IEEE. Reprinted with Permission, from Proceedings of COMPCON '88, March 1–3, San Francisco, CA.

information on the architecture can be found in the companion paper.

Processor Microarchitecture

The entire IU is implemented in a single 20,000-gate CMOS gate-array chip fabricated by Fujitsu. This gate-array is based on a 1.5 micron technology (with 10% gate shrink), yielding a worst case cycle time of 60ns (16.6 MHz) for the processor. One quarter of this gate-array is occupied by a 4K-bits register file and the other three quarters are used by the data path and control circuitry. The circuitry inside the IU has been partitioned, hierarchically, into blocks, sub-blocks and sub-sub-blocks allowing easy place and route and predictable post-layout wire delays for the entire chip. The processor chip has a total of 156 I/O signals and uses a 256 pin PGA (Pin Grid Array) package.

As shown in Figure 12.1., the chip consists of four major units.

1. *REGISTER FILE UNIT (R_UNIT)*—The R_UNIT contains a total of 120 32-bit general purpose registers, from which eight registers are global and the rest are divided into seven overlapped frames (windows) of 24 registers each. Although the MB86900 processor implements only seven windows, the actual number of windows is implementation dependent and future implementations can have more. A pointer in the Processor Status Register, called Current Window Pointer (CWP), is used to point to the current window in the register file. The register file has two read ports and a single write port. The uniform format of instructions allows reading both source operands of any instruction and writing the result of a previously fetched instruction into the register file, through the write port. The entire process occurs in a single cycle.

2. *EXECUTION UNIT (E_UNIT)*—This unit consists of a fast 32-bit carry-look-ahead ALU (which performs all arithmetic and logic operations), a 32-bit barrel shifter, condition code generation logic, load and store alignment logic, and related pipeline registers required to save the operands and

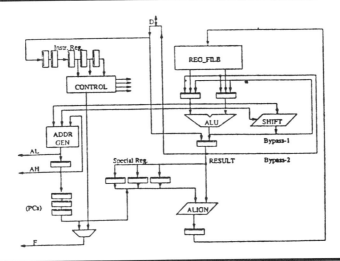

FIGURE 12.1. *Block diagram of the processor chip (IU).*

intermediate results. All arithmetic and logic instructions use the E_UNIT for a single cycle to complete their execution. The data path incorporates two bypass paths for handling dependencies between the operands and results of consecutive instructions. The first bypass path feeds the output of the ALU directly to the input of the operand registers. This bypass is activated when a source operand of an instruction depends on the results of its previous instruction. The second bypass path feeds the output of the result register to the input of the operand registers. It is activated when a source operand of an instruction depends on the result of the instruction prior to the previous instruction in the pipeline.

3. *INSTRUCTION FETCH UNIT (I_UNIT)*—This unit consists of the processor's program counters and instruction/data address generation circuitry. There are four program counters corresponding to the four stages of the instruction pipeline (see section on processor pipeline). These program counters are necessary and are used in the case of exceptions that may occur as late as the last stage in the

processor pipeline. This unit also includes the circuitry for the Trap Base register (TBR), Trap Type register (TT), Y register (used by multiply step instruction), and Window Invalid Mask register (WIM).

4. *CONTROL UNIT (C_UNIT)*—This unit implements the main state machine, instruction pipeline, instruction decoder, Processor Status Register (PSR), circuitry for exception/trap handling, and the interface to the cache and floating-point unit. The C_UNIT maintains a copy of the instructions that execute in different stages of the pipeline. The majority of the control signals for other units are generated in this unit.

Processor Pipeline

The processor has a four-stage deep pipeline. Each stage of the processor pipeline performs a subset of operations that are needed to complete the execution of an instruction. All operations performed in a given pipeline stage occur in one full clock cycle. A brief description of each pipeline stage follows:

1. Fetch Stage—In this stage of the pipeline, a new instruction is fetched. The fetched instruction enters the processor's pipeline at the completion of this stage.

2. Decode Stage—In this stage, the instruction is decoded and source operands are read from the register file. The source operands read during this stage are passed to both the E_UNIT and the I_UNIT for execution of the instruction in later stages. The decode stage of the pipeline is also used to generate the next instruction address (and in the case of branches, the branch target address). More precisely, while instruction $I(n)$ is being decoded in the decode stage, the address for instruction $I(n + 2)$ is being calculated by the I_UNIT.

3. Execute Stage—In this stage, the E_UNIT performs arithmetic and logic operations on the operands read during the decode stage. The results of these operations are saved in a

temporary result register before they are actually written into the destination register.

4. Write Stage—The write stage marks the end of an instruction execution in the pipeline. In this stage a decision is made whether to write the results into the register file, which means the instruction has completed successfully, or to prohibit any changes in the state of the processor. The write stage will abort if an exception is raised during the execution of that instruction.

As shown in Figure 12.2., four instructions can execute simultaneously in the processor pipeline. While instruction I(n) is being fetched, instruction I(n − 1) is being decoded in the decode stage, instruction I(n − 2) is being executed in the execute stage, and instruction I(n − 3) is writing its results into the destination register.

In this processor since branch instructions are delayed by one instruction, all taken PC-relative branches execute in a single cycle. This is done by fetching the target instruction before the condition codes are ready. If after evaluation of the condition codes it is determined that the branch should have not been taken, the processor ignores the target instruction and continues to fetch the next instruction in the sequence.

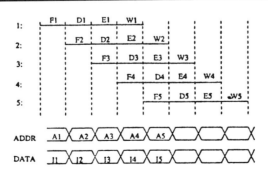

FIGURE 12.2. *Four-stage instruction pipeline.*

Instruction Buffer

The IU uses a dual-instruction buffer in order to keep the pipeline full at all times. These buffers are used to prefetch instructions during the execution of multiple-cycle instructions and to speed up the execution by utilizing the data bus more efficiently. The buffer is empty when the processor is executing a sequence of single-cycle instructions in a row. When a multiple-cycle instruction enters into the pipeline, its following instructions are prefetched into the buffer until the multiple-cycle instruction is complete.

Internal Instructions

All control circuitry in the IU has been implemented using random logic (no PLA's). The state machine and controls are designed so that each multiple-cycle instruction behaves like several consecutive single-cycle instructions. This is accomplished using *internal instructions* which are generated automatically by the IU and are injected into the processor's pipeline as they are needed. Load and store instructions are examples of instructions that need more than one cycle to complete. Figure 12.3. shows a single-word load instruction which takes one extra cycle and Figure 12.4. shows a single-word store instruction which takes two extra cycles in the pipeline to complete.

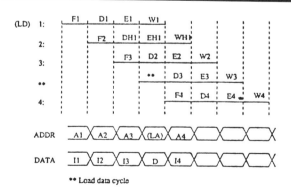

FIGURE 12.3. *Execution of a single-word load instruction.*

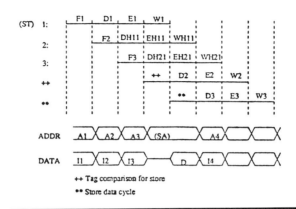

FIGURE 12.4. *Execution of a single-word store instruction.*

Traps and Exceptions

A given instruction may raise several exceptions (traps) during the course of its execution. When multiple traps are raised simultaneously, the trap handling logic guarantees that the highest priority trap is taken by the IU. Traps are vectored and an on-chip trap base address register (TBR) is used to point to the trap table. Traps may be synchronous such as privileged instruction trap or asynchronous such as external interrupts. The IU provides 15 External Interrupt Levels that are maskable (with the exception of Level-15) by a 4-bit Processor Interrupt Level. All external interrupts are ignored when traps are disabled. If a synchronous trap is detected while traps are disabled, the IU enters into an Error Mode and remains in that mode until it is reset externally. At reset the IU enters into an initial state and starts execution from memory address 'zero'.

Cache/Memory Interface

The IU uses two separate 32-bit busses, *A_BUS* and *D_BUS*, for address and data to access the storage. As shown in Figure 12.5, the address bus is divided into two parts: AL (low address, bits 17..0) and AH (high address, bits 31..16). AL and AH bits are overlapped

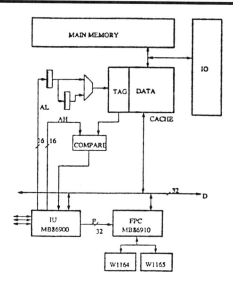

FIGURE 12.5. *A typical cache-based system configuration.*

in bits 16 and 17, allowing direct addressing of a cache with a size up to 256K bytes.

Every cycle in this processor is either an instruction fetch cycle, a load cycle, or a store cycle. For every instruction fetch, the IU sends the AL in the cycle before the fetch cycle. The AL is latched externally and used to fetch the instruction in the fetch cycle.

Within the same cycle, the cache tags are read and checked against AH. In the case of a cache-hit, the IU treats the fetched instruction as a correct instruction and continues to fetch the next instruction in the following cycle. However, if the cache is missed, the external cache controller logic must hold the IU in the cycle following the fetch cycle. This can be done by asserting one of the MHOLD input signals that forces the processor pipeline into a WAIT state for the duration of the time that the signal is asserted. During this period, the cache controller fills the missed cache line and strobes (using MDS signal) the missed instruction into the IU's instruction register. The IU, in this case, ignores the previous instruction and uses the new instruction as the correct one to be executed. The cache-miss for load and store instructions is handled in a similar way.

Since a new instruction address is sent every cycle before the tag comparison result for the previous address is ready, the cache address must be saved by the external circuitry for one extra cycle. This delayed address will be needed by the cache only in the case of a cache-miss; otherwise it is ignored.

Bus request/grant operations are implemented in very simple manner. Basically, the processor may be forced into a WAIT state in any cycle for any duration of time using BHOLD signal. A LOCK signal is provided and is asserted when the processor is in the middle of a multi-cycle bus transaction that should not be aborted. Normally, a device that needs the bus simply asserts the BHOLD signal in the first cycle that it sees the LOCK signal is inactive. Once the processor is in the WAIT state, AOE and DOE control signals may be used to turn off the output drivers of the chip. The LOCK signal is guaranteed to be deasserted for at least one cycle during any instruction, preventing the I/O from being locked out.

All I/O devices are memory mapped and load/store instructions are used to read from or write into the I/O devices. For every memory access, the IU sends out an 8-bit Address Space Identifier (ASI) field. Normally, ASI bits carry information such as processor mode (user/superuser) and the type of memory access (instruction/data). During the execution of alternate load/store instructions, these bits carry the ASI field specified by the instruction.

Floating-Point Unit Interface

In MB86900 processor, floating-point instructions are executed by the MB86910 floating-point controller chip, refered to here as FPC. The FPC, also designed using Fujitsu's 20,000 gate CMOS gate-array, consists of thirty-two 32-bit floating-point registers, a Floating-Point Status Register (FSR) and a Floating-Point Queue (FQ). The floating-point controller chip handles the execution of floating-point instructions as well as floating-point loads/stores concurrent with the execution of integer instructions.

Floating-point instructions and their addresses are sent to the FPC through a dedicated 32-bit *F_BUS* in two consecutive cycles. This information is maintained in the floating-point queue of the FPC and is used for later execution of the instruction by the arithmetic units (WTL1164 multiplier and WTL1165 alu). Each entry of the queue consists of two pieces of information: the floating-point instruction and its address. The contents of the queue can be read out and used by the trap handler when floating-point exceptions occur.

Both single and double precision load/stores are supported. For these instructions, the IU computes the memory address for the operands and the FPC either receives the data from the data bus (for loads) or puts the data on the data bus (for stores). The floating-point controller holds the processor when there is a dependency between the operands of loads/stores and the operands of previous instructions in the floating-point queue.

Branch on floating-point condition instructions behave very similar to the branch on integer condition instructions. The only difference is that the condition code bits for these instructions are generated by the floating-point controller. The IU enters into a wait state whenever it needs the floating-point conditions and these condition bits are not ready.

MB86910 does not implement square root (SQRT) and extended precision instructions. These instructions will generate floating-point exception if they are executed. Floating-point exceptions are signaled to the IU using FEXC signal. In general, these exceptions are asynchronous with respect to the processor's pipeline. The reasons are (1) integer instructions are executed concurrently with the floating-point instructions and (2) different floating-point instructions take a different number of cycles to complete their execution or generate an exception. In the MB86900 processor, floating-point exceptions are taken in a synchronous manner. This is done by taking the exception immediately, if the current instruction is a floating-point, or delaying the exceptions until the next floating-point instruction, if the current instruction is not a floating-point. All integer instructions with the exception of SWAP instruction are implemented by the IU.

MB86900 Performance

In addition to the cycle time, there are two other important factors that affect the performance. These are (1) the average number of cycles per instruction (CPI) and (2) the average number of instructions needed to complete a given task, which is a function of compilers and the efficiency of the instruction set. As was mentioned earlier, some instructions take more than one cycle to complete. Table 12.1 gives a summary of the number of cycles used to execute each instruction.

For large C programs an instruction mix ratio of about 15% loads, 5% stores, 15% taken branches and 5% untaken branches is observed. Based on the above table, the contribution of loads, stores, branches, annulled instructions, load interlocks (assuming 50% of the loads cause interlock with the next instruction), and jumps to the CPI, excluding cache-misses would be approximately 1.47. The contribution of cache-misses for a 128K-byte cache (with approximately 1% miss-ratio and 10 cycles miss penalty) would be:

$$CACHE\_MISS\_COST = 0.01 * (1 + 0.15 + 0.05) * 10 = 0.12$$

Instruction Type	# of cycles	# of Internal Instr.
Load (word/halfword/byte)	2	1
Load (double)	3	2
Store (word/halfword/byte)	3	2
Store (double)	4	3
Atomic Load and Store	4	3
Floating-point ops	2 + Cf	1
Jump and Rett	2	1
Branch (untaken)	2	0
Branch (taken)	1	0
All Other instructions	1	0

(Note: Cf is the number of cycles needed by the floating-point arithmetic unit to complete a floating-point instruction. This number varies depending on the type of floating-point operation. The WTL1164/1165 arithmetic units perform single precision add/multiply in 10 cycles, double precision add in 13 cycles, and double precision multiply in 15 cycles.)

TABLE 12.1. *Instruction execution times.*

Therefore, the average CPI for the processor would be:

$$CPI = 1.47 + 0.12 = 1.59$$

Conclusions

In this paper we described the first implementation of SPARC architecture on a single gate-array. With a worst case cycle time of 60ns and an average CPI of approximately 1.59, this processor delivers a performance that exceeds most existing 32-bit microprocessors. In this implementation, some instructions, such as loads and stores, take more than one cycle to complete, resulting in a slight increase in the average CPI. The reason for this is mainly due to limitations of the single 32-bit data bus, which is used in this design. The CPI can be improved in future implementations with a different bus structure.

The gate-array approach, chosen for this implementation, proved to be a low-risk, low-cost solution and resulted in early availability of functional parts which were used in debugging of prototype systems. The entire design of IU uses an equivalent of approximately 12000 2-input nand gates and a custom designed 3-port register file. This gate count includes the overhead for additional circuitry needed for a fully scannable design in order to facilitate testing of the chips. Both IU and FPC designs were simulated and verified using a large set of diagnostics. The extensive amount of simulations paid off eventually once the first silicon of these chips ran the multiuser Unix in a prototype system of SUN 4/200 work station.

Acknowledgments

The authors would like to thank all members of the MB86900 design team. K.G. Tan and Wayne Rosing managed this project. J.K. Lu, Rick Iwamoto and Larry Yang helped in logic simulation and design verification. Phil Mak, Susan Rohani and Quyen Vu helped in timing verification tools and other cad support. Will Brown wrote an architectural and machine cycle simulator. Ed Kelly and Robert Garner designed the Sun-4/200 processor board and helped design the IU/cache interface. Many others including Bill Joy, David Patterson, Steven Muchnick, Steve Kleiman, Dock Williams, David Weaver, David Hough, Richard Tuck, and Alex Wu helped in developing the architecture.

References

1. D.A. Patterson, "RISC." *Eighth Annual Symposium on Computer Architecture*, May 1981.

2. J. Hennesey, "VLSI Processor Architecture," *IEEE Transactions on Computers*, December 1984.

3. R. Garner et al., "The Scalable Processor Architecture (SPARC)," *this proceedings.*

4. S. Kleiman, D. Williams, "UNIX on SPARC," *this proceedings.*

5. S. Muchnick, C. Aoki, V. Ghodssi, M. Helft, M. Lee, R. Tuck, D. Weaver, A. Wu, "Optimizing Compilers for the SPARC Architecture: An Overview," *this proceedings.*

6. M. Namjoo and A. Agrawal, "Implementing SPARC: A High Performance 32-bit RISC Microprocessor," *Sun Microsystems Technical Publications*, Sun Microsystems, Inc., 1987.

7. MB86900 Processor Data Sheet, *Fujitsu Microelectronics Technical Publication*, Fujitsu Microelectronics, Santa Clara, CA, 1987.

Implementing SPARC: A High-Performance 32-Bit RISC Microprocessor

13

MASOOD NAMJOO • ANANT AGRAWAL

Designing better microprocessor performance can take two tracks. You can "turn up" the clock of an existing CPU; such is the case with Sun's MC68020-based computers, which offer performance gradients between 1.5 MIPS (million instructions per second) and 4 MIPS. Or you can improve CPU performance by developing and implementing an entirely new microprocessor architecture. Sun Microsystems took the latter approach for its Sun-4 family of workstations.

You no longer face architectural limitations when you devise and adopt a new CPU architecture. With a new architecture, such as SPARC (Scalable Processor ARChitecture), you pave the way for orders of magnitude performance jumps because you can incorporate new semiconductor technologies, such as GaAs (gallium arsenide), as they become available. A new CPU architecture can also take advantage of advanced microprocessor designs that smash previous barriers to faster, more powerful chips.

The SF9010IU processor is the first implementation of SPARC, Sun's new 32-bit RISC architecture. The SF9010IU is a high-performance microprocessor designed with Fujitsu's high-speed CMOS gate-array technology. With a worst-case cycle time of 60 ns, the sustained performance of the SF9010IU exceeds 10 MIPS when the CPU executes instructions from a reasonable-size cache. In a typical system, the SF9010IU works with a floating-point controller chip, two commercial floating-point arithmetic processors (Weitek W1164 multiplier and W1165 adder), and a cache that is a buffer between the main memory and the processor. The cache is an important factor in the performance of the SPARC processor and must be capable of delivering one instruction to the processor in every cycle. For this reason, the pipeline and control segments of the SF9010IU are optimized for a cache-based system.

The SF9010IU has a reduced-instruction-set-computer (RISC) architecture. The architecture defines a simple yet efficient set of instructions. Most of these instructions execute in a single cycle, resulting in a very low average number of cycles per instruction (CPI). Instructions that cannot finish in a single cycle, such as loads and stores, employ a minimum number of additional cycles.

Most instructions use only two different formats. In the first format, two registers (rs1 and rs2) are the source operands, and a third register (rd) is the destination operand. In the second format, a register (rs1) and a 13-bit signed, immediate value are the source operands, and a second register (rd) is the destination operand. The simplified format of instructions allows the source operands to be read immediately from the register file without any delay caused by the decoding of instructions. This format significantly decreases the cycle time, contributing to the processor's speed. The processor has a large on-chip register file that considerably reduces the overhead of load and store operations, allowing a peak execution rate of approximately one cycle per instruction when all operands are kept inside the processor's register file.

There are five major categories of instructions. The first category consists of arithmetic, logical, and shift instructions. Most of these instructions have two types: One type does not change the condition code bits, and the other type sets the condition code bits based on a computed result. The second category consists of instructions that read or write special registers such as the Processor Status register and Trap Base register.

A third category is made up of load and store instructions. These instructions operate on byte, halfword, word, and double-word operands. Special instructions are defined for use with multi-processor applications. These instructions are "atomic" in nature and perform a load from a memory location followed by a store into the same memory location without releasing the processor's bus until such time as the transaction is completed.

The fourth category consists of control-transfer instructions, such as conditional- and unconditional-relative branches with 22-bit word displacement, calls with 30-bit word displacement, absolute jumps, and returns. Branch instructions use a single delayed instruction. The delayed-branch concept is a simple way to improve the processor's performance by filling up the processor's pipeline with useful instructions while the target of the branch is being calculated. Normally, the target of a branch is not known until later in the processor's pipeline. Instead of waiting for the target calculation, the processor executes the following instruction and then runs the branch itself.

For conditional branches, the delayed instruction is always executed when the branch is taken (i.e., when the conditions are true). The architecture provides a simple mechanism to nullify the effect of the delayed instruction if the branch is not taken.

The fifth category is made up of floating-point and coprocessor instructions. The SF9010IU processor implements a rich set of single-precision and double-precision floating-point instructions that are fully IEEE compatible. These instructions are executed by the floating-point unit, which consists of a special floating-point controller chip and two Weitek floating-point arithmetic units (W1164 and W1165).

The entire SF9010IU processor is implemented in a single 20,000-gate gate-array chip fabricated by Fujitsu, using 1.5-micron technology with a typical gate delay of 1.2 ns. One quarter of this gate-array is occupied by a very large register file defined by the processor architecture, and the other three quarters are used by the data path and control circuitry. The design has been carefully partitioned in a hierarchical manner into blocks, sub-blocks, and sub-sub-blocks to allow easy routing and predictable post-layout wire delays for the entire chip. The processor chip has a total of 156 I/O signals and uses a 256-pin PGA (Pin Grid Array) package.

Processor Microarchitecture

As Figure 13.1 shows, the chip has four major units. Register File Unit—The Register File Unit contains a total of 120 32-bit general-purpose registers. Eight of these registers are global, and the rest are divided into seven overlapped frames (windows) of 24 registers each. Although the SF9010IU processor implements only seven windows, the actual number of windows is implementation-dependent, and future implementations can have more. A pointer in the Processor Status register, called Current Window Pointer (CWP), points to the current window in the register file.

As Figure 13.2 shows, each two adjacent register windows are overlapped by eight registers. Overlapped windows provide an efficient way to pass parameters during procedure calls and returns. Normally, during a procedure call, the "caller" puts its parameters in registers overlapping with the window used by the "callee" (next window). After the execution of the call, the window changes so the callee has direct access to the next window's parameters.

The register file has two read ports and a single write port. The uniform format of instructions allows reading both source operands of any instruction and writing the result of a previously fetched instruction into the register file, through the write port. The entire process occurs in a single cycle.

Execution Unit—The processor's Execution Unit consists of a fast 32-bit carry-look-ahead ALU (which performs all arithmetic and logical operations), a 32-bit barrel shifter, condition-code-generation logic, load-alignment and store-alignment logic, and related pipeline registers required to save the operands and inter-

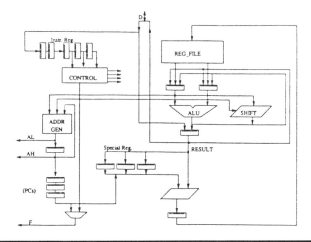

FIGURE 13.1. *Block diagram of SPARC processor.*

mediate results. All arithmetic and logic instructions use the Execution Unit for a single cycle to complete their execution. This process occurs even if dependencies exist between the operands and results of consecutive instructions. To work properly, the data path in the Execution Unit incorporates two bypass paths. The first bypass path feeds the output of the ALU directly to the inputs of the operand registers. This bypass is activated when a source operand of an instruction depends on the results of its previous instruction. The second bypass path feeds the output of the result register to the inputs of the operand registers. It is activated when a source operand of an instruction depends on the result of the instruction prior to the previous instruction in the pipeline.

Instruction Fetch Unit—The Instruction Fetch Unit contains the processor's Program Counters and instruction/data-address-generation circuitry. Four Program Counters correspond to the four stages of the instruction pipeline (see below). These Program

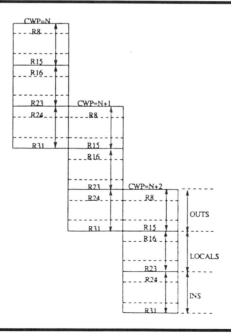

FIGURE 13.2. *Overlapped register windows in processor are more efficient for passing parameters during procedure calls and returns.*

Counters are used in the case of exceptions that may occur as late as the last stage in the processor pipeline. This unit also includes the circuitry for special registers, such as the Trap Base register (TBR), Trap Type register (TTR), Y register (used by multiply step instructions), and Window Invalid Mask register (WIMR).

Control Unit—The control core of the processor is the Control Unit. It implements the main state machine, instruction pipeline, instruction decoder, Processor Status register (PSR), circuitry for exception/trap handling, and the interface to the cache and floating-point unit. The Control Unit maintains a copy of the instructions that execute in different stages of the pipeline. The majority of the control signals for other units are generated in this unit and are dispatched to their destination units.

Processor Pipeline

The processor has a four-stage-deep pipeline. Each stage of the processor pipeline performs a subset of operations that are needed to complete the execution of an instruction. All operations performed in a given pipeline stage occur in one full clock cycle.

Fetch Stage—At this stage of the pipeline, the address of an instruction is sent out. Once the instruction is fetched, it enters the processor's pipeline at stage completion.

Decode Stage—In the Decode stage of the pipeline, the instruction is decoded, and source operands are read from the register file. The source operands read during the Decode stage of the pipeline are passed to both the Execution Unit and the Instruction Fetch Unit for later execution. The Decode stage of the pipeline also generates the next instruction address (and in the case of branches, the branch target address). More precisely, while instruction I(n) is being decoded in the Decode stage, the address for instruction I(n + 2) is being calculated by the Instruction Fetch Unit.

Execute Stage—While the instruction is in the Execution stage, the Execution Unit performs arithmetic and logical operations. The results of the operations in the Execution stage are saved in temporary registers before they are actually written into the register file. The decision to write the results into the register file is made during the last stage of the processor's pipeline.

Write Stage—In the Write stage of the pipeline, the processor either writes the results into the register file (which means the instruction has completed successfully) or prohibits any changes in the state of the processor. The Write stage aborts if an exception is raised during the execution of that instruction.

As Figure 13.3. shows, four instructions can execute simultaneously in the processor pipeline. While instruction I(n) is being fetched, instruction I(n − 1) is being decoded in the Decode stage. Instruction I(n − 2) is being executed in the Execution stage, and instruction I(n − 3) is writing its results into the register file. A given instruction can raise several exceptions (traps) during the course of its execution. When it raises multiple traps simultaneously, the trap-handling logic guarantees that the processor takes the highest priority trap.

Instruction Buffer and Internal Instructions

In order to keep the pipeline full at all times, the SF9010IU uses a dual-instruction buffer. This buffer prefetches instructions during the execution of multiple-cycle instructions and so speeds up the execution by utilizing the data bus more efficiently. The buffer is empty when the processor is executing a sequence of single-cyle instructions in a row. When a multiple-cycle instruction enters into the pipeline, its following instructions are prefetched into the buffer until the multiple-cycle instruction is complete.

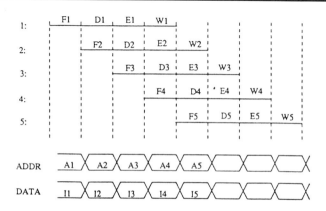

FIGURE 13.3. *The processor's four-stage instruction pipeline.*

In the SF9010IU processor all control circuitry uses random logic. For single-cycle instructions this task is straightforward. The control for multiple-cycle instructions lets the pipeline see each multiple-cycle instruction as several consecutive single-cycle instructions. This technique is accomplished by "internal instructions." The processor generates internal instructions automatically and injects them into the processor's pipeline as needed. Load and store instructions, for example, require more than one cycle to complete.

Figure 13.4. shows a single-word load instruction that takes one extra cycle in the pipeline and, therefore, uses one internal instruction to complete. In this case, the EH1 cycle fetches the load operand. Figure 13.5. shows a single-word store instruction that takes two extra cycles in the pipeline and, therefore, uses two internal instructions to complete. In this case, the store address is sent during the EH11 cycle, and the store data is sent during the EH21 cycle. Notice that the store address is available on the bus for two cycles, thus allowing the external logic to check the memory-write access before the data is written. After the completion of a multiple-cycle instruction, the processor first executes all instructions in the instruction buffer and then continues its normal operation by fetching instructions from the external cache.

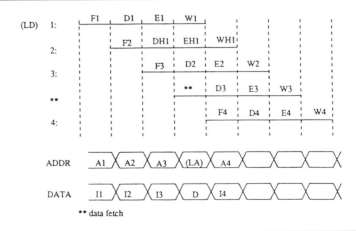

FIGURE 13.4. *A single-word load instruction takes one extra cycle in the pipeline.*

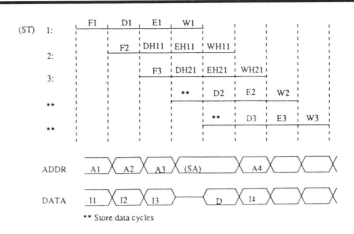

FIGURE 13.5. *A single-word store instruction takes two extra cycles in the pipeline.*

Traps and Interrupts

Execution of a given instruction can raise several traps or exceptions. The source of a trap can be internal (synchronous) or external (asynchronous). In both cases, the processor handles the traps in a similar manner. Traps are vectored. An on-chip trap-base address register points to the trap table. Interrupts are given to the processor using four interrupt input signals. Any logic level other than zero on these four inputs is detected by the processor as an external interrupt request. This value is compared with the current processor interrupt level, which can be set in the processor status register, and the interrupt is taken if the external interrupt request level is greater than the processor interrupt level. The highest-level interrupt (level-15) is nonmaskable.

When a trap is detected, the processor takes the following actions:

1. It saves the Program Counters corresponding to the trapped instruction and the instruction following the trapped instruction in the register file.

2. It aborts execution of the trapped instruction and flushes all fetched but unfinished instructions out of the pipeline.

3. It disables all traps. The processor's mode is set to the superuser mode and the Current Window Pointer is set to point to the next window.

4. It computes the trap address, based on the content of the Trap Base register and the Trap Type of the highest priority trap, and loads it into the Program Counter.

5. It restarts execution from the new trap address.

All external interrupts are ignored when traps are disabled. If a synchronous trap is detected while traps are disabled, the processor enters into an error mode and remains in that mode until the processor is reset externally. At reset, the processor enters into an initial state and starts execution from address 0.

Floating-Point Unit Interface

The SPARC processor executes integer instructions concurrently with floating-point instructions. The processor and its floating-point unit are tightly synchronized. All floating-point instructions are decoded inside the processor and are dispatched to the floating-point unit via a dedicated 32-bit bus. A few control signals are used for synchronization between the two chips. The floating-point controller consists of thirty-two 32-bit floating-point registers, the Floating-Point Status register (FSR), and the Floating-Point Queue (FQ). The Floating-Point Queue maintains information related to the instructions that have been dispatched to the floating-point controller but have not yet completed their execution. Each entry of the queue consists of two pieces of information: the floating-point instruction and its address. Functions of the floating-point controller chip include:

1. Maintaining the Floating-Point Status register and Floating-Point Queue.

2. Decoding floating-point instructions and generating proper control signals for the floating-point arithmetic units.

3. Detecting dependencies between floating-point instructions and signaling the processor to wait if necessary.

4. Executing floating-point load and store instructions (the memory address is computed in the processor).

5. Detecting floating-point exceptions and signaling the processor.

The SF9010IU uses both single-word and double-word floating-point load/store operations. From the pipeline point of view, floating-point load/stores behave exactly the same as integer loads and stores. Similar to the integer loads and stores, the memory address is computed by the processor. The only difference is that the floating-point controller either receives the data from the data bus (in the case of loads) or puts the data on the data bus (in the case of stores). Any exception raised during the execution of floating-point-loads and stores is detected and handled by the processor. The floating-point controller holds the processor in the event of a dependency between the operands of load/store and the operands of previous instructions in the floating-point queue.

Branch-on-floating-point condition instructions behave much like the branch-on-integer-condition instructions. The only difference is that the condition code bits for these instructions are generated by the floating-point controller. The processor enters into a wait state whenever it needs the floating-point conditions and these condition bits are not ready.

Once the processor encounters a floating-point instruction, the instruction and its address are sent to the external floating-point controller chip. The floating-point controller chip decodes the instruction and takes one of the following actions:

1. It holds the processor if a situation arises so that the floating-point controller must wait—for example, when the Floating-Point Queue is full.

2. It accepts the new instruction and enters the instruction and its address into the Floating-Point Queue for later execution. In this case, the processor advances to the next instruction without waiting, as if the floating-point instruction has been completed immediately.

Floating-point exceptions, in general, occur asynchronously

with respect to the processor's pipeline for the following reasons: (1) integer instructions are executed concurrently with the floating-point instructions; (2) different floating-point instructions take a different number of cycles to complete their execution or generate an exception. In the SF9010IU, floating-point exceptions are taken synchronously. When a floating-point exception is raised, two situations may occur:

1. If the current instruction in the integer unit is a floating-point instruction, the floating-point exception is taken by the processor only if no higher priority traps are pending.

2. If the current instruction in the integer unit is not a floating-point instruction, the floating-point exception is kept pending until the next floating-point instruction begins.

System Design Using a SPARC Processor

Figure 13.6 depicts a typical chip-set configuration with the SF9010IU chip, SF9010FP floating-point controller chip, Weitek W1164 multiplier chip, and Weitek W1165 ALU chip. These four chips are the core of any system designed around the SPARC processor.

Two separate 32-bit buses are used for address and data to access the storage. The cache is an essential part of the system and must be capable of delivering one instruction to the processor in every cycle. The processor bus cycles and the timing of I/O signals are optimized for cache-based systems. For example, the address bits are divided into two groups: low-address bits and high-address bits. The low-address bits (bits 17..00) are available earlier than the high-address bits (bits 31..16). In a cache-based system, this allows a designer to use the lower address bits to read the cache RAMs and cache tags, and the higher address bits to compare the tags later. The low-order and high-order bits of the address overlap in bits 16 and 17, allowing direct addressing of a virtual cache with a size up to 256K.

From a hardware point of view, the higher 16 bits of the address bus are taken directly from an on-chip Memory Address

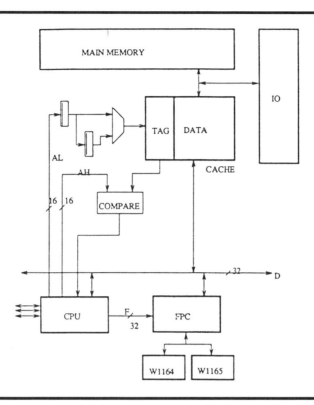

FIGURE 13.6. *A typical configuration of the SPARC SF9010IU chip set.*

Register that holds the address of the instruction or data to be fetched in that cycle. The lower 18 bits of the address are "unlatched" and sent a cycle earlier. These bits must be latched in an external Memory Address register before they are used. The processor provides necessary control signals that synchronize the internal and external Memory Address Registers. The processor also sends out an 8-bit Address Space Identifier (ASI) field for the instruction or data. Normally, these 8 bits carry information such as processor mode (user/superuser) and the type of fetch (instruction/ data). During the execution of alternate load and store instructions, these bits carry the ASI for load or store data.

Every processor cycle in this system is either an instruction fetch cycle, a load cycle, or a store cycle. When the processor sends out an instruction address, the cache is accessed and the instruction is fetched into the processor in the same cycle. This instruction may or may not be the correct instruction, depending on whether or not the instruction actually existed in the cache. Within the same cycle, the cache tags are read and checked. In the case of a cache-hit, the processor treats the fetched instruction as a correct instruction and continues to fetch the next instruction in the following cycle. However, if the cache is missed, the external cache controller logic must hold the processor operation in the cycle following the cycle in which the instruction is fetched.

The processor can do this step by asserting one of the MHOLD input signals. Assertion of an MHOLD signal forces the processor pipeline into a WAIT state while the signal is asserted. During this period, the cache controller fills the missed cache line and strobes (using an MDS signal) the missed instruction into the processor's instruction register when the register is ready. In this case, the processor ignores the previous instruction and uses the new instruction as the correct one to execute.

Since a new instruction address is sent every cycle before the tag comparison result for the previous address is ready, the cache address must be saved by the external circuitry for one extra cycle. The cache needs this delayed address in case of a cache-miss; otherwise it is ignored.

Instruction Type	Number of cycles	Number of Internal Instructions
Load (word/halfword/byte)	2	1
Load (double)	3	2
Store (word/halfword/byte)	3	2
Store (double)	4	3
Atomic Load and Store	4	3
Floating-point ops	2 + Cf	1
Jump and Rett	2	1
Branch (untaken)	2	0
Branch (taken)	1	0
All Other instructions	1	0

TABLE 13.1. *Summary of exception instruction execution times.*

In the SF9010IU, bus request/grant operations are implemented simply. Basically, the processor may be forced into a WAIT state in any cycle for any amount of time by a BHOLD signal. A LOCK signal is provided and is asserted when the processor is in the middle of a multi-cycle bus transaction that should not be aborted. Normally, a device that needs the bus simply asserts the BHOLD signal in the first cycle that the LOCK signal is inactive. Once the processor is in the WAIT state, AOE and DOE control signals can be used to turn off the output drivers of the chip.

All I/O devices are memory-mapped, and normal load/store instructions are used to read from or write into the I/O devices. The 8-bit ASI output signals determine the mapping of user space, superuser space, MMU, cache tags, and other I/O devices in the system. A set of alternate, privileged load and store instructions are defined and can be used to access any address space between 0 and 255 in the system.

SF9010IU Performance

Three major factors affecting the performance of any processor are the cycle time, the average number of cycles per instruction, and the relative code density, which is a measure of instruction-set effectiveness.

The design of the SF9010IU was analyzed carefully in order to identify the longest delay paths. The goal was to reach a typical cycle time of 50 ns or less. This goal was achieved through an iterative approach in which all internal or external paths that had a delay longer than 50 ns (typical) were either improved or redesigned. The worst-case cycle time for the SF9010IU is approximately 60 ns, allowing design of a system with 16.6-MHz clock rate.

Most instructions in the SF9010IU are executed in a single cycle. A small subset of instructions takes more than one cycle to complete. As noted earlier, these multiple-cycle instructions use one or more internal instructions to complete their execution. The table summarizes the exception instructions' execution times.

Based on the above table and a conservative instruction-mix ratio (15% loads, 5% stores, 15% taken branches, and 5% untaken branches), the average number of cycles per instruction (CPI), excluding a cache-miss penalty, would be about 1.3. Using a 128K cache, the miss ratio would be approximately 1%. With a 10-cycle cache-miss penalty, the CPI would be:

$$CPI = 1.3 + [0.01 * (1 + 0.15 + 0.005 * 10 = 1.42$$

With a cycle time of 60 ns, the above CPI translates into a 11.74 native-MIPS machine.

In general, the code generated for a given program in a RISC-based architecture is less dense than the code for a similar program in a non-RISC architecture because instructions in RISC machines are usually defined to be simple and efficient in order to reduce both the cycle time and the average number of cycles per instruction. Consequently, in comparison with non-RISC machines, the compiler can generate more code. In general, an optimizing compiler can significantly reduce this overhead.

The first implementation of the SPARC architecture, the SF9010IU, exceeds most existing commercial 32-bit microprocessors. This performance proves the effectiveness of SPARC and RISC architectures in general, paving the way to higher-performance implementations of this architecture in the near future. In order to achieve such high performance, the entire control logic was implemented through random logic, with as few levels of logic as possible. The SF9010IU was fully simulated with a simulation model that consisted of gate-level models of the SF9010IU chip, the floating-point controller chip, a high-level model of the cache, and Weitek chips. Many functional test cases were written by the designers (in assembly language) to verify the correctness of the design. These test cases checked the processor's data path and control logic by using a variety of instruction sequences and data patterns. The simulation model was also used to generate pin-test vectors for testing the ICs at the manufacturing stage. The extensive simulation paid off once the first silicon of the SPARC CPU ran the multiuser UNIX operating system in a prototype system. At more than 10 MIPS, the SPARC architecture and its first implementation, the SF9010IU, brings mainframe-level performance to desktop machines.

Acknowledgments

The authors would like to thank all members of the SF9010IU design team: K.G. Tan, Don Jackson, Le Quach, J.K. Lu, Susna Rohani, Quyen Vu, Robert Garner, Dave Patterson, Ed Kelly, Steve Kleiman, Will Brown; and Mark Hall and Karen Rohack.

References

1. John Hennesey, "VLSI Processor Architecture," *IEEE Transactions on Computers*, December 1984.

2. Dave Patterson, "RISC," *Eighth Annual Symposium on Computer Architecture*, May 1984.

3. Masood Namjoo and Anant Agrawal, "Preserve High Speed in CPU-to-Cache Transfers," *Electronic Design*, August 20, 1987, p. 91.

Design Considerations for a Bipolar Implementation of SPARC

14

Anant Agrawal • Emil W. Brown •
Joseph Petolino • James R. Peterson

Abstract

Sun Microsystems' Scalable Processor Architecture (SPARC™) defines an architecture that provides a migration path to higher performance levels as new technologies become available. Bipolar ECL processes such as the BIT1™ process from Bipolar Integrated Technology, make it feasible to implement the SPARC architecture in ECL cost effectively.

The cycle times of ECL machines are much shorter than those of CMOS machines and thus I/O and wiring delays become more significant. The well defined division between system and silicon considerations seen in CMOS microprocessor systems is not as obvious in ECL; many system concerns must be accounted for in the design of the silicon.

This paper describes the BIT1 ECL process, and design considerations which must be made for an ECL implementation of SPARC. Bus structures, cache concerns, interface considerations, and power density are all discussed.

VLSI ECL

In the past ECL had a well deserved reputation for low density and extremely high power levels. This has changed with the advent of BIT1. BIT1 maintains the high performance of ECL, but offers VLSI density and significantly reduced power when compared to other ECL processes. It provides minimum geometry transistors of 14 μm^2. Gates exhibit typical propagation delays of 300 ps and power dissipation of 300 μW. Using fully self-aligned transistors

1988 IEEE. Reprinted with Permission, from Proceedings of COMPCON '88, March 1–3, San Francisco, CA.

with polysilicon contacts and resistors, the BIT1 minimum feature size is 2 μm. The BIT1 process has demonstrated its high density potential with devices such as the B3110/20 floating point ALU and multiplier chip set, each of which contain more than 65,000 transistors. The B3110/20 offer the option of either TTL or ECL interfaces.

BIT1 allows three level series gating, which enables separate logic functions to share the same current tree. This feature saves devices and power, and enables complex functions to be implemented in a single gate delay. For example, a single gate delay two input multiplexer/latch requires less than 4000 μm^2, and a 32-bit add can be accomplished in four gate delays.

Bipolar transistors provide advantages both on and off the chip. A bipolar device is much better than a MOS device at driving large capacitive loads, due to better transconductance. This allows signals to be driven between chips at high speeds. Also, by using small voltage swings, gate delays and capacitive charging times are minimized. For example, at a 1 V/ns slew rate, a CMOS rail-to-rail transition would take about 2.5 ns to the 50% point while an ECL transition would take about 300 ps.

CMOS and TTL outputs are generally not designed to drive transmission lines, even though that is what they must do in a circuit board environment. Their uncontrolled output impedance, and the typical lack of termination make it difficult to maintain good signal quality. As TTL and CMOS chips strive for higher performance, the faster edge rates make system design even more difficult. Chip output overshoot and $\partial i/\partial t$ caused by gate transitions inside CMOS chips are a significant source of noise. With multiple outputs changing in the same direction, output overshoot can be significantly worse than for a single output transition, and the delay through the part may be longer than the specified delay. This is because CMOS and TTL delays are typically specified for a single output transition.

In the core of an IC, ECL has the advantage of using constant current, so signal transitions do not generate noise in the power supply and ground. The outputs of ECL chips are designed to drive transmission lines and have a slew rate that is matched to their propagation delay. With proper attention to return currents, the ECL system environment will be noise free.

System Considerations

SPARC implementations achieve high performance by reducing the number of cycles required to execute an instruction. The SPARC instruction set is optimized so that most instructions execute in one cycle. To execute instructions at this rate the memory system must provide one instruction every cycle, and in truly high performance designs it must also provide 20% to 30% additional bandwidth for loads and stores. To achieve this, all of SUN's SPARC based systems to date have used a tightly coupled Virtual Address Cache (VAC). By using virtual addresses, the penalty of address translation is avoided between the CPU and the cache. The VAC is designed as an integral part of the CPU rather than an adjunct part of the memory system.

The following few sections of this paper discuss some of the issues we have encountered implementing and incorporating SPARC in a high speed ECL system.

Transmission Lines

Unlike an NMOS or CMOS microprocessor with a cycle time in the 40 to 100 ns range, an ECL processor must be designed from conception to fit into a high speed transmission line environment. This includes considerations for characteristic impedance matching and trace delays.

The experience of designing machines based on SPARC processors has shown that the cache access path is likely to be one of the longest paths in the system. In an ECL system the cache access is even more critical because the address and data busses must be considered as transmission lines with trace delays that are a significant percentage of the cycle time. To minimize the trace delay of a transmission line it should have exactly one driver and one terminator. Consequently, we accepted as axioms that the cache address bus should only be driven by the CPU, and the cache data bus should only be driven by the cache RAMs. Furthermore, we believe that additional components such as discrete address latches or buffers would ultimately slow the cache access. Therefore, the CPU chip should drive the RAM array directly.

The implications of this are significant. All addresses from sources other than the CPU must pass *through* the CPU to address the cache, including cache fill addresses. The data bus from the cache cannot be bidirectional, so separate load and store busses are mandated. ECL RAMS typically provide separate data-in and data-out ports for this purpose. The axiom of allowing only the cache RAMs to drive the data bus implies that *all* data must pass through the cache RAMs, including non-cached data. This may require invalidating a cache line, or using a buffer to save the previous contents of the line.

Cache Organizations

Cache design is a major discipline in itself, but the number of options is quickly reduced by looking at the available technology and gaining an early understanding of the critical paths. Set-associative caches increase performance in multi-tasking environments by allowing some cache sharing. Two-way set associativity provides most of the gain. Unfortunately data selection between two associativities is always in the critical path and it depends on the result of the cache tag access and comparison. The result is a longer cycle time. The benefit of set-associativity did not justify the cycle time penalty in our studies of large application programs.

With ECL cycle times, the number of cycles required to process a cache miss will be greater than in slower CMOS/TTL systems, so low miss rates are even more important. We studied the effect of cache size by simulating large programs and found that the miss rate increases rapidly as the cache size decreases below 64-kilobyte. On the other hand, extremely large caches are not cost effective because miss rates may not drop below a certain threshold for real programs running on multi-tasking machines. Furthermore, a large cache requires physically long address and data busses, potentially increasing the cycle time. Based on the current RAM technology and future trends we believe that in ECL systems the cache size would be on the order of 128-kilobyte.

The CPU requires data and instructions at a rate that exceeds the capability of all but the fastest ECL static RAMs. RAMs with access times at or below 15ns are readily available today from several vendors. These RAMs range in size up to 64K bits. Access times are shrinking to the sub 10ns range.

Using an array of eight 16K×4 RAMs, it is possible to build a 32-bit wide, 64-kilobyte cache. Two of these arrays could be used to build a 128-kilobyte combined instruction/data cache or two separate caches for data and instructions. The combined cache can be organized in a 32-bit or a 64-bit width. Depending on the organization, a number of RAMs must be distributed evenly along the address transmission lines. These lines are heavily loaded, resulting in very low characteristic impedances due to capacitive effects. Propagation delay along these transmission lines, added to the processor's input and output buffer delays, is comparable to the read access time of the RAMs.

In earlier implementations of SPARC, memory reference instructions required multiple cycles. This was primarily due to the single 32-bit instruction/data bus between the cache and the processor. One of the goals of this design was to improve the load and store instruction performance. We looked at a number of alternatives which centered around various cache organizations.

One way to achieve our goal would be to provide independent access paths for data and instructions. Using two independent RAM arrays of 64-kilobyte each, a split instruction and data cache could be built. Each cache requires its own 32-bit address bus (the full 32-bits is required to do tag checking), and its own 32-bit data bus. Each address wire would be loaded with 8 data RAMs plus a few tag RAMs. The chip would require 64 output drivers for addresses, 32 inputs for instructions, 32 inputs for load data and 32 output drivers for store data. Thus 160 pins are required just for the busses to support this configuration.

A second way to achieve our goal would be to provide a single 64-bit interface to a combined instruction/data cache. This approach provides twice the required instruction-fetch bandwidth. By saving some of the excess instructions on the CPU chip, some cycles can be used to access data without reducing the instruction execution rate. The configuration easily supports the required additional bandwidth of 20% to 30% data accessses. The pin requirement for busses is 64 input pins, plus 32 address outputs and 32 store-data outputs for a total of 128. An added advantage of this scheme could be improved performance for floating-point double precision computation.

We also considered a number of techniques to decrease the

system cycle time, while still meeting the bandwidth requirement of greater than one word per cycle. In particular, we explored using a two-cycle cache access path. There are several possibilities which include (1) a interleaved cache in which odd and even words are accessed in parallel from two banks, (2) a pipelined access in which the latency of access is two cycles, but the data rate is one access per cycle, and (3) a duplicated cache in which the same data can be accessed from two different banks.

If we can depend on the processor to access words sequentially most of the time, it is productive to assign consecutive words to different cache banks. A pipeline that supports a stage between address generation and data return is used. The processor would require separate address busses for each bank, and would alternate their usage. Separate data-in busses would also be required. Stalls would occur whenever consecutive accesses are made to the same bank.

Another kind of pipeline can be designed if RAMs are available with internal address registers. This allows the first cycle of a two cycle access to be used in driving the address transmission line, and the second cycle in accessing the RAMs and sending the data back to the processor. This design relies on RAM vendors to produce special RAM parts.

The best choice among these possibilities is governed by the performance goals and the expected usage of the machine. We rejected the two-cycle access methods on the basis of pin requirements, complexity, and reduced performance.

Stores

The ECL RAM write cycle presents special problems because the write-pulse width specification is usually as long as or longer than the address access time, and there is address and data setup time to the pulse's leading edge and hold time from the pulse's trailing edge. There are two approaches. Allow the write cycle to increase the cycle time, or use multiple cycles to perform stores. Our data has shown that large SPARC programs execute about 5% store instructions and 15% load instructions. The remaining bandwidth is used to fetch instructions. Because the store percentage is quite low (mainly due to the large on-chip register file) we believe that it is better to have an additional cycle for stores than to allow a longer cycle time.

Chip Crossings

Once the timing of the primary cache access path is analyzed, attention must be given to the control signals. At high speeds, the cost of crossing any chip boundary can be as high as 60% to 80% of the system cycle time. This was considered from the very beginning of design when interfaces were being defined. We avoid interfaces that require more than one or two levels of logic in a chip crossing path and double chip crossings. These restrictions resulted in some interfaces being logically complex in order to accomplish simple functions, and forced some operations to use additional cycles. Tradeoffs were made between lengthening the cycle time and increasing the number of cycles required for frequent operations.

Since the cache interface in this design requires a large number of pins, care had to be taken when adding functionality at the cost of more pins. Most processor status information has been encoded into a single bus that provides more information to the external system than the earlier SPARC implementations.

Floating-Point Performance

Floating-point performance has historically been low in microprocessor based machines because the operations take longer than simple integer operations. Simple systems could not afford the multiple functional units that give supercomputers their floating-point speed. In the domain of ECL microprocessors however, the issue of floating-point performance cannot be ignored.

ECL densities are not yet sufficient to support floating-point hardware on the CPU chip, especially not multiple arithmetic units. BIT has developed the first ECL floating-point chip set that supports very high performance computation. The B3110/20 chip set can perform double precision multiply in 50 ns, and double precision add in 25 ns, without internal pipelining. This level of performance can lead to low latency as well as high throughput floating-point performance.

The B3110/20 in combination with the B3210 high-speed register file can be used as a floating-point co-processor with a SPARC microprocessor to provide performance unprecedented in a microprocessor based system. SPARC defines a floating-point instruction set which is compatible with the B3110/20, and supports concurrent operation between the two floating point chips as well as with the integer CPU.

Floating-point performance comes down to two cases: load/store limited problems and computational limited problems. Calculations such as a matrix times a vector are likely to be computation limited when the matrix is constant because the number of FLOPS is of order N^2, while the load and store operations are of order N. The Linpack bench-mark, which solves a system of linear equations, is load/store limited. The number of floating point operations per data word accessed is less than one. Thus the requirement for consistently good floating-point performance can be met by using the B3110/20, *and* by providing sufficient data bandwidth.

Cooling and Package Considerations

System designers using ECL must pay close attention to thermal management. Even though BIT1 gates provide lower power dissipation than other ECL technologies, an implementation which contains more than 20,000 BIT1 gates may dissipate 10 watts or more. This level of power requires special packaging techniques. BIT products are housed in ceramic pin grid array (PGA) packages designed to give users maximum flexibility in thermal management. These PGA packages use a cavity down configuration and incorporate a copper/tungsten slug brazed into the cavity. The silicon die is mounted directly to the slug using a silver glass paste. A path of low thermal resistance is thus provided from the silicon chip to the external area of the slug, and is estimated to be approximately 0.2° C/W.

To simplify thermal management at the system level BIT standard products have heat sinks attached to the slug. These thermal dissipators were designed to provide a low thermal resistance from junction to ambient, which ensures that the junction temperature does not exceed 125° C when the ambient temperature is 70° C or less, with 500 linear feet per minute (LFM) airflow across the heat-sink. Designers can also obtain BIT parts without a heat sink and attach their own, for added flexibility.

Using the standard heat sink, thermal concerns are reduced to airflow considerations and ambient temperature specifications. Although these standard devices are specified for 500 LFM and 70° C ambient temperature, a system may need to meet more stringent requirements. Since these specifications must be met at the device, any obstructions to the airflow upstream from the device must be accounted for. For example, if a B3120 is 0.5 inches downstream from a B3110, the upstream device will cause the downstream device to be subjected to a slightly higher temperature and lower airflow. If a part is dissipating 10 watts and causes 0.25° C/W rise in ambient temperature downstream, the downstream part will actually see 2.5° C higher temperature. Additionally, studies indicate that 0.5 inches downstream from a B3110, the airflow may drop by more than 100 LFM due to turbulence effects on the air-stream caused mainly by the heat sink. This decrease in airflow could be countered in a number of ways, such as increasing the upstream airflow, placing the devices orthogonal to the air-stream, or spacing the parts further apart.

The decisions that maximize performance also force a high pin count. With a large number of signal outputs, power supply allocation becomes very important. The potential for output ringing and cross-talk must be simulated and minimized. For example, the cache address lines must not be affected, after they have settled, by the transitions of outputs that have a different timing. A large percentage of all pads on a die may have to be allocated to power supplies. This helps reduce supply inductance to the output drivers which minimizes output ringing and cross-talk.

Conclusion

The implementation of a microprocessor in high speed technologies, such as the BIT1 ECL process, requires that system level design considerations be made a part of the chip design. Careful analysis of critical timing paths and accounting for wiring and I/O delays are some of the issues which must be solved when designing an ECL microprocessor.

The scalable nature of the SPARC architecture makes migration to ECL a natural progression, and the integration capabilities of BIT1 make such a migration possible.

Acknowledgments

The ECL implementation of the SPARC architecture is being carried out as a joint development program between Sun Microsystems and Bipolar Integrated Technology. In addition to the authors Trevor Creary, Tom Guthrie, Mike Klein, Arthur Leung, Dave Murata, Susan Rohani, Tom Tate, Jim Testa, Chris Yau, David Yen from Sun Microsystems and Bob Elkind, Duane Jacobson, Paul Kingzett, Jim Russell, and Mark Slamowitz from Bipolar Integrated Technology are contributing to the implementation and verification of the design. Thanks to Robert Garner for reviewing and suggesting improvements to this paper.

SPARC is a trade mark of Sun Microsystems. BIT and BIT1 are trade marks of Bipolar Integrated Technology.

References

"The SPARC Architecture Manual", Sun Microsystems, Inc., Mountain View, CA. Also published by Fujitsu Microelectronics, Inc., 3320 Scott Blvd., Santa Clara, CA 95054.

Robert Garner, Anant Agrawal, Fayé Briggs, Emil W. Brown, David Hough, Bill Joy, Steve Kleiman, Steven Muchnick, Masood Namjoo, Dave Patterson, Joan Pendleton, & Richard Tuck, "The Scalable Processor Architecture (SPARC)," This proceedings.

M. Namjoo, A. Agrawal, D. Jackson, Le Quach, "CMOS Gate Array Implementation of the SPARC Architecture," this proceedings.

M. Namjoo, et al., "CMOS Custom Implementation of the SPARC Architecture," this proceedings.

Bob Leibowitz, Greg Taylor, "ECL gains ground in battle against CMOS," Computer Design, April 1, 1987.

Jim Peterson, Bob Leibowitz, "Processor chip set shrinks latency, boosts throughput" Electronic Design, February 5, 1987.

George Wilson, "Creating Low-Power Bipolar ECL at VLSI Densities" VLSI Systems Design, May, 1986.

Bipolar ECL Implementation of SPARC

15

Anant Agrawal • Emil W. Brown • Dave Murata •
Joseph Petolino

Abstract

The Scalable Processor Architecture (SPARC™) defines a general purpose 32 bit RISC processor architecture. The simple nature of the architecture provides a migration path to higher performance levels as new technologies become available. The goal was to design an architecture that would scale with, or track, improvements in the circuit technology. It has been implemented in gate arrays, full custom CMOS and bipolar ECL technologies by four different vendors. A number of implementations in other technologies including BiCMOS and GaAs are under way.

This paper describes the bipolar ECL implementation of the SPARC architecture. Also, covered are some of the system level considerations that influenced the design of the processor.

Introduction

The design of the bipolar ECL SPARC processor (BIT B5000) was a joint effort between Sun Microsystems and Bipolar Integrated Technology Inc. When operating at speeds close to 100 MHZ the system design considerations greatly influence the micro-architecture and the I/O interface design of the processor. Sun provided the architectural and system design expertise and BIT provided the silicon expertise to make this program successful.

Technology

In the past, ECL was associated with low density and high power. Over the past few years this has changed with the introduction of low power, high density technologies from a number of vendors. The technologies that we chose to implement SPARC in is BIT1 from BIT. BIT1 provides minimum geometry transistors of 14 μm^2 and typical gates are biased by only 70 microamps of current. Gates exhibit typical unloaded propagation delays of 300 ps and power dissipation of 300 μW. Using fully self-aligned transistors with polysilicon contacts and resistors, the BIT1 minimum feature size is 2 μm.

The technology allows three level series gating. The open emitter outputs of several gates can be tied together with a single pull down current source to provide a 'wire OR' function, or the collectors of two or more differential pairs can be connected together (collector dotting) to provide NOR functions. All these features save devices and power, and enable complex functions to be implemented in a single gate delay.

Bipolar transistors provide advantages both on and off the chip. A bipolar device is much better than a MOS device at driving large capacitive loads, due to higher transconductance. This allows signals to be driven between chips at high speeds. Also, by using small voltage swings, gate delays and capacitive charging times are minimized.

CMOS and TTL outputs are generally not designed to drive transmission lines, even though that is what they must do in a circuit board environment. Their uncontrolled output impedance, and the typical lack of termination make it difficult to maintain good signal quality. As TTL and CMOS chips strive for higher performance, the faster edge rates make system design even more difficult. Chip outputs overshoot and $\partial i/\partial t$ caused by gate transitions inside CMOS chips are a significant source of noise. With multiple outputs changing in the same direction, output overshoot can be significantly worse than for a single output transition, and the delay through the part may be longer than the specified delay. This is because CMOS and TTL delays are typically specified for a single output transition.

In the core of an IC, ECL has the advantage of using constant current, so signal transitions do not generate noise in the power supply and ground. The outputs of ECL chips are designed to drive transmission lines and have a slew rate that is matched to their propagation delay. With proper attention to return currents, the ECL system environment will be noise free.

System Considerations

The cycle times of ECL machines are much shorter than those of CMOS machines and thus I/O and wiring delays become more significant. When designing processors running at very high speeds, system design considerations become very important. We carefully looked at the possible applications of the chip to make sure the I/O interface is suitable for designing high performance cost-effective systems. Based on the feedback from system designers we made significant changes to the micro-architecture, pipeline and I/O interface.

Cache

To meet the aggressive cycle time goals required very close coupling of the processor with the cache. Set associativity was rejected based on the fact that the set elements have to be multiplexed thereby increasing the cycle time. To avoid the penalty of address translation between the CPU and the cache, the address coming out of the processor is made virtual.

Most RISC architectures execute their instructions in a single cycle and thus require the memory system to provide one instruction every cycle and, in a truly high performance system, it must also provide an additional 20% to 30% bandwidth for loads and stores. We looked at two cache options to provide the necessary bandwidth: split instruction and data caches and a combined cache. Pin limitation on the processor would have limited the split caches to be 32 bits wide. We determined that a 64 bit interface to a combined cache was a better choice for several reasons. Double wide cache reduces the cache fill time and substantially increases the double-precision floating point performance, cache controls are simpler as only one cache needs to be controlled and the size of data and instruction regions in the cache are dynamically adjusted. A 64 bit bus enabled tje processor to fetch two instructions every cycle. These instructions are buffered on the chip. Thus when the cache and the data/instruction bus is busy doing data transfers, internally buffered instructions are used to keep the processor pipeline full. This achieves 80% to 90% of the benefit of the separate caches.

I/O Busses

Unlike an NMOS or CMOS microprocessor, an ECL processor must be designed from conception to fit into a high speed transmission line environment. This includes considerations for characteristic impedance matching and trace delays.

In an ECL system the cache access is very critical because the address and data busses must be considered as transmission lines with trace delays that are a significant percentage of the cycle time. To minimize the trace delay there should be exactly one driver on the net. This requires that the cache address bus be driven only by the processor, and the cache data bus be driven only by the cache RAMs. To achieve this, we made the critical buses uni-directional. Thus, there are separate load and store data busses.

Since only the processor can address the cache, all external sources of address must pass through the processor. This is achieved by providing the address to the processor over the non-critical, bidirectional *Address High Bus*. The processor, one cycle later sends it out on the cache address lines.

Since only the cache RAMs can drive the data bus, all data must pass through the processor. This is achieved by providing a passthrough mode in the chip that transfers the incoming data on to the *Data-Out Bus*.

To avoid additional delay due to external drivers we chose to drive the RAM arrays directly from the processor by providing two differential copies of the cache address bus. This reduces the address line trace delays. Differential lines reduce the static power on the chip and the transitional current.

To minimize trace delays the RAMs are placed as close together as possible, which reduces the effective line impedance. The address line drivers on the B5000 are designed to drive lines with impedances as low as 25 ohms.

Early Cache Address

The virtual address coming out of the chip is split into two busses. The *Address Low Bus*, used to address up to 512K byte of cache, and the *Address High Bus*, used for tag comparison. The pipeline of the processor expects the cache hit/miss signal one cycle after the cache access cycle. This provides more time for tag comparison and relaxes the timing constraints on the address high bus. Since the *Address Low Bus* is timing critical, the low address lines are latched on the processor using an early clock. This provides more time for cache access thereby improving the cycle time.

Matched Delays

In high performance system designs it is desirable to minimize clock skews without returning the board every time a critical component like the processor is replaced. This is achieved by a unique clock distribution and delay matching scheme. This is illustrated in Figure 15.1. The system clock is driven from an output of the processor. CAR_CLK is an early version of the SYS_CLK. The 'Matched Delay' corresponds to the delay from instruction register 'IR' to Cache address register 'CAR'. This scheme ensures that the timing relationship between cache address, cache write enables and system clock to CAR_CLK does not change with the replacement of the processor.

Pipeline

The B5000 supports a five stage pipeline; Fetch (F), Decode (D), Execute (E), Memory (M) and Write (W). Each stage is one clock cycle long. In the F stage two instructions are fetched into the processor. The D stage passes the instruction further down the pipe by decoding it and reading the operands from the register file. In case of branch and call instructions, the target address is computed in this cycle. In E stage the operands are operated upon by passing them through either the ALU or the shifter. This cycle is also used for generating address for memory reference instructions and evaluating condition codes in case of conditional branch instructions. Memory reference instructions use the M stage to perform the data transfers. The W stage marks the completion of an instruction. In this cycle, results are written into the register file.

Microarchitecture

Figure 15.2 illustrates the internal data-path of the B5000 integer unit. The chip could be viewed as comprising five distinct functional blocks.

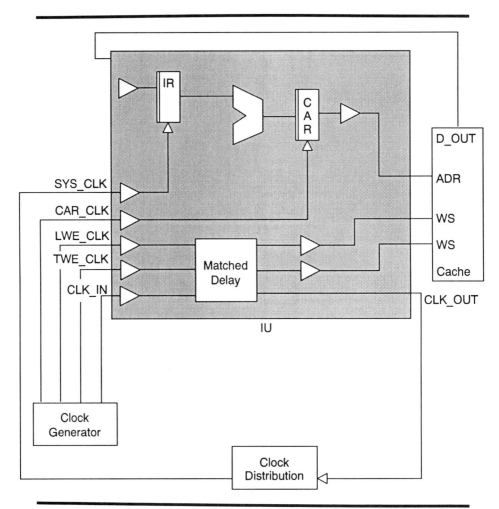

FIGURE 15.1.

F	D	E	M	W			
F	BUF	D	E	M	W		
	F	BUF	D	E	M	W	
	F	BUF	BUF	D	E	M	W
		F	BUF	BUF	D	E	M	W
		F	BUF	BUF	BUF	D	E	M	W

Pre-fetching queing and forwarding: This diagram illustrates the filling of buffers by fetching two instructions every cycle. Also, shown are the three forwarding paths.

```
(Load)n   F    D    E    M    W
   n+1    F   BUF   D    E    M    W
     n+2       F   BUF   D    E    M    W
     n+3       F   BUF  BUF   D    E    M    W
        n+4         F   BUF  BUF   D    E    M    W
        n+5         F   BUF  BUF  BUF   D    E    M    W
       Data         F
                    F
           n+6            F   BUF  BUF   D    E    M    W
           n+7            F   BUF  BUF  BUF   D    E    M
```

Load Instructions: When the instructions/data bus is busy transferring data, pipeline is kept busy by providing it instruction from the buffers.

TAKEN BRANCH

```
(SetCC)  n        F    D    E    M    W
(Bicc T) n+1      F   BUF   D    E    M    W
(Delayed Inst) n+2     F   BUF   D    E    M    W
          n+3          F   BUF  BUF
               n+4          F   BUF
               n+5          F   BUF
                  T         F    D    E    M    W
                T+1         F   BUF   D    E    M    W
                  T+2            F   BUF   D    E    M    W
                  T+3            F   BUF  BUF   D    E    M    W
```

UNTAKEN BRANCH

```
(SetCC)  n        F    D    E    M    W
(Bicc T) n+1      F   BUF   D    E    M    W
(Delayed Inst) n+2     F   BUF   D    E    M    W
          n+3          F   BUF  BUF   D    E    M    W
               n+4          F   BUF  BUF   D    E    M    W
               n+5          F   BUF  BUF  BUF   D    E    M    W
                  T         F   BUF
                T+1         F   BUF
                  n+6            F   BUF  BUF   D    E    M    W
                  n+7            F   BUF  BUF  BUF   D    E    M
```

Branches: Branch instructions initially assume branches are taken and fetch the target instruction. In the execute cycle if it is determined that the branch should not have been taken, the next instruction is executed from the instruction buffers. This results in both taken and un-takes branches to take a single cycle.

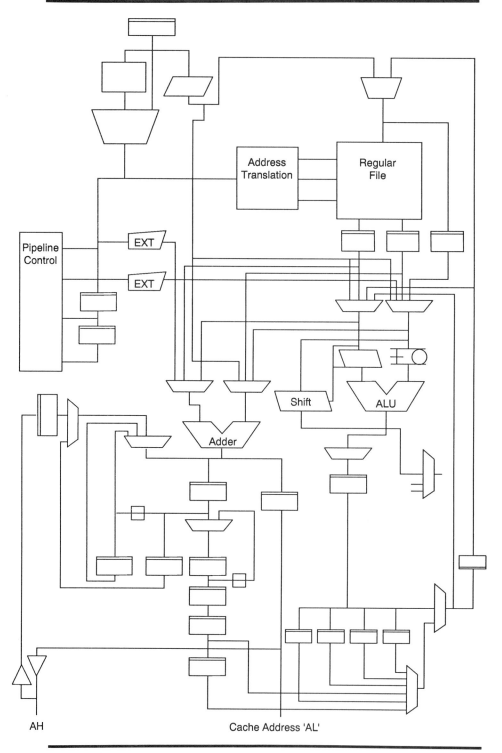

Address
Translation

Regular
File

Pipeline
Control

EXT

EXT

Shift

ALU

Adder

AH

Cache Address 'AL'

FIGURE 15.2.

The instruction buffers: As instructions are fetched into the chip, the unused instructions are saved in the buffers and used when the instruction/data bus is busy transferring data. This enables load instructions to execute in a single cycle. Due to the limited depth of the buffers, more than three back to back loads will require and extra cycle. Load data is passed through the data aligner *'Align'* before it is transferred either to the register file or the execution units.

The register file: It consists of a three ported RAM array with 128, 34 bit entries. Two of the bits are used to preserve half-word parity. In any given cycle two operands can be read and one written simultaneously into the register file. The array is divided into eight global registers and seven overlapping windows of 24 registers each. There is a block of eight redundant registers. On power-on the chip can be put in a diagnostic mode and a bad block of eight registers can be replaced by the redundant block.

The Execution Unit: It consists of a 32 bit carry look ahead ALU, a 32 bit barrel shifter and the associated pipeline registers. There are three bypass paths around the execution unit to support the five stage pipeline. This enables data-dependent integer instructions to execute without causing interlocks.

Address Unit: It consists of the 32 bit address adder for instruction and data and copies of the program counter corresponding to each stage of the pipeline. The address adder is designed to produce the low 16 bits of the address *AL* faster than the rest. *Al* is latched into the cache address register. *CAR* using an early clock and is used to drive the cache address bus *AL Bus*.

Control Unit: This unit maintains a copy of instruction for each stage of the pipeline and generates all the controls for the chip.

Table 15.1 shows the number of integer unit cycles it takes to complete various types of instructions. The numbers shown for memory reference instructions will vary depending on the number of consecutive loads and stores in the pipeline.

Coprocessor Interface

The B5000 supports two co-processor interfaces. One of them is a dedicated floating point interface, the other one could be used to interface to a user defined co-processor. Both the co-processors can

Instruction type	# of cycles
ALU	1
Shift	1
Branch (taken)	1
Branch (untaken)	1
Integer Load Single	1
Integer Load Double	2
Integer Store Single	2
Integer Store Double	3
Floating Point Load Single	1
Floating Point Load Double	1
Floating Point Store Single	1
Floating Point Store Double	1
Floating point operations	1

TABLE 15.1. *Instruction Execution Times*

operate concurrently with the integer unit. Control signals are provided to branch on condition codes generated by the co-processors. All exceptions detected by the co-processors are communicated to the integer unit. The store data bus is used to dispatch instructions from the integer unit to the coprocessors. Co-processors maintain their own copies of the program counter which are managed by the integer unit. In case of control transfer instructions the new program counter is sent to the co-processors over the store data bus.

Cooling and Package Considerations

The B5000 integer unit dissipates a maximum of 22 watts of power. The package-heatsink assembly is designed to be cooled with forced air. The chip is housed in a ceramic pin grid array (PGA) package designed to give users maximum flexibility in thermal management. These PGA packages use a cavity down configuration and incorporate a copper-tungsten slug brazed into the cavity. The silicon die is mounted directly to the slug using a silver glass paste. A path of low thermal resistance is thus provided from the silicon chip to the external area of the slug.

Conclusion

B5000 is the first commercial single chip 32 bit microprocessor to be designed in bipolar ECL technology. It represent the union of two emerging technologies; the RISC computer architecture and low power ECL. The scalable nature of the SPARC architecture made migration to ECL a natural progression, and the integration capabilities of BIT1 made such a migration possible. It is a low cost approach to achieving main-frame performance in desk-side machines.

Acknowledgments

The ECL implementation of the SPARC architecture was a joint development program between Sun Microsystems and Bipolar Integrated Technology. The authors would like to acknowledge the contributions of Don Clinkinbeard, Scott Dunagan, George Gennopoulous, Duane Jacobson, Amber Karr, Lisa Lowell, Tom Michel, Jim Peterson, Jory Radke, Jim Russell, and Mark Slamowitz from BIT and Trevor Creary, Daniel Chang, Tom Guthrie Arthur Leung, Dave Murata, Dan Nelsen, Joe Petolino, Renu Raman, Jim Testa, Thomas Tate, Rob Teigen, Kwok Tsang, Chris Yau, David Yen, Alex Yu, Vahe Avedissian, Susan Rohani and Yatin Trivedi from Sun Microsystems.

References

1. "The SPARC™ Architecture Manual", Sun Microsystems, Inc., Mountain View, CA. Also published by Fujitsu Microelectronics, Inc., 3320 Scott Blvd., Santa Clara, CA 95054.

2. Robert Garner, Anant Agrawal, Faye Briggs, Emil W. Brown, David Hough, Bill Joy, Steve Kleiman, Steven Muchnick, Masood Namjoo, Dave Patterson, Joan Pendleton, & Richard Tuck, "The Scalable Processor Architecture (SPARC)," COMPCON88, February 29, 1988.

3. M. Namjoo, A. Agrawal, D. Jackson, Le Quach, "CMOS Gate Array Implementation of the SPARC Architecture," COMPCON88, February 29, 1988.

4. A. Agrawal, Emil W. Brown, Joseph Petolino, James R. Peterson "Design Considerations For A Bipolar Implementation of SPARC COMPCON88, February 29, 1988

5. S. Kleiman, D. Williams "UNIX on SPARC COMPCONN88, February 29, 1988.

6. George Wilson, "Creating Low-Power Bipolar ECL at VLSI Densities" VLSI System Design, May 1986.

Implementing SPARC in ECL

Emil W. Brown • Anant Agrawal •
Trevor Creary • Michael F. Klein •
Dave Murata • Joseph Petolino

16

In 1987, as the first Sun 4 workstation moved into full production, an emerging emitter coupled logic technology caught Sun Microsystems' attention. ECL promised very large scale integrated densities at much higher operating frequencies than CMOS (complementary metal-oxide semiconductor) technology. The convergence of this technology with our Scalable Processor Architecture (SPARC) would for the first time enable a complete microprocessor to be implemented in ECL.

Sun initiated a joint development project with Bipolar Integrated Technology to implement SPARC using BIT's new bipolar process. Initial work indicated that a clock cycle time of 12.5 nanoseconds, an execution rate of 1.3 clock cycles per instruction, and benchmark performance of 60 million instructions per second and 12 million floating-point operations per second were achievable with an entry-level price of $100,000.

This was an aggressive goal considering that minisupercomputers then under development targeted clock rates of 25 to 40 megahertz and $200,000 to $500,000 entry-level prices. We were confident that the simplicity of SPARC would put the processor core on less than a dozen chips, and Sun's workstation heritage would fit the entire 80-MHz processor onto one circuit card. We minimized the cost by using air cooling, pin grid array and dual inline packaging, 10K technology, and conventional printed circuit boards.

We believe that early adoption of new technology is the key to creating competitive products. However, chip development can no longer be separated from system design since much of the system now resides on the silicon itself. With these factors in mind, we assembled a design team that consisted of an equal number of IC engineers and system or board-level designers. We knew that board-level issues such as RAM access characteristics, transmission line design, and clock skew control as well as system architecture would determine many of the requirements for the VLSI chips.

Here, we briefly review both ECL technology and the features of BIT's ECL technique and discuss how board and cache considerations influenced the chip designs. Discussion of the integer unit pipeline, system interface signals, and coprocessor interface concludes the article. The chip set, now completed, sells commercially from BIT as the B5000 series. See The B5000 Microprocessor box.

Technology

ECL is a digital bipolar technology generally used for applications in which cost and power dissipation are less important than switching speed. The relatively large bipolar transistors of a traditional ECL design resulted in circuits with lower integration density than their CMOS counterparts. In addition, the power dissipation in ECL was high because the gates had to be biased to drive longer, more capacitive internal signal lines.

BIT achieved a double breakthrough when it

- Reduced the physical size of the bipolar transistors, and
- Provided a typical unloaded gate propagation delay of 375 picoseconds, while biasing each gate with 70 microamperes of static current. More traditional ECL techniques use 200 μA to 1 mA to achieve comparable switching speed.

With three layers of interconnect metallization, the process is ideally suited for building VLSI devices.[1,2]

All three layers of metal distribute power on these devices to minimize the voltage drops along the bus and to avoid metal migration. A package with an embedded copper-tungsten slug having high thermal conductivity dissipates the power. The die bonds directly to the slug, which transfers the heat to the top of the package. A heat sink in a forced airstream dissipates the heat. The resulting thermal resistance (θ_{ja}) is about 2.5 degrees centigrade per watt.

An ECL inverter consists of a differenetial pair, a current source, a load resistor, and an output drive (Figure 16.1a). By adding transistors in parallel to the input transistor of the differential pair, we create an Or function. If we add another differential pair between the original pair and the load resistor, we create an And function.

This stacking of differential pairs is called series-gating. A traditional ECL process allows only two levels of series-gating. For example, the logic function (A + B)(C + D) can be implemented as one gate (Figure 16.1b). The BIT process allows three levels of series-gating, which supports functions such as (A + B)(C +D)(E + F), as shown in Figure 16.1c. The penalty for the additional functionality is an increase in the propagation delay; however, this increase is generally less than if the function was decomposed into two gates. Three levels of series-gating proved useful in constructing the shift registers that make up the diagnostic scan chain in the integer unit, or IU, and the floating-point controller, or FPC. The required multiplexer and latch functions combine into one gate.

ECL circuits can efficiently drive transmission lines at high frequencies. So the IU and the FPC each contain a set of low-

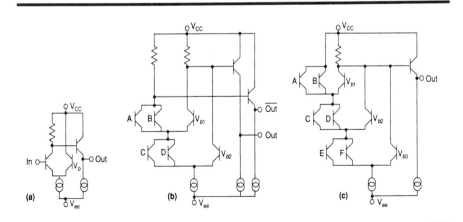

FIGURE 16.1. *An ECL inverter (a), a two-level series gate implementing the function (A + B)(C + D), and its complement (b), and a three-level series gate implementing the function (A + B)(C + D)(E +F).*

impedance (25-ohm) output drivers to drive system buses directly. We minimized the timing skew between these outputs by matching delays on the chip. We also designed package traces from the die to the pin to match the impedance of the drivers.

BIT technology supports two ECL interface standards, designated 10K and 100K. The 100K interface uses temperature compensation circuitry to minimize the temperature-induced shift in the switching threshold. The 10K interface specifies the amount of threshold shift that is allowed across the operating temperature range. All 100K circuits operate with a −4.5 volt supply, while 10K circuits operate at −5.2 volts. We chose to adhere to the 10K standard because it offers a wider selection of standard components. The cooling system maintains a maximum junction-temperature gradient of 25°C across the board to minimize differences in switching thresholds between devices. This system is necessary to maintain noise immunity and to control temperature-induced switching skew.

Board Design Influences

We started with several studies of cache designs. Although we looked at a variety of concepts, the simplest design offered the shortest access time, and the more complex designs did not offer comparable advantages.

We rejected set associativity because the set elements must be multiplexed, which inevitably increases the cycle time. We also discarded the idea of a nonpipelined, two-cycle access cache because branches become two-cycle instructions, reducing performance by 15 percent.

We strongly considered separate instruction and data caches, each with a 32-bit port. However, the lack of 64-bit data paths increases the cache miss penalty and adversely affects double-precision performance. Ultimately we chose a direct-mapped, write-back, 72-bit-wide (including parity), one-cycle access cache that contains instructions and data.

By fetching two instructions per cycle and using an instruction buffer on the IU, we achieve 80 to 90 percent of the performance advantage of separate caches. We designed the cache around a composite of several vendors' specifications for

16K × 4-bit and 4K × 4-bit RAMs. The write cycle takes longer than the read access time because address and data must be set up to the leading edge of the write pulse and held beyond its trailing edge. The write pulse itself is only slightly shorter than the access time.

The electrical and physical architectures are as important in high-speed ECL design as the logical architecture. Signal reflections and cross talk must be analyzed and minimized. In particular, we considered high-speed signal lines as transmission lines. They are driven from a single driver at one end of the wire. The wire must be daisy-chained from receiver to receiver and terminated at the other end by a DC impedance that matches the characteristic impedance of the line. To reduce cost, we did not specify differential transmission lines, except for lines carrying critical clock signals. We put power planes between signal planes and interleaved vertical and horizontal signal layers to manage cross talk on the printed circuit board.

Figure 16.2. illustrates the core of the processor and several basic decisions we made to minimize signal propagation delays:

- only the IU drives the cache address bus;
- the cache data bus only connects to the IU and the floating-point unit, or FPU; and
- the cache write operation does not limit the cycle time; it is preferable to use two cycles for each write.

As a result, all data entering the IU or FPU comes from the cache RAMs, and cache data must pass through the IU or the FPU to get to memory. Noncached data (such as system control registers, or power-on boot-strap code) moves through the cache. First, the cache controller saves the addressed word from the cache in a temporary register, writes the desired data into the vacated cache location, and from there into the IU or FPU, then restores the original cache data from the temporary register.

The CPU core seen in Figure 16.2 contains the SPARC integer unit, the five-chip FPU, the cache RAM array, the tag match chip, and four copies of the system data path gate array. The FPU consists of the controller, two register file chips, the double-

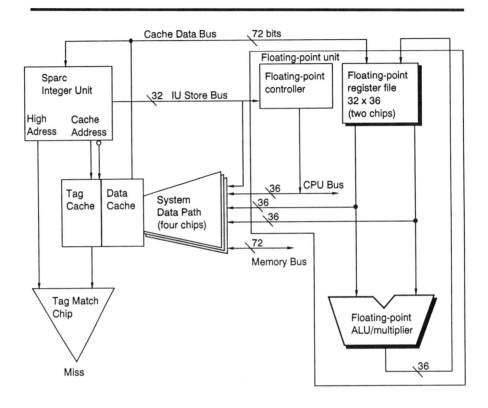

FIGURE 16.2. *The CPU core.*

precision ALU, and the double-precision multiplier. The tag match chip implements the cache miss logic and the tag portion of a four-entry translation (lookaside buffer) cache, or TLB. The system data path contains the data portion of the TLB and provides interconnections between the major units of the CPU via the CPU bus. It also contains the memory bus interface.

Cache Design

With each address pin of a RAM presenting 5 to 7 picofarads of loading in DIP form, the AC impedance of an address bus with the RAMs packed as closely as possible is about 25 ohms. With 25

RAMs (18 for data and parity, and 7 for tags), the delay on the address transmission line totals about 10 ns. By splitting the cache into two banks, each driven by its own copy of the address, we halve the delay time to 5 ns. We provided the IU with 25-ohm differential drivers for 16 address lines, enough to support a 512-Kbyte cache. A further split into four banks is possible by using external drivers, but these can add significant delay and skew.

We optimized the tag-access and compare operations for speed in several ways. First, the tag RAMs are four times smaller than the data RAMs and thus have a shorter access time. Second, we designed a high-speed ECL gate array (the tag match chip) to perform the tag match computation, and third, placed the tag RAMs so that they are the first to receive the address from the IU.

Systems with one-cycle access caches have in the past required RAMs with a read-access delay significantly shorter than the cycle time of the machine. We assumed that such RAMs would be unavailable, too expensive, or too small for this machine, so we designed the pipeline to allow extra time in the cache access stage. We "borrow" time from the address generation stage (see Figure 16.3), which operates in less than 7.5 ns. An on-chip cache address register (CAR) is clocked with an early clock to enable the next cache access to begin before the current one completes. We rely on the address transmission line and the RAMs to provide hold time for the data, despite the changing address.

As in previous SPARC implementations the store operation consists of a tag check followed by the actual cache write (on a cache hit).[3,4] In this implementation, the tag check takes one cycle, but the write takes two (see Figure 16.4). The write pulse straddles the second and third cycles because it must end before the early address changes, and the store data arrives one cycle later than the address. There must also be time to stop the write pulse from occurring if the tag check results in a cache miss. If the store instruction is followed by a nonmemory-access instruction, its execution will be overlapped with the third cycle of the store, reducing the effective cost of the store to two cycles.

The timing of store and swap (seen in Figure 16.4a) illustrates the critical placement of the write pulse between the arrival of the data and the end of the address. Integer load-double (Figure 16.4b) takes two separate load cycles. Integer store-double (Figure 16.4c)

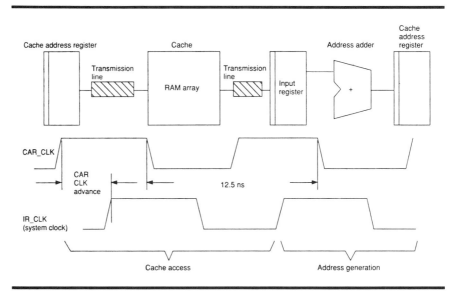

FIGURE 16.3. *Address generation.*

is the only three-cycle instruction. Floating-point store and store-double instructions take one cycle in the pipeline, although it takes three cycles to complete the cache write (Figure 16.4d).

IU Pipeline

SPARC offers a simple instruction set based on a register-to-register paradigm. Only load and store instructions access memory and the only addressing modes used by these instructions are register-plus-register and register-plus-immediate. Register specifiers appear in the same bit fields of every instruction. Branch instructions carry an immediate, program counter-relative offset.[5]

The simplicity of Sparc allows all of the instructions to fit neatly into a fixed pipeline which, on the B5000, consists of five stages: fetch (F), read (R), execute (E), memory (M), and write (W). (Note in The SPARC Architecture box that pipelining is not a required feature of any SPARC implementation.) Each stage completes its processing in one clock cycle. During the F stage instructions move from memory into the processor. Then the processor reads operands from the register file, decodes opcodes, and detects instruction dependencies in the R stage. The operands enter either the arithmetic and logic unit (ALU) or the shift unit in the E stage. Load and store instructions in the M stage fetch data operands from memory, and arithmetic instructions use it to move the arithmetic result back across the chip to the write port of the register file. In the W stage the processor writes the ALU result or the data from memory into the register file.

In the next clock cycle we use standard result-forwarding techniques to keep the pipeline full, even when an instruction's result is used.[6] We added a new data path to this implementation to allow load instructions to execute in one cycle, or two cycles when the next instruction requires the data being loaded. The hardware detects and handles the two-cycle case; compiler support is not required. We call this an interlock action and in general use it when an instruction encounters a resource conflict or data dependency and cannot be issued in the current cycle.

Figure 16.4 illustrates most of the multiple-cycle instructions. The integer store and store-double instructions require two and three cycles respectively because the IU register file does not have a third read port to access the stored data in the R stage. However, the floating-point load, load-double, store, and store-double instructions take just one cycle in the pipeline due to external 64-bit buses and the separate floating-point register file.

Instruction Queue

The B5000 contains a 64-bit data input bus on which two instructions can be fetched in parallel. One or both of these instructions will be inserted into a queue, which has a maximum depth of four instructions. The queue allows the pipeline to complete one instruction every cycle even when memory access instructions occasionally use the data bus (Figure 16.5). The B stage of the pipeline represents cycles in which an instruction stays in the queue. By cycle 4, the chip holds three buffered instructions. When a load instruction uses the data bus to access data (Figure 16.5 shaded M stage in cycle 4), the pipeline uses up one of the prefetched instructions to maintain full performance, and the queue depth drops to two instructions in cycle 5.

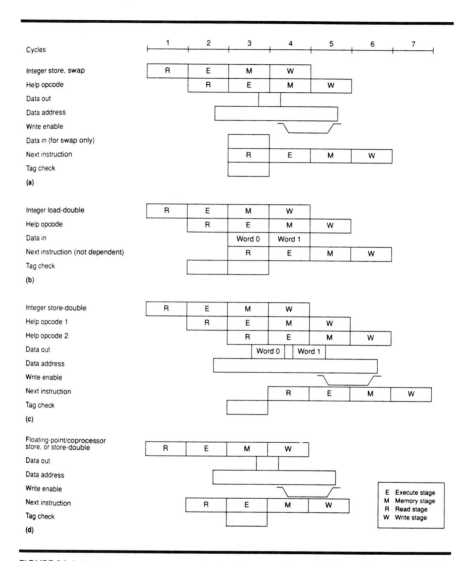

FIGURE 16.4. *Various memory access instructions require multiple cycles on the B5000: store and swap timing (a), integer load-double (b), integer store-double (c), and floating-point store and store-double (d).*

The maximum depth of the queue determines how much load and store traffic can be tolerated without reducing the rate of instruction completion. With four buffers the machine can execute three back-to-back load instructions with no degradation. Since

branches occur as frequently as every six cycles in typical programs, and cause the instruction queue to be flushed, we gain little
performance increase by having a maximum queue depth greater
than six or eight instructions. We chose a depth of four based on the
chip area budget and performance simulations.

Conditional Branching

The instruction following the SPARC branch instruction executes
before the control transfer occurs. This delay allows the machine to
execute a useful instruction while it adds the address of the branch
instruction to its immediate offset to form the target address. On
the B5000, the cache address for a given cycle issues late in the
previous cycle. Since the generation of this address is a critical
path, the B5000 predicts that every branch will be taken. It sends
out the target address late in the R stage, without regard to the
condition codes that are being computed in the same cycle by the
compare instruction (Figure 16.6 on the next page, cycle 2).

If the branch is *not* taken, the "fall-through" instruction (the
instruction sequentially following the delay instruction) is the next
instruction to execute. In most cases this instruction resides in the

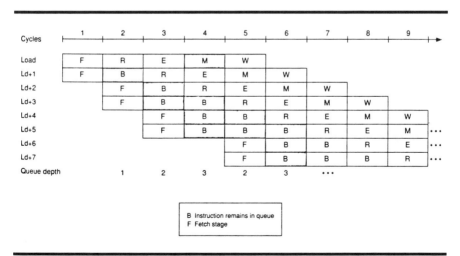

FIGURE 16.5. *By fetching two instructions in each fetch cycle, the on-chip instruction
queue fills as linear code executes.*

instruction buffers, and no penalty results. In the case illustrated, we show the branch itself being fetched as the target of a previous branch. Thus it enters the R stage directly after it is fetched. The branch resided at an even-word address, so its delay instruction was also fetched at the same time. Complexities arise when the fall-through or delay instructions are not in the instruction queue. These infrequent cases do not significantly affect performance, although they do complicate the logic design.

The instruction at the target address of a branch is always fetched in the E stage of the branch (Figure 16.6). In the subsequent cycle 3, when the compare (Cmp) instruction computes and makes known the condition codes, the target is either decoded immediately or discarded. If the branch is not taken, the prefetched instructions following the branch/delay pair (the fall-through instructions) execute, so no cycles are lost.

FPU, Coprocessor Interfaces

The B5000 implements the SPARC floating-point interface and coprocessor interface symmetrically, so discussion of the floating-point interface applies equally to the coprocessor. SPARC allows register-to-register floating-point operations to execute and complete in the "background" while the pipeline continues to execute integer instructions. However, a floating-point operation may complete by generating an exception, rather than an arithmetic result.

To pinpoint the instruction causing an exception, the FPC maintains a queue of pending instructions and their addresses. The queue can be read after an exception occurs to determine which instruction actually caused the exception and which subsequent instructions had been issued but not completed. Each entry of the queue contains an instruction and its address. The IU dispatches instructions on the store-data bus in the R stage of the pipeline. The addresses are generated on the FPC chip, which has a copy of the E stage program counter (called the XPC). The IU manages the XPC with its "increment XPC" control, and by loading it from the store-data bus following any control transfer. This design allows floating-point instructions to be dispatched at a rate of one every clock cycle.

When a dependency occurs between a floating-point arithmetic instruction and a floating-point memory access instruction, the FPC halts the IU until the arithmetic instruction completes. This process occurs in the W stage of the memory access instruction.

Three dedicated pins continuously carry the FPU's condition codes and a validation bit to the IU. The floating-point conditional branch instruction can thus execute in the pipeline as an integer instruction; it is not dispatched to the FPU. When a floating-point compare instruction is sent to the FPU, the unit invalidates the floating-point condition codes until the instruction completes. A subsequent conditional branch instruction must wait until the unit validates the condition codes.

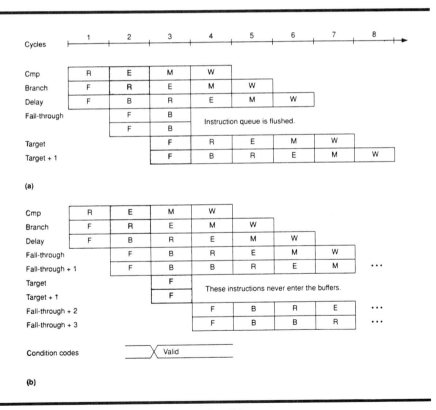

FIGURE 16.6. *Branches:taken (a) and not taken (b).*

Performance

The Dhrystone benchmark attempts to synthesize the frequency of occurrence of various high-level-language statements in operating system code. This benchmark is not a large program and doesn't really compute anything useful, but it has been run on many machines, from personal computers to mainframes. As a result, we find it useful as a one-dimensional measure of processor and compiler performance.

Reportedly, the Apple IIe with an 8-MHz 8086 processor executes 197 Dhrystones per second (version 1.1), and the IBM 3090/200 processes 31,250.[7] Simulation of the benchmark (version 1.1) on the B5000 indicates a rating of 104,000 Dhrystones/s, which is more than five times the rating of the Sun 4/260 workstation. Actual hardware results produced a rating of 103,000 Dhrystones/s. The difference occurs from process switching and the resulting cache misses.

From the Dhrystone simulation, we know that the B5000 should execute at the rate of 1.29 cycles per instruction and 62 million instructions per second. This is the expected average for integer benchmarks. Simulation of DAXPY (double-precision $A \times X + Y$) the double-precision inner-loop routine of the Linpack benchmark, on the B5000 has indicated a performance of 14 Mflops.

The B5000 ECl SPARC series of components represents a new approach to constructing high-performance computer systems at a relatively low cost. For the first time, we are able to design small ECL systems that perform at a level equal to large mainframe computers and approach that of today's supercomputers. In the future we can expect even more highly integrated bipolar and bipolar/MOS chips, further narrowing the gap between low-cost workstations and high-performance servers.

The B5000 Microprocessor

The B5000 SPARC integer unit is the first highly integrated ECL microprocessor. Its design took a custom cell-based approach in which nearly 600 unique logic gates were employed. The data path, in the center of the die, performs all of the 32-bit-wide operations and contains the 32-bit-wide registers. Routing in this section is primarily vertical. The control section on the left side of the die uses cells of a fixed vertical pitch and is routed vertically on the third layer of metal and horizontally on the second layer of metal. Bias and supply lines appear in fixed vertical positions and run horizontally.

The register file, a 3-port RAM, contains 4,352 bits, uses 70,000 transistors, and provides a read access time of 10 nanoseconds. Two rows of pads on a 4.5-mil pitch provide contacts for 213 signal wires and 87 power bond wires. By designing custom input and output logic, we minimized setup and hold windows and output delays. The B5000 contains 122,000 transistors and 77,000 resistors in a 279-pin grid array. Some features of the chip include:

- **Parity.** Parity checking on incoming data occurs across each byte, and two parity bits protect each general-purpose register. Parity violations cause synchronous traps to support graceful error recovery and reporting. Data and register file parity checking can be independently disabled.

- **Scan mode.** Most of the registers in the chip set can be connected into one shift register by asserting the scan mode pin. The entire shift register can then be read and written by clocking the part. This feature is useful in testing the part, debugging a system containing it, and diagnosing failures.

- **Pass-through mode.** Two address pass-through modes allow the external cache controller to index each 64-bit word in a cache block, or to index the entire cache. The data pass-through mode supports write-backs and cache interrogation by allowing data from the cache to be shunted directly through the chip to the store-data bus.

- **Delay matching.** The 32 pins of the cache address bus, the two write enables, and the clock output are designed to switch within a 0.5-ns time window. The clock output can generate the system clock, which strobes the cache data into the IU or the FPU, and the write enables can be positioned precisely with respect to the addresses to simplify write-cycle timing.

- **Direct drive.** Address lines 3–18 use 25-ohm complementary output drivers to allow the chip to directly drive a 64-bit cache RAM array as large as 512 Kbytes. An on-chip register, which contains the address of the latest cache miss, further supports direct addressing.

- **Redundancy.** A redundant block of eight general-purpose registers can be substituted for any one of 14 blocks of window registers to provide yield enhancement. On the IC tester, a small set of test vectors determines whether a bad block of registers exists, performs any substitution and indicates an encounter with one bad block. A simple firmware routine automatically performs the substitution in the system environment.

The SPARC Architecture

The reduced instruction-set computer, or RISC, architectures developed at the University of California at Berkeley form the basis of the Scalable Processor Architecture. SPARC contains only 32-bit-long instructions in three formats. Operand specifiers appear in fixed positions in the instructions to enable rapid register file access. Delayed control transfer instructions allow an instruction that follows a control transfer instruction to execute before the transfer of control occurs.

In Figure 16.7 we can see that Format 1 is used only by the subroutine Call instruction. This format has a 30-bit displacement, which allows a Call to any word-aligned address in the virtual address space. Formate 2 supports the SETHI instruction and the Branch instructions. The 22-bit displacement allows Branch instructions to span 16 Mbytes of the virtual address space. Format 3 supports all of the other instructions. It has three 5-bit operand specifiers, or two 5-bit operand specifiers and one 13-bit signed immediate constant. The three-operand version leaves 8 bits available for floating-point opcodes (fp-op), coprocessor opcodes (op), or alternate space identifiers (asi).

Integer computation occurs on only one data type, a 32-bit word, and always acts on operands from the register file. Only explicit memory load and store instructions access memory. Sparc supports word (32-bit), halfword (16-bit), and byte (8-bit) memory operations. All addresses must be aligned.

A windowed register file with two to 32 windows forms part of the SPARC architecture. Each window provides working storage for one subroutine of a program. Eight registers shared between adjacent windows support efficient passing of subroutine arguments. The save instruction, used at the beginning of a subroutine, advances to the next window while simultaneously performing an addition (usually to advance the stack pointer). The restore instruction permits return to the previous window when returning from a subroutine.

A separate set of 32 registers supports floating-point operations. All floating-point operations that refer to register operands implicitly access this set, including the floating-point memory load

Format 1 (CALL):

op	displacement
2	30

Format 2 (SETH)

op	rd	op	immediate
2	5	3	22

Format 2 (Bicc, FBfcc, CBCC):

op	a	cc	op	displacement
2	1	4	3	22

Format 3 (Remaining instructions, i-0):

op	rd	op	[s]	i	asi *or* fp-op	rs2
2	5	6	5	1	8	5

Format 3 (Remaining instructions, i-1):

op	rd	op	[s]	i	immediate
2	5	6	5	1	13

FIGURE 16.7. *SPARC instructions: 32 bits long in three formats.*

and store instructions. By their nature, floating-point arithmetic operations take longer than integer operations (using the same implementation), so SPARC allows floating-point operations to run for several cycles in parallel with integer operations. The separation of integer and floating-point data into two distinct register files eliminates direct dependencies between integer and floating-point instructions.

In Tables A and B we list each individual instruction and its variations. Note that some implied variations don't exist. For example, SPARC contains no instructions for signed store, alternate space floating-point load or store, shift left arithmetic, or floating-point convert to self.

While pipelining is not a part of SPARC, the instruction set design allows efficient pipelined implementations. By keeping the instructions simple, it is relatively easy to overlap the execution of several instructions at once.

Instruction	Data types	Data width	Variations	Notes
Memory operations				
Load	Signed	Byte, halfword	Alternate space[1]	—
Store	Unsigned	Word	Floating-point queue	—
		Double word	Floating-point status reg.	—
		Single, double	—	—
Swap		Word	Alternate space[1]	Atomic[2]
Load/Store	Unsigned	Byte	Alternate space[1]	Atomic[2]
Integer computational				
And, Or	—	Word	Not[3]	—
XOR	—	—	Set cc[4]	—
Add	—	Word	Set cc,[4] tagged[5]	—
Sub	—	—	Extended	—
MULSCC	Signed	Word		SEt cc[4]
Save	—	Word		Performs Add
Restore	—	Word		—
Shift	—	Word	Left, right	Shift by 0 to 31 bits
Read	—	Word	PSR,[6] WIM[7]	—
Write	—	—	TBR,[8] Y[9]	—
Control transfer				
Branch	Signed	22-bit displacement	Integer cc[4]	—
			Floating-point cc[4]	—
			Coprocessor cc[4]	—
			Execute delay[10]	—
			Annul delay[10] if not taken	—
Call	Signed	30-bit displacement	—	Delayed
Jump and Link	—	Word	—	Delayed
Return from trap	—	Word	—	Privileged, delayed

	Variations	Notes
	Byte	8 bits
	Halfword	16 bits
	Word	32 bits
	Double word	64 bits
	Single	32-bit floating-point value
	Double	64-bit floating-point value

[1] Access to one of 255 privileged, alternate address spaces
[2] Load and Store occurs indivisibly in memory
[3] The second operand is logically inverted.
[4] Condition codes
[5] The least significant two bits of the data act as simple type tags.
[6] Processor status register
[7] Window invalid mask
[8] Trap base register
[9] Y register (used by MULSCC as an accumulator)
[10] The instruction immediately following a control transfer instruction

TABLE A. *Three of the four general types of the Sparc instruction set.*

Instruction	Data types	
Conversion	Signed	Integer
FADD,FSUB	—	Single
FMUL, FDIV	—	Double
FCOMPARE	—	—
Square root	—	—
FMOVE	—	Single
FABSOLUTE	—	—
FNEGATE	—	—

TABLE B. *The fourth general type of the Sparc instruction set.*

Acknowledgments

The B5000 series resulted from a productive joint development between Sun and BIT. In addition to the authors, many people contributed to the project, including Daniel Chang, Arthur Leung, Dan Nelsen, Renu Raman, Jim Testa, Kwok Tsang, and Alex Yu at Sun, and the layout and design teams at BIT.

References

1. G. Wilson, "Creating Low-Power Bipolar ECL at VLSI Densities," *VLSI System Design*, May 1986.

2. "Electronics, Technology to Watch: Suprise! ECL Runs on Only Microwatts," *Electronics*, Vol. 59, Apr. 7, 1986.

3. M. Namjoo et al., "CMOS Gate Array Implementation of the SPARC Architecture," *Proc. Compcon 88,*IEEE Computer Society Press, Los Alamitos, Calif., 1988, p. 10.

4. M. Namjoo et al., "CMOS Custom Implementation of the SPARC Architecture," *Proc. Compcon 88*, IEEE CS Press, 1988, p. 18.

5. R.B. Garner et al., "The Scalable Processor Architecture (SPARC)," *Proc. Compcon 88*, IEEE CS Press, 1988, p. 278.

6. D.A. Patterson, "Reduced Instruction Set Computers," *Comm. ACM*, Vol. 28, No. 1, Jan. 1985, p. 8.

7. R.P. Weicker, *Comm. ACM*, Vol. 27, No. 10, Dec. 1984, p. 1013.

SPARC: An Open RISC Architecture

17

KEVIN M. KITAGAWA • RAYMOND M. LEONG

Introduction

The availability of commercial high-performance microprocessors has transformed the job of system designers by providing them with readily available and inexpensive standard engines to power their creations. Instead of expending effort to develop proprietary processors from scratch, designers are able to leverage the massive investments of semiconductor companies in general purpose microprocessors, operating systems, compilers, development tools, and technical support. Rather than defining a new architecture, the task of the designer becomes one of selecting a microprocessor from an array of offerings.

This flexibility has not come without cost: the typical systems company has become almost totally dependent on the microprocessor supplier. Instead of the major R&D cycle being dictated by the needs of the systems company, it is now driven by the time it takes the semiconductor company to bring out the next generation product. While a fast moving systems company may be able to turn major products in as little as 12 to 18 months, they must contend with a microprocessor supplier which might not accomplish an R&D cycle in two or three years. The long term result is predictable: increased design time, reduced innovation, stop-gap products, and ultimately loss of competitiveness.

There are two problems with the current situation in high-performance 32-bit microprocessors. First, innovation in each architecture is usually provided by only one semiconductor vendor. Thus the rate of architectural improvement is limited by the vendor's resources. This is true even when the product is available from alternate sources since the typical alternate source is really just a foundry. Second, the breadth of implementations that can be developed at one time is also restricted because only one vendor, with its limited areas of specialization, is responsible for the product line.

In response to this situation, a simple and powerful RISC architecture called SPARC (Scalable Processor ARChitecture), was created. SPARC is an open architecture. To data five semiconductor companies (Fujitsu Microelectronics, Cypress Semiconductor, Bipolar Integrated Technology, LSI Logic, and Texas Instruments) are actively developing chips based on the SPARC architecture. In addition, a increasing number of systems manufacturers are in the process of building products ranging from relatively inexpensive PC-class machines to supercomputers using their own implementations of the SPARC architecture. All these products are able to take advantage of the operating system and application software base already established for SPARC.

SPARC Architecture

In contrast to other RISC architectures whose initial features appear to have been defined primarily with high integration in mind, the SPARC architecture has been designed foremost with scalability in mind. The architecture has already scaled through several processes and will have quadrupled performance in only 18 months.

In the transitions through CMOS gate-array technology, semi-custom technology, full custom 0.8 micron CMOS, ECL, and finally GaAs, SPARC implementations have scaled from the initial 10 VAX MIPS to the current level of 24 VAX MIPS. Future versions of SPARC will provide up to 250 VAX MIPS within the next 2 to 3 years. This rapid incorporation of new semiconductor technologies has provided multiple price/performance points for SPARC which, with its common unchanged instruction set, is aimed at supporting a complete spectrum of platforms. For example, SUN Microsystems has released in the first year, three workstations based on just the first implementation of SPARC.

The SPARC architecture defines simple instructions, all 32 bits long, in five formats. Most instructions can be executed in a single cycle. Integer, IEEE Standard Floating Point and user-defined instructions can be executed concurrently with architectural support for program concurrency and precise traps. To maximize data locality, the SPARC architecture uses a non-destructive, triadic register model which reduces procedure call and return overheads significantly.

Other noteworthy features in the SPARC architecture include: hardware register interlock, multiprocessor and AI support instructions, and an 8-bit address identifier field (ASI) which can be modified by load and store instructions in the supervisor mode.

All registers in the Integer Unit (IU) are 32 bits wide. They are divided into 8 global registers and a number of register sets called windows. Each window contains 24 registers and they are grouped into In, Out, and Local registers. Adjacent windows overlap each other by 8 registers so that the Out registers of the previous window become the In registers of the current window and the Out registers of the current window become the In registers of the next window. This overlapping register window feature is illustrated in Figure 17.1.

Registers 0 to 7 are global registers addressable by all procedures. An active window contains registers labelled from R8 to R31. Each time a non-leaf procedure is called, the SAVE instruction in the calling sequence will decrement the current window pointer (CWP) to point to the next window. In doing so, the 8 Out registers (R8 to R15) of the calling window become the 8 In registers (R24 to R31) of the new window. By storing parameter information in the Out registers and invoking the SAVE command, the calling procedure can pass data easily into the new procedure. A reverse situation is initated when the RESTORE instruction is executed. The 8 In registers of the current window will become the Out registers of the previous window because the current window pointer will be incremented to point to the previous window, thus passing results stored in those registers back to the calling procedure. The last window is held unused to support fast trap handling. A special configuration register, Window Invalid Mask (WIM) is provided to specify the number of windows implemented in the Integer Unit.

SPARC Implementations

Fujitsu Microelectronics offered the first SPARC IU implementation in 1987 based on gate array technology. Cypress Semiconductor, a leader in custom CMOS technology, began shipping a

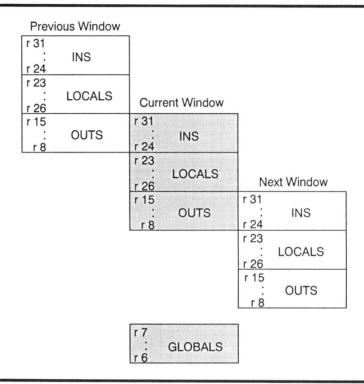

FIGURE 17.1.

full custom, 0.8 micron SPARC IU in 1988. An ECL implementation of the SPARC architecture from Bipolar Integrated Technology is scheduled for sampling in 1989. A description of the Cypress SPARC family of processors will be described in the following sections.

Cypress CY7C601 Integer Unit

The Cypress CY7C601 Integer Unit is a 0.8 micron full custom CMOS version of the SPARC architecture housed in a 207-pin Pin-grid Array package. It is presently offered at clock rates of 25 MHz and 33 MHz, and has a sustained integer performance of 24 VAX MIPS and floating point performance of 4.3 MFLOPS double precision Linpack.

The IU has five major functional units: a tri-ported register file; a four-stage instruction pipe with dual instruction buffers; a 32-bit ALU; a 32-bit adder for address calculations; and a load/store data aligner. Figure 17.2 shows a block diagram of the IU architecture.

The register file has 136 32-bit registers grouped into 8 register windows, 8 global registers, and all special registers defined in the SPARC architecture such as the Processor State Register

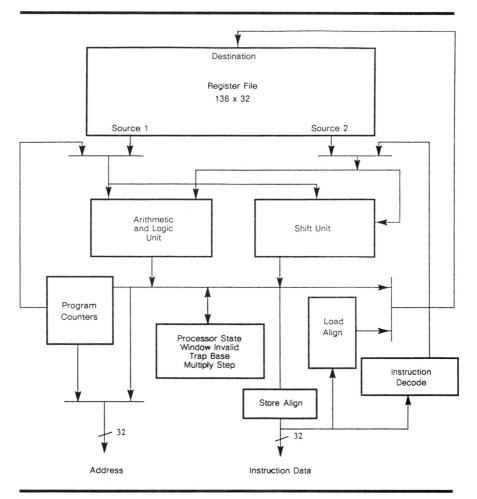

FIGURE 17.2.

and the Window Invalid Mask Register. The registers are tri-ported so each can be used as either source operand or result destination.

The 4-stage instruction pipe allows the IU to execute instructions at a rate approaching one instruction per clock. With the exception of load, store, jump, and return from trap instructions, all instructions are executed in a single clock cycle. Because the high speed ALU in the CY7C601 evaluates condition codes early in the execution cycle, even branch instructions (both taken and not taken) are dispatched in a single clock. Two instruction buffers are provided to keep the pipeline filled for maximum throughput.

The ALU performs all arithmetic, logical, and shift operations. Results from the ALU are written into the destination register in one clock cycle. Data sourced into the execution unit is obtained from either the register file or from the result of the previous instruction. This "internal forwarding" of ALU result into the next execution cycle improves performances by reducing the time spent on interlocking registers. Interlocking is necessary only when the result of a load instruction is used by the next instruction. Optimizing compilers can be programmed to avoid this instruction sequence to further reduce the interlock penality.

A separate 32-bit adder is provided on-chip to calculate PC-relative target addresses for branch instructions. Target addresses based on register indirect data are performed by the ALU.

Interface to memory is conducted over a 32-bit address bus, a 32-bit bi-directional data bus, 8 address space identifiers, and access control signals. Normally, the IU fetches a new instruction once every clock except when data load or stores are required. Accesses can be extended by asserting the MHOLD input of the IU. This simple interface allows easy connections with different memory system designs, including cache, static RAM, varies types of D-RAM arranged in direct of interleaved fashions, and EPROMs.

The load/store data aligner aligns the IU data to the correct boundary during load and store operations. In a load cycle, the LSB of the returning data from external logic is aligned with the LSB of the destination register. In a store byte cycle, the 8-bit data is aligned on a byte boundary and repeated on all four byte outputs. Store half word cycles are aligned on 16-bit boundaries and repeated on both the upper and lower halfwords.

The IU provides easy-to-use interfaces to two coprocessors: a floating-point unit and a customer-defined coprocessor.

Cypress' Floating-Point Solution

The Cypress CY7C608 Floating-Point Controller (FPC) and the CY7C609 Floating-Point Processor (FPP) together provide high performance single and double precision floating-point operations. The FPP supports IEEE standard 754-1985 single and double precision formats and performs add, subtract, multiply, divide, square root, compare, and convert functions. The FPC makes the CY7C609 FPP look like a SPARC floating point unit to the IU by supporting register to register move operations, floating point load and store functions, as well as maintainance of the floating-point queue. Instructions not implemented by the FPC such as extended precision operations will cause a trap. Both FPC and FPP are available in PGA packages with 299 pins in the FPC and 208 pins in the FPP.

The CY7C608 FPC contains a dual-port (one read port and one write port) 32 by 32 register file. Two registers are paired up to store double precision operands. The contents of these registers are transferred to and from external memory under control of the IU via floating point load and store instructions.

Each time the IU performs an instruction fetch, the FPC copies the information on the data bus as well as the address of the instruction into two 64-bit Decode Buffers. When the decoder in the IU detects a floating point instruction in the execution sequence, it will notify the FPC to process the instruction by activating one of two signals: FINS1 or FINS2. Assertion of FINS1 transfers the contents of decode buffer 1 into the three-level deep floating point queue while assertion of FINS2 causes the same operation on decode buffer 2. The execution unit extracts instructions from the output of the queue and converts them into code sequences understood by the FPP. Figure 17.3 is a block diagram of the FPC.

The floating-point queue keeps track of floating-point operations that are pending completion by the FPP when a trap occurs. The first entry of the queue contains the address of the floating-point operation which caused the exception as well as the actual instruction itself. The remaining entries in the queue contain other

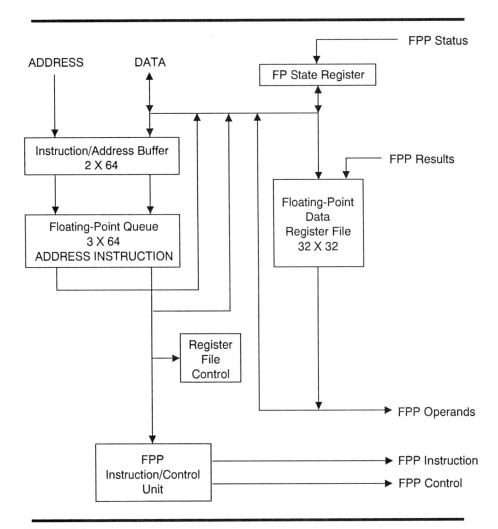

FIGURE 17.3.

floating-point instructions that has not finished when the exception is detected. Precise trap handling is possible with the information supplied by the floating point queue. A connection diagram between the CY7C601 IU and the CY7C608/CY7C609 is shown in Figure 17.4.

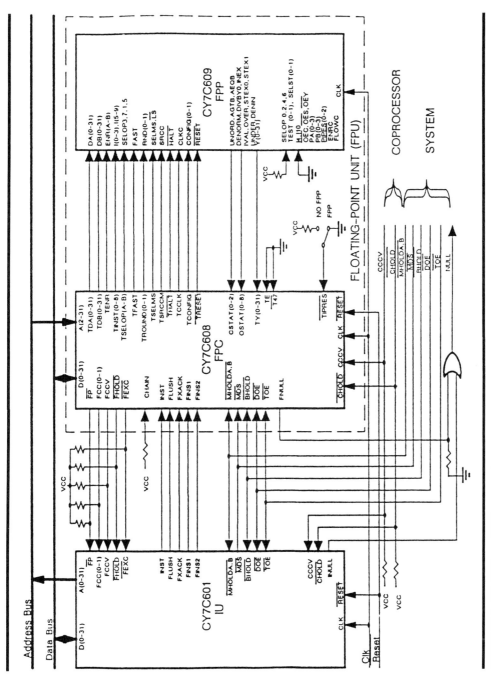

FIGURE 17.4. *IU, FPC, and FPP connections.*

Cypress CY7C604 Cache Controller/Memory Management Unit

The CY7C604 Cache Controller/Memory Management unit (CMU) provides hardware support for a demand paged virtual memory environment with the Cypress CY7C601 32-bit RISC processor and CY7C157 16K by 16 cache RAMs. It conforms fully to the SPARC Reference MMU specification. A block diagram of the CMU is shown in Figure 17.5.

Page size is fixed at 4 K-bytes. The CMU translates 32-bit virtual addresses from the processor into 36-bit physical addresses. Up to 4096 contexts are supported on-chip via 12 context bits. High-speed address look-up is provided by a 64-entry fully associative Translation Look-aside Buffer (TLB). Each entry contains the virtual to physical mapping of a 4 K-byte page. If a virtual address finds a match in one of the TLB entries, the physical address translation contained in that entry will be delivered to the outputs of the CMU. If the virtual address from the processor has no corresponding entry in the TLB, the CMU will perform address translation for the virtual address using a four-level page table map (one context table and three page tables).

The second level page pointers of the last successful instruction and data translations are cached on-chip to speed up the address translation process. Because of the locality characteristics exhibited in most programs, the chance of reusing the cached page pointers are high. The CY7C604 CMU also allow frequently used pages to remain in memory by providing a TLB locking mechanism.

Each "matched" TLB entry is checked for protection violation automatically and violations are reported to the CY7C601 Integer Unit as memory exceptions. Pages can be declared as non-cacheable by clearing the cacheable (C) bit in the TLB. A random replacement algorithm is used to replace TLB entries.

In the cache controlling capacity, the CMU provides 2K direct-mapped tag entries and supports both write through and copy black cache policies. The cache can be locked and line size is set at 32 bytes. Since multiple virtual address can be mapped into the same physical address, address aliasing is checked each time a

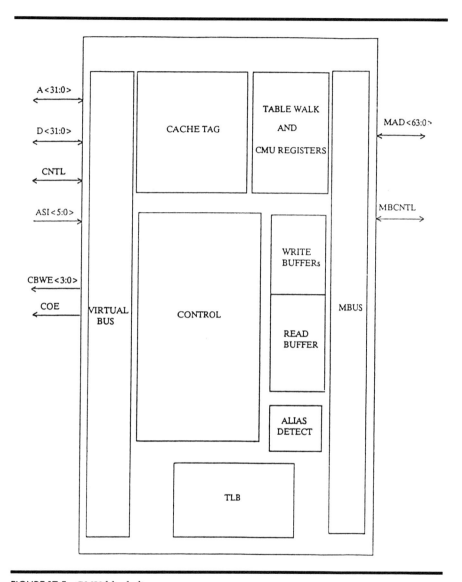

FIGURE 17.5. *CMU block diagram*

cache line is replaced. If the new virtual address is mapped to the cache line selected for replacement, the CMU will cancel the main memory access and modify the cache tag accordingly.

The CMU provides 3 types of on-chip buffer to enhance data

transfers between cache memory and main memory: a 32-byte line buffer, a 32-byte read buffer and 4 write buffers. The line buffer is used to store the modified line being evicted from the cache, allowing main memory read to proceed as soon as the physical bus is acquired. The read buffer stores data from main memory temporary before they are written into the cache memory. The write buffers are used in the write through mode only to capture address and data from the IU during write cache hits, allowing the IU to continue processing while the buffer contents are transferred into main memory over the physical bus.

Communications to and from main memory is conducted via the Module (M) Bus. The M bus has 64 multiplexed address and data lines and is capable of burst accesses. For systems requiring more tag or TLB entries, additional CMUs can be used with each processor.

Cypress's advanced 0.8 micron double-metal CMOS process is used to fabricate the CMU and it will be available in 2 packages: a 208-pin plastic quad flatpack and a 244-pin PGA.

For multiprocessing applications, Cypress offers the CY7C605 CMU-MP. This CMU is a superset of the CY7C604 and as such, fully conforms to the SPARC Reference MMU Specification. It contains both virtual and physical cache tags and is capable of concurrent bus snooping. A data consistency protocol similar to the one defined in the Future Bus is implemented in the CY7C605 to maintain data integrity among processor modules. Both direct data intervention with memory reflection and direct data intervention without memory reflection modes are supported.

Cypress CY7C157 Cache RAM

The CY7C157 16K by 16 cache RAM is designed to interface directly to the CY6C601 IU and the CY7C604 CMU. Two speed versions are available; the user can choose the 20 nS or the 24 nS version to suite their system requirements. Since byte writes are an essential part of IU operations, 2 write inputs are provided to support this function. A self-timed write cycle is initiated automatically whenever one or both write inputs are sampled low at clock fall.

Three latches are provided on-chip to simplify interface to the

IU: an address latch captures the IU address at the rising edge of each clock, an input data latch supplies write data to the RAM core until the store function is completed, and an output data latch ensures that the 5 nS data hold time required by the IU is satisfied. The CY7C157 cache RAM is fabricated in double metal CMOS technology and packaged in a 52-pin PLCC.

Summary

The SPARC is designed to offer multiple price/performance points over a wide variety of semiconductor technologies. New implementations of SPARC will be able to quickly take advantage of new semiconductor technologies as they become available and the Cypress SPARC product line is a good example. SPARC can and will provide a single architecture for systems ranging from PCs to supercomputers, with binary compatibility across all platforms.

SPARC Development Tools

Optimizing Compilers for the SPARC Architecture

STEVEN S. MUCHNICK • CHRISTOPHER AOKI •
VIDA GHODSSI • MICHEL HELFT • MENG LEE •
RICHARD TUCK • DAVID WEAVER • ALEXANDER WU

18

Introduction and Overview

This paper discusses Sun Microsystems' user programming model for the SPARC architecture [SPAR87], and the optimizing compilers for the SPARC-based Sun-4 workstations. The architecture and its first implementations are discussed in [GarA88, ChuQ88, Goss88, Solt88] and [Klei88] describes the Sun implementation of UNIX for SPARC. Here we concern ourselves with two broad areas: how the compilers use the architecture and the design of the compilers themselves.

SPARC (Scalable Processor ARChitecture) is a new architecture for computer systems designed by a team of Sun hardware and software engineers. The architecture is licensed by Sun to chip manufacturers for implementation. Sun provides compilers for C, FORTRAN 77 with VMS™ extensions, Pascal and Modula-2 for SPARC, all based on the same code generation and optimization technology. In addition, Sun provides Common Lisp and will provide Ada™ for SPARC (derived from third-party products) and others provide or will provide Smalltalk [Smal87], Prolog, Mainsail and other languages. We deal with support for the first set of languages in depth here and mention some of the others peripherally.

As a reduced instruction set computer (RISC) architecture, SPARC is designed to achieve high performance by making the things which account for the overwhelming majority of real com-

1988 IEEE. Reprinted with Permission, from Proceedings of COMPCON '88, March 1–3, San Francisco, CA.

puting as fast as possible, while not unduly slowing down other operations. Judicious application of this principle results in an architecture which has a relatively simple set of operations and only a few addressing modes. As seen by a compiler, SPARC is in the Berkeley RISC II and SOAR tradition [Kate83, UngB84], with register windows, delayed branches and delayed loads with hardware interlocks, a floating-point coprocessor, and a few special instructions to support tagged data. All instructions are 32 bits long and most take only a single machine cycle to execute.

Since there are only a few choices (or, in many cases, only one) for the proper instructions and addressing modes to use for a given operation, compilers can generate locally optimal code for expressions with relative ease, leaving more time available for the developers to address questions of the run-time environment and global code optimization.

The remainder of the paper is structured as follows. Sections 2 and 3 discuss the register and addressing models used by our compilers. Section 4 discusses synthesized instructions, i.e. functions provided by single instructions in CISC architectures which are generally performed by instruction sequences in RISCs. Section 5 presents SPARC'S support for tagged data and efficient trapping. Section 6 begins the discussion of the SPARC compilers. Section 7 discusses issues of source language compatibility between previous Sun architectures and SPARC. Section 8 discusses our global and peephole optimizers and Section 9 presents the effects of optimization on code quality and code space. Section 10 presents conclusions. The Appendix describes the notation used in SPARC assembly language.

Registers

The effective use of registers is typically among the most important resource allocation issues for a compiler. The load/store nature of RISC architectures makes this even more so. Garner et al. [GarA88] describes SPARC's register model in some detail. Here we provide a synopsis of the features of greatest importance to the compiler writer and then describe how our compilers use the registers.

SPARC provides three sets of registers visible to the user program at any time (see Table 18.1):

- Global integer registers
- Global floating-point registers
- Windowed integer registers

Global integer register g0 is special in that it reads as zero and discards values written to it. The other global integer registers are managed by software using the caller-saves protocol (i.e. around a subroutine call, the caller saves and restores the registers containing live values). These registers could be used for global variables and pointers, either visible to the programmer or maintained as part of the program's execution environment. For instance one could, by convention, address global variables by offsets from one or more global registers, allowing quick access to 2^{13} bytes of global storage per register so dedicated [ChoC87]. The global floating-point registers are also managed entirely by software. Our compilers use them as caller-saved register variables and temporaries.

The windowed registers are further subdivided into three sets: the *ins*, *outs*, and *locals*. A save instruction may be executed as part of a procedure prologue changing the machine's interpretation of register numbers so that the calling procedure's *outs* become the called procedure's *ins*, and a new set of *locals* and *outs* is provided. In our compilers, the save also allocates a new stack frame, by setting the new stack pointer from the old one. Similarly, the restore instruction executed in a procedure epilogue restores the register number interpretation to the caller's state, and simultaneously cuts back the stack. The overlap of *in* and *out* registers provides a way to pass most parameters in registers. One of the *outs* receives a call's return address, and another is the caller's stack pointer, which becomes the callee's frame pointer. This leaves six registers for user parameters[1] (additional parameters are passed on the memory stack). A procedure returns a value by

---

[1] Six is more than adequate, since the overwhelming majority of procedures take fewer than six parameters. The average number of parameters, measured statically or dynamically, is no greater than 2.1 [Weic84].

Register Names

Register numbers	Alternate numbering	Names	Windowed?
r24 to r31	i0 to i7	*ins*	yes
r16 to r23	l0 to l7	*locals*	yes
r8 to r15	o0 to o7	*outs*	yes
r0 to r7	g0 to g7	*globals*	no

Distinguished Registers

Register	Use
g0	zero value & discard result
sp (same as o6)	stack pointer
fp (same as i6)	frame pointer
o7	return address

TABLE 18.1.

writing it to one or more of its *in* registers, where it is available to the caller in the corresponding *out*. Unused *in* registers and all the *locals* are available for a procedure's automatic storage and temporaries.

Since an implementation can provide only a bounded set of windows, provision is made for a trap to occur when a procedure is entered if all windows are in use, and when a procedure is exited if the window being returned to does not have the proper values in it. The operating system can then spill or refill register windows, respectively, as needed.

Addressing and Stack Models

SPARC's computational instructions obtain all their data from registers and immediate fields in instructions and put their results in registers. Only load and store instructions access memory. The load and store instructions have two addressing modes, one which adds the contents of two integer registers and one which adds the contents of an integer register and a 13-bit signed immediate. The semantics of g0 makes an absolute addressing mode available also.

All but one of the integer computational instructions use the same means to specify their operands and results, i.e. one operand comes from a general register and the other either comes from a register or is a sign-extended 13-bit immediate, and the result is stored in a register. The exception is the sethi instruction, which is used to construct 32-bit constants and addresses for access to global data. It loads an immediate 22-bit constant into the high end of a register and zeros the other 10 bits. Thus, for example, the sequence (see the Appendix for a description of the assembly language)

```
sethi      %hi(loc), %i1
ld         [%i1+%lo(loc)], %i2
```

can be used to load the word at address loc into i2. While the need for an extra instruction to construct 32-bit constants and addresses may appear to be a disadvantage, it is fully in line with RISC design principles—it helps make the common cases fast without significantly slowing down the low frequency ones. Constants are usually short, so the sethi is rarely needed, and the address construction is frequently optimizable to a single instruction because %hi(loc) turns out to be a loop invariant.

Despite the number of registers available to the programmer, many procedures still require a memory stack frame. The stack frame may contain several sorts of things:

- Parameters beyond the sixth, if any;
- Parameters, which must be addressable, are stored in the stack at entry to a procedure, since registers do not have memory addresses;
- A one-word hidden parameter, used when the caller is expecting to be returned to a C-language *struct* by value; it gives the address of stack space allocated by the caller to receive the value;
- Space for the window overflow trap handler to store the procedure's *in* and *local* registers;
- Automatic variables which must be addressable, including automatic arrays and automatic records;
- Some compiler-generated temporaries;

• Space for saving floating-point registers across calls.

Automatic variables on the stack are addressed relative to fp, while temporaries and outgoing parameters are addressed relative to sp. When a procedure is active, its stack frame appears as in Figure 18.1.

Synthesized Instructions

We use the term synthesized instruction to refer to one which is generally provided in a more complex architecture, such as the DEC VAX or IBM 370, but which is replaced by a series of instructions or a special-case subroutine call in a RISC system. In SPARC the most important instances of synthesized instructions are for procedure call, procedure entry, multiply and divide.

Procedure Call and Entry

Rather than providing a complex procedure call instruction like the DEC VAX's CALLS [VAX79], which takes an argument count and list of arguments and sets up the stack frame in addition to passing control to the procedure, SPARC provides two instructions which can be used to invoke a procedure, namely call and jmpl, each of which occupies a single cycle plus a delay slot. The call instruction takes a 30-bit PC-relative *word* displacement from the instruction; it branches to the target address and stores the return address in o7. Jump and link (jmpl) takes a target address which is the sum of two registers or a register and an immediate, and stores the return address in a specified register. Additional instructions are required to pass parameters and to move from one register window to the next. The latter is done by the save instruction as part of the entry-point sequence of the called routine, and a corresponding restore instruction is done on exit. The save and restore also set the callee's stack pointer and reset it for the caller.

Aggregate Value Return

Some programming languages, including C, some dialects of Pascal, and Modula-2, allow the user to define functions which return an aggregate value, such as a **C struct** or a Pascal **record.** Since such a value generally does not fit into the registers, another value-returning protocol must be used to return the value in memory. Reentrancy and efficiency considerations require that the memory used to hold such a return value be allocated by the function's caller. The address of this memory area is passed as the one-word hidden parameter mentioned in the above section. Because of the lack of type safety in the C language, a function should not assume that its caller is expecting an aggregate return value and has provided a valid memory address. Thus some additional handshaking is required.

When a procedure expecting to be returned an aggregate function value is compiled, an unimplemented instruction (unimp) is placed at the point to which the callee would ordinarily return. The immediate field in this instruction is the low-order twelve bits of the size in bytes of the aggregate value expected. When an aggregate-returning function is about to return its value

		Previous Stack Frames
fp, old sp →	. . .	
	Local stack space for addressable automatic variables	Current Stack Frame
	Dynamically allocated stack space	
	Local stack space for compiler temporaries and saved floating-point registers	
	Outgoing parameters past the sixth	
	6 words into which callee may store register arguments	
	One-word hidden parameter (address of caller-allocated space for aggregate return value)	
sp →	16 words in which to save *in* and *local* registers	
	↓ Stack Growth (Decreasing Memory Addresses)	

FIGURE 18.1. *Memory stack layout for an active routine.*

in the memory allocated by its caller, it first tests for the presence of this unimp instruction in the caller's instruction stream. If it is found, and the size is appropriate, the function returns control to the location following the unimp instruction. Otherwise, no value can be returned. Conversely, if a scalar-returning function is called when an aggregate value is expected, the function returns as usual, executing the unimp instruction and causing a trap. For example, suppose we define in C a pair-of-integers type PAIR

```
typedef struct pair
{      int first;
       int second;
{      PAIR;
```

and call

```
PAIR p13;
p13 = make_pair(1,3);
```

with make_pair defined by

```
PAIR  make_pair(m,n)
       int m, n;
{      PAIR p;
       p.first = m;
       p.second = n;
       return p;
}
```

Then the call to make_pair generates

```
add       %sp,LP15,%o0        !    construct 1-word hidden
                                   parameter
st        %o0, [%sp+64]       !    and save it in stack frame
mov       1,%o0               !    set up first argument
call      _make_pair               ! call the routine
mov       3,%o1               !    set up second argument
                              !    in delay slot of call
unimp     8
sub       %fp,8,%o1           !    move the returned value
ld        [%o0],%o2           !    to its destination
ld        [%o0+4],%o3
st        %o2,[%o1]
st        %o3,[%o1+4]
```

and returning the structure from the subroutine is carried out by a special leaf routine which does the following (on entry to it, i7 contains the address of the call to make_pair, o0 contains the address of the struct being returned, and o1 contains the number of bytes the called routine expects to return):

```
        ld      [%i7+8],%o3         !   fetch 2nd instruction
                                        beyond the call
        and     %o1,0xfff,%o4       !   extract low-order 12
                                        bits of size
        sethi   %hi(UNIMP),%o5      !   put high-order 20
                                        bits of unimp in o5
        or      %o4,%o5,%o5         !   combine opcode and
                                        size
        cmp     %o5,%o3             !   compare with 2nd
                                        instr. beyond call
        bne     LE12               !   branch to return if
                                        no match
        nop
            . . .
! copy the struct from [%o0], using the same loop the compiler
! does for large structure assignment
            . . .
        add     %i7,4,%i7   !  bump return address beyond unimp
LE12:
        jmp     %i7+8       !  return
        restore             !  restore register window
```

Integer Multiplication and Division

SPARC provides no integer multiply, divide or remainder instructions, so these operations are synthesized from more elementary instructions. There is a multiply step instruction mulscc[2], but even that is not used to multiply variables by constants. Instead multiplication by constants known at compile time is done using sequences of shifts and adds (subtracts are used also if overflow detection is not an issue). For example, multiplication by 30 in a C program is done by the following sequence:

```
        sll     %o2,1,%o2      !      2 * x → x
        sll     %o2,4,%o3      !      16 * x → y
        sub     %o3,%o2,%o2    !      y − x → x
```

---

[2] The "cc" indicates that the instruction sets the integer condition codes.

Multiplication of variables by variables and all divisions and remainders other than by powers of 2 are done by calling special leaf routines. Based on statistics gathered from running an instrumented version of the system, the routines are biased so as to terminate quickly for the common cases, namely either operand being short in a multiply and the operands of a divide or remainder being about the same length. For example, for multiplication the length of the smaller operand determines the cycle count as follows:[3]

Length (in bits)	Cycles
1 to 4	18
5 to 8	25
9 to 12	33
13 to 16	41
17 to 32	60

TABLE 18.2.

Our measurements show that over 90% of var × var multiplications have at least one nonnegative operand. They also show that over 90% of the time one of the operands is at most seven bits long and 99% of the time one is at most nine bits long. Combining the statistics on the distribution of operands presented in [MagP87] with our own measurements, we estimate that the average multiplication (including both the constant- and variable-operand cases) takes under six cycles and the average var × var subcase takes about 24 cycles.

Tagged Data Support & Explicit Trapping

In addition to the ordinary add and subtract instructions, SPARC provides versions which interpret the low-order two bits of a word as a type tag. If the tags of the two operands are not both zero (or if arithmetic overflow occurs in the add or subtract operation) the

---

[3] These are for the case of a nonnegative multiplier. Negative multipliers require one more cycle for operands up to 16 bits long and up to four more cycles for longer operands.

integer overflow condition code bit is set and (optionally) an overflow trap occurs. These tagged arithmetic instructions are intended
to be used in implementations of languages such as Common Lisp
and Smalltalk which allow polymorphic functions. Sun Common
Lisp currently uses the tagged instructions and has never existed
in a form which did not use them [Kaph87]. They cut the time
necessary to do fixnum (integer) addition and subtraction from six
cycles to three (or five to two, if the delay slots of the branches
below can be filled productively). In particular, if one tags fixnums
with the low-order two bits zero, then adding two tagged values in
registers can be done by

taddcc	%11,%12,%o1	!	add tagged & set cond. codes
bvs	nonfixnum	!	branch on overflow or nonzero tag
nop			

instead of

or	%11,%12,%o1	!	extract or of tags
and	%o1,3,%o1		
bnz	nonfixnum	!	branch on nonzero tag
add	%11,%12,%o2		
bvs	nonfixnum	!	branch on overflow
nop			

ParcPlace Smalltalk does not currently use the tagged instructions (and may never do so) because of some incompatible historical choices made in its tagging mechanism. The implementors
estimate that they would increase overall performance about 2.5%
[Deut87], but the Sun-4 is already the fastest Smalltalk engine
available by a large margin anyway [Smal87].

Ada [Ada83] provides for the raising of exceptions during
expression evaluation for certain operand values, but does not
require an exception until the data value is actually stored. Thus,
for example, one can compute an expression with halfword data in
32-bit arithmetic and only raise an exception if the final result is too
large to store in a halfword. SPARC's explicit trap on condition
instruction ticc accomodates this optimization by allowing one to
generate (assuming 11 contains the value of the expression and g3
has been previously set to 2^{16}) the code

| subcc | %g3,%11,%g0 | ! | set cond. codes & discard arith. result |
| tleu | overflow | ! | trap on ≤ unsigned |

once before the store, rather than after each operation. Thus there is no loss of efficiency in implementing Ada arithmetic compared to architectures like the VAX which provide halfword arithmetic.

SPARC Compilers

As noted above, Sun provides SPARC compilers for C, FORTRAN with VMS Extensions, Modula-2 and Pascal. All four are based on the same technology as used in our previous Sun-2 and Sun-3 compilers, as described in [GhoM86]. Since that paper describes the basic technology in detail, we concentrate here on the new SPARC-oriented components and the additional optimizations which have been added recently for all Sun architectures.

The SPARC versions of the C, FORTRAN and Pascal compilers include global optimization and all four include a new code generator, assembler and peephole optimizer targeted to SPARC. The compilers are structured as shown in Figure 18.2. The component names which may not be familiar are as follows:

- *aliaser* determines which variables may at some time point to the same location;
- *iropt* is the global optimizer;
- *cgrdr* translates the Sun IR intermediate code used by the global optimizer into the PCC trees [John81] expected by the code generator;
- *c2* is the assembly level optimizer.

The arrows describe the path followed when global optimization and inlining are both enabled. When either is disabled, certain components are skipped, in some cases depending on the source language being compiled.

In contrast to our Sun-2 and Sun-3 compilers, which ran *c2* as a separate pass before the assembler, the SPARC *c2* is integrated into the assembler and operates on an internal linked-list form of the assembly language. This results in nontrivial savings in compilation time, since we read and write one less intermediate file.

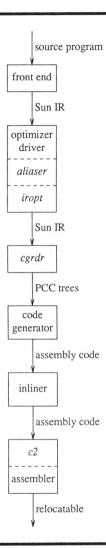

FIGURE 18.2. *Structure of the SPARC optimizing compilers.*

The compilers support several levels of optimization which require various amounts of compilation time and produce various qualities of code. For example, the C compiler has four levels of optimization (in addition to the "no optimization" level):

O1 This invokes only the peephole optimizer.

O2 This and the following levels invoke both the global and peephole optimizers. At the O2 level, expressions involving global variables and pointers are not candidates for optimization.

O3 Expressions involving global variables are optimized, but worst case assumptions are made about pointers.

O4 This level traces, as assiduously as possible, what pointers may point to.

In general, the amount of compilation time required and the speed of the resulting code increase as the optimization level increases. However, it is interesting to note that O3 and O4 almost always produce the same code, but that compilation with O4 tends to be slightly faster because it typically uses less virtual memory. Some examples for which O4 does produce better code than O3 are C programs which take the addresses of local variables and then dereference them and Pascal programs containing with statements.

Source-Language Compatibility

Efficient use of the SPARC architecture requires more stringent interpretation of a few points in the programming languages we support, and particularly in C. The following are a few examples:

1. Pointer punning

   The Sun-2 and Sun-3 architectures support accessing (4-byte) words on any even-byte boundary in memory, though one pays a significant performance penalty for references to data not aligned on boundaries corresponding to their sizes. SPARC loads and stores, in contrast, trap if the memory address is not aligned on the corresponding boundary. So, for example, casting a C character string pointer to a pointer to an integer is likely to produce a trap when it is dereferenced. Similarly, passing a pointer to a short integer as a parameter to a routine which expects a pointer to an integer may produce a trap.

2. Aggregate construction

For the same reason as item (1) above, the rules for aligning and packing elements of data aggregates are different on SPARC than on previous Sun systems. For example, a C structure containing a character item followed by a pointer item will have the pointer item placed on a word boundary on SPARC, but on only an even boundary for Sun-2 or Sun-3. This applies to all Sun languages, not just C.

3. Aggregate and union parameter passing

Because previous Sun architectures pass parameters in the memory stack, because of their less stringent alignment restrictions, and because C does not require type checking across procedure call boundaries, it is possible on Sun-2 and Sun-3 systems to pass, e.g., three integers as separate parameters to a routine expecting to receive a single parameter which is a structure consisting of three integers. This should always have been an error, and on SPARC systems it is. A similar mismatch occurs if an element of a union is passed to a routine expecting to receive a parameter of the union type.

4. Variable-type argument lists

On previous Sun architectures it was possible, in most cases, to write routines which accepted arguments of varying types in C without using the varargs macros, though this was highly non-portable. SPARC requires that varargs be used, since most parameters are passed in registers by default.

Also, again because most parameters are passed in registers on SPARC, our new compilers differ from our Sun-2 and Sun-3 compilers in the order of evaluation of parameters to procedure calls. Depending on the evaluation order is, of course, highly non-portable anyway.

The conversion of our compilers to SPARC was, in addition, taken as an opportunity to obsolete a few constructs in C which most programmers have long ago stopped using, namely the so-called old-fashioned initializers and assignment operators (see Sec. 17 of the C Reference Manual[KerR78]). In addition, we now treat enumerated type values as integers.

The Global and Peephole Optimizers

The SPARC global optimizer *iropt* is shared with our Sun-2 and Sun-3 compilers. Tailoring it for one architecture or another involves describing the register model to the global register allocator and tuning a few other components in minor ways, such as to determine which types of common subexpressions are worth reevaluating rather than saving and the degree of loop unrolling appropriate to use. Note that we use the term "global optimizer" in the sense in which it is most frequently used in the compiler literature—to refer to an optimizer which works on whole procedures, rather than basic blocks; our global optimizer currently makes no attempt to do interprocedural optimization.

The global optimizer performs the following optimizations:

1. Loop-invariant code motion
2. Induction-variable strength reduction
3. Common subexpression elimination (local & global)
4. Copy propagation (local & global)
5. Register allocation (modified graph coloring)
6. Dead code elimination
7. Loop unrolling
8. Tail recursion elimination

Inlining of language-defined (and user) routines is done by a separate pass after code generation and before peephole optimization. The peephole optimizer does

1. Elimination of unnecessary jumps
2. Elimination of redundant loads and stores
3. Deletion of unreachable code
4. Loop inversion
5. Utilization of machine idioms
6. Register coalescing
7. Instruction scheduling

8. Leaf routine optimization

9. Cross jumping

10. Constant propagation

Most of these optimizations are discussed in [GhoM86], and so we shall discuss only the new ones in detail here, namely tail recursion elimination, loop unrolling and leaf routine optimization, and make a few comments about inlining and instruction scheduling as they apply to SPARC.

Tail Recursion Elimination

Given a self-recursive procedure whose only action upon being returned to is to itself return (and to always return the same value, if any), tail recursion elimination converts the body of the procedure into a loop. Thus, for example, the following C routine to insert a node into a linked list

```
void  insert_node(n,1)
      int n;
      struct node *1;
{     if (n > 1->value)
          if (1->next == nil) make_node(&1->next,n);
          else insert_node(n,1->next);
}
```

is compiled as if it were

```
void insert_code(n,1)
     int n;
     struct node *1;
{loop:
     if (n > 1->value)
         if (1->next == nil) make_node(&1->next,n);
         else
         {  1 = 1->next;
            goto loop;
         }
}
```

On SPARC this typically saves register window overflows and underflows and on all Sun architectures it saves stack allocation, manipulation and deallocation.

Call by reference (or the ability to pass the address of a local variable to another routine, as found in C) poses some tricky issues when combined with recursion. The following Pascal program illustrates this:

```
program tailrec(output);
var x, y: integer;
procedure f(var a, b: integer; n: integer);
     var c: integer;
     begin
          c := 0;
          if n = 0
          then begin
               a := 4;
               writeln(b)
          end
          else if n = 1
          then
               f(b,c,0)
          else
               f(b,c,1);
     end;
begin
     f(x,y,2);
end.
```

During the third recursive invocation of f( ), with n = 0, a and b point to the previous two invocations' local variables c, respectively. If tail recursion elimination folds the c's into a single location, the program prints 4, rather than 0. Thus it may be essential that two invocations of a tail-recursive routine have different stack areas for their local variables. Our optimizer detects this situation and suppresses the tail recursion elimination.

A trickier situation occurs in C: one can call a routine with different numbers of parameters in different calls, so that a tail recursive call inside the routine might have more parameters than some call from outside it, resulting in different stack space requirements. Currently the global optimizer has no way to detect this, since we do not attempt interprocedural data flow analysis and optimization.

Loop Unrolling and Instruction Scheduling

Loop unrolling replaces the body of a loop with several copies of the body, adjusting the loop control code accordingly. While this optimization is generally valuable for loops with constant bounds, since it reduces the overhead of looping, it is particularly valuable for an architecture like SPARC because it typically increases the effectiveness of instruction scheduling.

We apply loop unrolling to loops which satisfy four conditions. Namely, the loop must

1. contain only a single basic block (i.e. straight-line code)
2. generate at most 40 triples of Sun IR code[4]
3. contain floating-point operations
4. have simple loop control

If the conditions are satisfied, the loop body is copied once. A special compiler flag makes it possible to unroll more copies in the relatively rare cases where that is appropriate.

SPARC has branches with a one-instruction delay and with an option to annul conditionally (i.e., not execute) the delay slot instruction. SPARC's load instructions may overlap with the execution of the following instruction, if that instruction does not use the value loaded. Also, it allows integer instructions and one or more floating-point instructions (how many is implementation-dependent) to proceed in parallel. The implementation used in the Sun-4, in particular, allows one floating-point additive operation and one floating-point multiplicative operation at the same time. So the Sun-4 instruction scheduler must pay attention to scheduling as many as four types of operations at once:

1. A branch or load
2. An integer unit instruction other than a branch or load

---

[4] This restriction is imposed in order to keep the unrolled blocks of code relatively short, so as not to expand the object code unduly.

3. An additive floating-point instruction

4. A multiplicative floating-point instruction

It uses the technique described in [GibM86] and, in general, is quite effective. For example, for the Stanford benchmark, adding instruction scheduling to the other optimizations performed at level O3 increases performance on the individual benchmark components by anywhere from 8 to 20%. Measured statically, our scheduler utilizes all but 5% of the branch delay slots in the Stanford benchmark and fills 49% of them without resorting to annulment. Also statically, about 74% of loads are scheduled so that the immediately following instruction does not use the target of the load, and almost all the remaining 26% are in basic blocks which are so short that there is no possible alternative.

In-Line Expansion

In-line expansion provides a way for the compiler writer or user to specify assembly language code sequences to replace source-language calls. The expansion is done by a separate pass between code generation and peephole optimization.

As (a trivial) example of inlining, one can specify that instead of generating a call instruction for add(j,k) in the C routine example below

```
int  example(j,k)
     register int, j, k;
{    int i;
     i = j − k;
     i = add(j,k);
     return i;
}
int  add(a,b)
     int a, b;
{    return a + b;
}
```

the compiler should use the in-line expansion template

```
.inline   _add,8
add       %o0,%o1,%o0
.end
```

While such expansions save execution time by replacing procedure calls by in-line code, their greatest benefit comes from introducing opportunities for further optimization in the peephole optimizer. In the above example the peephole optimizer discovers, after inlining that add( ) has no side effects, so that the value of i is computed by i = j − k is dead and hence its computation can be removed—something it could not have determined without the in-line expansion, since we do not do interprocedural analysis.

The SPARC architecture defines an interface for a second implementation-defined coprocessor (in addition to the floating-point unit). Inlining could profitably be used to provide smooth, efficient access to its operations from higher-level languages.

Leaf Routine Optimization

As mentioned in leaf routines (routines which call no others) are comparatively common (refer to earlier discussion on procedure call and entry). If a leaf routine uses few registers and needs no local stack, it can be entered and exited with the minimum possible overhead by omitting the save and restore and adjusting the register numbers used in it correspondingly. This also reduces the number of register window overflows and underflows incurred. For example, the trivial routine

```
int  leaf(i,j)
    int i, j;
{   int k;
    return i + 3 * j;
}
```

would be naively compiled as

```
_leaf:
        save  %sp,−64,%sp    !  slide register window and stack
        sll   %i1,1,%o1      !  2 * j --> %o1
        add   %i1,%o1,%o0    !  3 * j --> %o0
        add   %i0,%o0,%i0    !  i + 3 * j --> value register
        jmp   %i7+8          !  return
        restore             !  and restore register window
```

but with leaf routine optimization as

```
_leaf:
    sll   %o1,1,%o2    !   2 * j --> %o2
    add   %o1,%o2,%o1  !   3 * j -- %o1
    jmp   %o7+8        !   return (delayed branch)
    add   %o0,%o1,%o0  !   and put i + 3 * j --> value register
```

Saving a minimum of two cycles, and possibly significantly more—if it causes fewer register window overflows to be incurred and if it saves a large amount of stack space. While this optimization frequently does not make very much difference, it is occasionally significant. For example, in our standard benchmark of C compiler performance (i.e. measuring the compiler itself, not the code it produces) when compiled with O3 optimization, it reduces register window overflows by 15%.

Compiler Performance Analysis

In this section we present several sorts of performance comparisons, evaluating SPARC-based Sun-4 systems against MC68020-based Sun-3 systems, and showing the effects of various types of optimization on the Sun-4.

Sun-4 vs. Sun-3 Performance

The benchmark numbers which follow provide a very quick comparison of two varieties of Sun-3's with the Sun-4. We close the section with a Sun-4 vs. Sun-3 comparison of code and total program size (Tables 18.3 through 18.6).

The Sun-3/100 Series is based on a 16.67 MHz Motorola MC68020 with a 16.67 MHz MC68881 Floating-Point Processor and an optional Sun Floating-Point Accelerator (FPA), while the Sun-3/200 Series is based on a 25 MHz Motorola MC68020 with a 20 MHz MC68881 Floating-Point Processor and an optional Sun FPA. In both cases the Sun FPA is based on the Weitek 1164/1165 floating-point arithmetic units running at 16.67 MHz. The Sun-4/200 Series is based on the Fujitsu SPARC SF9010 Integer Unit (IU) and Floating-Point Controller (FPC) and the same Weitek 1164/1165, all running at 16.67 MHz. The measured Sun-3 and Sun-4 systems were all running either SunOS Release 3.2 or Release 4.0 and, in all cases, were running globally optimizing compilers at the −O3 level of optimization.

Dhrystone in C (Version 1.1) Dhrystone instr. per sec.	
Sun-3/100	3850
Sun-3/200	7140
Sun-4/200	19000

TABLE 18.3.

C compiler (in C) times in seconds	
Sun-3/100	11.7
Sun-3/200	6.4
Sun-4/200	3.2

TABLE 18.4.

	Stanford (Hennessy) in C times in milliseconds		
	Sun-3/100 +FPA	Sun-3/200 +FPA	Sun-4/200
Perm	752	412	110
Towers	950	484	175
Queens	302	176	90
Intmm	404	248	150
Puzzle	1816	1088	553
Quick	344	200	97
Bubble	390	232	120
Tree	1242	696	203
Mm	498	376	253
FFT	840	584	461

TABLE 18.5.

The first benchmark we consider is Weicker's Dhrystone [Weic84] program, Version 1.1, in C. This is a synthetic integer-only benchmark which attempts to simulate the performance of systems code, but which, to a considerable extent, measures string copy and string compare.

100 × 100 Linpack in FORTRAN (rolled loops) MFLOPS		
	single	double
Sun-3/100 + FPA	0.62	0.40
Sun-3/200 + FPA	0.86	0.46
Sun-4/200	1.6	1.1

TABLE 18.6.

Next we consider the Sun-3 C compiler compiling a section of itself.

The Stanford or Hennessy benchmark suite consists of several routines which compute permutations, solve some puzzles (Towers of Hanoi, Eight Queens, and Forest Baskett's blocks puzzle), multiply matrices (integer and floating-point), compute a floating-point fast Fourier transform, and sort in three different ways (quick, bubble, and tree). Only the components below the double line involve floating point.

The Linpack benchmark [Dong86] is a FORTRAN program which measures solving of linear equations and which has been measured on many machines. The case we report here is for 100 × 100 matrices with rolled loops.

Effect of Optimizations

In this section we compare the effects of the optimizations performed by the global and peephole optimizers in various ways, in all cases by observing their effects on the Stanford benchmark (Tables 18.7 through 18.10). Our first table compares the effect on SPARC code of the four levels of optimization provided by the C compiler: O1, O2, O3 and O4. In all tables in this section, the numbers represent percentage improvements in execution time[5] over totally unoptimized code. For these benchmarks, O1 improves the code's execution time by an average of 21%, O2 by an average of 57%, and both O3 and O4 by an average of 59%, though

---

[5] For example, the number 54 at the intersection of row Towers and column O2 in the first table indicates that Towers compiled with O2 optimization runs in $(100 - 54)\% = 46\%$ of the time a totally unoptimized version of Towers requires.

Effect of Optimization Levels Percentage improvements				
	O1	O2	O3	O4
Perm	28	62	62	62
Towers	26	54	57	57
Queens	16	58	58	58
Intmm	17	55	56	56
Puzzle	28	68	73	73
Quick	27	60	63	63
Bubble	25	64	73	73
Tree	13	77	81	81
Mm	14	45	47	47
FFT	16	28	28	28

TABLE 18.7.

Global vs. Peephole Percentage improvements		
	O3, no peephole	O3
Perm	28	62
Towers	35	57
Queens	40	58
Intmm	46	56
Puzzle	54	73
Quick	40	63
Bubble	53	73
Tree	74	81
Mm	35	47
FFT	25	28

TABLE 18.8.

there is considerable variation from one benchmark component to another.

Next we compare the effect of O3 optimization for SPARC with and without the peephole optimizer.

On the average, doing only the global optimizations in O3 improves the code by 43%, compared to full O3's 59%.

Finally, we show the effect of the accumulation of optimiza-

	1	2	3	4	5	6	7	8
	Effect of Individual Optimizations Percentage improvements							
Perm	24	24	17	17	14	23	62	62
Towers	21	23	22	23	18	28	57	57
Queens	17	20	16	−16	0	3	58	58
Intmm	16	17	23	14	25	26	56	56
Puzzle	28	28	38	−6	21	20	73	73
Quick	24	29	25	4	0	4	63	63
Bubble	25	25	22	−6	1	0	73	73
Tree	11	63	61	62	59	66	81	81
Mm	16	16	22	13	20	21	47	47
FFT	12	12	12	−3	9	10	26	28

TABLE 18.9.

tions for SPARC. In particular, this table shows the effect of accumulating the optimizations done at level O3, in the order they are ordinarily performed. Each run includes peephole optimization, but only those global optimizations listed here:

Column 1: No global optimizations.

Column 2: Column 1 plus tail recursion elimination.

Column 3: Column 2 plus loop-invariant code motion.

Column 4: Column 3 plus induction-variable strength reduction.

Column 5: Column 4 plus common subexpression elimination.

Column 6: Column 5 plus copy propagation.

Column 7: Column 6 plus global register allocation.

Column 8: Column 7 plus loop unrolling (i.e. all global optimizations).

Note that some of the percentages are negative—in some cases the optimizations performed up to that point slow the code down. This is because some optimizations are done to create opportunities for

| | Programs with dynamic linking (after static linking) | | | | | |
| | sizes | | | | ratios | |
	Sun-3 text	Sun-4 text	Sun-3 total	Sun-4 total	text	total
ccom	188416	204800	310768	318640	1.09	1.03
troff	65536	81920	675136	691848	1.25	1.02
mailtool	65536	73728	90112	98304	1.13	1.09
make	65536	81920	88704	105648	1.25	1.19

TABLE 18.10.

later ones and we make no effort to clean up the code after each individual one. Also, note that the O1 percentages listed above and the column 1 percentages here are different, even though they both include only peephole optimizations. This is because the code produced for a C program by invoking O1 generates PCC trees directly, while the code measured in column 1 goes through the Sun IR phase, resulting in somewhat different code.

Code and Program Size

In this section we compare code and total program size for several large programs. We would include the Stanford benchmark, but it is too small to show a significant difference, due to UNIX's predilection for rounding sizes up to the next full page. Instead, we show ratios of sizes for the C compiler front end, the troff text formatter, the window-based mail handler, make, and the C and pixrect[6] libraries, compiled on the Sun-3 and Sun-4 with O2 optimization (Table 18.11).

The measurements were all collected on SunOS Release 4.0 systems and hence include the effects of shared libraries [GinL87]. With the advent of shared libraries, most executables are built without libraries linked in and are linked to shared instances of them dynamically at runtime. This results in considerable savings of both disk and memory space in return for a small time penalty.

---

[6] The pixrect library is one of the lower layers of the Sun View window system.

Static and dynamic libraries					
	sizes				ratios
	Sun-3 text	Sun-4 text	Sun-3 total	Sun-4 total	text	total
libc (static)	206832	223656	225160	255984	1.08	1.14
libpixrect (static)	104720	168048	129520	168448	1.60	1.30
libc (dynamic)	286720	311296	311296	393216	1.09	1.26
Libpixrect (dynamic)	114688	163840	122880	180224	1.43	1.47

TABLE 18.11.

The first table below shows sizes of the various programs after they have been linked, but before libraries have been linked into them.

The second table shows sizes of both static and dynamic versions of two libraries. The dynamic (i.e. shared) versions are larger because of the need to generate position-independent code and code to address separate copies of global variables for each use of the library.

Thus with O2-level optimization, SPARC code and whole programs are usually only marginally larger than Sun-3 code and whole programs, though code is occasionally as much as 60% larger and whole programs as much as about 50% larger.

Conclusions

The primary design considerations for SPARC were to provide an architecture which (1) is scalable through several technologies and performance levels, (2) is well-matched to available and near future compiler technology, (3) provides in its first implementation a significant performance improvement over previous Sun processors, and (4) could gain wide acceptance as an industry standard. This paper has concentrated on the second and third goals.

We have shown our compilers' model of the SPARC architecture, which is general enough to cover most modern programming languages and exploits SPARC's inherent performance to a considerable degree.

Opcode	Meaning
add	add
and	logical and
bne	branch on not equal
bnz	branch on not zero
bvs	branch on overflow set
call	call subroutine
cmp	compare (pseudo-op)
jmp	jump (pseudo-op)
ld	load word
mov	move register to register (pseudo-op)
nop	no operation (pseudo-op)
or	logical or
restore	restore previous register window
save	move to next register window
sethi	Set high 22 bits
sll	shift left logical
st	store word
sub	subtract
subcc	subtract and set condition codes
tadcc	tagged add and set condition codes
tleu	trap on less than or equal unsigned
unimp	unimplemented instruction

TABLE 18.12.

We have discussed the structure of our compilers and the effects of optimization. Optimization is very much more important to realizing the full performance of RISC systems than for the more traditional CISC systems, and consequently we expect to continue adding capabilities to our global and peephole optimizers over time.

Appendix, Reading SPARC Assembly Language

The notation used for SPARC assembly language in this paper (Table 18.12) is a subset of the full language, which is explained in [Asse88]. Instructions are written with an optional label field terminated by a colon ":", followed by the operation code, and the arguments. Comments begin with an exclamation point "!" and run to the end of the line. In all cases source operands precede the result operand.

The opcodes used in the paper and their meanings are as follows:

Pseudo-operations which generate no code, such as .inline and .end, are written with a leading period ".".

The registers are named as described at the end of Section 2, except that in the assembly language each is preceded by a percent sign "%". The names "%sp" and "%fp" are synonyms for the stack and frame pointers, respectively. The %hi( ) operator extracts the high-order 22 bits of its (32-bit) operand and %lo( ) extracts the low-order 13 bits.

The first operand of a three-operand instruction is always a register name. The second may be either a register name or a (13-bit signed) constant.

Storage is addressed by writing a sum in square brackets "[ ]". In a few other contexts, such as the target address of a jmp, the address is written as a sum, but without the brackets.

References

[Ada83] *Reference Manual for the Ada® Programming Language*, ANSI/Mil-Std-1815 A, United States Dept. of Defense, Jan. 1983, p. 11–9.

[Asse88] *Sun-4 Assembly Language Reference Manual*, Sun Microsystems, Mountain View, CA, Part No. 800-1788-05, 1988.

[ChoC87] Frederick Chow, Stephen Correll, Mark Himelstein, Earl Killian & Lawrence Weber, How Many Addressing Modes are Enough?, Proc. of Second Intl. Conf. on Arch. Support for Prog. Lang. and Oper. Syst., *SIGPLAN Notices*, vol. 22, no. 10, Oct. 1987, pp. 117–121.

[ChuQ88] Chueh, R. & L.T. Quach, CMOS Gate Array Implementation of SPARC, *Proc. of the 1988 COMPCON Conf.*, San Francisco, Mar. 1988.

[Deut87] Deutsch, L. Peter, Personal communication, 22 Oct. 1987.

[Dong86] Dongarra, John J., Performance of Various Computers Using Standard Linear Equations Software in a Fortran Environment, Tech. Memo. 23, Argonne National Lab., Argonne, IL, 17 Feb. 1986.

[GarA88] Garner, Robert, Anant Agrawal, Will Brown, David Hough, Bill Joy, Steve Kleiman, Steven Muchnick, Dave Patterson, Joan Pendleton & Richard Tuck, The Scalable Processor Architecture (SPARC), *Proc. of the 1988 COMPCON Conf.*, San Francisco, Mar. 1988.

[GhoM86] Ghodssi, Vida, Steven S. Muchnick & Alex Wu, A Global Optimizer for Sun FORTRAN, C and Pascal, *Proceedings of the Summer 1986 USENIX Conference,* June 1986, pp. 318–334.

[GibM86] Gibbons, Philip B. & Steven S. Muchnick, Efficient Instruction Scheduling for a Pipelined Architecture, *Proc. of SIGPLAN Symp. on Compiler Constr.,* Palo Alto, CA, June 1986.

[GinL87] Gingell, Robert A., Meng Lee, Xuong T. Dang & Mary S. Weeks, Shared Libraries in SunOS, *Proc. of the Summer 1987 USENIX Conf.,* June 1987, Phoenix, AZ, pp. 131–146.

[Goss88] Goss, L., CMOS Custom Chip Implementation of SPARC, *Proc. of the 1988 COMPCON Conf.,* San Francisco, Mar. 1988.

[John81] Johnson, S.C. A Tour Through the Portable C Compiler, Bell Laboratories Memo, Jan. 1981.

[Kaph87] Kaphan, Shel, Personal communication, 23 Oct. 1987.

[Kate83] Katevenis, Manolis, *Reduced Instruction Set Computer Architectures for VLSI,* Ph.D. dissertation, Computer Science Div., Univ. of California, Berkeley, 1983. Also published by M.I.T. Press, Cambridge, MA.

[KerR78] Kernighan, Brian W. & Dennis M. Ritchie, *The C Programming Language,* Prentice-Hall, Englewood Cliffs, NJ, 1978.

[Klei88] Kleiman, Steven & Dock Williams, SunOS on SPARC, *Proc. of the 1988 COMPCON Conf.,* San Francisco, Mar. 1988.

[MagP87] Magenheimer, Daniel J., Liz Peters, Karl Pettis & Dan Zuras, Integer Multiplication and Division on the HP Precision Architecture, *Proc. 2nd Intl. Conf. on Arch. Support for Prog. Lang. and Oper. Sys.,* Palo Alto, CA, Oct. 1987.

[Smal87] Smalltalk 80 on the Sun-4—Call for Beta Testers, *Smalltalk-80 Newsletter,* No. 11, Sept. 1987, p. 5.

[Solt88] Soltesz, L., A High Performance, High Density Bipolar Implementation of SPARC, *Proc. of the 1988 COMPCON Conf.,* San Francisco, Mar. 1988.

[SPAR87] *The SPARC Architecture Manual,* Sun Microsystems, Mountain View, CA, Part No. 800-1399-07, 1987.

[Unga87] Ungar, David, Ricki Blau, A. Dain Samples & David Patterson, Architecture of SOAR: Smalltalk on a RISC, *Proc. of 11th Annual Intl. Symp. on Comp. Arch.,* Ann Arbor, MI, June 1984.

[VAX79] *VAX11 Architecture Handbook,* Digital Equipment Corporation, 1979.

[Weic84] Weicker, R.P., Dhrystone: A Synthetic Systems Programming Benchmark, *CACM,* vol. 27, no. 10, Oct. 1984.

Development Tools for RISC: An Array of Tools for SPARC Designs

19

MAX BARON • KIM INGRAM • Kevin M. Kitagawa

Abstract

With the development of RISC technology, system performance is rapidly approaching a 100 MIPS. To remain competitive system developers must take full advantage of such advances. This paper describes the array of hardware and software tools available allowing developers to take advantage of the rapidly increasing SPARC technology by substantially reducing the development cycle for SPARC-based systems.

Introduction

The advent of RISC architectures has reduced the time expected between major improvements in microprocessors, SPARC™, or Scalable Processor ARChitecture, is a powerful but simple architecture that can be implemented with a minimum number of transistors and therefore the pace of such improvements has been and continues to be the fastest in the industry.

Several implementations are now available from semiconductor manufacturers such as Fujitsu Microelectronics, Cypress Semiconductor, LSI Logic, and BIT. The first Integer Unit (IU) implementation, from Fujitsu, only requires approximately 12,000 gate equivalents (plus 4,000 gate equivalents for a 7 register-window file). The small gate count places SPARC in the best position for implementation in very high speed technologies such as ECL and GaAs.

Simplicity of architecture has also allowed the fastest turnaround of new chipsets by semiconductor design teams. Three chipsets ranging from 10 to 20 integer VAX 11/780 equivalent

MIPS have been brought to market within the past 12 months. Two additional implementations, extending both the performance range (40–50 VAX 11/780 MIPS) and integration capability, will be available within the next 6 months. Floating point performance for the above implementations will range between 1.1 to 15.0 MFLOPS DP Linpack.

This rapid scaling of performance has created a demand for quick turnaround of system designs. System houses need to be able to track and take advantage of new microprocessor implementations. While designing implementations of its SPARC architecture, as well as during the development of its SPARC-based workstations, Sun has developed powerful tools to support all design phases ranging from definition of system architecture to software and hardware design. These tools will support all implementations of SPARC. This article is intended to provide an overview and capabilities of the tools which provide an improved system development cycle (Figure 19.1) where interdependencies between debugging software and hardware are reduced.

Hardware Development
System Design

SPARC based systems are easy to design. The processor's operations are easy to monitor, simplifying system test and debug. Nonetheless, good development tools are necessary, since they play a crucial role in reducing the length of the development cycle. To that purpose, system design tools have been stressed for SPARC to support designers from the very early stages of architecture definition, through the board level design stage, to final debug and integration.

System Architecture Definition

A system designer must first make architectural level decisions about his hardware. Criteria for these decisions include: expected workload, required throughput and response, and price. An architectural definition that will meet the specifications will be defined from these decisions. Some design teams rely on their past experience to make such decisions. Although, this can be done by

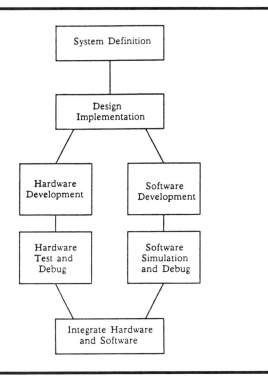

FIGURE 19.1. *System development cycle.*

few engineers, most of the time, their expertise is not available. Also, design decisions based on experience from previous failures will not always result in error free designs.

To be competitive, a system architecture must not only take full advantage of the capabilities of the microprocessor and other system resources, it must be designed correctly the first time. To help the system designer create the optimal system architecture, the SPARC Architectural Simulator (SPARCsim) was developed. SPARCsim is based on the architectural simulator that was used in the design of the Sun–4 family workstations.

SPARCsim allows the system designer to execute software representative of the expected workload on an architecture simulation of the SPARC and the associated system resources: memory management, caches, memory mapped devices, etc. The system designer can explore the interaction between workload and different resource configurations, and reach optimal solutions without wasting money and valuable time. SPARCsim generates workload traces, which not only can be used by user-specific simulators, but also can be used for the evaluation of generated code quality.

Having developed the system architecture, the system designer now can define the functional reference specification. This will allow the software designers to develop code based on these specifications, in parallel with hardware development. The quality of the software can be monitored and significant departures from the specifications flagged for improvement or design change.

Design Implementation

Detailed hardware design can now be started with good assurance that system-level changes are unlikely. The hardware designer can concentrate on the task of board-level design and simulation. Component level emulation is needed at this level of design. This emulation has to be fully integrated into CAD/CAE packages to give the designer the environment needed for hardware design and simulation.

Valid Logic is one of the companies providing state-of-the-art computer aided design tools for SPARC on Sun Workstations. These tools allow a designer to develop schematic drawings and simulate the logic to verify the hardware before committing to printed circuit board layout. Full simulation of a SPARC based design is supported by a SPARC H/W-S/W emulator, now part of Valid's Realproducts™ hardware simulation systems.

At this design level, changes impact only the schematic, and testing simply requires re-executing the simulation. Thus the breadboard phase of a SPARC-based design can be eliminated. The designer can go directly to layout for a prototype, especially when using high frequency chipsets performing at 20 VAX 11/780 MIPS at 33 MHz.

Prototype

Once the prototype is verified by simulation, it undergoes layout and fabrication. The prototype is then used in the initial tests and validation of hardware. This phase is necessary to eliminate errors associated with board layout and fabrication. While microprocessor hardware emulators may speed up prototype debug, their availability generally lags chip availability, especially in the case of very high frequencies of operation. To be competitive, systems designers must provide products long before emulators are available. System debug is therefore partitioned into two phases. First, hardware is debug to a minimal level of functionality and second, software monitors are used to bring the hardware to full functionality. Software monitors are inexpensive tools which can be used very effectively in the debug stage of new microprocessor hardware. Bringing up the hardware to the level of functionality required to use a software monitor is a simple task.

A number of different software monitors are available for use. The software monitors available with a number of SPARC evaluation boards perform many of the functions of a processor emulator. They allow uploading and downloading of code, setting of breakpoints, manipulation of data in registers and memory, single-stepping, and assembly/disassembly of user code. A logic analyzer provides a real-time trace capability allowing the designer to monitor the processor signals during software execution and compare them if required, to the results of the same program running on either a CAD/CAE emulator or SPARCsim.

The software monitor—logic analyzer approach provides a low cost debugging solution. It also has the ability to run the hardware at full processor speed, since none of the processor signals need to go through any emulator hardware.

Software Development

Software development usually begins on a UNIX-based development system. Using the software development and management tools on UNIX, the engineering team can begin to design and implement the modules of the application. Developers are free to use the usual UNIX tools such as text editors, compilers, assemblers, make, RCS, SCCS and so on. The application itself can make use of many of the libraries available from UNIX.

For SPARC targeted development, engineers can choose from two platforms. Although the native environment is based on the Sun–4 workstation, code can also be developed on a Sun–3 in a cross-development environment based on SunOS, a converged version of UNIX System V and Berkeley 4.3. SunOS delivers state-of-the-art virtual memory management, shared libraries, and dynamic linking, as well as the distributed services, administration, and security services. A typical software development cycle is shown in Figure 19.2. The unique software tools which assist in this cycle are discussed below.

Using the text editors available on the Sun platform source modules can be created and compiled. Available compilers for SPARC based development are: C, FORTRAN, Pascal, LISP and Ada. C, FORTRAN, and Pascal share the underlying language base tools. The set of language base tools includes a SPARC code generator, a global optimizer, a peephole optimizer, an assembler, a linker, and libraries.

High-Performance Optimization

The first phase of the compilation process involves scanning and parsing the source language. From this, the compiler generates an intermediate language called SunIR. SunIR was designed to remedy the shortcomings of the older PCC intermediate representation, which did not provide enough information to support the extensive control and data flow analysis required to perform global optimization.

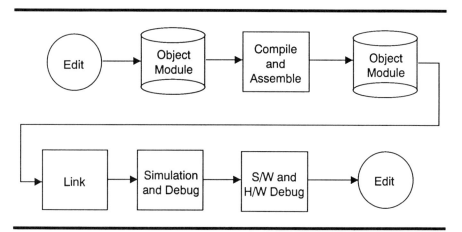

FIGURE 19.2. *Software development cycle.*

The global optimizer, IROPT, reads the SunIR code produced by the compiler front-end. A series of data-flow analyses and transformations are applied to the module, such as local and global common subexpression elimination, local and global copy propagation, loop-invariant code motion, tail-recursion elimination, dead code elimination, and global register allocation. IROPT fully handles memory aliasing, a difficulty in globally optimizing code from languages (such as C and Pascal) which have pointer variables. The use of the global optimizer has resulted in measured performance improvements of 10 to 80 percent, compared to unoptimized code.

Output of IROPT, in SunIR form, is read by the code generator, which produces SPARC assembly language. This assembly language is then processed by the peephole optimizer. Here instruction scheduling, register coalescing, brand chaining, creation of "leaf" routines, utilization of machine idioims, and several other straight-line code optimizations take place. The resulting code is then assembled into relocatable object code and linked with run-time libraries, system libraries or other compiler libraries, as needed.

Software Simulation

At this point, programmers can use SPARCsim to test and debug the object modules prior to the availability of actual target hardware. Not only does this save time, but the programmer does not have to contend with hardware implementation bugs. The simulator provides two levels of simulation: user-level and supervisor-level. User-level simulation is used to test programs such as compilers and linkers, where priviledged operations are not required. Supervisor-level simulation is used to develop operating system software. SPARCsim is rich with features to help the programmer. It contains debugging tools similar to the *adb* debugger available under the UNIX operating system. The debugger is an assembly-level symbolic debugger that supports breakpoints, single-stepping, and set/display of memory and registers, dynamic execution tracing, disassembly, etc. The simulator provides complete execution traces that can feed into other analysis tools, such as the SPARC Trace Analyzer (STA) tool. STA reports instruction counts, machine cycle counts, and the percentages of each. This feature helps the programmer pinpoint areas where execution time can be improved.

Debugging Support

After the software has been tested and debugged using the simulator, the designer can begin to test the debugged software on actual debugged hardware. Several programming support tools are available to assist at this stage of development. One such tool is *dbxtool*, a sophisticated symbolic debugger based on the 4.2BSD symbolic debugger, *dbx*, whose user interface is window-based and mouse-driven. By using the mouse instead of the keyboard as the primary input mechanism, *dbxtool* eliminates the need to type variables, line numbers, breakpoints, and most other commands. *Dbxtool's* windows give a view of the program being debugged and also detailed information about the state of the program, thus affording two qualitatively different perspectives on the debugging problem.

The debugger supports the entire edit-compile ("make")-link-debug cycle in a single integrated context. For example, when correcting a bug in the source code, the programmer enters the correction in the *dbxtool* source code subwindow. Then types make in the command subwindow, and *dbxtool* changes the module, recompiles it, and re-links the new object code into the program. The programmer then clicks the run button with the mouse, which reloads the program and restarts execution on the remote target system. For debugging support of remote non-UNIX target systems, there is a remote debugger *rdbxtool/rdbxmon*. The host component (rdbxtool) of the remove debugger not only provides full source-code symbolic debugging capabilities of *dbxtool* on a Sun workstation, but remote communication to a SPARC-based target system via serial link or ethernet. *rdbxtool* has the underlying functionality of *dbxtool* but also provides remote communications via serial link and/or Ethernet to the SPARC target. The target component (*rdbxmon*) is modular and configurable for any SPARC based target and allows downloading of programs, setting of execution breakpoints, and examining and modifying registers and memory, etc. In addition, the monitor provides initialization of the board, and diagnostics.

Conclusion

Fast system design turnaround time is crucial to a system houses in their competition with one another. Powerful system development tools are needed to maximize the productivity of system designers and programmers, thus minimizing the time delay between idea inception and finished product. The SPARC system H/W and S/W development tools provide a complete, highly efficient development environment, allowing their user to be first out with new products. These tools include third party hardware debug tools, such as Valid Logic, simulation tools, native and cross-compilers, remote debugging support, all available on a standard Sun development platform.

Sun's SPARC Embedded Development Tools

20

Kenji B. Armstrong

Introduction

The success of any embedded development project is often a reflection of the quality of the tools available to it. Developers wishing to use SPARC (Scalable Processor ARChitecture) as their processor have access to wide range of tools available on SPARC-based workstations, as well as Personal Computers. These tools range from editors to compilers, simulators, and remote debuggers. Sun is able to offer SPARC developers a package of tools running under SunOS which can contribute greatly to their success. The SPARC Embedded Development Toolkit (indicated by shading in Figure 20.1) consists of the SPARC Architectural Simulator (SPARCism)—an instruction-level simulator, RDBXtool—a windowed source level remote debugger, and SPARCmon—a monitor construction package. When used from system conception through implementation, these tools can aid the SPARC embedded developer in getting a product "out the door" expediently and with high quality.

SPARCsim

The SPARC Architectural Simulator (SPARCsim) is an instruction-level simulation tool which allows the embedded system designer to create a hardware system model upon which binary executables can be run. A trace facility and analysis tool are also available for analyzing the results of a particular execution run of a program. These powerful capabilities can play an important part in various phases of the design cycle:

1. Initial system analysis where hardware tradeoffs can be analyzed using actual code.

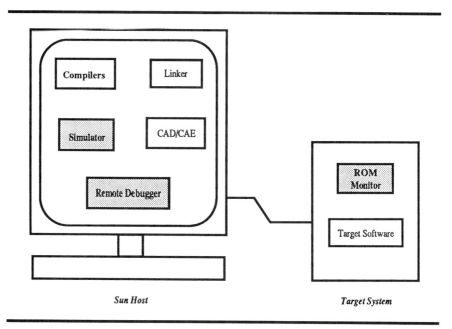

FIGURE 20.1. *SPARC development tools.*

2. Software design where software can be debugged on "perfect" hardware resulting in more mature and bug-free code before integration. Also, multiple programmers can have access to a hardware implementation prior to hardware and software integration. Traditionally, it has been costly to create prototypes to accommodate every programmer.

3. Hardware and software integration where more mature software results in a smoother integration period. In addition, existence of the software model allows the software designer to analyze possible problems which may have appeared during this phase.

SPARCsim has a modular architecture upon which to build a simulation model. It consists of a binary core encompassing an integer unit (IU), floating point unit (FPU), and simulation support

(See Figure 20.2). The integer unit emulates various implementations of the SPARC architecture (the Fujitsu Microelectronics MB86900, MB86901/LSI Logic L64801, Cypress Semiconductor CY7C601/LSI Logic L64811, and BIT B5000 chips). The floating point unit handles floating point instructions with cycle times supplied by a capabilities file. An example capabilities file is provided for user modification. Also available is a capabilities file for the Cypress CY7C602. Simulation support is provided in the form of the user interface, parameter input upon simulation start-up, debugger support, and hooks for additional user-provided simulation models.

The rest of the SPARCsim system architecture is built upon the binary core (see Figure 20.2). Here is where the flexibility of

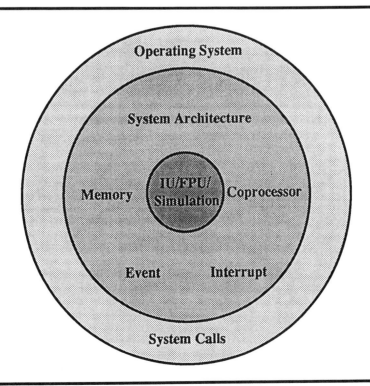

FIGURE 20.2. *SPARCsim architecture hierarchy.*

SPARCsim is revealed. The simulator provides mechanisms to model various entities present in an embedded system. Thus, support is provided for memory, system events, interrupts, co-processors, system architecture specific components, and even an operating system emulation. Each of these modules is created in C and can call other C routines or programs.

The memory support gives access to the memory interface of the SPARC Integer Unit. Devices that respond to memory requests can be simulated and attached to this interface. SPARCsim allows the building of a hierarchy of these memory devices so that a system including caches, memory management units, and memory-mapped I/O devices can be simulated.

The system event support provides the capability of scheduling time-dependent events. These events can be scheduled to occur per period of machine cycles or instructions. This mechanism allows the creation of system events such as periodic clocks or allows the simulation of device latency, such as disk head seek times.

The interrupt support provides the capability of responding to simulated external interrupts within the user created architecture. Support is provided for handling various types of interrupts: persisting, such as the TBE (Transmitter Buffer Empty) status line of a serial I/O device; non-persisting, such as the finished processing command of a disk controller; and missed interrupts, such as an unacknowledged non-persisting interrupt from a Counter/timer circuit (CTC). Interrupts can appear to the processor as either edges or levels.

The coprocessor interface provides the capability of simulating a coprocessor that would connect to the SPARC coprocessor interface. It is flexible enough to accommodate the range of uses for which coprocessors may be created. Features included are queues, registers, and the capability of handle cycle counting.

System architecture specific needs are handled in the simulator support interface. These system architecture specific routines fall into three categories: architecture-dependent command line options; initialization and re-initialization of the architecture-dependent parts of the simulation; and, handling user input destined for the configurable modules. Therefore, flexibility is built into SPARCsim to allow a variety of means for passing data between the user, the binary core of the simulation, and the configurable modules.

Finally, an environment can be added which provides operating system simulation. SPARCsim can be run in two modes, machine or user. In machine mode, the programmer must supply all the code running the system. This includes initialization routines and trap handlers. This mode is very useful for bootstrap software and supervisor level software. The second mode, user, provides an environment for the application programmer who usually does not worry about the low level activities. SPARCsim provides a model of a generic Sun–4 SPARC machine with a minimal set of SunOS 4.x system calls handled. Enough system call support is provided for simple I/O, use of the heap, and to allow the programmer to ignore the details of setting up the underlying hardware, as though programming for the usual UNIX System C programming environment. This was found useful in the performance test of critical algorithms. The embedded designer may choose to create a custom hardware system model with a custom operating system to provide to applications progammers.

Once a model of the hardware and software environment is created, SPARCsim provides the user with many capabilities for software development. It includes a symbolic debugger which can set breakpoints, single-step instructions, examine/modify memory, symbolically disassemble the code, and keep a trace buffer of executed instructions. With the trace analysis features (see Figure 20.3), cycle counts can be studied, executed instruction mixes can be viewed, and SPARC unique events can be examined (such as window overflows and underflows). This allows fine-tuning of the code for greater efficiency. SPARCsim can play an effective role in the development of an embedded system by providing a powerful simulation environment in which to develop software. At the same time, it can uncouple the dependencies between software and hardware resulting in fast development time. SPARCsim is shipped with source modules created to simulate a Sun–4 architecture, a Mizar SPARC board architecture, and a Cypress chip set including a cache/memory management unit. These example systems allow the embedded designer to get a running start on the creation of modules specific to their systems. For those who need it, the SPARCsim core is also licensable in source code format.

```
SPARC TRACE ANALYZER V-5
Integer Unit Version 4
Floating Point Unit Version 4

OBJECT FILE: `a.out'

TRACE SEGMENT: SUPERVISOR

instructions executed: 0
instructions annuled: 0
cycles used: 0 (assumes 100% cache hit)
includes 0 untaken branches
includes 0 cycles for pipeline interlocks
includes 0 cycles for FPU or Coprocessor dependencies
load instructions in which rD - rS[1,2]: 0

TRAPS:

INSTRUCTION PAIR DATA

TRACE SEGMENT: USER

instructions executed: 580501
instructions annuled: 11
cycles used: 690663 (assumes 100% cache hit)
includes 30050 untaken branches
includes 40053 cycles for pipeline interlocks
includes 0 cycles for FPU or Coprocessor dependencies
load instructions in which rD - rS[1,2]: 3
```

LOAD INSTRUCTIONS

opcode	attributes	count	percent	cycles	percent
ldsb	mem	3	0.00%	3	0.00%
ldsh	mem	10049	1.73%	10049	1.45%
lduh	mem	20000	3.45%	20000	2.90%
ld	mem	50009	8.61%	50009	7.24%
total		80061	13.79%	80061	11.59%

STORE INSTRUCTIONS

opcode	attributes	count	percent	cycles	percent
sth	mem	6	0.00%	12	0.00%
st	mem	30012	5.17%	60024	8.69%
total		30018	5.17%	60036	8.69%

SETHI INSTRUCTIONS

opcode	attributes	count	percent	cycles	percent
sethi		30011	5.17%	30011	4.35%
total		30011	5.17%	30011	4.35%

FIGURE 20.3. *Sample trace analysis output.*

RDBXtool

Often an embedded system consists only of limited system resources in the form of memory and on-board coding and debugging capabilities. Effective software development and debugging on these systems is difficult, if not impossible. RDBXtool, residing on a Sun host, is a remote debugger which allows the connection of the target embedded system to the more powerful Sun host system for software development and debugging. The only requirements on the target system are a serial port, for communications to the host, and a monitor which supports the Remote Debugging (RDB) protocol.

Code development is greatly enhanced on the Sun host with its large memory, disk system, windowed interface, and networking capabilities. Software developers have available the wealth of tools available under SunOS for program development. These include editors, assemblers, compilers, and profilers. Debugging is enhanced by the capabilities provided by RDBXtool.

RDBXtool is based upon the same interface as *dbxtool*, a bit map window and mouse-based, fully symbolic, source code-level debugger, which is familiar to many programmers on Sun workstations. This main window interface is divided into five subwindows (see Figure 20.4):

- Status—Gives the overall status of the debugging session, including the location at which execution has stopped, and the line numbers of the lines in the source subwindow

- Source—Displays the source text of the program being debugged; allows setting breakpoints (indicated by a stop sign icon); provides the capability of editing the source file; indicates the present location with an arrow icon

- Button—Contains user configurable buttons for frequently used commands; clicking on the button causes the associated command to be executed

- Command—Provides an interface for entry of commands not associated with a button; provides a history of commands issued during the debugging session; displays the output for most commands

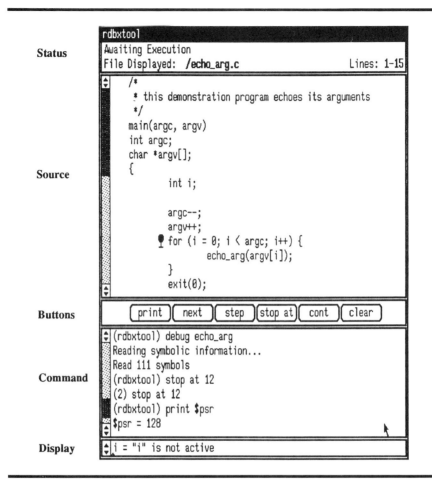

Status

Source

Buttons

Command

Display

```
rdbxtool
Awaiting Execution
File Displayed: /echo_arg.c                          Lines: 1-15
    /*
     * this demonstration program echoes its arguments
     */
    main(argc, argv)
    int argc;
    char *argv[];
    {
            int i;

            argc--;
            argv++;
          for (i = 0; i < argc; i++) {
                    echo_arg(argv[i]);
            }
            exit(0);
```

[print][next][step][stop at][cont][clear]

```
(rdbxtool) debug echo_arg
Reading symbolic information...
Read 111 symbols
(rdbxtool) stop at 12
(2) stop at 12
(rdbxtool) print $psr
$psr = 128
```

```
i = "i" is not active
```

FIGURE 20.4. *RDBXtool example window.*

• Display—Allows monitoring the values of selected user variables

RDBXtool provides many functions expected in a debugger. One such function is breakpoint manipulation. A user can set a breakpoint by selecting a source line (point at with cursor then click the mouse button) in the Source subwindow, then clicking on the "stop at" button in the Button subwindow. These breakpoints can be displayed and removed. Another powerful capability is the ability to set conditional breakpoints. A breakpoint can be set so that it can only occur when the value of an arbitrary C expression is true, e.g.:

stop at 73 if ((i==5) && (ptr−>next==foo[n]))

A breakpoint can also be set to occur only when the value of a specified variable changes. This is particularly useful for pinpointing when the value of a variable is getting unexpectedly changed during execution. The display of pertinent information is also important to the software designer and RDBXtool provides a full set of capabilities. A user is able to see the values of all SPARC registers (window and special purpose), variables, symbolic addresses, and memory locations in decimal, hexadecimal, octal, as machine instructions, floating point numbers, or even characters or strings as appropriate. Because the tool knows the types of all variables, it can even display complex variables such as a structure consisting of integers, characters, and pointers.

Other capabilities of RDBXtool include the ability to create aliases of commands and sets of commands, searching for specific strings in the source file, assigning values to variables, printing function call backtraces, and of course, starting, stopping, continuing, and single-stepping (by line or through entire procedures).

The final and most differentiating feature of RDBXtool to the embedded designer is the capability for communicating with a target system. Commands are provided to set the baud rate for communication, open the communication path, and download code to the target. Communication is accomplished via the RDB (Remote DeBugging) protocol talking over a serial communication link. Physical layer communications is presently supported via RS-232C.

RDB Protocol

The RDB protocol is an application level protocol whose full specifications are provided along with the RDBXtool package. It requires a host component and a target system server component. The protocol was designed to minimize the memory impact on the target system. The host system is responsible for providing:

- the debugger user interface
- source file handling
- expression evaluation
- symbol and string table information
- section and file header information

The target system server provides all the services needed to control and report on the execution of the remote program, such as:

- initializing and starting the program
- reading and writing memory locations
- setting and clearing breakpoints
- reading and writing registers

The RDB Protocol was designed with the following criteria in mind:

1. The protocol must be independent of the host and target operating system

2. The protocol must be independent of the host and target system architectures

3. The protocol must be independent of the object file format used to store a target program

4. The protocol must be simple and non-intrusive; it should require a minimal amount of system resources from the target machine.

5. The protocol must provide the following debugging capabilities:

- initialize a remote program for running
- start a remote program running
- single-step a remote program
- set and clear breakpoints
- read and write memory locations on the target machine

• read and write registers on the target machine

• suspend the execution of a remote program

• continue the execution of a remote program

• terminate the execution of a remote program

The protocol supports the exchange of binary data in the industry standard External Data Representation (XDR) format developed by Sun, which allows the debugging of a SPARC target from either a SPARC or a non-SPARC host system. This enables any type of host to be used, even one with a different native byte ordering than SPARC (such as an Intel processor architecture). This protocol is used by RDBXtool in versions for the Sun–3 (Motorola 680×0) and Sun–4 (SPARC) systems.

SPARCmon

The third component of Sun's embedded development toolkit is SPARCmon. SPARCmon is a package of source code for the creation of an on-board monitor for a SPARC target system. It consists of system components and library routines primarily coded in C with some assembly language routines. Because it is a toolkit of routines, SPARCmon is not delivered in a PROM format, however, full source code is provided. This gives the SPARC software developer a head start in coding for the SPARC system, as well as proven example code from which to work. SPARCmon can be a base upon which to build more complex software systems. The major components of SPARCmon are the Core (initialization and trap handlers), Command Interpreter, Process Control, Floating-point Support, Debugger Interface, I/O Interface, Download Interface, and Utility routines.

The Core module consists of the initialization routines and trap handlers. Board specific initialization routines have been separated to make porting easier. The trap handlers deal with traps in both the monitor and the target code. Also included is debugger support, register window underflow and overflow code, as well as code for returning to a saved process state. Additionally, there is a mechanism for temporarily intercepting traps, which is suitable for applications like peek and poke routines.

The Command Interface provides a table-driven command parser and a set of command routines to provide basic monitor functionality. The user can customize this command set by adding, deleting, or replacing commands. The entire command interface can even be replaced if desired.

The Process Control module is a set of framework routines, structures, and utilities which together with the trap handlers provide single target process control and debugging functions. It provides the underlying functionality required by the Command Interface and Remote Debugger Interfaces.

The Floating-point code includes a set of trap handlers which provide basic floating-point support. This includes handlers for IEEE exceptions, simulation of unimplemented and unfinished floating-point operations, and software emulation of floating-point (if no FPU is present). The Debugger Interface employs the same RDB protocol as used by RDBXtool. SPARCmon implements the debugger server part of the communication link. This protocol allows source level debugging of the target task. This section may be replaced with a user provided protocol to communicate with other debuggers.

The I/O Interface provides a standard way to interface with user provided device drivers. These drivers need to be provided for board specific devices. The interface also handles the communications for the command interface via a console and to the host system using the RDB protocol.

The download interface provides the facility for downloading code from a host system. Three different formats for downloading data are supported:

1. Motorola S-record—a de facto industry standard format for embedded systems

2. Fast download—disjoint blocks of code are transferred, such as text or data segments

3. Raw byte download—a byte stream is passed with address and size

Utility routines are included to aid the user in the creation of a monitor and target code. These include a library of C type functions for character and string manipulation, as well as conversion routines for converting among ASCII, decimal, and hexadecimal. Routines are also provided for debugging capabilities.

Because SPARCmon is meant for the creation of monitors, it is implemented with both simplicity and modularity in mind. Thus, the embedded designer can "mix-and-match" functionality as desired or can add or remove functions easily. Sections of the monitor can be removed as development proceeds and their need diminishes to minimize the size of the ROM. The approximate memory usage for an example system is given in Table 20.1 (memory in kilobytes).

These figures are taken from the Mizar MZ 7170 (a SPARC-based VME bus board) version of a SPARCmon PROM. These numbers will vary as user supplied target code and board specific drivers and initialization routines are created. To aid the designer in creating a stand alone monitor, the entire source code of the Mizar PROM is included with the product.

Section	Text	Data	Bss
Core	21	8	2
Command	34	0	1
Process	2	0	0
Floating-point	30	0	1
RDB server	10	0	1
I/O	14	0	6

TABLE 20.1. *Mizar MZ 7170 memory estimates.*

Summary

Embedded system design using SPARC has the same rewards as other chip implementations with the additional benefits of a high performance RISC processor and the use of an open, standard architecture. From SPARCsim's use in the conceptualization and implementation stages through RDBXtool and SPARCmon's use in the hardware/software integration stages, the SPARC embedded designer gains both a head start in development and an efficient development environment. These tools, combined with the others available for SPARC, can lead to a more productive design cycle and a quality product.

References

1. 2.0 SPARCsim Installation Guide, Sun Microsystems, Inc., June 1990, 800-3548-10

2. 2.0 SPARCsim User's Guide, Sun Microsystems, Inc., June 1990, 800-3550-10

3. 2.0 SPARCsim Configuration Guide, Sun Microsystems, Inc., June 1990, 800-3549-10

4. SPARC Remote Debugger—RDBXtool Installation Guide, Sun Microsystem, Inc., April 1990, 800-3337-10

5. SPARC Remote Debugger RDBXtool User's Guide, Sun Microsystems, Inc., April 1990

6. SPARC Debugging Monitor—SPARCmon Installation Guide, Sun Microsystems, Inc., April 1990, 800-3360-10

7. SPARC Debugging Monitor—SPARCmon User's Guide, Sun Microsystems, Inc., April 1990, 800-3361-10

8. SPARC Debugging Monitor—SPARCmon Internals Manual, Sun Microsystems, Inc., April 1990, 800-3386-10

9. Remote Debugging Protocol Specification, Sun Microsystems, Inc., May 1990, 800-3335-10

Software Considerations for Real-Time RISC

21

JERRY FIDDLER • ERIC STROMBERG • DAVID N. WILNER

Introduction

The latest wave of new microprocessor architectures bears some significant differences from previous computers. These architectures, known as RISC, for Reduced Instruction Set Computer, include the SPARC, the Motorola 88000, the AMD 29000 and the MIPS. They bring with them the promise of extremely high computing speeds. However, they present important and difficult challenges to the software designer, particularly for real-time use. This paper describes some of those challenges and some of the solutions. The SPARC microprocessor and the VxWorks implementation for that processor are used as examples.

RISC

Although the acronym RISC is used to label these architectures, the reduced instruction set is only one of the things that makes RISC processors different from the more traditional CISC (Complex Instruction Set Computer) machines.

As Table 21.1 shows, the intent of RISC architectures is to provide an architecture that can be made to run very fast, by running very simply and by minimizing interaction with the world outside the CPU itself. This allows a degree of optimization within the CPU that would be much more difficult with CISC machines. For example, many RISC CPUs make extensive use of pipelining and overlapping of multiple instruction execution. It also means that many functions that, with CISC architectures, are performed as complex instructions in hardware, are now off-loaded to the

Reprinted with permission from Wind River Systems, Alcemeda, CA 94501.

CISC	RISC
Large instruction set (>100)	(50–75)
More complex instructions (most instructions microcoded.)	Simpler instructions (little or no microcode
Complex addressing modes	Most instructions operate only on register operands
Variable size instructions	Fixed-format instructions
Small internal register set (≤32)	Large internal register set (32–256)
Most instructions require multiple machine cycles	Most instructions require one machine cycle
Slower clock speeds (≤30 MHz)	Faster clock speeds (25–100 MHz)

TABLE 21.1. *Differences Between CISC and RISC*

software. This allows the software to optimize complex functions, instead of using microcoded instructions that might not be exactly optimal for a specific purpose and might actually be slower.

The Nature of Real-Time Systems

Real-time systems have some very different needs than general purpose computers. The major difference is that general purpose machines need to be optimized for throughput, while real-time systems need to be designed around worst-case latency and determinacy. In a real-time system, the correct answer delivered a microsecond late is wrong. A system that always responds in 100ms might be much better than a system that responds in 1 μsec on average, but occasionally takes 150ms.

To a much greater degree than a general-purpose system, a real-time system is typically event-driven. Events come in from the real-world and the system responds. These events might be a character being received, a satellite coming on line, or a nuclear plant overheating. In almost all cases, events arrive at the CPU by means of an interrupt. Because of this, fast, deterministic interrupt response is critical in a real-time system.

Another difference is that real-time systems tend to be much more intensively multitasking than general-purpose systems. Consider a UNIX system, for example. Even though there are multiple tasks, there is very little interaction between the tasks. By contrast, in a real-time system all the tasks are typically cooperating to perform a single function—control a machine, for instance. Therefore, there tends to be much more communications between tasks, as well as between task-level and interrupt level.

Perhaps the most obvious difference between real-time and general-purpose systems, though, is speed. In a general-purpose system, task context switch times of 1–100ms are respectable. In a real-time system, because of the intensity of the multitasking, context switch times of $<100\mu sec$ are more the norm.

It is important to note that speed is the last difference discussed here and not the first. Even though it might be the most obvious difference between the two types of systems, it is really only as a result of the deep architectural differences that the speed issue becomes important, or even makes sense.

The Challenges and Benefits of Using RISC in Real-Time

Although RISC was not developed specifically for real-time, RISC chips can perform extremely well in a real-time environment. However, RISC CPUs must be used somewhat differently than CISC and some real-time system implementation concepts need to be re-examined.

Register Usage & The Nature of a Task Context

Within a multitasking system, each task exists within its own *context*. This context is basically a model of the computer in which the task operates. It is the job of the operating system to set up the context each time the task is run and save it each time the task is suspended or pre-empted.

In existing real-time OS's, the task context is almost always a model of the entire CPU. If the CPU has 32 internal registers, each task has its own copy of those 32 registers that are swapped in and out with the task. In a CISC machine, that is entirely reasonable, since the number of registers is small. In a RISC, though, there might be hundreds of registers. Swapping all of them in and out for each task can take a significant amount of time. In a general-purpose computer, where task context switch times are in the many-millisecond range, this doesn't matter much. But in a real-time system it can be very significant. In VxWorks, for instance, a task context switch on the 68020 microprocessor takes 17 μsec. Swapping a large number of registers in and out during that amount of time is simply not possible.

The approach we have taken in VxWorks is to rethink the nature of a task context. Instead of defining a task context as being a model of the entire CPU architecture, we allow the application to define a subset of the architecture for each task. In order to explain, a short explanation of SPARC register windows is in order.

In the SPARC, the internal registers are arranged in overlapping *register windows*. There may be between 6 and 32 register windows, each window having 24 working registers. In addition, there are 8 global registers. At any time, only one window is visible. The windows are arranged in a circular file. Each register window has 8 *in* registers, 8 local registers and 8 *out* registers. The *out* registers for one window are the same as the *in* registers for the next. There is a *current window pointer (CWP)* that keeps track of which window is currently active. On a function call, the *CWP* increments and on a return, it decrements. A *window invalid mask (WIM)* has a bit for each window and keeps track of whether there is valid data in that window. If a function call is made and the next register window has data in it already, a window overflow trap is generated. Likewise, if a function return is executed and the previous window has no valid data, a window underflow trap is generated. It is the job of the operating system to handle both of these traps.

The point of the register window architecture is to speed subroutine invocation by minimizing memory references required to pass and return parameters. However, if all the registers had to be saved and restored as part of each task's context, this architecture could significantly slow down context switch speed. Fortunately there are several techniques used in VxWorks to turn the register window architecture to advantage in context switching.

First, VxWorks saves only those registers windows that are actually in use by a task at the time of the context switch. This is usually much less than the entire register window set. The window *invalid mask* is used to determine which windows are in use by a task at the time of the context switch. Furthermore, when a task is switched back in, only a single register window needs to be restored. The window *invalid mask* is set to indicate that only that window is valid. Subsequent returns from subroutines will cause window underflow traps causing the other register windows to be reloaded as needed.

A more significant optimization would be to use the register windows as a sort of register "cache" in which register windows are not saved at all except as required to make room for register sets that need to be loaded. In this technique, when switching tasks it is only necessary to find a free window for a single register window of the incoming task. If a window is already available at the time of the switch, then NONE of the outgoing tasks register windows need to be saved at the time of the switch. At worst, if all register windows are in use at the time of the context switch, a single register window of the outgoing task must be saved to make room for a window of the incoming task. Later, if additional register windows are required by other tasks, the windows in use must be saved. However, if a task gets to run again before some of its register windows have been used by others, then the entire saving and restoring of those windows has been avoided. It is even possible to have repeated switching among several tasks without saving or restoring a single register!

A final optimization would be to allow an application to allocate a register window or set of windows to specific tasks or groups of tasks. For instance, one high speed task might be allocated one or two register windows of its own. Context switching to or from that task NEVER requires saving or restoring its register windows!

Development

Most real-time systems are written in a high-level language, but debugged in assembly language. This alternative is reasonable, if less than optimal, in a CISC architecture, because there is usually a relatively clear correspondence between one high-level language statement and several assembly language instructions. On a RISC machine, there might be no such clear correspondence. Because of the minimal instruction set and the rich register set, the available compilers perform extensive optimization, move variables in and out of registers in order to operate on them there and count on overlapping execution of multiple instructions. Therefore, it might be difficult or impossible to make sense of the generated assembly language, understand where any particular variable is stored at any given time, etc.

The solution is to provide source-language debugging. VxWorks/SPARC works with a special version of Sun Microsystems dbxtool debugger, known as dbxWorks. This allows source language debugging of a real-time target from an attached Sun workstation. This way, the debugger can keep track of what's where and the programmer can debug in a language he/she can easily understand.

Interrupts

In any operating system, interrupts operate in their own context. The usual technique is to save any registers that may be modified immediately upon the occurrence of an interrupt, then restore them when the interrupt returns. The issues here with RISC are similar to those already described relating to task context switch. One solution for SPARC would also follow this pattern. If the application designer wishes, he/she could set aside one or more register windows specifically for interrupt usage. Those windows would not need to be saved or restored at all, except for nested interrupts. This technique could drop interrupt latency to near zero.

General Operating System Facilities

There is another issue with using RISC in real-time that is harder to define or quantify. This is the issue of "appropriateness" of the real-time operating system and development tools. The new generation of RISC CPUs brings promise of 5–100 MIPS in the next two years. This power, combined with large, cheap memory capacity, can lead to new, more advanced applications. Many applications that once required special purpose hardware, or supercomputer speed, can now be done far more cheaply and flexibly in software on one or more single board computers.

The fly in the ointment is the available real-time operating software. The previous generation of software may have been appropriate for the previous generation of hardware. But using a 100 MIPS processor with a real-time "kernel" that does little more than switch tasks is analogous to building a spacecraft with a hammer and saw: the tools are not in scale with the job at hand.

The VxWorks approach is to provide a very rich real-time environment and leverage off UNIX to provide development and host support. Some of the tools provided in VxWorks are:

Network—

VxWorks contains a complete port of the BSD4.3 network environment, including TCP/IP, UDP, sockets and higher level tools like *rlogin, ftp, telnet*, etc. It also contains all of the inter-network tools, for transparent gateways between networks. Communications is transparent between UNIX and VxWorks, multiple VxWorks systems, or multiple UNIX systems.

Remote File Access (NFS)—

Diskless real-time systems can use any NFS server (or any UNIX system) as a remote file server over any network medium..IP

Remote Procedure Calls (RPC)—

RPC allows a task to call a subroutine without regard to where that subroutine actually executes. It might execute on the same CPU or a different CPU on the network, on a UNIX system or a VxWorks system. The subroutine is simply called and results returned.

Multiprocessing Tools—

VxWorks provides tools to configure multiple CPUs on a backplane with exactly the same communication mechanisms as used over the network. Thus multiprocessing systems can communicate using sockets or remote procedure calls, rlogin, (remote login) to each other, use each other as remote file servers, etc. Because of the gateway capabilities, all CPUs sharing a backplane can communicate over an attached network, using one of the CPUs in the box as a gateway between the network and the backplane.

Development Tools—

VxWorks provides high-level development tools such as a C interpreter shell, a loader that loads *a.out* or COFF files directly, load-time linkage, extensive performance and debugging tools, remote source language debugging, extensive exception handling and logging facilities, etc.

A Rich Operating System Environment—

The operating system contains extensive facilities for intertask communications and synchronization (UNIX-compatible signals, pipes, semaphores), a UNIX-compatible real-time I/O and file system, memory management and utility routines (linked lists, ring buffers, string handling, etc.).

Conclusion

Although the high-speeds available with RISC are very attractive, it is important to think carefully about implementation strategies. To move system software from CISC to RISC without reexamining basic concepts is likely to lead to no gain in performance and perhaps even a loss. The first VxWorks RISC implementation, for the SPARC, uses the differences of the RISC environment and some of the specific advantages of the SPARC, to great advantage. It also provides a direct migration path from current technologies for application software and provides a set of tools appropriate to the power of the underlying hardware.

SPARC for Real-Time Applications

22

Kim Ingram

The Real-Time Market

The characteristics of a real-time system are not necessarily restricted to fast and compact. Computer systems that control real-time events are not only required to achieve the correct answer, but to achieve the answer within the defined timeframe. With real-time applications, the correct answer at the wrong time is simply the wrong answer. These strict requirements are due to the fact that real-time involves time-critical events, such as satellites in space, flight control and even automated factory control.

Real-Time Environment

Ten years ago, when system performance was 0.1 MIPS, on-board memory was small (16K), and application programs were written in assembly code, traditional real-time environments proved adequate. Current technology, however, has brought processor performance up to 100 MIPS and on-board memory of 16 MBytes. Programs are larger and more complex and are written in high-level languages like C.

Despite this technology evolution, real-time designers have been left with somewhat archaic tools and design philosophies. Recently, however, software vendors have developed methods to take advantage of the power of UNIX as a development environment, while, at the same time, achieving the high performance, integrated solutions required by real-time.

In these new methods, the host development platform typically utilizes UNIX with its facilities to edit, compile, load and store real-time code that can be run and debugged on the target system (Figure 22.1). As with previous methods, the real-time software resides on each real-time processor and handles the debugging, testing, and running of real-time applications. Recent industry advancements have added networking capabilities, high-level source debugging tools, and remote procedure calls. These additional facilities allow faster, more efficient code development and improved run-time performance.

System Requirements

The nature of real-time applications dictate certain unique requirements. Perhaps the foremost of these is system performance. Real-time applications often push the limit of computer technology, and it is the rare real-time application that does not benefit from higher performance.

Real-time systems must also be able to react rapidly to external interrupts. Reaction times are typically comprised of four elements: 1. the time it takes for the system's CPU to perceive the

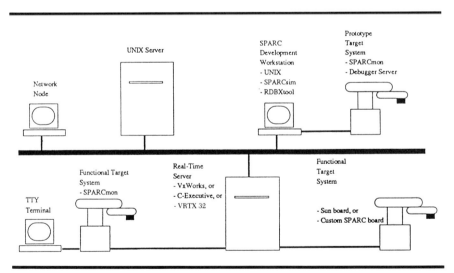

FIGURE 22.1. *Currently, the SPARCRISC chip is available for real-time target systems on VME boards from Ironics, Force, and Sun and is available by itself for in-house board designs from the SPARC semiconductor manufactures. SPARC is supported by real-time operating systems from Wind River Systems (VxWorks), JMI (C-Executive), and Ready Systems (VRTX 32). SPARC development tools provided by Sun include high-level symbolic debugging (RDBXtool), target monitors (SPARC monitor), and C cross computers, compilers.*

external event (the interrupt latency); 2. the time it takes to end gracefully the process that is running at the time of the interrupt (including saving necessary data registers); 3. the time it takes to load the process required by the interrupt (memory fetches); and 4. the time it takes to run the new process. (Ending the old process and loading the new one is called "context switching.")

In addition to providing high performance and reacting quickly to interrupts, real-time systems must be predictable. This means the systems' response-time must be deterministic. A system that has a fast average response is ill-suited for real-time applications if the response time also has a large variance.

Real-time operating systems have not traditionally utilized the development environment and networking capabilities found in UNIX due to the high memory overhead that such functionality requires. However, real-time operating systems today allow developers to take advantage of an outstanding software-development environment including debugging and simulation tools without sacrificing real-time operating system performance or target hardware real estate.

This UNIX debugging functionality is especially important because it is impractical to debug machine code produced by RISC compilers. This is because the reduced instruction set and the ability to pipeline instructions that characterize RISC architectures allow high levels of compiler optimization which often makes machine code difficult to understand. However, using the integrated UNIX/real-time operating system development environment described above, developers can attain the advantages of high-level symbolic debugging of RISC-based code.

Why RISC is Good for Real-Time
RISC vs. CISC: Speed

RISC technology is attractive to real-time developers because, as a rule, it is faster than CISC technology. RISC designs execute simple, symmetric instructions extremely fast. Although RISC must execute more instructions (approximately 10–20%) to accomplish the equivalent of CISC instructions, the speed of RISC enables programs to execute 2 to 5 times faster. This is a result of

RISC's smaller, fixed-format instruction set; its ability to execute instructions using fewer clock cycles (approximately 1.6 cycles per instruction) than CISC architectures; the faster clock speeds at which RISC chips run; and larger internal register sets (discussed below).

RISC is also cost effective. LSI Logic, a SPARC semiconductor manufacturer, provides a $10-per-MIP price-performance ratio. The competitive nature of the SPARC semiconductor market (with six independent SPARC semiconductor vendors) will continue to foster price-performance advances.

RISC vs. CISC: Scalability

Because RISC chips are inherently more simple than CISC chips (having approximately one-tenth the number of transistors), they can be altered to take advantage of technological advances more rapidly. For example, the currently available 65 MIPS ECL SPARC implementations and the soon-to-be available GaAs SPARC implementations will precede comparable CISC implementations by years. RISC simplicity and SPARC's scalability also facilitate chip-set integration.

SPARC: Unique Advantages for Real-Time

SPARC offers real advantages over other RISC and CISC technologies. These advantages include faster processing as well as reduced context-switching and interrupt-latency times. SPARC also offers systems designers architectural flexibility, allowing for custom I/O and databus (standard or Harvard) specification.

Speed

SPARC chips are the highest performance RISC chips available today. The 80 MHz ECL SPARC chips from Bipolar Integrated Technologies (BIT) and 40 MHz CMOS SPARC chips from Cypress-Ross Technologies are current performance leaders. Because six independent semiconductor manufacturers are concurrently designing and producing SPARC implementations, competitive market forces ensure the continuation of rapid price/performance improvements. Table 22.1 compares various RISC chips.

Mfg	Arch	Tech	Clock	Reg	VAX MIPS
BIT B5000	SPARC	ECL	80 MHz	120	65
Cypress CY7C601	SPARC	CMOS	40 MHz	136	29
Fujitsu MB86930	SPARC	CMOS	40 MHz	136	33
LSI L64811	SPARC	CMOS	33 MHz	136	24
Fujitsu S-25	SPARC	CMOS	25 MHz	120	15

Key:
Mfg = manufacturer. SPARC is available from multiple manufacturers (BIT, Cypress-Ross, LSI, Fujitsu, Texas Instruments, and Philips). LSI will be offering the L64811 at 25, 33, and 40 MHz with performance identical to the CY7C601.
Arch = architecture. All are RISC architectures.
Tech = process technology.
Clock = clock speed.
Reg = number of registers. Note: SPARC chips can have up to 520 registers.
VAX MIPS = One VAX MIPS is a unit of performance equal to the speed of a VAX 11/780. A rating of n number of Vax MIPS means that the chip is n times faster than the 11/780.

TABLE 22.1.

Register Windows

A common, but erroneous, belief is that the suitability of a chip for real-time applications is inversely proportional to the number of registers the chip has. This is thought to be true because it is also commonly believed that all active registers must be saved before an interrupt can be serviced. Were this the case, a chip with many registers would present two problems for the real-time application: first, a large number of registers containing an interrupted process might need to be saved before high-priority processes could be loaded and run. Second, it would probably be impossible to predict how many registers would need to be saved. This would make the application's reaction time non-deterministic. **In fact, however, SPARC's abundance of registers is an asset for real-time developers, not a liability.**

SPARC's register window design is outlined in Figures 22.2 and 22.3. As discusssed there, the register design offers speed advantages for passing data from one process to the next. It also offers speed and deterministic advantages when registers are dedicated to processes (including interrupt handling). Using the windows in a cache-like manner also increases performance.

SPARC's Register Windows

SPARC is defined by an architectural specification with many different implementations possible. SPARC is not a single chip or implementation. Therefore, it cannot be said that SPARC has "X" number of registers. However, today, SPARC chips manufactured have at least seven register windows each of which contains 16 registers. Additionally, the chips have eight global registers (for a grand total of at least 120 registers). Clearly, present SPARC implementations have more registers than most other RISC technology and more than any CISC implementation. The SPARC architecture allows implementations to have a range of 2 to 32 register windows. A 32-register window implementation would have 520 registers (32 windows × 16 registers per window + 8 global registers = 520 registers).

SPARC employs an overlapping register window design. Each register window actually has 24 registers divided into three groups of eight: eight "in" registers, eight "local" registers and

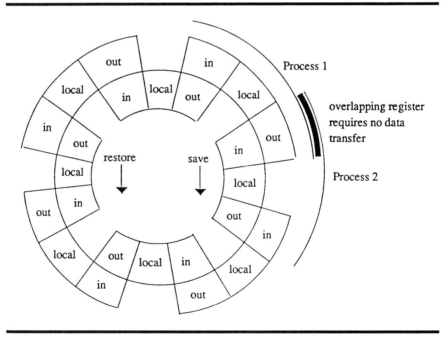

FIGURE 22.2. *SPARC's register windows.*

eight "out" registers. Each window shares its "out" registers with the next windows "in" registers: they are the same registers. Thus, passing the output of a process from register window to register window requires no actual movement of data from register to register.

Dedicated Register Windows

SPARC's registers can be used several ways to reduce context-switching times and ensure deterministic behavior. One example is the ability to allow register windows to be dedicated to processes. If a process has a window dedicated to it, the process is always available without reference to memory. Context-switching under these conditions can be reduced to as little as 5 microseconds or less, depending on the operating frequency of the SPARC implementation. No memory access is required for such a context-switch.

In the example illustrated below, four register windows (indi-

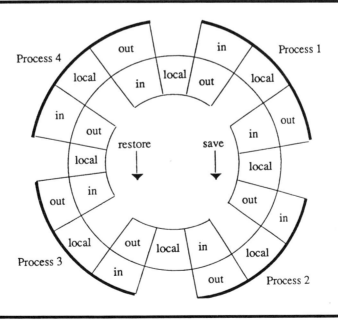

FIGURE 22.3. *Register windows dedicated to processes.*

cated by a dark outline) are reserved (dedicated) for four processes. Note that the windows between the reserved windows are invalid since they are reserved for trap handling. Also, note that the reserved windows have all 24 registers available since they are not overlapping valid windows.

Dedication of register windows can be used to reduce interrupt latency as well as to reduce context-switching. This is accomplished by reserving a window for trap handling processes required to service interrupts.

Cache-like Register Windows

SPARC allows other register-based context-switching optimizations. Real-time operating systems can treat the register windows in a cache-like manner. Here, windows are saved only if there is no window available to load the initial window of the required process. Thus, if a window is available at the time of the interrupt, no registers need be saved. Under these conditions, context-switching can occur multiple times between high and low priority processes without any memory references if both tasks fit in the register windows at the same time.

Another SPARC optimization uses the Window Invalid Mask pointer to determine windows in use at the time of the interrupt. Only the active window, not the entire register window set, is saved before the interrupt is serviced. When the interrupted process is restored only a single register window is loaded. As the reinstated process requires the additional windows, SPARC's Window Underflow trap prompts their restoration.

Dedicated and cache-like SPARC windowing techniques offer bounded, deterministic performance significantly faster than CISC technology.

Summary

The real-time market poses special hardware and software challenges. Software development tools must be integrated into real-time operating system environments, and embedded processors must be fast and predictable.

RISC architectures offer speed enhancements over CISC architectures. Sun Microsystem's RISC architecture, SPARC, which is available from independent semiconductor manufacturers, currently offers advantages to the real-time market above and beyond those offered by other RISC chips. SPARC has a rich set of UNIX-based development tools that can be utilized by networked real-time operating systems. Additionally, SPARC's register window design offers many options for reducing interrupt latency and memory fetch times, and for increasing the determinant nature of the chip's performance.

Real-time developers requiring state-of-the-art processor performance and optimal development and deployment platforms, should carefully evaluate SPARC.

System Software

SunOS on SPARC

STEVE R. KLEIMAN • D. WILLIAMS

23

This paper describes the port of SunOS, a derivative of the UNIX operating system, to the SPARC™[1] RISC CPU. SPARC makes tradeoffs between hardware and software complexity. Operations implemented by microcode on CISC CPUs are supported by low-level operating system routines.

Hardware Architecture

SPARC specifies both integer and floating-point execution units. SPARC implementations also require a surrounding system architecture. The system architecture used in the port of SunOS to SPARC is called Sun-4™. The specific implementation of the Sun-4 architecture that was used is called the Sun-4/200 series. The core of the Sun-4 architecture contains a SPARC Integer Unit (IU), an optional SPARC Floating-Point Unit (FPU), a memory management unit (MMU), an optional virtually addressed cache, an optional VMEbus interface and several control registers.

Virtual Memory Management

The SPARC CPU has no built-in knowledge of the Sun-4 MMU. It merely emits addresses and processes memory exceptions. The MMU provides both protection and mapping.

Sun-4 Memory Mapping Hardware

The Sun-4 MMU consists of a two-level static-RAM based translation table (see Figure 23.1). The first-level translation table is called the segment map. Each entry in the segment map contains an index into the second-level table, which is called the page map. Entries in the page map contain the actual physical page address,

1988 IEEE. Reprinted with Permission, from Proceedings of COMPCON, '88, March 1–3, San Francisco, CA.

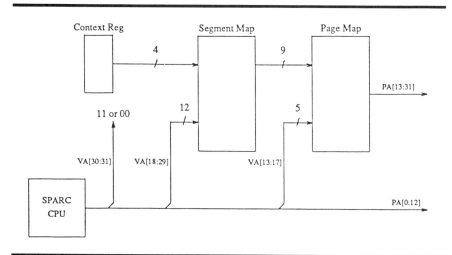

FIGURE 23.1. *Sun-4/200 MMU.*

protection information and statistics bits. Pages contain 8 kilobytes of memory. Page map entries are grouped into 32 entry units called *page map entry groups* (PMEG). Each PMEG maps 256 kilobytes of memory. Entries in the segment map are grouped into units called contexts. The context used to translate the current virtual address is provided by the context register. Each context represents a memory mapping of a virtual address space for a process. The Sun-4 architecture does not require that the entire 32-bit virtual address space for a process be mappable. An implementation may choose to mark a part of the middle of the virtual address space as permanently invalid. Thus, depending on the implementation, the "hole" in the middle of a process will grow or shrink. The Sun-4/200 has 16 contexts each having 1 gigabyte of mappable virtual address space; 512 megabytes at the top, and 512 megabytes at the bottom.

Virtual Address Layout

The typical layout of a SunOS process is shown in Figure 23.2. The kernel occupies the top 128 megabytes in all contexts to allow the kernal to switch freely among them. The kernal stack is contained in the per process global structure called the *u area.* The *u*

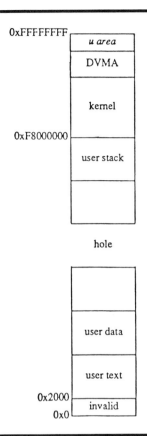

FIGURE 23.2. *Virtual address layout.*

area resides at the very top of the address space so it can be addressed absolutely. The upper 1 megabyte of the address space is also used by external I/O devices. Memory requests from these devices are translated through this portion of the MMU to provide fully mapped memory access. This technique is called Direct Virtual Memory Access (DVMA).

MMU Management

The operating system allows more runnable processes and more total virtual address space than can be accommodated by the MMU at any one time. Therefore the MMU is managed as a cache of entries. For example, when a process is started, it initially runs in a context which is reserved by the kernel for processes without contexts. The user portion of the address space of this context is completely invalid. When the process exits the kernal and attempts to run user code it gets a page fault. The kernel then tries to allocate a free context and a free PMEG to the process to provide the mapping capability to satisfy the fault. If an unused context and/or PMEG cannot be found, one is taken away from another process.

Virtual Address Cache

On the Sun-4/200 the SPARC CPU accesses main storage through a virtually addressed cache. On such caches there is a problem of cache consistency between *synonyms*; i.e. two or more virtual addresses which map to the same physical address[2][3]. One solution is to turn off the cache for those pages which have synonyms. Sun-4 allows cached synonyms if the virtual addresses are the same modulo the cache size[4]. On the Sun-4/200 the cache size is 128 kilobytes. The machine-dependent layer of the SunOS kernel maintains a list of all mappings to a physical page. When a new mapping to a physical page is requested by the virtual memory subsystem, the new virtual address is checked against the current mappings to see if it is the same modulo the cache size. If it is, all the mappings may be cached. Otherwise, the old mappings are flushed from the cache and the pages are marked non-cacheable. SunOS contains mechanisms[5] which allow the machine-dependent layer to pick appropriate cache-consistent virtual addresses for mappings where the user does not insist on a particular virtual address. The machine-independent layer of SunOS has no knowledge of the virtual cache.

Trap Handling

Trap handlers on SPARC are the very lowest level of software. They do many things normally reserved for microcode in CISC architectures. Trap handlers can be split into three broad categories: 1) window overflow and underflow, 2) generic traps and interrupts, and 3) floating point.

Processor State

This paper assumes that the reader is familiar with the concept of register windows in general and SPARC[1] in particular. However, before going further, we review some of the SPARC processor state that is of particular interest to trap handlers:

- Current Window Pointer (CWP). A field in the Processor State Register (PSR) which contains an integer index which points to the current active register window. Decrementing the CWP moves to the "next" window. Incrementing it moves to the "previous" window.

- Window Invalid Mask (WIM) register. Any register window may be declared invalid by setting the corresponding bit in this register. Normal instructions that cause window motion cannot enter invalid windows.

When a trap is taken, further traps are disabled, the CWP is decremented (regardless of the value of the WIM), the program counters (there are 2) are saved in registers in the next window, and processing continues at the appropriate vector.

Traps and Register Windows

The purpose of the window overflow and underflow trap handlers is to give user programs the illusion that they have an (effectively) infinite supply of overlapping register windows. Conceptually these register windows form a normal LIFO stack (see Figure 23.3). Normally a program uses the SAVE instruction to "push" a new window on the stack, or a RESTORE instruction to "pop" a window from the stack. In actuality the register windows are implemented as a ring (see Figure 23.4). Eventually, new register windows wrap around to overwrite previously used windows. This is called a window overflow. When the register window wraps around software must save the contents of the old window in memory. Similarly, the software must restore previously used register windows when the register file is emptied (window underflow). The software detects window overflow and underflow by marking at least one window between the least recently used window and the most recently used window as invalid in the WIM.

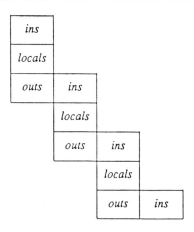

FIGURE 23.3. *Register window model.*

If a SAVE or RESTORE instruction would move the current window to one that is marked invalid, the instruction traps instead.

If the software were to use all the implemented register windows, the *out* registers for the last window would overlap the *in* registers for the least recently used window. In addition, since the CWP is decremented in the trap sequence, the software must ensure that at least one window is available to handle a possible trap whenever traps are enabled. Thus, even though there are n implemented windows only n-1 are available for general use. The window which is marked invalid to detect overflow and underflow also serves to guarantee that there will be at least one window (the invalid window) which is free for use by the trap handler. However, it is likely that the *in* registers for the trap window are in use by the program that took the trap and the *out* registers for the trap window may be in use as the *in* registers of the least recently used window. Thus, the trap handler may always use the local registers in the trap window, but it may not use the *in, out,* or *global* registers without first checking whether they are in use and possibly saving and restoring them.

It is not required that one use register windows in this way. For example, one can provide one register window for users, one

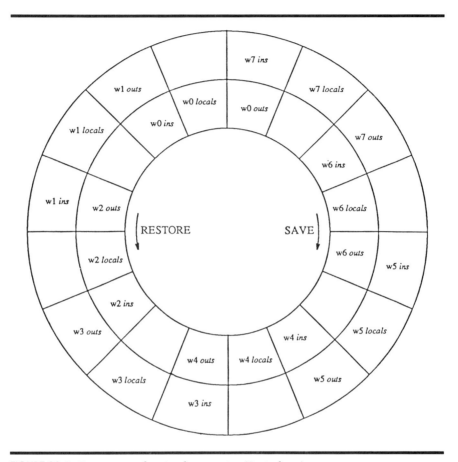

FIGURE 23.4. *Register window implementation (8 windows).*

register window for the operating system, and several other windows for interrupt handlers. In this mode of operation, general software should not attempt to use SAVE or RESTORE instructions, but should instead use only the 32 registers in one window. The different window contexts can be protected from each other by marking register windows as invalid through the Window Invalid Mask register (WIM). Context switching would involve just setting the CWP to point to the appropriate register window and saving/restoring the global registers. This effectively removes the advantages[6] of register windows.

Window Overflow and Underflow Trap Handlers

The window overflow trap handler is responsible for saving one or more of the least recently used windows to memory. There are at least two alternative places to save overflowed register window data; On the normal program stack or on a special window save stack. In a virtual memory environment, saving window data on a separate window save stack has the advantage that it is relatively easy to make the top of the window stack be always resident in memory. This means that the window overflow and underflow trap handlers do not have to test for residency before doing the actual save or restore of the window data. However, a separate window save stack effectively doubles the stack maintenance effort since two independent growable regions must be maintained. Because of this we chose the former alternative. The trap handlers designate one of the *out* registers in each window as a pointer to a 16-word save area for window overflow or underflow. In general, this register is also used as the stack pointer. The stack pointer must be maintained whenever traps are enabled since traps may happen at any time.

Simulation data[7] has shown that saving and restoring one window at a time is the simplest and most effective algorithm for handling overflow and underflow.

Simple Window Trap Handlers
A simple trap handler assumes that reading or writing words to the window save area pointed to by the stack pointer will not cause a trap. If it does, a reset trap occurs. This means that the stack pointer must be aligned to a word boundary and must point to a valid area of memory. The trap handler assumes that the WIM is initialized to a value with only one bit set, which invalidates the window before the initial CWP. The algorithm is as follows:

```
window_overflow:
        !
        ! Current window is marked invalid. Next
        ! window must be saved and marked invalid.
        !
        save;                   ! go to next window
        %wim = ror(%wim, 1);    ! rotate WIM right by 1
        save window data (ins and locals) to stack
```

```
        restore;                    ! back to trap window
        rett;                       ! return from trap
window_underflow:
        !
        ! Previous window is last active window.
        ! The window before that is marked invalid
        ! and must be restored. The window before
        ! that becomes the new invalid window.
        !
        %wim = rol(%wim, 1);    ! rotate wim left by 1
        restore; restore;           ! back 2 windows
        restore window data (ins and locals) from stack
        save; save;                 ! go to trap window
        rett;                       ! return from trap
```

In many SPARC implementations it is faster to load and store doublewords than to load and store words. The SunOS trap handlers assume that the stack pointer is doubleword-aligned so that they can use the load doubleword and store doubleword instructions to save and restore windows.

Full Window Overflow and Underflow When running in a multi-programming environment, such as UNIX, the window trap handlers must do more checking before actually saving or restoring a window. The system must make sure that the save area is aligned and is resident in memory. If the save area is misaligned or is non-resident then the overflow trap handler must temporarily save the overflow window to an internal buffer so that the system can continue.

The operating system can run the register file in one of two ways: 1) save the entire register file on system entry and restore it on system exit, or 2) share the register file with the user. The first approach has the advantage of making the trap handler less complex. Sharing the register file with the user has that advantage of possibly not saving or restoring user windows that have not overflowed/underflowed. This can improve the performance of interrupts and simple system calls. The algorithm below assumes that the register file may contain both user and supervisor windows.

```
window_overflow:
        save;                       ! go to next window
        %wim = ror(%wim, 1);    ! rotate wim right by 1
```

```
            if (window to be saved is a user window) {
                    if (%sp & 7) {
                            save window data to internal buffer
                            goto user_alignment trap;
                    }
                    if (stack is writable) {
                            save window data to stack
                    } else {
                            save window data to internal buffer
                            if (user_trap)
                                    goto user_page_page_fault;
                    }
            } else {                        ! system window
                    save window data to stack
            }
            restore;                        ! back to trap window
            rett;                           ! return from trap
window_underflow:
            %wim = rol(%wim, 1);    ! rotate wim left by 1
            restore; restore;       ! back 2 windows
            if (user_trap) {
                    if (%sp & 7)
                            goto user_alignment_trap;
                    if (stack is not readable)
                            goto user_page_fault;
            }
            restore window data from stack
            save; save;                     ! back to trap window
            rett;                           ! return from trap
```

Generic Trap Handlers

A generic trap handler is a standard preamble and postamble for any non-window trap that requires register windows. Examples of this type of trap are page faults, interrupts and system calls. Certain other traps may not require the use of the generic trap handler, but they must work in the restricted environment left immediately after a trap.

The generic trap preamble first saves the global registers and the PSR. Then it checks for a window overflow condition. If there is an overflow condition it must save the next window. Next, if the trap is an interrupt it must set the appropriate processor interrupt level. Lastly, it re-enables traps and dispatches the trap to higher-level code.

The generic trap postamble first checks for a window underflow condition. If there is an underflow condition it restores the previous window. Then it restores the global registers and the PSR. When restoring the PSR it must make sure that the CWP field reflects the current CWP, not the CWP at the time of the trap, as these may be different (see Context Switching below). Lastly, it returns from the trap, which reexecutes the instruction which took the trap.

In a multi-programming environment it is also necessary to make sure that kernel data is not accessible to the user. Since, the user and the kernel share the register file the generic trap postamble must "clean" (zero) the register windows used by the kernel before returning to the user.

Page Faults Page faults use the generic trap handler. When a page fault on data is taken, the page fault handler must compute the address of the fault. It may do this by decoding the faulted instruction and computing the effective address. On the Sun-4, the effective address of a data fault is latched in an external register. The register is read by the page fault handler to determine the faulted address.

VMEbus Interrupts After the preamble, the VMEbus interrupt handler reads an external system register to get the VME interrupt vector and complete the interrupt acknowledge cycle. The vector is then used to find the correct interrupt handler to call.

Floating-Point Trap Handlers A bit in the Processor State Register enables the SPARC floating-point unit. Processes are started with the FPU disabled. When a process executes its first floating-point instruction, a trap is generated. The floating-point trap handler enables the FPU, initializes the FPU registers to NaNs, and marks the process as using the FPU so that a context switch will save the FPU state.

SPARC defines a set of floating-point operations (FPops) that an implementation may provide. FPops which are not implemented are simulated by the kernel for compatibility. Configurations without an FPU generate traps on every execution of a floating-point instruction. The floating-point trap handler calls a simulator for floating-point operations in this case. The simulator runs at the lowest interrupt priority until it completes. Interrupts can be taken during simulation but the kernel will not context switch until the simulator finishes.

A SPARC FPU may execute several FPops in parallel while other non-floating-point IU operations are proceeding. The number of FPops that may execute in parallel is implementation-dependent. A queue in the FPU stores the necessary state for all the concurrently executing FPops when exceptions occur. The floating-point unit and trap handler together guarantee a user model (ANSI/IEEE 754 compatible) in which the floating-point instructions appear to finish in sequence, even though they are executing in parallel.

Exceptions are generated asynchronously, by the FPU yet are only taken by the IU synchronously when another floating-point instruction is encountered in the instruction stream. The trap handler for floating-point exceptions normally gets control at a point where the IU has advanced the program counter many instructions after the FPop that generated the exception. The floating-point queue contains sequence of address/instruction pairs which are the current set of instructions being executed by the FPU. The trap handler dumps the queue and takes action appropriate to the type of exception. The following exceptions may be generated (with the noted actions):

- IEEE exceptions—The kernel sends a signel to the user with a code and the address of the instruction generating the exception.

- Unfinished FPops—An implementation may not be able to fully implement correct handling of some instructions in all cases. The trap handler simulates the instruction in this case.

- Unimplemented FPops—An implementation may not implement all FPops. The trap handler simulates the instruction.

Context Switching

The general procedure for context switching is shown below:

```
cswitch:
            store stack pointer
            store PC (return address)
            save global registers (if required)
            save floating point registers (if required)
            flush active register windows to the stack
            save;save;  . . .NWINDOWS—2 times
            restore floating point registers (if required)
            restore global registers (if required)
            load new return address
            load new stack pointer
        restore;
        return;
```

The main action that is unique to register window architectures is flushing the register windows to the stack. One way to do this is to do NWINDOWS—2 SAVE instructions, where NWINDOWS is the number of implemented windows in the ring. The reason we can do two less than the number of windows is that one window is always invalid and we don't have to flush the window that the context switch is operating in. The restore at the end of the context switch (part of the normal return sequence) is guaranteed to cause an underflow which fetches the window data from the new stack.

This is the method the kernel uses to context switch. However, it is undesirable to have user programs know how many windows are implemented on a particular implementation of SPARC. Therefore, a process may use a special software trap instruction which causes the kernel to flush its register windows. Also note that a process which is context switched may return to a different window than the one it left. Therefore, users never know which register window (CWP) they are in currently.

Measurements of the Sun-4/200 kernel (which has seven implemented windows) suggest that on average three active register windows are flushed to the stack.

Kernel Context Switching

Switching processes in the kernel is more complicated than ordinary context switching. After the state of the old process has been saved, the context switch routine must switch kernel stacks by switching the MMU entries for the *u area*, which is at a fixed address. Before this can be done, the current stack must be flushed out of the virtual address cache. This is the most expensive operation in kernel context switching (about 75% of the context switch time). It is possible to avoid this by not requiring the UNIX *u area* to reside at a fixed address. After this, the context switch routine loads the context register with the context number of the new process, if it has one. If it doesn't, it uses the reserved kernel-only context.

Conclusions

The most difficult part of porting SunOS to SPARC was dealing with the register windows. Once the trap handler "microcode" was written the port proceeded much like for other microprocessors. The simplicity of RISC architecture allowed processor state saving to be tailored exactly to the needs at hand, without extra overhead. Simple instruction restarting provided easy exception handling.

References

1. R. Garner, A. Agrawal, W. Brown, D. Hough, W.N. Joy, S.R. Kleiman, S. Muchnick, D. Patterson, J. Pendelton, R. Tuck, "The Scalable Processor Architecture", *Compcor. Conference Proceedings*, March 1988.

2. A.J. Smith, "Cache Memories", *ACM Computing Surveys,* September 1982.

3. R. Cheng, "Virtual Address Cache in UNIX", *USENIX Conference Proceedings*, Summer 1987.

4. Sun Microsystems, Inc., "Sun-4 Architecture: A Sun Technical Report".

5. R.A. Gingell, J.P. Moran, W.A. Shannon, "Virtual Memory Architecture in SunOS", *USENIX Conference Proceedings*, Summer 1987.

6. D.A. Patterson, C.H. Sequin, "RISC I: A Reduced Instruction Set VLSI Computer", *Proceedings of the 8th Symposium on Computer Architecture*, May 1981.

7. Y. Tamir, C.H. Sequin, "Strategies for Managing the Register File in RISC", *IEEE Transactions on Computers*, vol. C-32, no. 11, November 1983.

SunOS Multi-Thread Architecture

Mike L. Powell • S.R. Kleiman • S. Barton
D. Shan • D. Stein • M. Weeks

24

Abstract

We describe a model for multiple threads of control within a single UNIX process. The main goals are to provide extremely lightweight threads and to rationalize and extend the UNIX Application Programming Interface for a multithreaded environment. The threads are intended to be sufficiently lightweight so that there can be thousands present and that synchronization and context switching can be accomplished rapidly without entering the kernel. These goals are achieved by providing lightweight user-level threads that are multiplexed on top of kernel-supported threads of control. This architecture allows the programmer to separate logical (program) concurrency from the required real concurrency, which is relatively costly, and to control both within a single programming model.

Introduction

The reasons for supporting multiple threads of control in SunOS fall into two categories, those motivated by multiprocessor hardware and those motivated by application concurrency. It is possible to exploit multiprocessors to varying degrees depending on how much the uniprocessor software base is modified. In the simplest case, only separate user processes can run on the additional processors; the applications are unchanged. To allow a single application to use multiple processors (e.g., array processing workload), the application must be restructured.

The second category of reasons for multiple threads of control is application concurrency. Many applications are best structured as several independent computations. A database system may have many user interactions in progress while, at the same time, performing several file and network operations. A window system can treat each widget as a separate entity. A network server may indirectly need its own service (and, therefore, another thread of control) to handle requests. In each case, although it is possible to write the software as one thread of control moving from request to request, the code may be simplified by writing each request as a separate sequence and letting the language, library, and operating system handle the interleaving of the different operations.

These examples are not intended to be exhaustive, but they indicate the opportunities to exploit powerful hardware and build complex applications and services with this technology. The examples show that the user model for multiple threads of control must support a variety of applications and environments. The architecture should, where possible, use current programming paradigms and preserve software compatibility.

As is true of many system services today, the programmer's view of the multiple threads of control service is not always identical to what the kernel implements. The software view is created by a combination of the kernel, run-time libraries, and the compilation system. This approach increases the portability of applications and systems, by hiding some details of the implementation, while providing better performance by allowing library code to do some work without involving the kernel.

The remainder of this paper is divided into five sections. The first section gives an overview of the architecture and introduces our terminology. The second section discusses our design goals and principles. The third section gives additional details of operation and interfaces and how the UNIX process model is reinterpreted in the new environment. The fourth section gives some performance data and operational experience. The last section compares this architecture with others.

The terminology of multiprocessor and multithreaded computation is, unfortunately, not universally agreed upon. We have chosen terms that are most common and have tried to be consistent, but the reader is warned that some people use these words with other meanings. Examples of other models can be found in the last section of this paper.

Multi-Threading Architecture Overview

The multi-threaded programming model has two levels. The most important level is the thread interface, which defines most aspects of the programming model. That is, programmers write programs using threads. The second level is the lightweight process (LWP), which is defined by the services the operating system must provide. After describing each level, we explain why both levels are essential.

Threads

A traditional UNIX process has a single thread of control. A thread of control, or more simply a thread, is a sequence of instructions being executed in a program. A thread has a program counter (PC) and a stack to keep track of local variables and return addresses. A multi-threaded UNIX process is no longer a thread of control in itself, instead, it is associated with one or more threads. Threads execute independently. There is in general, no way to predict how the instructions of different threads are interleaved, though they have execution priorities that can influence the relative speed of execution. In general, the number or identities of threads that an application process chooses to apply to a problem are invisible from outside the process. Threads can be viewed as execution resources that may be applied to solving the problem at hand.

Threads share the process instructions and most of its data. A change in shared data by one thread can be seen by the other threads in the process. Threads also share most of the operating system state of a process. Each sees the same open files. For example, if one thread opens a file, another thread can read it. Because threads share so much of the process state, threads can affect each other in sometimes surprising ways. Programming with threads requires more care and discipline than ordinary programming, because there is no system-enforced protection among threads.

Each thread may make arbitrary system calls and interact with other processes in the usual ways. Some operations affect all the threads in a process. For example, if one thread calls exit (), all threads are destroyed. Other UNIX system services have new interpretations; e.g., a floating-point overflow trap applies to a particular thread, not the whole program.

The architecture provides a variety of synchronization facilities to allow threads to cooperate in accessing shared data. The synchronization facilities include mutual exclusion (mutex) locks, condition variables, and semaphores. For example, a thread that wants to update a variable might block waiting for a mutual exclusion lock held by another thread that is already updating it. To support different frequencies of interaction and different degrees of concurrency, several synchronization mechanisms with different semantics are provided.

As shown in Figure 24.1. threads in different processes can synchronize with each other via synchronization variables placed in shared memory, even though the threads in different processes are generally invisible to each other. Synchronization variables can also be placed in files and have lifetimes beyond that of the creating process. For example, a file can be created that contains database records. Each record can contain a mutual exclusion lock variable that controls access to the associated record. A process can map the file, and a thread within it can obtain the lock associated with a particular record that is to be modified. When the modification is complete, the thread can release the lock and unmap the file. Once the lock has been acquired, if any thread within any process mapping the file attempts to acquire the lock, that thread will block until the lock is released.

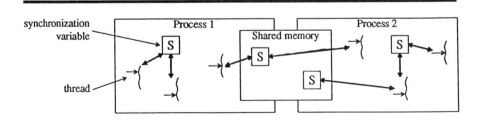

FIGURE 24.1. *Synchronization variables.*

Lightweight Processes

Threads are an appropriate paradigm for most programs that wish to exploit parallel hardware or express concurrent program structure. For those situations that require more control over how the program is mapped onto parallel hardware, and to optimize the costs of concurrent execution and synchronization, a second interface is defined.

In the SunOS multithread architecture, a UNIX process consists mainly of an address space and a set of lightweight processes (LWPs[1]) that share that address space. Each LWP can be thought of as a virtual CPU that is available for executing code or system calls. Each LWP is separately dispatched by the kernel, may perform independent system calls, incur independent page faults, and may run in parallel on a multiprocessor. All the LWPs in the system are scheduled by the kernel onto the available CPU resources according to their scheduling class and priority.

Threads are implemented using LWPs. Threads are actually represented by data structures in the address space of a program. LWPs within a process execute threads as shown in Figure 24.2. An LWP chooses a thread to run by locating the thread state in process memory (a). After loading the registers and assuming the identity of the thread, the LWP executes the thread's instructions (b). If the thread cannot continue, or if other threads should be run, the LWP saves the state of the thread back in memory (c). The LWP can now select another thread to run (d).

When a thread needs to access a system service by performing a kernel call, taking a page fault, or to interact with threads in other processes, it does so using the LWP that is executing it. The thread needing the system service remains bound to the LWP executing it until the system call is completed. If a thread needs to interact with other threads in the same process, it can do so without involving the operating system. As Figure 24.2 shows, switching from one thread to another occurs without the kernel knowing it. Much as the UNIX stdio library routines (such as fopen () and fread ()) are implemented using the UNIX system calls

---

[1] The LWPs in this document are fundamentally different than the LWP library in SunOS 4.0. Lack of imagination and a desire to conform to generally accepted terminology lead us to use the same name.

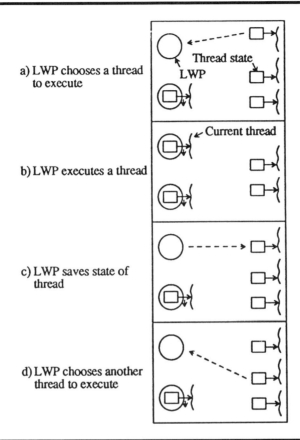

a) LWP chooses a thread
   to execute

b) LWP executes a thread

c) LWP saves state of
   thread

d) LWP chooses another
   thread to execute

FIGURE 24.2. *LWPs running threads.*

(open () and read ()), the thread interface is implemented using the LWP interface, and for many of the same reasons.

An LWP may also have some capabilities that are not exported directly to threads, such as a special scheduling class. A programmer can take advantage of these capabilities while still retaining use of all the thread interfaces and capabilities (e.g., synchronization) by specifying that the thread is to remain permanently bound to an LWP.

Threads are the primary interface for application parallelism. Few multithreaded programs will use the LWP interface directly, but it is sometimes important to know that it is there. Some languages define concurrency mechanisms that are different from threads. An example is a Fortran compiler that provides loop level parallelism. In such cases, the language library may implement its own notion of concurrency using LWPs. Most programmers can program using the threads interface and let the library take care of mapping threads onto the kernel primitives. The decision of how many LWPs should be created to run the threads can be left to the library or may be specified by the programmer.

Why Have Both Threads and LWPs?

One might wonder why it is necessary to have two interfaces that are so similar. The multithreaded architecture must meet a variety of different expectations. Some programs have large amounts of logical parallelism, such as a window system that provides each widget with one input handler and one output handler. Other programs need to map their parallel computation onto the actual number of processors available. In both cases, programs want to have complete and easy access to the system services.

Threads are implemented by the library and are not known to the kernel. Thus, threads may be created, destroyed, blocked, activated, etc., without involving the kernel. LWPs are implemented by the kernel. If a thread wants to read from a file, the kernel needs to be able to switch to other processing when the LWP blocks in the file system code waiting for the I/O to finish. The kernel has to preserve the state of the read operation and continue to when the I/O interrupt arrives. However, if each thread were always known to the kernel, it would have to allocate kernel data structures for each one and get involved in context switching threads even though most thread interactions involve threads in the same process. In other words, kernel-supported parallelism (LWPs) is relatively expensive compared with threads. Having all threads supported directly by the kernel would cause applications such as the window system to be much less efficient. Although the window system may be best expressed as a large number of threads, only a few of the threads ever need to be active (i.e., require kernel resources, other than virtual memory) at the same instant.

Sometimes, having more threads than LWPs is a disadvantage. A parallel array computation divides the rows of its arrays among different threads. If there is one LWP per processor, but multiple threads per LWP, each processor would spend overhead switching between threads. It would be better to know that there is one thread per LWP, divide the rows among a smaller number of threads, and reduce the number of thread switches. By specifying that each thread is permanently bound to its own LWP, a programmer can write a thread code that is really a LWP code, much like locking down pages turns virtual memory into real memory.

A mixture of threads that are permanently bound to LWPs and unbound threads is also appropriate for some applications. An example of this would be some real-time applications that want some threads to have system-wide priority and real-time scheduling, while other threads can attend to background computations.

By defining both levels of interface in the architecture, we make clear the distinction between what the programmer sees and what the kernel provides. Most programmers program using threads and do not think about LWPs. When it is appropriate to optimize the behavior of the program, the programmer has the ability to tune the relationship between threads and LWPs. This allows programmers to structure their application assuming extremely lightweight threads while bringing the appropriate degree of kernel-supported concurrency to bear on the computation. To some degree, a threads programmer can think of LWPs used by the application as the degree of real concurrency that the application requires.

Summary

Figure 24.3 shows all of the pieces in one diagram. The assignment of threads to LWPs is either controlled by the threads package or is specified by the programmer. The kernel sees LWPs and may schedule these on the available processors.

Process 1 is the traditional UNIX process with a single thread attached to a single LWP. Process 2 has threads multiplexed on a single LWP as in typical coroutine packages, such as SunOS 4.0 liblwp. Processes 3 through 5 depict new capabilities of the SunOS multithread architecture. Process 3 has several threads

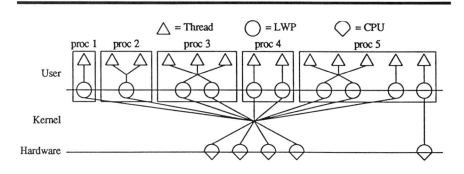

FIGURE 24.3. *Multithread architecture examples.*

multiplexed on a lesser number of LWPs. Process 4 has its threads permanently bound to LWPs. Process 5 shows all the possibilities; a group of threads multiplexed on a group of LWPs, while having threads bound to LWPs. In addition, the process has asked the system to bind one of its LWPs to a CPU. Note that the bound and unbound threads can still synchronize with each other, both within the same process and between processes in the usual way.

Design Goals

Having described the overall thread model and language used to describe the model, we can now describe the goals of the architecture. The following goals are approximately in order of importance.

- The architecture should describe structures and mechanisms that work among threads in the same program, between different programs (processes), and between processors (whether the processors are executing in the same or different processes).

- The architecture should support threads that are as cheap as possible. Threads within a program should not be forced to cross protection boundaries to synchronize or context switch, nor should threads require excessive kernel resources.

- The architecture must support both multiprocessor and uniprocessor implementations.

- All current UNIX semantics should be provided in user programs and libraries wherever possible. The degenerate case of a process being constructed of an address space and one lightweight process must provide complete UNIX semantics.

- Different lightweight processes should be able to do independent simultaneous system calls.

- The mechanisms defined in the system should be simple and fundamental. For example, there should be a method of using threads that does not force the threads library to use malloc (). This prevents interference with other application or language runtime system memory allocators.

The following are not exactly goals, but are principles that were used to help design the architecture.

- Per-thread state must be kept to a minimum. Each additional piece of state above the minimum necessary must be justified so as not to add undue "weight" to a thread.

- An address space with one thread (and, therefore, one lightweight process) should behave like a standard UNIX process; the addition of a new thread (and possibly a lightweight process) that does not interact with the first thread should not change the behavior of the first thread.

- The opportunity should be provided for different implementations. For example, by allowing but not requiring threads to share the whole address space, by allowing but not requiring threads to be multiplexed on lightweight processes, and by allowing but not requiring synchronization primitives to be executed in user mode.

- Wherever possible, equivalent semantics to UNIX should be provided, even if that does not seem like the best way to implement the function. Alternative operations should be added to do things the "right" way.

• The process is the unit of work. Threads are resources of the process and are applied to the work of the process in much the same way as file descriptors. For example, threads in other processes are invisible.

Multithreaded Operations
System Calls

The base programmer interface for functions other than those relating to threads or multithreading is the System V Interface Definition, Third Edition (SVID3). In general, most current UNIX system calls remain unchanged. The main difference is that system calls that block do so to the lightweight process and, therefore, to the thread that executes them. However, programmers must understand that threads and LWPs share almost all the programmer visible process resources such as address space and file descriptor table. This can lead to several potential trouble spots:

• Because file descriptors are shared, if one thread closes a file, it is closed for all threads. Care must be taken with seeks before reads or writes, because another thread could change the seek position before the read or write (this is similar to what happens now when a parent and child process share a file descriptor).

• There is only one working directory for each process. If one thread changes the working directory, it is changed for all of them.

• There is only one set of user and group IDs for each process, so if one thread changes one of these, it is changed for all of them. Because these can change concurrently, the kernel must ensure that the values are sampled, atomically, only once per system call.

• Multiple threads may manipulate the shared address space at the same time via mmap (), brk (), or sbrk ().

• Programs must not make assumptions about "the" stack, because there may be several.

Threads and Lightweight Processes

One lightweight process is created by the kernel when a program is started, and it starts executing the thread compiled as the main program. Additional threads are created by calls to the library specifying a procedure for the new thread to execute and a stack area for it to use.

Depending on the implementation, on the library, or on programmer supplied parameters, a thread may be associated with the same or different lightweight processes during its lifetime. There may be a one-to-one relationship between threads and lightweight processes, or one or more lightweight processes may be multiplexed by the thread library among a set of threads. Ordinarily, a thread cannot tell what the relationship between lightweight processes and threads is, although for performance reasons, or to avoid some deadlocks, a program may require there to be more or fewer lightweight processes.

When a thread executes a kernel call, it remains bound to the same lightweight process for the duration of the kernel call. If the kernel call blocks, that thread and its lightweight process remain blocked. Other lightweight processes may execute other threads in that program, including performing other kernel calls. The same principle applies to page faults.

There is no systemwide name space for threads or lightweight processes. Thus, for example, it is not possible to direct a signal to a particular lightweight process from outside a process or to know which lightweight process sent a particular message.

Thread State

The following state is unique to each thread:

- Thread ID
- Register state (including PC and stack pointer)
- Stack
- Signal mask
- Priority

• Thread-local storage

All other process state is shared by the threads within the process.

Thread-Local Storage

Threads have some private storage (in addition to the stack) called thread-local storage. Most variables in the program are shared among all the threads executing it, but each thread has its own copy of thread-local variables. Conceptually, thread-local storage is unshared, statically allocated data. The C library variable errno is a good example of a variable that should be placed in thread-local storage. This allows each thread to reference errno directly, and it allows threads to interleave execution without fear of corrupting errno in other threads. Thread-local storage is potentially expensive to access, so it should be limited to the essentials, such as supporting older, nonreentrant interfaces.

It is implementation-dependent whether a thread is absolutely prevented from accessing another thread's stack or thread-local variables, but a correct thread must never attempt to do so.

Thread-local storage is obtained via a new #pragma, supported by the compiler and linker. The contents of thread-local storage are zeroed, initially; static initialization is not allowed. In C, thread-local storage for errno would be declared as follows:

```
#pragma unshared errno
extern int errno;
```

The size of thread-local storage is computed by the run-time linker at program start time by summing the thread-local storage requirements of the linked libraries. This prevents the exact size of thread-local storage from being part of the library interface.Once the size is computed it is not changed (e.g., by future dynamic linking in the process). This restriction prevents the size of thread-local storage from changing once a thread is started. Thus, thread-local storage requirements are known at thread start-up time and can be allocated as part of stack storage. More dynamic mechanisms (such as POSIX thread-specific data [POSIX 1990]) can be built using thread-local storage.

Thread Synchronization

Threads synchronize with each other using facilities supplied by the implementation that present a standard set of semantics. The following synchronization types are supported:

- Mutual exclusion (mutex) locks
- Counting semaphores
- Condition variables
- Multiple readers, single writer locks

The architecture allows a range of implementations of each synchronization type to be supported. For example, mutual exclusion locks may be implemented as spin locks, sleep locks, or adaptive locks, etc.

These facilities use synchronization variables in memory. The variables may be statically allocated and/or at fixed address (within the alignment constraints of the variable). The programmer may choose the particular implementation variant of the synchronization semantic at the time the variable is initialized. If the variable is initialized to zero, a default implementation is used.

Synchronization variables may also be placed in memory that is shared among processes. The programmer can select an implementation variant of each synchronization type that allows the variable to synchronize threads in the processes sharing the variable. Synchronization primitives apply to the shared variable as part of the underlying mapped object. In other words, synchronization variables may be shared among processes even though they are mapped at different virtual addresses.

Synchronization variables that are not in shared memory are completely unknown to the kernel. Synchronization variables that are in shared memory or in files are also unknown to the kernel unless a thread is blocked on them. In the latter case, the thread is temporarily bound to the LWP that is blocked by the kernel, as in a system call.

Signal Handling

Each thread has its own signal mask. This permits a thread to block some signals while it uses state that is also modified by a signal handler. All threads in the same address space share the set of signal handlers, which are set up by signal () and its variants, as usual. If desired, it would be possible for a particular application to implement per-thread signal handlers using the per-process signal handlers. For example, the signal handler can use the ID of the thread handling the signal as an index into a table of per-thread handlers. If the threads library was to implement per-thread signal handlers, it must decide on the correct semantics when several threads have different combinations of signal handlers, SIG_IGN, and SIG_DFL. In addition, all threads would be burdened with the handler state. For this reason, we felt that library support of per-thread signal handlers was overly complex and possibly confusing to the application programmer.

If a signal handler is marked SIG_DFL or SIG_IGN, the action on receipt of the signal (exit, core dump, stop, continue, or ignore) affects all the threads in the receiving process.

Signals are divided into two categories: traps and interrupts. Traps (e.g. SIGILL, SIGFPE, SIGSEGV) are signals that are caused synchronously by the operation of a thread, and are handled only by the thread that caused them. Several threads in the same address space could conceivably generate and handle the same kind of trap simultaneously. Interrupts (e.g., SIGINT, SIGIO) are signals that are caused asynchronously by something outside the process. An interrupt may be handled by any thread that has it enabled in its signal mask. If more than one thread is enabled to receive the interrupt, only one is chosen. Thus, several threads can be in the process of handling the same kind of signal simultaneously. If all threads mask a signal, it will pend on the process until a thread unmasks that signal. As in single-threaded processes, the number of signals received by the process is less than or equal to the number sent.

For example, an application can enable several threads to handle a particular I/O interrupt. As each new interrupt comes in, another thread is chosen to handle the signal until all the enabled threads are active. New signals will then pend waiting for threads to complete processing and re-enable signal handling.

Threads may send signals to other threads within the process via a new interface; thread kill (). In this case, the signal behaves like a trap and can be handled only by the specified thread. The programmer may also send a signal to all the threads via sigsend ().

A thread cannot send a signal to a specific thread in another process because threads in other processes are invisible.

Threads that are not bound to LWPs may not use alternate signal stacks. Adding alternate signal stacks to the unbound thread state was deemed too expensive to implement, because this would require a system call to establish the alternate stack for each context switch of a thread requiring it. Threads bound to LWPs may use alternate stacks as this state is associated with each LWP.

Nonlocal Goto

setjmp () and longjmp () work only within a particular thread. In particular, it is an error for a thread to longjmp () into another thread. Therefore, it is possible to longjmp () from a signal handler only when the setjmp () was executed by the thread that is handling the signal.

Thread Interfaces

Most of the interfaces available to threads are those that are available to UNIX processes in single-threaded UNIX. As mentioned above, some of those interfaces have different implications in a multithreaded environment, but the intent is to provide "UNIX semantics" as the ordinary programming model. This section describes some of the additional interfaces needed to create and manage threads.

The syntax of the interfaces is shown in Figure 24.4.

Thread Creation thread_create () creates a new thread. If stack_addr is not NULL, stack_size bytes of memory starting at stack_addr are used for the thread stack. In this case, any thread-local storage is also placed on the stack so as not to interfere with stack growth. This allows a language run-time library to control thread storage, without interference, with its memory allocator. It is machine dependent whether the initial stack pointer is at higher or lower addresses in the specified stack. If stack_addr is NULL, the stack is allocated from the heap. If stack_size is not zero, the stack will be of the specified size. Otherwise a default stack size is used. Zeroed thread-local storage is also allocated to the thread. thread_create () returns the ID of the new thread. The thread IDs have meaning only within a process. The initial thread priority and signal mask is set to the same values as its creator. When the new thread is started, it begins execution by a procedure call to func (arg). If func returns, the thread exits (calls thread_exit ()). The flags argument provides the following (or'able) options:

- THREAD_STOP
  The thread is to be immediately suspended after it is created. The thread will not run until another thread executes thread continue () to start it. If THREAD_STOP is not specified, the thread is immediately runnable.

- THREAD_NEW_LWP
  A new LWP is created along with the thread. The new LWP is added to the pool of LWPs used to execute threads.

- THREAD_BIND_LWP
  A new LWP is created and the new thread is permanently bound to it.

- THREAD_WAIT
  Specifies that another thread will eventually wait for this thread to exit. This also means that the thread ID of a thread created with THREAD_WAIT will not be reused until the waiting thread returns. If the thread is not created with THREAD_WAIT, the thread ID may be reused at any time after the thread exits.

Thread Concurrency Control thread_setconcurrency () sets the degree of real concurrency (i.e., the number of LWPs) that unbound threads in the application require to n. The number of LWPs permanently bound to threads is not included in n. If n is zero (the default), the library automatically creates as many LWPs for use in scheduling unbound threads as required to avoid deadlock. This number can be incremented by creating a thread with the THREAD_NEW_LWP flag. If n is less than the current maximum, LWPs are removed from the pool. thread_setconcur-

```
thread_id_t
thread_create (char *stack_addr,
    unsigned int stack_size,
    void (*func) (),
    void *arg,
    int flags);

int
thread_setconcurrency (int n);

void
thread_exit ();

thread_id_t
thread_wait (thread_id_t thread_id);

thread_id_t
thread_get_id ();

int
thread_sigsetmask (int how,
    sigset_t *set,
    sigset_t *oset);

int
thread_kill (thread_id_t thread_id,
    int sig);

int
thread_stop (thread_id_t thread_id);

int
thread_continue (thread_id_t thread_id);

int
thread_priority (thread_id_t thread_id,
    int priority);

void
mutex_init (mutex_t *mp,
    int type,
    void *arg);

void
mutex_enter (mutex_t *mp);

void
mutex_exit (mutex_t *mp);

int
mutex_tryenter (mutex_t *mp);
```

```
void
cv_init (condvar_t *cvp,
    int type
    void *arg);

void
cv_wait (condvar_t *cvp,
    mutex_t *mutexp);

void
cv_signal (condvar_t *cvp);

void
cv_broadcast (condvar_t *cvp);

void
sema_init (sema_t *sp,
    unsigned int count,
    int type,
    void *arg);

void
sema_p (sema_t *sp);

void
sema_v (sema_t *sp);

int
sema_tryp (sema_t *sp);

void
rw_init (rwlock_t *rwlp,
    int type,
    void *arg);

void
rw_enter (rwlock_t *rwlp,
    rw_type_t type);

void
rw_exit (rwlock_t *rwlp);

int
rw_tryenter (rwlock_t *rwlp,
    rw_type_t type);

void
rw_downgrade (rwlock_t *rwlp);

int
rw_tryupgrade (rwlock_t *rwlp);
```

FIGURE 24.4. *Thread interface functions.*

rency () guarantees only that this degree of concurrency is available to application threads. The actual number of LWPs employed by the library at any one time may vary.

The number of LWPs automatically created by the library (n = 0) is sufficient to avoid deadlock, but it may not be enough to avoid poor performance; the library may create too few or too many LWPs. The programmer may tune the number of LWPs by creating threads with the THREAD_NEW_LWP flag or using thread_setconcurrency () as required by the application.

- *Thread termination*
  thread_exit () terminates the current thread and deallocates thread resources allocated by the threads package.

- *Waiting for threads*
  thread_wait () blocks until the specified thread exits. It is an error to wait for a thread that was created without the THREAD_WAIT attribute, to wait for the current thread, or to have multiple thread_wait () s on the same thread. If thread_id is NULL, then any thread marked THREAD_WAIT that exits causes thread_wait () to return. If a stack was supplied by the programmer when the thread was created, it may be reclaimed when thread_wait () returns successfully. thread_wait () returns the ID of the thread that exited if the wait is successful. After thread_wait () returns successfully, the returned thread_id is unusable in any subsequent thread operation.

  An alternate interface for this function is waitid () with id_type equal to one of the following:

P_THREAD
  waitid () waits for the thread specified by id.
P_THREAD_ALL
  waitid () waits for any thread marked
  THREAD_WAIT.

The exit status of a thread is always zero.

Thread identification: thread_get_id () returns the thread ID of the caller.

Thread signal mask: thread_sigsetmask () or sigprocmask () sets the thread's signal mask.

Thread signaling: thread_kill () causes the specified signal to be sent to the specified thread. An alternate interface for this function is sigsend () with id_type equal to one of the following:

P_THREAD
 sig is sent to the thread within the process
 specified by id.
P_THREAD_ALL
 sig is sent to all the threads within the process.

Thread execution control: thread_stop () prevents the specified thread from running. If thread_id is NULL, then the current thread is immediately stopped. thread_continue () initially starts a thread or restarts a thread after thread_stop (). The effect of thread_continue () may be delayed, but thread_stop () does not return until the specified thread is stopped.

Thread priority control: thread_priority () sets the priority of the specified thread. If thread_id is NULL, the current thread is used. The priority must be greater than or equal to zero. Increasing the specified priority gives increasing scheduling priority. The old priority is returned. If the specified thread is not running then it may or may not execute immediately even though its new priority is greater than a currently executing thread.

Thread synchronization: The thread synchronization facilities are designed to synchronize threads both within a process and between processes. When a synchronization variable is initialized, the programmer must specify whether the synchronization variable is to be shared among processes. The programmer can usually also specify other variants such as extra debugging, spin waiting, etc. The programmer may bitwise-or THREAD_SYNC_SHARED into the variant type to specify that the variable is to be shared among processes.

 Any synchronization variable that is statically or dynamically allocated as zero may be used immediately without further initialization, and provides the default implementation variant in the default initial state. A dynamic initialization with an implementation variant type of zero also specifies the default implementation variant.

Mutex locks:
Mutex locks provide simple mutual exclusion. They are low overhead in both space and time and are, therefore, suitable for high-frequency usage. Mutex locks are strictly bracketing in that it is an error for a thread to release a lock not held by the thread. Mutex locks are used to prevent data inconsistencies in critical sections of code. They may also be used to preserve code that is single threaded.

mutex_enter () acquires the lock, potentially blocking if it is already held; mutex exit () releases the lock, potentially unblocking a waiter. mutex_tryenter () acquires the lock if it is not already held. mutex_tryenter () can be used to avoid deadlock in operations that would normally violate the lock hierarchy.

Condition variables:
Condition variables are used to wait until a particular condition is true. Condition variables must be used in conjunction with a mutex lock. This implements a typical monitor.

cv_wait () blocks until the condition is signaled. It releases the associated mutex before blocking, and reacquires it before returning. Since the reacquiring of the mutex may be blocked by other threads waiting for the mutex, the condition that caused the wait must be retested. Thus, typical usage is:

```
mutex_enter (&m) ;
. . .
while (some_condition) {
    cv_wait (&cv, &m) ;
}
. . .
mutex_exit (&m) ;
```

This allows the condition to be a complicated expression, as it is protected by the mutex. There is no guaranteed order of acquisition if more than one thread blocks on the condition variable.

cv_signal () wakes up one of the threads blocked in

cv_wait (). cv_broadcast () wakes up all of the threads blocked in cv_wait (). Since cv_broadcast ()causes all threads blocking on the condition to recontend for the mutex, it should be used with care. For example, it is appropriate to use cv_broadcast () to allow threads to contend for variable amounts of resources when resources are released.

Semaphores: The semaphore synchornization facilities provide classic counting semaphores. They are not as efficient as mutex locks, but they need not be bracketed so that they may be used for asynchronous event notification (e.g., in signal handlers). They also contain state so they may be used asynchronously without acquiring a mutex as required by condition variables.

sema_p () decrements the semaphore, potentially blocking the thread. sema_v () increments the semaphore, potentially unblocking a waiting thread. sema tryp () decrements the semaphore if blocking is not required.

Multiple readers, single writer locks: Multiple readers, single writer locks allow many threads simultaneous read-only access to an object protected by this lock simultaneously. It allows only one thread to access an object for writing at any one time, and excludes any readers. A good candidate for a multiple readers, single writer lock is an object that is searched more frequently than it is changed. For brevity, this type of lock is also known as a readers/ writer lock.

rw_enter () attempts to acquire a reader or writer lock. type may be one of the following:

- RW_READER Acquire a readers lock.
- RW_WRITER Acquire a writer lock.

rw_exit () releases a readers or writer lock. rw_tryenter () acquires a readers or writer lock if doing so would not require blocking. rw_downgrade () atomically converts a writer lock into a reader lock. Any waiting writers remain waiting. If there are no waiting writers, it wakes up any pending readers. rw_tryupgrade ()

attempts to atomically convert a reader lock into a writer lock. If there is another rw_tryupgrade () in progress or there are any writers waiting, it returns a failure indication.

Lightweight Process State

A lightweight process consists of a data structure in the kernel used for processor scheduling, page fault handling, and kernel call execution. It also contains state that is private to the LWP and an association with a process (address space). The following programmer-visible state is maintained by the kernel and is unique to each LWp within a process:

- LWP ID
- Register state (including PC and stack pointer)
- Signal mask
- Alternate signal stack and masks for alternate stack disable and onstack
- User and user+system virtual time alarms
- User time and system CPU usage
- Profiling state
- Scheduling class and priority

All other process states are shared by the LWPs within the process.

Note that even though the CPU usage, virtual time alarms, and alternate signal stack are available to each LWP, this state is not kept for each thread that is multiplexed on LWPs. Threads that require this state must be bound to an LWP. Whether the LWP state includes a separate stack area known to the kernel or not is implementation dependent. Of course, the lightweight process runs with a stack.

Signals

A new signal, SIGWAITING, is sent to the process when all its LWPs are waiting for some indefinite, external event (e.g., in poll ()). The default handling for SIGWAITING is to ignore it. The threads package can use the receipt of SIGWAITING to cause extra LWPs to be created as required to avoid deadlock. This is similar in functionality to the architecture described in [Anderson 1990].

While SIGWAITING is sent for "indefinite" waits, supposedly short-term blocking for things like page faults or file system I/O may take a long time relative to the speed of the CPUs. It may be desirable to define an alternate signal that is sent in these cases.

Time, Interval Timers, and Profiling

There is only one real-time interval timer per process, so it delivers one signal to an address space when it reaches the specified time interval. Library routines may implement multiple per-thread timers using the per-address space timer when that functionality is required. Each LWP has two private interval timers: one decrements in LWP user time, and the other decrements in both LWP user time and when the system is running on behalf of the LWP. When these interval timers expire, either SIGVTALRM or SIGPROF, as appropriate, is sent to the LWP that owns the interval timer.

Profiling is enabled for each LWP individually. Each LWP can set up a separate profiling buffer, but it may also share one if accumulated information is desired. Profiling information is updated at each clock tick in LWP user time. The state of profiling is inherited from the creating LWP.

Resource Usage

The resource limits set limits on the resource usage of the entire process (i.e., the sum of the resource usage of all the LWPs in the process). When a soft resource limit has been exceeded, the LWP that exceeded the limit is sent the appropriate signal. The sum of the resource usage (including CPU usage) for all LWPs in the process is available via getrusage ().

Process Creation and Destruction

The fork () system call attempts to duplicate the existing UNIX semantics. It duplicates the address space and creates the same LWPs in the same states as in the original. This duplicates the threads in the original process. Calling fork () may cause interruptible system calls to return EINTR when the calls are made by any LWP (thread) other than the one calling fork ().

A new system call, fork1 (), causes the current thread/LWP to fork, but the other threads and LWPs that existed in the original process are not duplicated in the new process. fork1 () is defined as follows:

```
int fork1 ();
```

The return values are similar to fork ().

Both the exit () and exec () system calls work as usual, except that they destroy all the LWPs in the address space. Both calls block until all the LWPs (and, therefore, all active threads) are destroyed. When exec () rebuilds the process, it creates a single LWP. The process startup code then builds the initial thread.

Why have both fork ()and fork1 ()? UNIX fork () seems to have two generic uses: to duplicate the entire process (the BSD dump program uses this technique), or to create a new process in order to set up for exec (). For the latter purpose, fork1 () is much more efficient because there is no need to duplicate all the LWPs. There are, however, dangers to using fork1 (). First, since threads are maintained by the threads library as data structures, the threads library must take care that after fork1 () only the issuing thread remains in the new address space, which is a duplicate of the old one. Secondly, the programmer must be careful to call only functions that do not require locks held by threads that no longer exist in the new process. This can be difficult to determine as libraries can create hidden threads. Lastly, locks that are allocated in memory that is sharable (i.e., mmap () 'ed with the MAP_SHARED flag) can be held by a thread in both processes, unless care is taken to avoid this. The latter problem can also arise with fork ().

Having fork () completely duplicate the process is the semantic that is most similar to the single-threaded fork (). It allows both generic uses, and there are fewer pitfalls for the programmer. Having fork1 (), which forks only one thread, permits optimized fork () and immediate exec () (e.g., system ()).

Scheduling

LWPs (and bound threads) can change their scheduling class and class priority via the priocntl () system call. A new scheduling class for "gang" scheduling is available for implementations of fine grain parallelism. The LWP may also ask to be bound to a CPU, depending on the scheduling class.

Debugging

The /**proc** file system has been extended to reflect the changes to the process model required by the addition of multithreading at the process level. Of necessity, a kernel process model interface can provide access only to kernel-supported threads of control, namely LWPs. Debugger control of library threads is accomplished by cooperation between the debugger and the threads library, with the aid of the /**proc** file system to control the kernel-supported LWPs.

The details of the proc file system and some of the enhancements for multithreading support can be found in [Faulkner 1991].

Performance

All the performance numbers in this section were obtained on a SPARCstation 1+ (Sun4/65), which is a 25Mhz SPARC platform. The measurements were made using the built-in microsecond resolution real-time timer. The numbers reflect an untuned prototype system.

Thread Creation Time

The first measurement is for thread creation time. It measures the time consumed to create a thread using a default stack that is cached by the threads package. The measured time only includes the actual creation time, it does not include the time for the initial context switch to the thread. The results are shown in Table 24.5.

The ratio column gives the ratio of the creation time in that row to the creation time in the previous row.

Measurements were taken for creating both bound and unbound threads. Bound thread creation involves calling the kernel to also create an LWP to run it. Unbound thread creation is done without kernel involvement.

	Time (usec)	Ratio
Unbound thread create	56	—
Bound thread create	2327	42

TABLE 24.5

Thread Synchronization Time

The second measurement is for thread synchronization time. It measures the time it takes for two threads to synchronize with each other using two synchronization variables, as shown below:

```
sema_t sl, s2;
thread1 ()
{
    . . .
    start_timer ();
    sema_v (&sl);
    sema_p (&s2);
    t = end_timer ();
    . . .
}
thread2 ()
{
    . . .
    sema_p (&s2);
    sema_v (&sl);
    . . .
}
```

The numbers presented in Table 24.6 are the results of the above measurement divided by two, since there are actually two synchronizations involved. The ratio column gives the ratio of the synchro-

	Time (usec)	Ratio
Setjmp/longjmp	59	—
Unbound thread sync	158	2.7
Bound thread sync	348	2.2
Cross process thread sync	301	.86

TABLE 24.6. *Thread synchronization time.*

nization time in that row to the synchronization time in the previous row.

The first measurement is a simple routine that does a setjmp () and longjmp () to itself. It is presented as a baseline for thread switching time. The next two measurements are for unbound and bound threads synchronizing within a process. The last measurement is for threads in two different processes synchronizing through a file in shared memory.

Comparison with Other Thread Models

This section addresses the similarities and differences between the SunOS multithread (MT) architecture and other commercially available multithread interfaces. Instead of comparing procedural interfaces, the discussions concentrate on comparing and contrasting architectural issues. The comparisons underscore what we believe are the key differences rather than being comprehensive.

Mach Release 2.5 C Threads

Mach Release 2.5 C Threads [Cooper 1990], [Tevanian 1987] exemplifies a thread interface that provides the programmer with the means to express concurrency, independent of the underlying system support. While this is a desirable trait, Mach 2.5 C Threads does not acknowledge the existence of a second layer of abstraction (i.e., LWPs) and, therefore, does not allow the programmer to control the degree of kernel resources it uses. In many useful applications, the programmer must know and manipulate the degree of actual kernel resources required. For example, a window system programmer must know that extremely lightweight threads are available, since a window system may use thousands. A micro-tasking Fortran run-time library relies on kernel-supported threads that are scheduled on processors as a group. Database programmers may require a mixture of the two situations. In addition, there may be aspects to kernel-supported threads that are too "heavyweight" to export to lightweight threads (e.g., virtual time) and are required by some applications.

In Mach 2.5, C Threads libraries have been constructed that map threads directly to kernel-supported threads or multiplex threads on kernel-supported threads, but one application cannot have both types at the same time. In addition, there can be no direct access to "heavyweight" features of kernel-supported threads, since that would allow only a one-to-one mapping between threads and kernel-supported threads.

Newer versions of Mach [Golub 1990] have corrected some of these deficiencies by extending the C Threads interface to provide a two-level model similar to ours. In the new library, C Threads are multiplexed on Mach kernel threads. In addition, new C Threads interfaces allow C Threads to bind to Mach kernel threads.

The main difference between the C Threads synchronization primitives and the SunOS MT architecture primitives is the scope of operation. C Threads does not explicitly support the use synchronization variables allocated in mmap'ed memory even though Mach virtual memory supports the sharing of memory between tasks. The SunOS MT architecture does support this. It also allows the placement of synchronization variables in files to control access to the file data, and having the lifetime of such synchronization variables be greater than that of the creating process.

C Threads supports per-process signal state. There is no per-thread signal mask. There is no way for a thread to control when it can handle a signal except by preventing all the threads in a process from handling it. When a particular thread is in a critical section of code with respect to the signal handler, it must block the interrupt for all threads. This can cause severe performance problems in heavily asynchronous applications. The alternate solution for C Threads is Mach IPC. Mach IPC, however, does not allow asynchronous interruption of a computation. For example, an application that creates a thread to perform some long computation may wish to terminate the computation regardless of results. There is no way to interrupt the computation unless it is coded to occasionally poll for IPC. This forces the programmer to change the computation code so that polling is done frequently enough to respond to a termination request, but not so frequently as to slow down the computation.

Chorus

Chorus [Armand 1990] intentionally avoided user-level threads because of a perceived impact on real-time requirements. For example, the two levels of scheduling interfere with the requirement that the highest priority runnable thread is always allowed to run. SunOS meets this requirement by allowing a thread to bind to an LWP and, thus, achieve a systemwide scheduling priority. In addition, the bound thread can ask that the underlying LWP be made a member of a real-time scheduling class, which provides more exact scheduling control.

Chrous threads each have a signal mask and a vector of signal handlers. The effect of receipt of an asynchronously generated signal and combinations of catching SIG_DFL, and SIG_IGN are computed. If one or more threads are catching the signal, it is delivered to all catching threads (broadcast delivery). Otherwise, if any thread has set the handler to SIG_IGN, the signal is discarded. Otherwise the default action is taken on the process. The main deficiency in this model is that broadcast delivery can cause "synchronization storms" when the handling threads try to synchronize. It also causes much extra work for the kernel. Lastly, broadcast makes the number of signals delivered to a process uncountable in a nonqueuing signal implementation. For example, if several threads are waiting for a keyboard interrupt, and two are sent, some threads will receive two signals while others will receive one.

The per-thread signal handlers add some code modularity, at the cost of complexity in the handling of SIG_DFL and SIG_IGN as noted above. The modularity added is relatively minor because asynchronous signals are mostly controlled by the application, not the library. In addition, serial handling of the same signal within a thread is still a problem, just as it is in single-threaded UNIX.

University of Washington

The variant of the Topaz [McJones 1989] operating system by the University of Washington [Anderson 1990] implements a portable threads interface with lightweight user-level threads that use kernel resources only as required. In most cases, threads can synchronize without kernel involvement, while at the same time, I/O, page faults, and other blocking operations do not stop the entire process. This approach has the same advantages as our threads multiplexed on LWPs. However, programmer control over the use of kernel resources is not supported.

The main underlying difference between the University of Washington work and the SunOS MT architecture is that the University of Washington work uses lightweight "scheduler activations" that do upcalls into user space to give schedulable execution contexts to the threads package. An upcall by a new scheduler activation informs the threads package whenever a scheduler activation currently in use by the process blocks in the kernel. This gives the threads package the opportunity to schedule another runnable thread. This is similar to the function of the new SIGWAITING signal in our architecture. This signal also gives the threads library the opportunity to schedule a runnable thread by first creating a new LWP. The main difference is that the current definition of SIGWAITING is much more coarse than the way scheduler activations are used. The former is sent only when the LWP blocks in an indefinite wait. The latter is sent whenever the thread blocks in the kernel for any event. In the future, we plan to experiment with sending signals on "faster" events.

The University of Washington approach gives much finer-grained control over scheduling threads on processors, though it is not clear that this is an absolute requirement. In general, the SunOS MT architecture satisfies most of the requirements that motivated the University of Washington group. The critical observation made by both efforts was that the kernel need not be invoked for every thread operation.

POSIX P1003.4a

Comparison with POSIX P1003.4a Pthreads [POSIX 1990] is somewhat difficult at this time, as it is a moving target. Currently (pre Draft 10) it seems that the signal model is a direct superset of the SunOS model. In addition, there seems to be support for the two-level threads model in the scheduling interfaces. However, the interaction between synchronization variables and mapped files (P1003.4) is missing.

Sun LWP library

The Sun LWP library [Kepecs 1985] supplied in SunOS 4.0 is a classic user-level-only threads package. It contained no explicit kernel support. Threads (called LWPs) synchronized with each other without kernel involvement. If an LWP called a blocking system call or took a page fault, the entire application blocked. This could be mitigated somewhat by using a nonblocking I/O library instead of the standard UNIX I/O interfaces. The nonblocking I/O library uses kernel-supported asynchronous I/O facilities to mimic standard I/O interfaces and allows the package to switch LWPs when one blocked on an indefinite I/O. The application was still blocked when a page fault was taken.

The SunOS multithread architecture completely supersedes this interface in functionality.

Summary

The SunOS multithreading architecture provides the following advantages:

- The two-level (threads and LWP) model allows the programmer to decouple logical program parallelism from the relatively expensive kernel-supported parallelism. Programmers can rely on the availability of extremely lightweight threads.

- The architecture allows the programmer to control the degree of real concurrency the application requires or allows the threads package to automatically decide this.

- The architecture has a uniform synchronization model between threads both inside and outside a process.

- The programmer can control the mapping of threads onto

LWPs to achieve particular performance or functionality without leaving the threads model.

- The programmer can control the allocation of stacks and thread-local storage. This allows coexistence with different memory allocation models (e.g., garbage collection).

- A minimalist translation of the UNIX environment to threads allows higher-level interfaces such as POSIX Pthreads to be implemented on top of SunOS threads.

References

[Anderson 1990] T.E. Anderson, B.N. Bershad, E.D. Lazowska, H.M. Levy, "Scheduler Activations: Effective Kernel Support of the User-Level Management of Parallelism", Department of Computer Science and Engineering, University of Washington, Technical Report 90-04-02, April 1990.

[Armand 1990] F. Armand, F. Herrmann, J. Lipkis, M. Rozier, "Multi-threaded Processes in Chorus/MIX", Proc. EUUG Spring 1990 Conference, Munich, Germany, April 1990.

[Cooper 1990] E.C. Cooper, R.P. Draves, "C Threads", Department of Computer Science, Carnegie Mellon University, September 1990.

[Faulkner 1991] R. Faulkner, R. Gomes, "The Process File System and Process Model in UNIX System V", Proc. 1991 USENIX Winter Conference.

[Golub 1990] D. Golub, R. Dean, A. Florin, R. Rashid, "UNIX as an Application Program", Proc. 1990 USENIX Summer Conference, pp. 87–95.

[Kepecs 1985] J. Kepecs, "Lightweight Processes for UNIX Implementation and Applications", Proc. 1985 USENIX Summer Conference, pp 299–308.

[McJones 1989] P.R. McJones and G.F. Swart, "Evolving the UNIX System Interface to Support Multithreaded Program", Proc. 1989 USENIX Winter Conference, pp 393–404.

[POSIX 1990] POSIX P1003.4a, "Threads Extension for Portable Operating Systems", IEEE.

[Tevanian 1987] A. Tevanian, R.F. Rashid, D.B. Golub, D.L. Black, E. Cooper, and M.W. Young, "Mach Threads and the UNIX Kernel: The Battle for Control", Proc. 1987 USENIX Summer Conference, pp University of California at Berkeley in 1984.

Understanding the Application Binary Interface

SPARC INTERNAL WHITE PAPER

25

The concept of the application binary interface (ABI) has received a considerable amount of attention recently as a solution to the perennial problem of how to develop and distribute software that will run across a wide range of UNIX-based systems. The ABI is a document that comprehensively defines the binary system interface between applications and the operating system on which they run.

To understand the benefits of a standard ABI, just consider the market for DOS software. With a common DOS ABI, developers needed to write just one version of their product. Retailers carry just one "shrink-wrapped" package on their shelves. Users can purchase a DOS package, confident that it will install easily and run on their PC compatibles. Without doubt, this standardization —which the microcomputer industry stumbled upon quite unconsciously—is a major reason for the huge library of software applications now available for PCs.

This standardization has come about because of two factors: PC-DOS is a proprietary operating system controlled by one company; and it is tied to one architecture.

How can the UNIX software developer realize the same benefits, given the multiplicity of computer architectures and the varieties of UNIX implementations? AT&T and Sun Microsystems, along with other UNIX International members, have developed the notion of the ABI for UNIX System V Release 4. The ABI precisely addresses this issue and provides binary portability across different vendors' UNIX platforms.

At present, few value-added resellers (VARs) or distributors who resell UNIX software even attempt to shrink-wrap their products. Rather, they typically cut fresh tapes or disks on demand for a particular platform. In the future, however, it will be practical for the reseller to stock limited numbers of versions of any one application. This will be true even though System V Release 4 implementations on different platforms have been created by different vendors, because the ABI provides a well-defined, complete, and verifiable interface.

The ABI will alter the economics of UNIX software substantially. Because software vendors need to produce far fewer versions of an application to reach the entire UNIX marketplace, their costs—for porting, testing, distributing, and supporting software—will diminish. This favorable leverage will lead to the availability of more, and less expensive, applications on UNIX platforms.

ABI: A Closer Look

The ABI specifies the complete environment, including system services, libraries, files, calling conventions—everything an application needs to run—plus the file formats, media, and installation procedures to be used to package and install the application. The ABI is a contract: system vendors promise to run any software that conforms to the ABI and software developers promise to write applications that run on any ABI platform.

Because UNIX runs on many architectures and the ABI is a binary interface, the ABI is actually a family of specifications. The SPARC ABI, for example, comprises two sections: the generic part, which describes those aspects constant across all hardware architectures, and a SPARC-specific part, which describes details specific to SPARC machines. ABI specifications are being developed for many architectures, including SPARC, Intel's x86 and Motorola's 680x and 88000.

Contents of the ABI

An ABI document is defined based on several standards, including POSIX 1003.1, ANSI C, X Window System Version 11, System V

Interface (SVID) Definition 89, and X/Open Portability Guide 3rd Edition (XPG3). The content of the ABI specification is very detailed and exhaustive. It includes both generic and processor-specific groups.

The generic ABI contains software installation and packaging/media specifications; file formats such as character representations and object file formats, called extended linkage format (ELF); libraries such as system, C, network, and RPC; and applications environments such as file system structure, commands, and window systems—which are optional.

The processor-specific ABI contains machine interfaces such as data representation and function-call sequence; operating system interfaces to determine such items as address space, page size, and process stack; coding samples, dynamic lining tables, and system data interfaces such as header files.

ABI Features

What distinguishes the ABI from the implicit binary standards that exist? It has the following advantages: precision and completeness, an evolution path, and new technology.

Precision and Completeness

Existing binary interfaces are usually derived from a particular implementation and are incomplete and ill-defined, leaving the door open for obscure bugs in new versions. The ABI, on the contrary, is explicitly defined and is thus verifiable. This allows both hardware vendors and application vendors to easily implement the ABI standard with confidence.

Evolution Path

Because the ABI definition process is open and vendor-neutral, many parties support its evolution. In addition, the technology of dynamic linking enables the smooth evolution of the standard-old software can be supported with compatibility libraries while new software can use the latest system features.

New Technology

Dynamic linking is an important addition to the ABI because it allows scalability. Using this feature, applications can run on platforms with widely different characteristics. All external references are not statically bound into the application; details of hardware configuration and system interface are only linked-in at load time so that the appropriate shared libraries are used. This allows an application, for instance, to take advantage of a floating point co-processor if it exists on a particular platform.

Software Distribution Mechanisms for UNIX

Many different schemes have been devised for selling or distributing software for UNIX. In the early days, UNIX was usually distributed as source, and the user compiled and built the operating system and programs needed. Other formats used include object files, executable files, intermediate code, and assembly language (sometimes encrypted with keys obtained from the vendor, sometimes requiring conference calls between the hardware vendor, the software vendor, and the local UNIX guru to make it work).

Source distribution of software is a UNIX tradition. It has the advantage that a single-source product can be sufficient for all architectures. Customers may also modify the software to meet their needs. In theory, source distribution should provide the way to reach the widest market at the least cost.

In practice, however, source is an unacceptable medium for most end users. Many customers are unable to cope with source. Not only do most machines not have compilers, but most people are not willing to learn the complex compilation procedures needed for non-trivial applications. Many machines have insufficient memory of disk space to compile modern applications. Moreover, truly portable software is extremely difficult to write, especially when the application uses many system features or when performance is important. It is common for "portable" software to include machine-dependent portions for each machine it has been ported to.

Many software vendors also find source an inadequate distribution vehicle. Source compromises the intellectual property of the vendor, greatly increasing the opportunities for piracy and reducing the incentive to invest in better software. Furthermore, the software vendor cannot exactly control the end product, leading to potential support problems as well.

In summary, source may be a acceptable medium for certain groups of expert customers, but it is not usable for mass-market software.

The Intermediate Alternative

Using the intermediate code, such as UCSD P-code or other architecture-independent formats of software, has some advantages over source. With this approach, the source is partially compiled and a presumably portable representation of the program is distributed. The user compiles the intermediate code to the appropriate machine during installation, the intellectual property of the developer is somewhat more secure and the compilation system needed for most intermediate code is fairly simple. Intermediate code, like source, may be portable to multiple architectures, although there may be some assumptions such as word size, data formats, or byte order.

Unfortunately, such intermediate forms have many of the same disadvantages of source—the problems have just been moved down a level. Truly portable intermediate forms are just as unsatisfactory as truly portable source. The performance, correctness, and quality of the software depends on the compiler. Testing is still difficult because the developer does not know what machine the software depends on the compiler. Testing is still difficult because the developer does not know what machine the software will run on, but the user has less ability to fix bugs that are exposed by a particular configuration. The application vendor still faces support and quality assurance problems, because assumptions have to be made about the user's environment and the correctness of translators and the translation procedures.

Intermediate code is better than source in some ways, but still poses support problems and requires some user sophistication. The Open Software Foundation (OSF) has proposed a form of intermediate code, known as "Architecture-Neutral Distribution

Format (ANDF)" as a solution the UNIX software distribution issue. ANDF and ABI are not mutually exclusive concepts: the hardware-dependent translation mechanism on the target system may choose to generate an executable that adheres to the ABI for that architecture.

Historically, binary distributions have had some problems. The most popular binary standards are based on proprietary systems. The interfaces are often poorly specified, because there is only on implementation and it is considered sufficient to run the application on that one system to know that it meets the standard. Binaries often depend on more than just the architecture—for example, a program that runs only on certain versions of the system. Because the standard is not well-documented, such problems are usually found only after the product has shipped.

Nevertheless, it is clear that binary solutions offer the best mechanism. From the point of view of the user, shrink-wrapped binaries require the least effort. For high-volume software vendors, binary standards make possible the creation of highly optimized applications and allow for easy manufacturing and support.

Implementation

UNIX International (UI) has proposed the ABI as the binary standard for UNIX software distribution. The ABI conforms to the POSIX and X/Open standards; it has also been subject to wide industry review. UI hopes the benefits of the ABI to both the hardware vendor community and software vendors are so great, the ABI will become the shrink-wrapped standard for UNIX.

The ABI will continue to evolve and UNIX International will work with the industry to refine the ABI. SPARC International will work with UNIX International to refine the SPARC-specific portion of the ABI. In addition, SPARC International will administer the compliance process for the SPARC ABI.

SPARC Compliance Definition

26

SPARC INTERNATIONAL WHITE PAPER

The idea behind SPARC

The SPARC microprocessor architecture was designed to run lots of applications on lots of different system platforms. And because SPARC's architecture allows implementations that are both powerful and scalable, it serves as an ideal platform for the most powerful software—for anything from laptops to supercomputers.

SPARC is the first and only microprocessor architecture designed for implementation in a variety of ways by a variety of competing microprocessor vendors. So microprocessor vendors compete not only in price (as they do with second-sourcing), but in quality and variety. The result is a whole buffet of implementation choices. This is completely new to the microprocessor business, where entire markets have always balanced on a single vendor's proprietary microprocessor architecture.

SPARC was created when Sun Microsystems recognized that monopolies were no longer acceptable at any level, and that history had passed the point where one microprocessor vendor could or should be in a position to offer their proprietary architecture as a standard for the whole world.

SPARC and UNIX are the only standards capable of creating and supporting a substantial popular market for the next generation of applications, and—because SPARC is scalable—for generations to come.

In fact, that market already exists, because SPARC is also the first and only new microprocessor architecture ever accompanied to market by thousands of native applications. Virtually the entire library of applications written for Sun workstations has been ported to the SPARC platform, and countless new applications are being designed, because ISVs know the market is there, and it will include not only Sun's SPARC systems, but those of many other system vendors.

SPARC International's Role

Unlike every other microprocessor ever designed, SPARC is not proprietary to a single vendor. While it was designed by Sun Microsystems, and Sun continues to license it, SPARC standards, and the trademarks that affirm those standards, are the responsibilities of SPARC International, an independent organization of SPARC silicon, system and software vendors, as well as interested individuals. It is SPARC International that publishes the SPARC Compliance Definition. Through its committee structure, SPARC International will specify the SCD to include important compatibility standards for windowing operations, graphics libraries, internationalization, networking, fonts, and other extensions.

The SCD allows SPARC International members to create a broad base of binary-compatible SPARC products that can be verified with openly agreed-upon standard definitions. Binary compatibility allows ISVs to develop "shrink-wrap" software that will run on any compliant hardware platform.

The SCD specifications give SPARC International members control over the operating environment for which they will develop compatible products in coming years. Therefore, the SPARC operating environment defined in the SCD builds upon product families and standards that already exist. The core of the SCD is the UNIX operating system. The first version, SCD 1.0, is based on Sun Operating System (OS) 4.0.3, a derivative of Berkeley UNIX. SCD 2.0 is based on the industry-standard UNIX System V, Release 4.0 (SVR4). Future extensions and enhancements will be added to the SCD as the SPARC software portfolio gradually migrates to SVR4 and SCD 2.0. This migration strategy will efficiently and effectively leverage the 3400+ SPARC applications already available for SunOS into the SVR4 library. SPARC International expects the largest percentage of SVR4 applications will be delivered from the SPARC sector of the SVR4 market, by means of this migration strategy.

The fact that SPARC-compatible software products are already shipping for both Sun OS and SVR4 makes the process of defining and specifying migration much more manageable for SPARC vendors than for those using other RISC architectures. Smooth migration offers increased market opportunity for participating vendors and a corresponding increase in the volume of SPARC systems and applications. RISC architectures that lack a clear migration strategy will find their system and application software bases fragmented rather than unified. A graphical representation of the migration process is shown in Figure 26.1.

While SVR4 has ABIs for many different microprocessors, only the SPARC ABI has the benefit of a migration strategy that leverages a large and unified body of existing applications. Not only is a SPARC system company (ICL) today the only vendor shipping both SVR4 and a growing portfolio of SVR4 applications, but this migration strategy will add those applications to the thousands already running on SPARC systems with SunOS—and will ultimately turn both together in to a volume substantial enough to

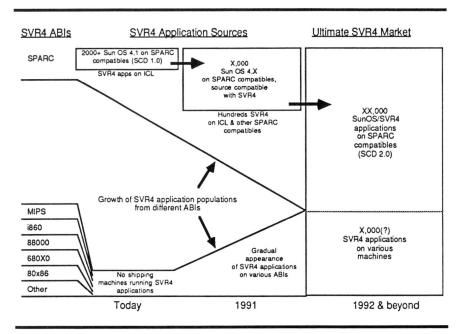

FIGURE 26.1. *A graphical representation of the migration process.*

rival both the DOS and Macintosh OS marketplaces in library size. The volume of systems and users will also grow at the same rate.

While UNIX is at the core of the SCD 1.0 specifications, it is important to recognize that the SCD concept provides a framework for defining standard operating environments that apply to *all* segments of the expanding SPARC market. Demand for standards in various SPARC segments, as expressed by SPARC International members, will drive the development of the specific SCD components most required by the majority of interested members. A near-term priority of SPARC International is developing real-time operating system compliance definitions for the SPARC embedded controller market.

SCD Compliance

Compliance with SCD is the most important and immediate step a SPARC systems vendor can take to verify, and assure the market, that a system is binary compatible. ISVs can then separately submit applications for compatibility testing on SPARC systems verified to be compliant in the SPARC International Laboratory.

From the ISV's perspective, testing compliance on SCD-verified SPARC systems opens the door to a rapidly increasing base of compatible installed systems. As a result, ISVs can redirect R&D, testing and productization costs associated with porting to product improvements. This benefits systems vendors by opening broader distribution channels for binary-compatible software, which in turn, will drive system market growth.

The broad availability of verified, compatible systems and applications ultimately benefits users who can choose from a variety of computers supported by a range of software—all at competitive prices.

Committee Work Behind the SCD

The SCD is developed by SPARC International's compatibility and compliance committee. The work of the committee is intended to make the standards migration as smooth and representative of members' interests as possible. To that end, the committee manages the evolution and expansion of the SCD. The committee monitors existing and emerging open standards and migration paths, incorporates them as appropriate, and periodically submits revised and expanded compliance definitions for ratification by the SPARC International board of directors.

The committee also works in conjunction with SPARC International's technical staff and advisors. In this role, it helps to develop mechanisms that verify compliance to evolving SPARC International standards and provide processes to extend and enhance the broader SPARC operating environment.

SPARC Compliance Definition Testing

To satisfy customers that SPARC products are, indeed, binary compatible, and to allow vendors to credibly claim the same, SPARC International has established compliance testing suites at both the systems and applications levels.

Over time, SPARC International will release SCD conformance tests and verification suites for the various SCD releases. SCD 1.0 system-level testing is available today, and SCD 2.0 compliance testing is being defined.

The SCD 1.0 test suite, available through SPARC International's testing center, is described in test specifications that are available through SPARC International.

ISVs that wish to test for SCD 1.0 compliance may run their software on the operating environment designated for a SPARC platform. For SCD 1.0, the SPARC reference platform in the SPARC International testing laboratory is Sun Microsystems' SPARCstation 1 running SunOS 4.1. For SCD 2.0, the testing laboratory's SPARC reference platform will be ICL's DRS6000 SPARC minicomputer/server running SVR4. While SPARC International's technical staff will test applications on a range of SCD-verified systems, these two machines have been approved by SPARC International as "Gold Seal Standards" for their respective operating systems and compliance definitions. These machines will be used to resolve compliance issues for specific applications.

SPARC International's role in supporting ISVs' compliance efforts is an extremely important one. SPARC International will help to manage and resolve issues of application compatibility *before* they become issues to end users—in contrast the anarchy that prevailed in the early days of PC industry development. This will also give users confidence in SPARC systems and applications.

Trademark Licensing and Administration

Once vendors have successfully completed compliance testing, they will need a way to let the universe of potential end users know that their products are compatible with other SPARC products at the binary level. This is the purpose of SPARC International's trademark licensing program. The program also informs end users of the SCD and architecture versions to which products comply.

The SPARC trademarks are among the most important assets of SPARC International as an independent organization, and of the distributed community of SPARC vendors. To demonstrate the proliferation of compatible software and hardware through active use of the trademark by SPARC International members if fundamental to the expansion of the market for SCD-compliant SPARC products.

The trademark licensing program will allow vendors to license the general trademarks and obtain powerful leverage from other SCD-verified hardware and software vendors. At the same time, the licensing program will allow vendors to apply for and obtain exclusive use of specific derivatives of the SPARC trademark, so they may create strong specific product identities.

To maximize the effectiveness of brand identity development, SPARC International will closely monitor both compliance and use of the trademarks. And to extend the reach of the SPARC brand worldwide, SPARC International will also coordinate cooperative promotional programs.

A Closer Look—SPARC Compliance Definition 1.0

SCD 1.0 is a formal definition of the requirements for software compatibility between SPARC systems that are shipping today, and for application software that can be distributed as one set of binaries across all compliant SPARC platforms.

SCD 1.0 specifies all components of the system software environment that applications typically require, including operating system software, window system and graphics libraries. As such, it is the first practical step by SPARC International to provide its members with reference documentation. When strictly adhered to, this documentation enables vendors to develop compatible SPARC systems that will support a large "shrink-wrap" software application base.

SCD 1.0 addresses two technical requirements. First, it specifies the environment (the minimal set of system files, directories and components of the operating and window systems) that the system vendor must have present for a SCD-verified application to be developed, compiled and run on a particular SPARC platform. Second, SCD 1.0 specifies the run-time environment (the binary interface and the specifications for the dynamically linked libraries) required by a SPARC system to load and run a binary-compatible application.

The SCD can be thought of as a specification for both development and run-time environments. System vendors may qualify for SCD verification merely by complying with the SCD run-time specifications, which may be important for low-end SPARC systems.

SCD 1.0 consists of two sections: the operating system specification and the window system and graphics specification. SPARC Compliance Definition 1.0 builds upon the environment found on Sun workstations. It consists of Sun OS 4.0.3, the SunView 1.75 window system, the (Version 11, Release 4) window system, ONC/NFS, and C (Sun OS 4.0.3) compilers.

Available SCD 1.0 System Software

Sun OS Release 4.0.3, including its libraries and utilities, are distributed in the Portable SPARC Sun OS Source Release Tape. Vendors submitting systems for conformance testing must supply all of the SCD 1.0 files that result from building the operating system, libraries and utility suites. The parts of Sun OS 4.0.3 not required by SCD 1.0 are generally machine- or system-dependent.

A portable version of Sun OS 4.0.3, including ONC/NFS and C compiler for SPARC system vendors is commercially available through Interactive Systems Corp. Interactive has designed its Sun OS version to be portable across various SPARC implementations by removing inappropriate, non-SPARC Sun code and by breaking out and documenting the hardware-dependent portions of the operating system. Interactive also offers the SunView 1.75 window system for Sun OS 4.0.3. In addition, Interactive, a leading UNIX porting and development house, will offer assistance in porting Sun OS to a particular SPARC hardware design.

Assuring SCD 1.0 Compliance

To become SCD 1.0 verified, system developers are required to support the X.11 window system as well as SunView 1.75. Many applications available today are written for X.11, and ISVs should expect its presence on any conforming system. Specifically, the system must support the X library, Xlib. A full specification of the Xlib library and its contents can be found in "Xlib-C Language Interface, X Window System, X Version 11, Release 2" (Massachusetts Institute of Technology, 1988).

Licensing Sun OS 4.0.3 and SunView 1.75 from Sun (either directly or through distributors) assures systems vendors that they will conform to the SCD development platform—assuming the port is done correctly. Today, more than 2000 applications run on SPARC systems under Sun OS 4.0.3. Many of these already meet SCD 1.0 specifications and run on non-Sun SPARC platforms without modification.

Emerging Guidelines—SPARC Compliance Definition 2.0

For SPARC compatible systems, SCD is not only a specification for today, but a roadmap to the future. SPARC International recognizes that the future of standards lies with AT&T's System V, Release 4.0, and it is basing SCD 2.0 on SVR4 and AT&T's System V Application Binary Interface (ABI) specification.

The ABI specification contains two components: the processor-independent, generic specification and the processor (SPARC)-specific supplement. These two manuals should be consulted for strict adherence to the SCD 2.0 binary interface conventions. SPARC International is participating in ABI specification reviews, and will test for ABI compliance as part of the SCD 2.0 verification process.

Development Platforms for SCD 2.0

ISVs can begin to develop SCD 2.0 code in several ways. They can develop applications under an SCD 1.0-derived operating system, keeping in mind the changes that are outlined in the Sun OS compatibility and Migration Guide and SPARC International's forthcoming guidelines. The first implementation of SVR4 is available now on a minicomputer/server from ICL. Using the ICL platform, ISVs can develop SVR4 native code that will run on all other future SPARC CD 2.0-verified SPARC platforms.

A substantial number of commercial applications now run on currently-shipping SVR4-based SPARC systems from ICL. In ensuing months, increasing numbers of SPARC system vendors will move to SVR4, and application developers will have a wider range of platforms for native SVR4 development and porting.

Windowing and Graphics in SCD 2.0

To be SCD 2.0-verified, system vendors must support X Windows, as they did under SCD 1.0. However, SunView 1.75 will no longer be part of SCD, starting with version 2.0. System vendors may optionally support the X.11/NeWS window system licensed as part of SVR4 from AT&T.

To support the X.11 window system-based applications in SCD 2.0, system vendors must support the X library, Xlib, as well as the X Toolkit Intrinsics, a library that provides the framework for building X-based window toolkits. More information on Xlib, and the X Toolkit Intrinsics is located in the C Language X Interface, X Window system manual from MIT and in AT&T's Processor Independent System V Applications Binary Interface specification.

Graphics libraries available as part of the X.11 window system—such as PEX, the PHIGS Extensions to X—may also be required as part of SCD 2.0. More detailed information on the SCD 2.0 graphics interfaces will be available with the SCD 2.0 specification, which is scheduled for release in September 1990.

One SCD-approved window system toolkit is the XView toolkit for the X Window System. It is included on the X.11 distribution tape and is a standard component of SVR4. The XView toolkit is nearly interface-compatible with the SunView toolkit so that applications can move directly to X.11 with only minimal porting. The SCD specification will have more detailed information on approved X.11 window toolkits, how those toolkits should be supported by SPARC system vendors, and how they can be used by ISVs.

Migrating from SCD 1.0 to SCD 2.0

The number of ISV applications that system vendors can run on their platforms is one of the key factors in the commercial success of any hardware platform. Currently, most of the applications that run on SPARC systems comply with SCD 1.0. It will take time for these ISVs to migrate their applications to the SVR4 base and comply with SCD 2.0.

While SPARC International encourages developers to migrate their applications to SVR4 as soon as possible, the organization realizes that it cannot dictate a mass-migration for the full population of ISVs. Therefore, SPARC International offers unique advantages to members during the transition period from SCD 1.0 to SCD 2.0. Since SPARC/UNIX systems vendors are already shipping product at both ends of the migration path, SPARC International will test and verify compliance for both SCD 1.0 and 2.0 by the end of 1990. This dual operating environment approach gives SPARC users and ISVs a level of flexibility lacking with other microprocessor architectures—CISC or RISC.

System vendors that currently offer a Sun OS derivative will begin to offer SVR4-based systems in the near future as their product schedules allow. Until then, they will continue offering Sun OS derivatives. The decision of individual system vendors to offer these SVR4-compliant systems will vary with the availability of their key applications under SVR4, the markets they address, and the price, performance and functionality of their particular system.

SPARC International recommends that ISVs who wish to run on future SPARC systems begin incorporating SVR4 into their product plans today. Migrating an application from an SCD 1.0-derived operating system to SVR4-based SCD 2.0 will require some porting effort. Sun Microsystems will update and publish its Sun OS 4.0.x Compatibility and Migration Guide, and SPARC International will publish a like document that describes the differences between SCD 1.0 and SCD 2.0. ISVs who follow the porting guidelines in these documents can minimize the porting effort required to move to SCD 2.0.

About SPARC International

SPARC International is a not-for-profit service corporation that supports its members by promoting and directing the evolution of the SPARC microprocessor architecture and operating environment through many means. It also is a central component of the open computing strategy set in motion by Sun Microsystems in July 1987. Under that strategy, the responsibility for evolving SPARC technology, developing and marketing compatible SPARC products and building SPARC brand identity, would be distributed worldwide to a broad base of technical and commercial vendors through open licensing practices.

SPARC International's role as an independent organization is to serve those functions that are centralized in the traditional proprietary market model created by established microprocessor vendors. By contrast with that model, the chief strength of the SPARC model is its distributed nature. SPARC International serves as the enabling technical, informational and administrative infrastructure for the distributed SPARC community.

SPARC International's members include semiconductor manufacturers, workstation and multi-user systems vendors, software developers, universities and users. Members may join at affiliate, ISV/VAR, associate and executive levels. Members have control of, and participate in, technical committee work as their market interests dictate and their level of membership allows.

System Configuration

Concept To System: How Sun Microsystems Created SPARCstation1 Using LSI Logic's ASIC System Technology

27

ANDREAS BECHTOLSHEIM • TOM WESTBERG • MARK INSLEY •
JIM LUDEMANN • JEN-HSUN HUANG • DOUGLAS BOYLE

The Making of a New Generation of Desktop Computers

On April 12, 1989, Sun Microsystems announced SPARCstation™ 1, the world's first all ASIC desktop workstation. SPARCstation 1 combines more power and features than any other desktop system. This white paper tells the SPARCstation 1 story, from concept to system. It is a story of cooperation and commitment between two companies, Sun and LSI Logic. It is also a story of the power of ASIC technology and the design methodology necessary to develop the workstation that will change the future of desktop computing.

Evolving Market Needs

In researching trends in the computer industry as a whole and the workstation community in particular, Sun defined four fundamental end-user needs:

- Greater functionality
- Improved price/performance

• Compact size

• Improved reliability

Sun established the goal of developing a RISC-based system that delivers more power with more features than any other desktop computer in the world. Additionally, Sun wanted to develop an ergonomically designed package that would be smaller, quieter and cooler than any workstation available in the marketplace. And finally, Sun committed to developing the most reliable, highest quality system—one that would be designed for high volume manufacturing and easy servicing by end users.

To achieve these goals against a stringent time-to-market deadline, Sun needed to develop hardware, firmware and software in parallel. Moreover, the traditional off-the-shelf design solutions would not meet the compact packaging, quality and reliability, plus performance/ functionality and pricing goals.

To make SPARCstation 1, Sun needed to work with advanced semiconductor and CAD technologies throughout the process, starting with the conceptual phase of design and continuing through the silicon production. Sun turned to LSI Logic, a leading supplier of both semiconductors and design tools.

LSI Logic: A Single Source for Chips and Tools

Originally an "ASICs only" company, LSI Logic now supplies a complete end-to-end system-design solution, combining high-quality hardware development tools with state-of-the-art standard part and semicustom IC fabrication capabilities. LSI Logic is unique in that it supplies gate-array and cell-based ASICs, a comprehensive set of design tools and standard ASICs such as the SPARC processor in the SPARCstation 1. Furthermore, a single source for software and hardware provided one contact for Sun's support, cementing the technical "partnership" necessary to bring the SPARCstation 1 to market quickly.

The ASIC Decision

Sun chose ASIC technology to implement the SPARCstation 1, because ASICs provide the control and flexibility to define and optimize the system logic while maintaining a high level of integration. By reducing the number of chips, boards and connections, the mean-time-between-failure (MTBF) increases.

ASICs Allow System-Level Simulation

An ASIC design methodology creates the opportunity to simulate the entire system before building the prototype. Since LSI Logic's Modular Design Environment™ [MDE™] software provides accurate and fully functional timing models, Sun Microsystems could perform a complete simulation of the entire system. System-level simulation at this scale provides an environment of complete controllability and observability, and therefore yields high productivity.

ASICs Provide an Easy Upward Migration Path

By using an ASIC design methodology, Sun has a complete gate-level description of the entire CPU support system. As a result, the opportunity exists to migrate the current designs to future ASIC technologies.

In making this migration, all that is necessary is to point the design description at a new ASIC library. Higher degrees of integration and faster chips are achievable with a minimal design effort, thus opening future options for Sun Microsystems.

Current gate-array technology makes it possible for a semicustom vendor to provide prototype samples in only three weeks. With LSI Logic's accelerated turnaround, a customer can receive silicon in as little as one week.

Low-Cost Surface-mount Package Technology

For packaging the gate arrays, Sun chose surface-mount technology. These low-profile packages reduce the PC board area and are extremely cost effective. At the time of product development, plastic quad flat packs (PQFPs) were selected because they were the most cost effective packages available with high pin counts.

Choosing an Architecture

For the processor itself, Sun chose to use RISC, leveraging the established SPARC architecture of the Sun-4. The power of the

SPARC architecture would meet the new workstation's performance goals and compatibility with the Sun-4 would give access to the large software base required for rapid market acceptance. Moreover, the elegant simplicity of the SPARC architecture would allow LSI Logic to implement the processor using its Modular Design Environment software in time for system simulation.

The Design Team

The SPARCstation 1 design team consisted of seven ASIC design engineers: five Sun engineers to design all the ASICs and perform system-level simulation, and two LSI Logic engineers. One of the two LSI Logic engineers developed the SPARC Integer Unit (IU) and the other supported ASIC development at Sun.

Design Methodology

Before IC design began for the SPARCstation 1, Sun defined complete specifications for each individual device. These comprehensive descriptions included chip-to-chip interfaces, allowing separate designers to work independently.

Chip	Product	Transistors	Package
SPARC IU	LCB15	90,000	179-pin CPGA
Cache controller	LMA9K	36,000	160-pin PQFP
MMU	LMA9K	20,000	120-pin PQFP
Data buffer	LMA9K	12,000	120-pin PQFP
DMA controller	LMA9K	36,000	120-pin PQFP
Video data buffer	LMA9K	16,000	120-pin PQFP
RAM controller	LMA9K	10,000	100-pin PLCC
Clock	LMA9K	4,000	44-pin PLCC

Key:
LCB15 = 0.9-micron Cell-based ASIC
LMA9K = 0.9-micron Channel-Free™ Array
CPGA = Ceramic Pin Grid Array
PQFP = Plastic Quad Flat Pack
PLCC = Plastic Leadless Chip Carrier

TABLE 27.1.

The first step was to partition the system into major functional blocks. As shown in Table 27.1, eight major partitions were mapped into eight separate ASICs. Partitioning the logic into several ASICs, rather than one, kept the pin count below the chosen 160-pin maximum pin count of the PQFP package and kept individual component costs as low as possible.

The design included standard parts only when they did not compromise the design objectives. Sun chose to use standard parts for the SCSI and Ethernet interfaces, since ASICs did not provide any higher integration for these functions in this application. No PLAs or TTL standard logic parts were used.

Chip Design
Control Logic

For the synthesis of control logic and state machines in the system, Sun used in-house logic synthesis tools based on public-domain software from the University of California. The output of these tools was piped into a netlist extractor that created a circuit design description in LSI Logic's netlist format.

Datapath Logic

To design and optimize datapaths, Sun Microsystems used LSI Logic's schematic editor (LSED) to connect complex library elements such as adders and register files. LSED allows the description of any number of components at any number of hierarchy levels and is fully integrated into LSI Logic's MDE suite of software design tools.

Chip-Level Verification

Designs were verified at the chip level before releasing any data for system-level simulation. Simulation vectors were developed using LSI Logic's interactive graphical waveform editor, LWAVE. With LWAVE, designers merely sketch out the waveform they want using a simple mouse-driven drawing editor, rather than writing a test generation program. LWAVE then generates simulation vectors automatically.

Since finding and fixing bugs in this chip-level simulation is faster and more efficient than finding them at the system level, this first stage of verification sped up the overall design process.

For chip-level simulation, Sun used LSI Logic's LSIM event-driven digital simulator. LSI Logic then used its hardware-accelerated counterpart, ZSIM, to run extensive verification simulations of the SPARC IU. ZSIM uses an optimized version of the Zycad hardware accelerator, developed by Zycad exclusively for LSI Logic.

Building a System-Level Model

System-level simulations can be difficult because different components may be supplied by different vendors. The Ethernet chip, for instance, is a vital component in the SPARCstation 1. It would have been impractical to design a gate-level model of the chip just for system-level simulation. For system-level simulation, it is therefore mandatory that the simulator support behavioral models in combination with gate-level models. This mixed-mode simulation is possible with MGSIM, LSI Logic's behavioral and gate-level multi-chip simulator.

Gate-level models were used for all the ASICs. For the industry-standard parts, behavioral models were written in LSI Logic's behavioral modeling language, BSL. Behavioral models in the system included SRAM, DRAM, Ethernet and SCSI. In addition, a UART model was built into the modeled system to process system messages and LED models were used to display diagnostic data.

Running System-Level Simulation

To run the system-level simulation, a powerful approach was employed. Approximately 4,000 lines of SPARC assembly language were developed to diagnose the system. These programs were assembled and loaded into the behavioral models of the DRAM.

By applying a system-reset pulse and a 20-MHz system clock, the simulated workstation would then proceed to execute instructions. The system simulation environment was used for system integration. Numerous problems were discovered and corrected in the process of getting the first instruction to simulate.

The engineers were very productive because they were working in the ideal environment of system simulation. Many of the problems encountered on the laboratory bench—such as failing components, difficulty in probing, and the long time required to implement design changes—were avoided.

By running the MBSIM multi-chip simulator on a Sun 4/260, each simulation clock was simulated in three real-time seconds.

Timing Verification

Timing verification was performed at both the chip and the system level. At the chip level, LSI Logic offers LCAP for static timing analysis. LCAP was used to verify internal timing and extract interface timing parameters for each chip's datasheet. Additionally, since LSI Logic's MBSIM multi-chip behavioral simulator supports actual delays, Sun was able to run system simulations over each process corner. For example, Sun was able to simulate the system using a best-case cache and a worst-case SPARC IU. This was simply accomplished by modifying a system specification file.

Transmission line effects between components (inter-chip) were controlled by choosing appropriate output buffer drive strengths and were modelled with RC delays in the MBSIM simulator.

The Final Stages of Design
Test Vector Generation

The vectors used during the manufacturing test of each individual ASIC were developed by either writing the vectors manually using LWAVE, or by extracting vectors from the mixed-mode system simulation. The ability to write diagnostic routines in assembly language, via system-level simulation techniques, made test vector development much easier. Once the vectors were simulated, LTEST was used to extract the vectors and to generate a complete test program in the appropriate IC production tester format.

Design Release to LSI Logic

Once the design was functionally complete, it was released to LSI Logic for a formal review. The design review process included:

1. Reviewing the bonding diagram for compliance to mechanical and electrical rules.
2. Reviewing the clocking scheme.
3. Evaluating the design for potential race conditions and dynamic hazards.
4. Identifying overloaded nets.
5. Evaluating skew sensitivity of the test vectors.

Layout and Backannotation

After the design had been reviewed, the chips were sent to layout. Layout was completed in one to seven days for each chip, depending on the size of the design. Following layout, a SEGLEN file was generated. This file contains accurate wire delay information based on the actual layout, rather than the prelayout estimates used for earlier design verification. The SEGLEN file was then transferred back to Sun for backannotation. Once the layout-sensitive delays had been calculated, the system simulation was rerun for final verification. Chip-level timing analysis was then repeated to compile the final datasheet.

Upon approval of the post-layout delays, the chips were released to manufacturing, with prototype turnaround time of between five to ten days for all the chips.

The Final Product: SPARCstation 1

The SPARCstation 1 packs unprecedented levels of performance and functionality into a desktop package. All of Sun's original system goals (performance, functionality, packaging, quality and reliability, compact size, low power consumption and high integration) were met.

At $8,895 (less than $725/MIPS), the SPARCstation 1 can race through applications at 12.5 MIPS and 1.4 MFLOPS with up to 64 MB of main memory, and coupled with its graphics, high speed expansion slots, audio input/output capabilities and over 500 SPARCware applications, it sets a new standard for desktop computing.

The SPARCstation 1 is smaller than a typical PC. By using leading-edge ASIC technology, the motherboard is the same size as a standard sheet of paper—8.5 × 11 inches. The entire system fits in a package measuring 16″ square and less than 3″ high. Since almost all components are low power CMOS devices, the board consumes less than 12 watts. The power consumption for the entire system is about the same as a light bulb.

Lessons Learned

The extensive system-level simulation resulted in a remarkably fast system "bring up." The schedule called for booting UNIX in three months. It actually happened in four days.

After one day to boot the PROM monitor and three days to boot UNIX, SPARCstation 1 was alive and kicking, announcing "hello, world" to the rest of Sun. This first-time success was due mainly to mixed-mode simulation. With multi-chip MBSIM (multi-chip behavioral simulation), SPARCstation 1 was completely simulated and deemed fully functional before any silicon was cast. In fact, while the design team awaited delivery of prototypes, they successfully booted UNIX on the simulated workstation.

The main lessons learned in this project were the importance of using comprehensive and accurate behavioral models during system simulation, and accurate gate-level models during chip-level simulation. The small number of bugs that were found were all traced to missing test cases and were later reproduced in the simulation. All of the end cases and corner conditions that were simulated worked correctly in the prototype.

A Successful Partnership

The overall success of the project was a direct result of Sun Microsystems forging a close technical relationship with LSI Logic, the world's leading supplier of ASIC technology and services. This relationship allowed Sun to:

- Use ASIC technology and closely-coupled design tools to achieve maximum integration and performance.
- Use system-level simulation to realize "right-the-first-time" system design.

The SPARCstation 1 project is a dramatic demonstration of how LSI Logic helped SPARCstation 1's design team turn bold new system concepts into a world-class product.

SBus Takes I/O Performance Into the '90s

DAVE EVANS

28

SBus' open bus architecture is emerging as a high-performance I/O interconnect that is optimized for the technologies of the 1990s. SBus is both a chip interconnect that links high-speed ASICs and an I/O expansion bus for desktop and other high-performance workstations and servers. It is not, however, a replacement for a backplane bus such as Futurebus+.

First introduced as part of Sun's SPARCstation 1 desktop RISC computer, SBus' small 83.82 mm × 146.7 mm (3.3″ × 5.8″) size made it possible to add postcard-sized expansion cards right to that system's motherboard. Its flexible, microprocessor-independent architecture can be implemented in many different versions by system and board vendors and will span several generations of workstations. And since SBus is freely licensed to developers, a market for add-in cards has been established.

SBus provides the memory bandwidth necessary for high-performance RISC CPUs and permits low-latency access by I/O devices such as Ethernet and SCSI. It features low static power dissipation, so that it can be used in both desktop and portable machines. In addition, SBus lets designers take advantage of the technologies that are expected to dominate in the future: CMOS and surface mount.

Important features of SBus include:

- 32-bit data bus
- 32-bit virtual address
- Direct virtual memory addressing (DVMA) for SBus masters
- 28-bit physical address for each slave device
- Synchronous operation

- Clock frequency ranging from 16.67 MHz to 25 MHz
- Transfers ranging from 1 to 64 bytes
- CMOS-compatible driving and loading so that CMOS ASICs can be connected directly to the SBus
- Machine-independent code for auto-configuration and boot devices
- Geographical device selection
- Fair arbitration between masters

Clock speeds, memory bandwidth requirements, I/O bandwidth requirements, and system integration will all continue to increase during the 1990s. SBus will facilitate these trends.

SBus Geared for Future System Improvements

SBus was designed under the assumption that system clock speed will progressively increase with time. Therefore, one of its main features is synchronous operation. Although the seven SBus interrupt lines are allowed to be asynchronous, the other 75 signals are sampled on the rising edge of a fixed frequency clock, which must be in the range of 16.67 MHz to 25 MHz.

The advantages of having SBus be synchronous with the main CPU are well worth preserving, since running the I/O bus asynchronously to the processor greatly increases the complexity of logic needed in the interface. This is why SBus is designed to run at any frequency between 16.67 MHz and 25 MHz. On systems where the CPU operates at a frequency greater than 25 MHz, SBus can be clocked at some integer division of the processor frequency. For example, in a 40-MHz system, the SBus frequency can be set at 20 MHz.

SBus Configured for Memory Bandwidth Improvements

SBus can be implemented in several different configurations. The two most common are host-based and symmetrical; they are differentiated by the connection between the CPU and SBus. In host-based systems, the CPU has both special access to the MMU and a special path through the SBus controller that bypasses the MMU. The host-based configuration saves the CPU the clock cycles required for the address translation, but increases the cost of the SBus controller. Current SBus machines such as the SPARCstation 1+ use the host-based model, with their main memory located on the SBus.

In symmetric SBus systems, all masters on SBus use the SBus controller to translate virtual addresses to physical addresses. With this configuration, the CPU can have a private memory bus in order to increase its performance while allowing an optimized I/O interface.

As processor speeds increase in the '90s, so will the demands on memory. To accommodate the need for larger memory bandwidth, main memory can be moved off SBus and put on a faster, wider bus that has an interface to both the CPU and SBus. In addition to this change, the SBus implementation could be symmetric configuration, with the CPU acting as just another SBus device.

Virtual Memory Addressing Helps Future Integration

A major SBus design feature is the use of virtual addresses at the hardware level by all masters on the bus to specify the source and destination of data. This eliminates the need for software to translate addresses for all I/O tasks. An MMU in the SBus controller has the responsibility of translating these addresses to the appropriate SBus slot and physical address.

In addition, SBus allows any master to talk to any slave on the bus. This means that in any transfer between two I/O devices, SBus automatically provides a two-fold performance improvement over other bus architectures that require all traffic to "stop-over" in main memory. This feature will become increasingly important to overall system performance as further integration results in more intelligent expansion devices.

For example, the SBus interface for disk controllers may one day enable the CPU to set up a copy from one disk to another on different controllers by first determining both the free inodes on the destination disk and the occupied area on the source disk, and then queueing up the data transfers for the controllers to perform.

Future Multimedia Uses

The developing interest in multimedia means that simply increasing I/O bandwidth won't be enough in the future: the need for low bus latency will also be important. Since multimedia data occurs in real-time, any data lost cannot be recovered. Therefore, it is necessary to design for worst-case latency.

The 64-byte burst transfers provided by SBus are a good compromise between bus bandwidth and latency, as increasing bus bandwidth by even 10% would double the latency. By requiring all transfers to complete within 255 clock cycles, the worst-case latency—with a maximum of eight masters (assuming three clock cycles for address translation)—is only about 124 microseconds at 16.67MHz (8 * (256 + 3) clock cycles).

While some SBus applications may need 64 bytes of buffer memory, most SBus devices will not require much—if any—buffer memory due to the ability of SBus slaves to regulate the rate at which data is transferred.

The ability of any SBus master to talk to any slave also has advantages for multimedia, because it makes synchronous operation simpler and more reliable than if all messages had to be placed in system memory.

SBus Design Allows Expansion

Sun designed SBus with features that let users expand the types and quantity of I/O devices connected to the system without affecting the host motherboard. These features will allow SBus developers to build cards that attach directly to the platform as newer, faster technologies evolve. For example, SBus could conceivably be used in the future as a high-bandwidth connection between a portable CPU and a desktop expansion unit containing disks and other I/O devices.

SBus expansion cards use a 96-pin high-density connector of

which 82 pins are used for signalling and 14 pins are used for +5V, +12V, −12V and ground. To keep power supply requirements down to a reasonable level in desktop or portable machines, each expansion card is limited to 2 amps at +5V and 0.03 amps each at +12V and −12V. By limiting the power consumption to about 11 watts per SBus expansion board, no cooling is inherently necessary, unlike most other bus architectures, in which some amount of airflow is required.

While the expansion boards are small, SBus' height specifications allow active components to be placed on both sides of the board, resulting in a surface area of 38.28 square inches. Double-width boards are possible if more space is needed. This small form factor means that up to four SBus options can reside on the 9U, double-height Eurocard used with VME. In contrast, other bus architectures restrict component heights so that the bottom surface of the card is all but unusable for most active components.

Installing SBus expansion boards is easy for end users thanks to the use of a configuration PROM containing machine-independent FORTH code on each expansion board. The system retrieves configuration information from the expansion board upon power-up.

An Open Bus Architecture

SBus is an open specification, which means that system and board developers can implement SBus designs free of any licensing restrictions or encumbrances from Sun. In this way, Sun encourages third-party vendors to offer added value to Sun systems via the SBus expansion slots. Currently, there are more than 60 SBus products from at least 35 card and system vendors. Products include 24-bit true-color boards, additional Ethernet cards, serial prot extenders, additional networking products and graphics or imaging boards.

Sun is committed to the SBus as its I/O interconnect on future products. The success of the SPARCstation family as the installed-base leader in the RISC/UNIX marketplace is opening up many opportunities for developers of SPARCstation add-in cards in traditional applications such as CAE, CASE and AI, as well as new applications among financial and business users. SBus' high performance, low cost and open architecture make it well-suited to handle the ever-increasing performance ranges of computer systems in the 1990s—and beyond.

SPARC MBus Overview

BEN CATANZARO

29

Introduction

The move towards higher levels of integration, higher clock rates and smaller packaging are now migrating to the point where backplane buses are not required to tie significant subsystems together. MBus, Sun's SPARC module interconnect bus provides a short physical connection media, synchronous operation with clock rates to 40 Mhz, 64 bit data transfers, and support for uniprocessor and multiprocessor implementations. What was once provided on a backplane bus can now be built on a single board. The MBus module interconnect allows for critical subsystems to be integrated more cleanly and more cost effectively making way for the development of more economical desktop systems and embedded applications. In addition, MBus provides a roadmap for system evolution without hardware redesign thus providing considerable performance enhancements well beyond the life span any single processor evolution.

MBus supports the following feature set:

- Fully synchronous operation at 40 Mhz
- 64 GigaBytes physical address space
- Multiplexed address/control with 64-bits of data
- Burst transfers up to 128-Bytes
- Centralized arbitration, reset, interrupt, clock distribution & timeout
- Uniprocessor and multiprocessor module interconnect through pin-compatible interface, and multi-master operation
- CMOS and Bi-CMOS compatibility, TTL voltage levels
- Provides for asynchronous processor operation

- Multiprocessor support—Arbitration with parking, signals and transactions to support write-invalidate cache coherency schemes

MBus Design Goals

MBus development stems from a critical need for a standard interface between the processor plus the cache and the rest of the system (see Figure 29.1). This interface is key to satisfying the high performance requirements and variety of protocol constraints in system architectures. Once implemented, this interface creates a technical partition allowing for enhanced development by independant groups, be they engineering groups or companies with different requirements or capabilities. MBus provides a common microprocessor pin-out standard which has already created a move among several different semiconductor manufacturers to design SPARC processors to this standard. The common pin-out is a side effect of RISC architectures, specifically SPARC, becoming an open standard. Systems manufacturers, led by companies such as Sun Microsystems, ICL and Xerox, need a common pin-out to enable quick upgrades for the ever-increasing variety of SPARC processors. This move towards a common pin-to-pin interface has allowed Sun's SPARC semiconductor vendors to develop SPARC

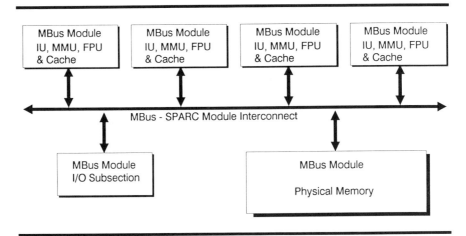

FIGURE 29.1. *Basic MBus level I system configuration.*

compatible support devices, cache controllers for example, independently of Sun. The Cypress/Ross Technology 7CY604 SPARC cache controller/MMU and the LSI Logic L64815 SPARC cache controller/MMU are the first chips to appear which integrate an interface to the MBus. LSI Logic has announced that its next-generation Lightning SPARC processor incorporates the MBus interface. Other implementations of SPARC chips are expected to follow the MBus standard as well.

MBus provides a rapid process to integrate new processors into systems because of the levels of compatibility provided. Systems incorporating MBus may take advantage of new higher performance processors much sooner, without the need for hardware re-design often required by other architectures. One of the primary goals of the MBus definition was to define a physical bus carefully at a specific point within the overall system architecture such that Sun, and other system manufactures, could avoid the problems associated with having a different processor/memory bus for different processor implementations. By defining the bus carefully at the memory side of the cache and memory management unit (MMU), the problem of having a different physical bus with each SPARC implementation was solved. The same benefits apply to SPARC system developers. Every implementation of SPARC now provides for MBus pin-compatibility, communication, and migration to higher levels of system performance without any modifications to the system hardware. Additional benefits are also realized through the economic advantages brought about by the added longevity to a products duration in the marketplace.

From a technical perspective, performance requirements were, of course, a major consideration. The SPARC MBus was designed with enough bandwidth to accommodate SPARC processors for the next three to five years. This led to the definition of a 40Mhz bus with 64 bit data transfer capability to achieve a substaned bandwidth of 80 megabytes per second as well as a peak bandwidth of 320 megabytes per second. In addition to providing high performance levels, the MBus also achieves levels of simplicity and cost constraints for system developers. To this end MBus has been designed to use TTL input voltage levels allowing designers to use standard off-the-shelf CMOS devices while also providing for high speed operation. This has proven to be a very successful cost saving measure for MBus system and module designers. The 40-MHz clock rate was selected as the highest speed at which CMOS chips could operate using a bus of only a few inches on standard PC boards. The 40 Mhz operation for the bus was also a special area of concentration mainly because it's fast enough that the overall electrical environment becomes a critical parameter effecting optimum operating criteria. To this end SPICE models were created that aided in the design and the timing verification at this high clock rate. MBus-based systems can be built at clock rates of 25 Mhz and 33 Mhz as well.

The 64-bit data transfer capability not only doubles the bandwidth from only 32-bits, but it was also very important to define and build a bus that would at the least have a lifetime of 3 to 5 years knowing that only 32-bits would have limitations within a very short time. MBus provides 36 bits for physical addressing permitting an addressing capability of 64 GBytes for high performance desktop systems and more than enough addressing capability required for embedded systems applications. In order to help reduce the number of pins a multiplexed address/data scheme was selected.

The protocol definitions were also an important aspect as MBus beginnings indicating an evolution towards the next generation of Sun's system architectures. This accounts for the distinction between Level I and Level II as defined by the MBus protocol specification.

MBus—Value Added

Unlike other processor/memory bus architectures that can support only a single processor implementation, MBus supports current SPARC implementations and will support future SPARC implementations as well.

MBus is an endorsement to Sun's Open Architecture philosophy. MBus provides an opportunity for third party companies, also third party Sun competitors—compatibles and clone makers, to add value more easily than they could in the past. MBus makes it easier for these companies to add value by adding a higher performance SPARC processor with an MBus interface while also adding value to an MBus memory subsystem. At the hardware level, MBus is clearly an endorsement to the Sun/SPARC open architecture that multiple module manufactures can target with specific value-added products. For these manufactures the key reference documents are the SPARC Architecture Reference Manual version 8.0 & the MBus Level I & Level II Protocol Specification. For board and system developers wanting to build MBus-based modules the suggested reference document is the MBus Module Design Specification. The Module Design Specification provides the information necessary to build MBus modules that will work in Sun Microsystems MBus-based systems.

MBus Centralized Functions

MBus centralized functions are those functions which are not controlled within a specific MBus module but instead supported as central functions on the bus (see Figure 29.2). These include Bus Arbitration, Interrupts, Reset, Clock, and Timeout. A brief description of each is provided here:

- *Bus Arbitration*: Arbitration between processors for ownership of the bus is controlled by external Arbiter logic. The arbitration scheme, or protocol, employed is implementation specific and can vary with each system. Regardless of protocol, MBus specifies that no more than one processor at any given time will drive the bus. This is made possible because the arbiter asserts only one bus grant signal at any instance interleaved with dead cycles between successive transactions of different masters. This allows for cleaner electrical characteristics since there is no driver overlap resulting from multiple masters attempting to gain access to the bus simultaneously. This also allows for simpler, less costly termination of the bus. Upon acquiring ownership of the bus and completion of a transaction, a master is not required to give up the bus. MBus specifies that the current master may continue to own the bus, thus allowing other operations to be performed immediately until another master issues a request. This feature, refered to as "Parking", permits multiple

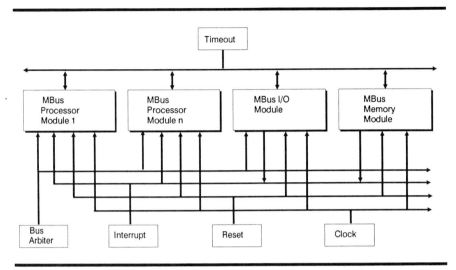

FIGURE 29.2. *MBus centralized functions & connectivity.*

address & data sequences by the same module without having to waste time asserting bus control to gain access to the bus once again.

• *Interrupts*: Interrupt distribution is a system issue unique to each vendors implementation. MBus basically provides the interrupt capability, at the hardware level, which can be configured to suit the application at hand. The interrupt request lines—IRL [3:0] are unique to each processor module and therefore are provided by each vendors implementation.

• *Reset*: Reset logic external to any specific master module generates the appropriate reset "RSTIN" signal to all master modules. The appropriate reset lines should be accommondated on MBus-based boards to satisfy the overall system reset requirements.

• *Clock*: MBus clock specifications is 40 Mhz. This does not preclude system implementations at lower clock rates of 25 or 33 Mhz. Clock distribution is a system implementation issue which should include all master, slave and other appropriate logic. Clock distribution at clock rates of 40 Mhz requires special attention. An essential requirement for the MBus to run at 40 Mhz is that the System clock skew be as small a value as possible. For this reason MBus module developers should refer to the MBus Module Design Specification.

• *Timeout*: Timeout is a system implementation issue. Typically, associated system logic, sometimes referred to as watchdog logic, monitors relinquish & retry acknowledge cycles. Upon timeout of an pre-determined number of cycles an error signal is generated to flag the error event.

MBus—Level I and Level II Protocols

The MBus specification defines two levels of compliance, Level I and Level II. A uniprocessor system implementation should conform to the Level I specification while Level II describes the signals, transactions, and protocols for building cache coherent, shared memory multiprocessing systems. An overview of Level I & II is presented here.

Level I Protocol

MBus Level I protocol has many characteristics which are similar to SBus, Sun's System Expansion Bus. This is due to the fact that MBus adheres to some of the same principals of partitioning since MBus serves explicitly for processor/memory interconnect where SBus serves only as a system expansion bus (see Figure 29.3). As shown, MBus and SBus can be used in the same system configuration thus providing a high-performance computer system with separate and distinct buses. In this example MBus provides a 40 Mhz, high-speed, pin-compatible interface for multiple MBus processor modules with a direct connection to physical memory. SBus is used only as the I/O interconnect to expansion slots where optional expansion I/O can be inserted for added system level functionality. In this example, the interconnection between MBus and SBus is accomplished by an LSI Logic L64852 MBus to SBus Controller (M2S). The LSI Logic L64852 provides a high perfor-

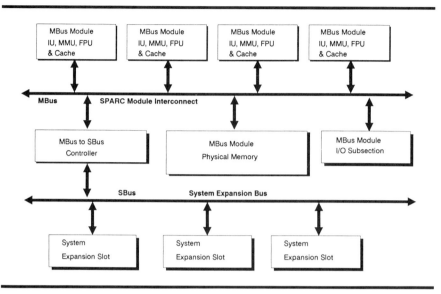

FIGURE 29.3. *MBus modular system configuration.*

mance interface from the 64-bit 40-Mhz MBus to the 25-Mhz 32-bit SBus while also supporting major MBus functions.

In addition to the enhanced performance capability made possible by the 40 Mhz operation, the system developer may also elect to design an MBus system at 25 or 33 Mhz at the onset without the connector provisions normally required for plug-in modules. This basic approach allows system vendors the flexibility to migrate their system capabilities at a cost effective pace by providing module interchangeability at a later time.

MBus modules are basically subsystems which at a minimum contain a single SPARC processor. Other, more advanced, higher performance modules contain dual processors, cache, FPU, arbitration logic, clock, and synchronization circuitry (see Figure 29.4).

Module developers will need to run SPICE models when building modules that have not been analyzed, such as the MBus compatible devices available from SPARC vendors. In these cases, ASIC devices will be required in order to interface to the MBus.

MBus module developers should take note of the MBus mod-

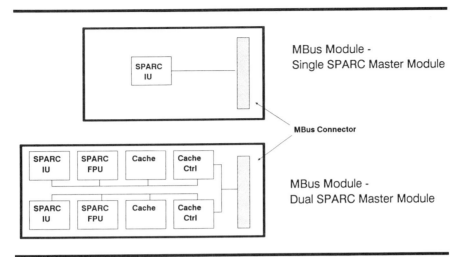

FIGURE 29.4. *MBus modules—Single & dual master examples.*

ule connector which has been selected as the standard connector for MBus interconnections. The connector is the AMP "Microstrip" connector. This connector provides high reliability, ease of installation, a fool-proof keying scheme, and is widely available in the marketplace. These features satisfy the SPARC module concept of being able to provide field-upgradable performance. The AMP connector also provides excellent electrical performance, i.e., low capacitance and low inductance to meet the aggressive MBus cycle time of 25ns. Module developers should refer to the MBus Protocol Specification or the MBus Module Design Specification for more details on the connector's pin-out assignments.

As MBus provides for fully synchronous 40 Mhz clock rate, processors with clock rates above 40 Mhz can also be incorporated to run asynchronously. In such an application, additional clock circuitry and synchronization logic on the processor module maintains complete synchronization with the bus. The advantage here is the performance enhancement realized from the move to higher performance SPARC processors as they become available. A 50 Mhz SPARC processor, for example, with cache, can run independently from the rest of the system. Here again, the primary attribute of MBus is realized by the system designer in that MBus allows the designer to buffer the system architecture from processor changes thus avoiding costly system re-design to accommodate new processors. This is also a key advantage for embedded system designers where now specific embedded systems can be designed to a single interface, MBus. This saves the designer from redevelopment and debug cycles while providing performance options at later points in time with no hardware modifications to the rest of the system.

The transactions and signals described in the MBus Level I protocol specification are as follows (refer to the MBus Protocol Specification for more information):

Level I transactions: READ & WRITE—These Read & Write bus transactions are initiated by LOAD & STORE operations of 1 byte to 128 bytes. Any operation longer than 8 bytes is performed in Burst Mode. Typically in these types of operations the slave device on the bus controls the data transfer rate.

Level I signals:

• 64-Bit address/data lines

• Address strobe

• Encoded bus acknowledge

• Bus arbitration (Cf)

• Interrupt lines (Cf)

• Reset (Cf)

• Asynchronous error

• Module ID

• Clock (Cf)   (Cf) Centralized Functions

The majority of the Level I signals listed above are rather basic and straight foward and will therefore not be discussed here. The reader is refered to the MBus Level I protocol specification for more detail. The one signal within this group that is unique is the Module ID. The Module ID serves as an identifier by which a specific module can be addressed for purposes of re-connecting in order to complete a previously suspended operation. The Module ID also serves a key function during system configuration. For more specifics on the Module ID and configuration mapping refer to section 4.3, MBus Configuration Address Map, in the MBus Specification.

MBus Level II Protocol

MBus Level II enhances basic Level I capabilities by introducing symmetric multiprocessing (SMP). For Sun, MBus SMP capability evolved as a logical extension that could be incorporated in all future SPARC systems. SMP is also the direction for Sun's Operating System, SunOS. SMP capability allows for a fully symmetric UNIX OS whereby all processors within a system can be used for any part of the processing. For Sun, as well as for SPARC system vendors, this brings the advantage of being able to produce low cost, modest size systems ranging from a single SPARC processor module to a complete integrated module solution with symmetric multiprocessing capability.

MBus facilitates the design of multiprocessor systems by allowing small numbers of processors to be tied together directly using the MBus. Large numbers of processors (such as those that number in the hundreds or thousands) must be tied together using more elaborate interconnection schemes. In addition, the MBus protocols allow the processor module to have its own internal cache or even a large second-level cache (see Figure 29.5 A & B). Multiprocessor implementations with MBus-based microprocessors is therefore trivial because all the cache coherence logic is built into the MBus protocol and associated microprocessor module. Multiple chips need only be wired in parallel to build a multiprocessor system.

Also within the context of multiprocessing support, it is worth noting that MBus does not provide for interprocessor communication, TLB consistency, or other complex protocols for reasons that the support be limited to a small scale multiprocessing implementation, i.e., no more than eight processors. Interprocessor communications, specifically interrupt distribution, as mentioned earlier, is a system issue which is unique to each system vendors implementation. MMU/TLB consistency and flushing of virtual

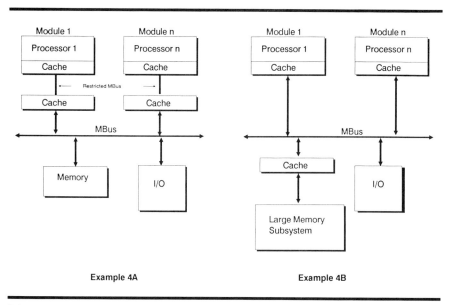

FIGURE 29.5. *A & B: Second-level cache examples.*

caches are also operations which must be handled through inter-processor communication. The protocols in which these operations are conducted can vary thus requiring flexibility and need to be handled by software. MBus basically provides the interrupt hooks, at the hardware level, which can be configured to suit the application at hand. The rest must be handled via software message passing which for small scale systems would be comparable in efficiency to doing it in hardware. Handling this type of operation in software is an equally workable solution when considering that the frequency of these events cannot be accurately specified.

Level II multiprocessing support introduced two additional signals, SHARED & INHIBIT, and four transactions which provide a basic foundation for cache consistency in multiprocessing systems. The SHARED & INHIBIT lines are typically part of a cache control block within a processor module which perform the hardware Writes & Reads. This control block may also contain the snooper or Bus Watcher logic. The four MBus Level II transactions include Coherent Read, Coherent Invalidate, Coherent Read and Invalidate, and Coherent Write and Invalidate. These MBus Level

II transactions allow for the control and maintenance of cache consistency. In the current mode of operation, MBus Level II only supports Write-Back caches in order to maintain cache consistency. In this mode a STORE into the cache does not perform a WRITE operation. This type of operation has the advantage of keeping bus traffic to a minimum. For multiprocessor systems however, this operation typically results in a condition where the cache is no longer consistent with main memory. The key concern in multiprocessing systems then becomes a matter of how to keep a cache which is not consistent with main memory consistent with other caches (see Figure 29.6). Cache coherency, or consistency, can only be maintained when all caches preceive the same memory image. In an MBus implementation, since all coherent transactions assume cache transfers of 32 bytes at a time—either the cache line is 32 bytes or if it is longer than 32 bytes the cache coherency is managed on sub-line basis of 32 bytes, in this manner cache lines of 64 and 128 bytes can be handled efficiently at a sub-block at a time. A cache line can be in any of the following states:

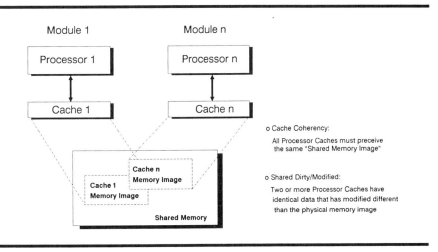

FIGURE 29.6. *Cache coherency in multiprocessor designs.*

• *Exclusive Clean*; a copy of the physical memory image is also in module 1 cache. No other copies exist in the system.

- *Exclusive Dirty/Modified*; sole owner is module 1 cache but the memory image has been modified.
- *Shared Clean*; a copy of the memory image exist in two modules, all identical to the physical memory image
- *Shared Dirty/Modified*; two modules have identical data that has been modified different than the physical memory image. In this case, in order to maintain cache consistency we must actually control the identicalness of the data.
- *Invalid*

These built-in capabilities aide the designer of small scale multiprocessing system by providing a mechanism for maintaining cache consistency of cache blocks. (refer to Figures 29.7. A through 7 D):

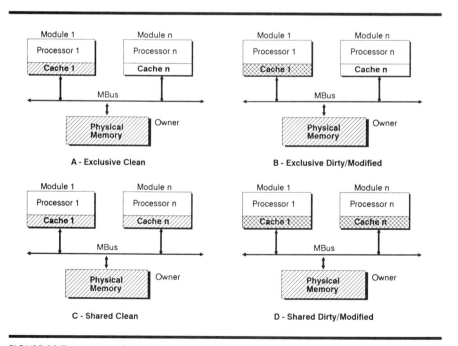

FIGURE 29.7. *MBus cache consistency states.*

Summary

Sun's SPARC module interconnect bus, MBus, provides a critical cost/performance trade-off that allows for development of more cost effective desktop systems and embedded applications. In addition, MBus provides a road map for system evolution without hardware re-design thus providing substantial performance enhancements well beyond the life span of any single processor evolution. MBus is the first generation of processor buses which will provide easy processor upgrade paths for Sun and for SPARC system developers. MBus makes possible, for the first time, a common microprocessor pin-out standard which has already created a drive towards RISC architectures, specifically SPARC, becoming an open standard. With this standard, the ability to integrate new processors into systems is accelerated significantly because of the levels of compatibility provided. The need for hardware re-design often required by other architectures is no longer a consideration as well as problems associated with having a different processor/memory bus for different processor implementations.

The benefits to SPARC system developers are very clear—pin-compatibility, migration to higher levels of system performance without any modifications to the hardware, as well as economic advantages brought about by the added longevity to any single product's duration in the marketplace.

Understanding MBus

Kevin M. Kitagawa

30

Why MBus?

Designing successive generations of microprocessor-based systems brings many problems upon the designer. One must think about how to make systems better, faster, and less expensive, without changes to the system architecture. Eliminating these changes eliminates the required system software changes. Upgrade paths of existing machines already in the field must also be considered.

Historically, making systems faster meant either a redesign of the system to accommodate the faster clock speeds required or an upgrade to a better microprocessor. These changes increased performance, but hopefully they did not extensively change the system architecture, thus keeping compatibility between both system and application software. This is, however, an expensive upgrade solution, requiring extensive hardware changes to existing machines in order to take advantage of the performance gains. The SPARC MBus allows an elegant systems upgrade path to take advantage of the latest microprocessor technology.

Multiprocessing for Better Performance

MBus also allows the building of high-performance shared-memory multiprocessor (MP) systems. This has become an increasingly popular and relatively inexpensive method to increase system performance beyond that of which current uniprocessors are capable. It allows multiple instructions to be executed in parallel resulting in faster system performance. A shared-memory MP system is one where system memory is a shared resource allowing both instructions and data to be shared among processors. The price/performance ratio is favorable for multiprocessors, since it allows the interconnection of multiple, relatively low-cost microprocessors. The price of a uniprocessor-based system of equal performance would be much greater.

Why Doesn't Everyone Do MP?

Although multiprocessing brings gains in performance, it also brings about problems that make efficient, tightly coupled, multiprocessor systems difficult to design. Accesses made from one processor to shared memory can drastically reduce other processors performance by increasing the effective memory access time. Getting access to the bus contributes to this access time. Concurrent requests to shared memory must be serialized to handle the possibility of memory contention between two processors trying to access the same location in memory. Private caches for each processor in the system will help reduce memory accesses, but the use of caches introduces another problem. The sharing of instructions and data between processors will result in multiple copies of the same data residing in memory and the private caches. Consistency must be maintained in the system to ensure only those copies that are correct are being used.

Enter MBus

The SPARC MBus is a private, high-speed interface that connects SPARC processor modules, physical memory module and I/O modules. It not only allows the design of efficient multiprocessor systems, but also, easily upgradable modular systems. MBus provides a standard pin interconnect between local modules that reside on the same printed circuit board. It is *not* intended for use as a general system expansion bus. Figure 30.1 shows a block diagram of what a typical MBus-based system may look like.

MBus Features
Overview

The SPARC MBus Interface is a fully synchronous 64-bit, multiplexed address and data bus that supports multiple masters at 40 MHz. It supports data transfers of up to 128 bytes and can support up to 64 Gigabytes of physical address space. Data transfers larger than 8 bytes occur as burst transfers allowing MBus to achieve a peak bandwidth of 320 MBytes/s. Bus arbitration among masters is defined to be handled by a central bus arbiter. Requests

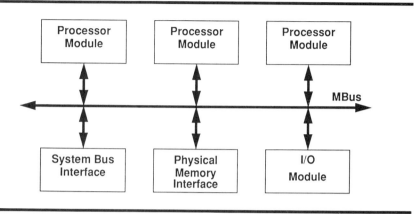

FIGURE 30.1. *Typical MBus system.*

from MBus modules are sent to the arbiter, and ownership is granted to the module with the highest priority. System Reset, Bus Arbitration, Interrupt Distribution, Bus Time-out, and MBus Clock are centralized functions that must be supported by the system. They do not belong to any particular module. A module ID mechanism allows each module to be uniquely identified and addressed to aid in system configuration.

A typical MBus cycle begins after an MBus module requests and is granted the bus. The module then initiates a transaction by supplying an address during an address phase. The bus slave that responds to the transaction either sources or sinks the data and then supplies an encoded acknowledgment to the bus master, signifying either a successful or unsuccessful data transfer. Figure 30.2 shows the timing of a typical MBus transaction. The data rate is controlled by the slave. The master must be able to accept a burst read, or source a burst write, of the requested size, at the maximum data rate of the bus. The arbitrary number of cycles is dependent on the data rate and can be zero for the maximum data rate on MBus.

When a successful data transfer is acknowledged, the bus-master will release the bus. Multiple acknowledgments are sent in the case of burst mode on each bus cycle. An unsuccessful data transfer can be stopped immediately, and the slave can signal for

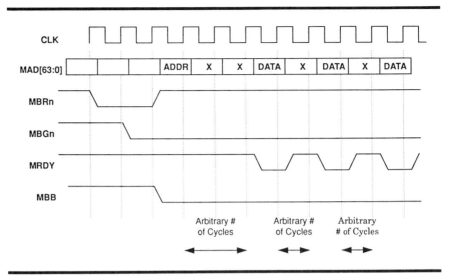

FIGURE 30.2. *MBus transaction timing.*

the master either to Retry or Relinquish and Retry. A Retry tells the master to stop the current transaction and restart it by reissuing the transaction from the beginning. A Relinquish and Retry tells the master to give up the bus and try to regain ownership before reissuing the transaction.

MBus Levels

The MBus specification has defined two levels of compliance. Level 1 includes the basic signals and transactions needed to design a complete uniprocessor system. Level 2 adds the additional signals and transactions needed to design a fully symmetric, cache coherent, shared memory multiprocessor system.

Level 1 Signals and Transactions Level 1 includes all the signals and transactions to support a uniprocessor system.

Table 30.1 summarizes the Level 1 signals. MBus defines a 64-bit multiplexed address and data bus MAD [63:0] as shown in Figure 30.3. During the data phase, this bus contains the data of the transaction. During the address phase, the lower 36 bits con-

Symbol	Description	Output	Input	Line Type	Signal Type
CLK	MBus Clock	Clock Driver	Mast/S1/Arbiter	dedicated	Bi-state
MAD[63:0]	Address/Control/Data	Master/Slave	Master/Slave	bussed	Tri-state
MAS	Address Strobe	Master	Slave	bussed	Tri-state
MRDY	Data Ready indicator	Slave	Master	bussed	Tri-state
MRTY	Transaction Retry Ind.	Slave	Master	bussed	Tri-state
MERR	Error indicator	Slave	Master	bussed	Tri-state
MBR	Bus Request	Master	Arbiter	dedicated	Bi-state
MBG	Bus Grant	Arbiter	Master	dedicated	Bi-state
MBB	Bus busy indicator	Master	Arbiter/Master	bussed	Tri-state
IRL [3:0]	Interrupt Level	Interrupt Logic	CPU Modules	dedicated	Bi-state
ID [3:0]	Module Indentifier	System	MBus Modules	dedicated	Bi-state
AERR	Asynchronous error out	Module	Interrupt Logic	bussed	Open Drain
INTOUT	Interrupt Out	I/O Modules	Interrupt Logic	dedicated	Bi-state
RSTIN	Module reset in signal	Reset Logic	Master	Imp. depend.	Bi-state
SCANDI	Scan Data In	System	Modules	dedicated	Bi-state
SCANDO	Scan Data Out	Modules	System	dedicated	Bi-state
SCANCLK	Scan Clock	System	Modules	dedicated	Bi-state
SCANTMSI	Scan Tap Control 1	System	Modules	dedicated	Bi-state
SCANTMS2	Scan Tap Control 2	System	Modules	dedicated	Bi-state

TABLE 30.1. *Level 1 signals.*

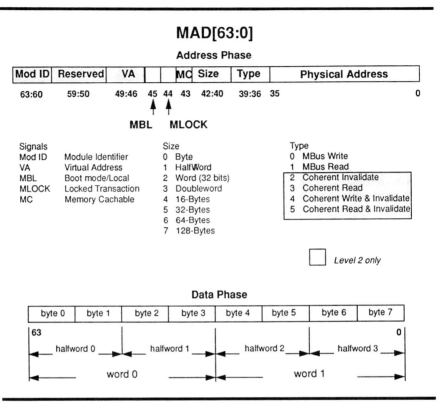

FIGURE 30.3. *Memory address and data—MAD [63:0].*

tain the physical address of the transaction. The upper bits during this phase contain transaction-specific information, such as transaction type and data size.

Level 1 MBus supports two transactions, Read and Write:

- Read

  A Read transaction merely reads a specified size of data, where size is from 1 to 128 bytes. Reads of greater than 8 bytes occur as burst transfers. Reads of less than 8 bytes will have undefined data on the unused bytes. A module that issues a Read transaction must be able to receive the data at the maximum rate of the MBus for the duration of the transaction.

• Write

A Write operation writes a specified size of data, where size is from 1 to 128 bytes. Writes of greater than 8 bytes occur as burst transfers. Writes of less than 8 bytes will have undefined data on the unused bytes. A module that issues a Write transaction must be able to source the data at the maximum rate of the MBus for the duration of the transaction.

Level 2—Cache Coherency and MBus

The system performance bottleneck in designing a shared memory MP system tends to be bus bandwidth. Reducing the amount of memory accesses over the bus is, therefore, essential. Using private caches for each processor can significantly reduce the bus traffic, since most memory references will access only the cache without the need of a bus transaction. The choice of memory update policy can also affect system performance. A write-back (or copy-back) memory updated policy is where stores only modify the cache line and do not immediately update main memory. The data are only written out when required. A write-through, memory-update policy stores the data to the cache and immediately updates main memory. Since the amount of memory accesses on the bus are significantly reduced, the write-back policy further enhances system performance.

MBus modules include a private cache in order to reduce memory bus traffic. Either write-back or write-through caches are supported, but in order to be cache consistent in Level 2, the caches in MBus systems must be write-back. MBus caches must also have a write-allocate policy where the contents of the cache line are updated on a write-miss.

While a write-back cache reduces bus traffic, it also introduces a problem, since a cache can have modified line that is inconsistent with memory. When another module requests that line, the most up-to-date copy must be provided. This problem is solved by MBus by implementing a write-invalidate, ownership-based protocol modeled after that used by the IEEE Futurebus. A line of data is said to be owned when there is one (and only one) cache in the system that is responsible for writing it back to memory as well as supplying the line when requested by another cache. If no cache is the owner, memory is considered the owner. This allows any cache to read a given line, but allows only the cache that owns the line to be able to write to it. Each cache listens to each bus transaction which is also called snooping the bus, and takes actions, if necessary, to maintain the consistency of any local copies of the line.

Cache States   A cache line can be in one of the following states:

- *Invalid (I):* Cache line is not valid.
- *Exclusive Clean (EC):* Only this cache has a valid copy of this cache line, and it is consistent with memory.
- *Exclusive Modified (EM):* Only this cache has a valid copy of the cache line, but the data have been modified and are different from memory. This cache is the OWNER of the cache line and supplies the data whenever there is a request for this memory location or memory needs to be updated.
- *Shared Clean (SC):* This cache line exists in one or more other caches. This line is consistent with the most up-to-date copy of this memory location, which is held by the owner of this cache line.
- *Shared Modified (SM):* This cache line exists in one or more other caches. This cache is the OWNER of the cache line and supplies the data whenever there is a request for this memory location or memory needs to be updated.

Level 2 Signals and Transactions   Level 2 MBus adds the Coherent Read, Coherent Invalidate, Coherent Read and Invalidate, and Coherent Write and Invalidate transactions, as well as two additional signals, MBus Share ($\overline{\text{MSH}}$) and MBus Inhibit ($\overline{\text{MIH}}$). All Coherent transactions have SIZE = 32 bytes.

- $\overline{\text{MSH}}$
  The Cache Block Shared signal is asserted by all caches that have a valid copy of data requested in a Coherent Read. It is asserted in the second cycle after the address is received.
- $\overline{\text{MIH}}$
  The Memory Inhibit signal is asserted by the owner of a

cache line to tell the main memory module not to supply the data for the current Coherent Read or Coherent Read and Invalidate. The owner will supply the data to the requesting cache. It is asserted in the second cycle after the address is received.

• Coherent Read
The Coherent Read transaction is similar to the Read transaction with a data size of 32 bytes (MBus line size). It also maintains cache consistency in the system. When a Coherent Read is issued by a module, all other modules "snoop" the bus. If another cache has a copy of the data *and* owns it, that cache asserts $\overline{MSH}$ and $\overline{MIH}$ during the A+2 cycle and supplies the data no sooner than cycle A+6. If there are multiple copies of the data, only the cache that owns the data will supply the data. All caches that have a copy of the data will assert $\overline{MSH}$ active and mark their copies as SHARED if not already done so. Otherwise, main memory suplies the data, and the requesting cache marks its data exclusive. An example of when Coherent Reads are issued by a module is in response to a cache miss on a processor read.

• Coherent Invalidate
The Coherent Invalidate transaction invalidates all copies of a line in a system. When a Coherent Invalidate is issued by a module, all other modules "snoop" the bus. If a module has a valid copy of the cache line, it immediately invalidates the line. Caches do not have to assert $\overline{MSH}$. One module (normally a memory controller) is responsible for acknowledging a Coherent Invalidate transaction.

The Coherent Invalidate MBus transaction is issued when a processor is writing to a cache line that is marked shared. Because MBus follows the write-invalidate cache consistency protocol, the module must invalidate all other copies of the line in the system. Doing so, the module takes ownership of the cache line, and the write is performed.

• Coherent Read and Invalidate
The Coherent Read and Invalidate combines a Coherent Read and a Coherent Invalidate. This reduces the number of Coherent Invalidate transactions on the bus. When a Coherent Read and Invalidate transaction is issued on the bus, and

if a cache owns the line, it will assert $\overline{\text{MIH}}$ to inhibit memory and supply the data. Once the data have been transferred successfully, the cache will then invalidate its entry. All other caches that have a valid copy of the cache line immediately invalidate their cache line upon seeing this transaction on the bus.

The Coherent Read and Invalidate transaction is issued, for example, on a processor write miss to read data from the current owner for write allocation. The module knows that it needs to fill the line and invalidate all other entries before the processor write can take place.

- Coherent Write and Invalidate
A Coherent Write and Invalidate combines a Coherent Write and a Coherent Invalidate. This was again included to reduce the number of Coherent Invalidate transactions on the bus. When a Coherent Write and Invalidate transaction is issued, any system cache with a valid copy of the line will immediately invalidate its entry. The cache that issued the transaction will then transfer the line to main memory. Software flush, block copy, or block fill are examples of when this transaction will be issued.

Transaction Acknowledgments

A master that has issued a transaction must be able to accept any acknowledgment. Normally, the slave will acknowledge a Valid Data Transfer, but can indicate that an error has taken place. Acknowledgments for any transaction are encoded on the $\overline{\text{MERR}}$ $\overline{\text{MRDY}}$, and the $\overline{\text{MRTY}}$ signals. Table 30.2 lists the encoding of these three bits.

An Idle Cycle indicates that either there is no bus activity or the bus is not transferring data. This can occur when there is a need to insert wait states or during dead cycle to prevent driver overlap.

Relinquish and Retry happens when a slave device cannot accept or supply data immediately. This tells the requesting master to release the bus immediately, giving another master the possibility of using the bus. The suspended transaction waits until bus ownership is attained. Once it regains the bus, the same transaction is issued again from the beginning. An exception is for the

MERR	MRDY	MRTY	Definition
H	H	H	Idle Cycle
H	H	L	Relinquish and Retry
H	L	H	Valid Data Transfer
H	L	L	Reserved
L	H	H	ERROR1 (Bus Error)
L	H	L	ERROR2 (Time-Out)
L	L	H	ERROR3 (Uncorrectable)
L	L	L	Retry

TABLE 30.2. *Transaction acknowledgment bit encoding.*

Coherent Invalidate, whichturns into a Coherent Read and Invalidate.

Valid Data Transfer indicates that valid data have arrived. On writes, it indicates that the data have been accepted and that the writing master shall stop driving the accepted data. The next data during a write burst will be driven onto the bus in the cycle immediately following $\overline{\text{MRDY}}$ being asserted.

ERROR1 indicates that an external bus error has occurred. ERROR2 indicates that a time-out has occurred, for example, from a system watchdog timer. ERROR3 indicates that an uncorrectable error has occurred and is mainly used by memory controllers.

Retry is similar to the Relinquish and Retry acknowledgment except the master will not relinquish control of the bus. The master immediately retries the transaction.

MBus System Issues

Centralized Functions

• System Reset
MBus systems must provide a mechanism for system reset. All moduels should have a reset input ($\overline{\text{RSTIN}}$) from some central reset logic that resets all the logic on a module to its initial state and drives its external signals inactive or tristate. Level 1 modules can also have a reset out signal (RSTOUT) that will perform a system reset.

• Bus Arbitration

Bus arbitration among masters is handled by an external bus arbiter. MBus does not specify the algorithm used by the arbiter and assumes the system designer will choose one that best suits the application. The only requirement is that fair bandwidth allocation be maintained.

Arbitration is overlapped with the current bus cycle. A requesting module requests the MBus by asserting its dedicated MBR signal and then waits for assertion of its dedicated grant signal $\overline{\text{MBG}}$. Upon receiving its grant, the requesting master can start using the bus as soon as the previous master releases the bus busy signal ($\overline{\text{MBB}}$). The requesting master asserts $\overline{\text{MBB}}$ immediately to acquire and hold the bus. A requesting master will not own the bus if it does not immediately assert $\overline{\text{MBB}}$ as soon as it is granted the bus. The requester, upon receiving a grant, immediately removes its request for the bus on the next clock edge. The arbitration protocol creates a dead cycle between transactions to ensure there will be no bus contention among back-to-back reads or writes from different masters.

The bus arbiter prioritizes requests and issues grants accordingly. A grant remains asserted until at least one cycle after the current master has deasserted $\overline{\text{MBB}}$, and it may be removed at anytime after this in response to assertion of requests from other masters. Bus parking is implemented, and if no other requests are asserted, the grant to the current owner remains asserted.

• System Interrupts

Each module has a dedicated set of interrupt request lines. A central system interrupt handler takes care of the distribution, status, priority, and level of system interrupts. Corresponding interrupt levels to the module correspond to the SPARC interrupt levels and are level-sensitive. Refer to the SPARC Architecture manual for more detail on the SPARC interrupt levels.

Bus Time-out and MBus System Clock are also to be implemented as centralized functions.

Memory Subsystems

During an MBus transaction, all caches snoop the bus to see whether they have a valid entry in their cache that needs to be modified in some way. For example, if a Coherent Read or Coherent Read and Invalidate is issued by an MBus module, all other modules are required to inhibit memory ($\overline{\text{MIH}}$ asserted) and supply the data (owned), or to mark their copy shared. Memory controllers will react to the assertion of $\overline{\text{MIH}}$ by immediately aborting the transaction, allowing the owner to supply the correct data. Memory controllers are also responsible for acknowledging Coherent Invalidate transaction.

MBus does not specify system details on how memory controllers handle memory errors, but it does provide mechanisms to report such errors. For example, a memory controller that supports error detection and correction may send a Retry Acknowledgment for a correctable error. Any of the Error Acknowledgments or the asynchronous error signal (AERR) may be used to signal an error.

Reflective Memory

Main memory can react to a Coherent Read in two ways. If the memory controller supports reflective memory it, will update main memory when the cache that owns the data sends it across the bus. The cache controllers must know that the memory controller supports reflective memory in order to mark their cache entries correctly. When the system has a memory controller that supports reflective memory, the cache entries will be marked clean, since they now reflect the most recently modified data. If the memory controller does not support this feature, the memory will not be updated, and the cache entries will be marked modified.

Figure 30.4 shows the MBus transaction that gets issued on the bus depending on the actions of the local cache. The vertical axis lists the processor-cache action, and the horizontal axis shows the state of that cache. The intersection of the two shows two things: the transaction that gets issued as well as the state of the cache after the transaction is completed.

Figure 30.5 shows the cache states and actions in response to a

Present Cache State

Processor Transaction		Invalid (I)	Exclusive Clean (EC)	Shared Clean (SC)	Exclusive Modified (EM)	Shared Modified (SM)
Read Hit	MBus Transaction Issued	N/A	None	None	None	None
	Cache State after Transaction		EC	SC	EM	SM
Read Miss	MBus Transaction Issued	Coherent Read	Coherent Read	Coherent Read	Coherent Read + Write	Coherent Read + Write
	Cache State after Transaction	EC/SC	EC/SC	EC/SC	EC/SC	EC/SC
Write Hit	MBus Transaction Issued		None	Coherent Invalidate	None	Coherent Invalidate
	Cache State after Transaction		EM	EM	EM	EM
Write Miss	MBus Transaction Issued	Coherent Read Invalidate	Coherent Read Invalidate	Coherent Read Invalidate	Coherent Read Invalidate + Write	Coherent Read Invalidate + Write
	Cache State after Transaction	EC	EM	EM	EM	EM

MBus Transaction Issued

Cache State after Transaction

FIGURE 30.4. *Transaction effects on cache states.*

MBus transaction. The vertical axis show the MBus transaction issued and the horizontal shows the state of a cache that is snooping the bus. The intersection shows which signals are asserted as well as the change in cache state due to the transaction.

An Example To illustrate the dynamics of MBus, let's assume a simple system as shown in Figure 30.6, where we have a physical nonreflective memory module (MEM) and three processor modules (PM), each having a processor, floating point unit, cache controller and cache RAM, and a SPARC Reference memory manage-

Present Cache State

MBus Transaction		Invalid (I)	Exclusive Clean (EC)	Shared Clean (SC)	Exclusive Modified (EM)	Shared Modified (SM)
Coherent Read Reflective Memory			M̄S̄H̄	M̄S̄H̄	M̄S̄H̄/M̄ĪH̄ Send Data	M̄S̄H̄/M̄ĪH̄ Send Data
		N/A	SC	SC	SC	SC
Coherent Read Non-Reflective Memory			M̄S̄H̄	M̄S̄H̄	M̄S̄H̄/M̄ĪH̄ Send Data	M̄S̄H̄/M̄ĪH̄ Send Data
		N/A	SC	SM	SM	SM
Coherent Invalidate						
		I	I	I	I	I
Coherent Read &Invalidate						
		I	I	I	I	I
Coherent Write &Invalidate						
		I	I	I	I	I

Snooping Cache Action

Cache State after Transaction

FIGURE 30.5. *MBus transaction effects on cache states.*

ment unit. For simplicity, the memory module is only 32 bytes large, and each processor module only has one cache line (32 bytes) corresponding to the memory address. This example will run through a series of events to illustrate both MBus transactions and the cache line state changes that take place. Each event will cause an MBus transaction and state change. Note that in a real

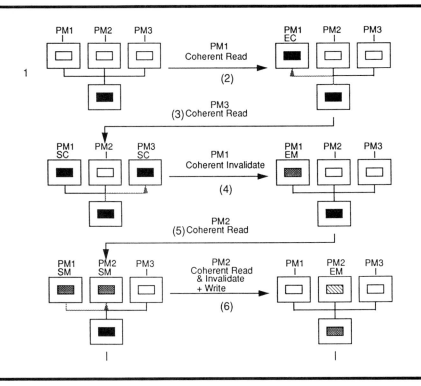

FIGURE 30.6. *System state changes—An example.*

MBus system, this would not occur, since most events will not cause a module to issue an MBus transaction. Please refer to Figures 30.4 and 30.5 for explanations of which transactions are being issued and how the caches are being affected.

1. Initially, the cache line in all processor modules have an invalid state, and memory owns the data.

2. Processor 1 executes a read and gets a read miss. In response to this, PM1 issues a Coherent Read, obtains data from memory, and marks the line exclusive clean.

3. Now, Porcessor 3 wants the data, so PM3 issues a Coherent Read. Memory supplies the data, PM1 plus $\overline{\text{MSH}}$ active and both PM1 and PM3 mark their entries as Shared Clean.

4. Processor 1 needs to write data into the cache and needs to own the cache line in order to do so. PM1 will issue a Coherent Invalidate to invalidate any other copy of the data to take ownership. It also updates its cache and marks its entry as Exclusive Modified. PM3, with a valid copy of the data, immediately invalidates its entry.

5. A Read Miss occurs in PM2 and a Coherent Read is issued. PM1 snoops the bus and sees that it owns the requested data. It then asserts $\overline{\text{MIH}}$ to inhibit memory from supplying the data and supplies the data to the requester. $\overline{\text{MSH}}$ is also asserted at this time. Both PM1 and PM2 mark their caches Shared Modified. If this particular system had supported reflective memory, the caches would have been marked Shared Clean, since memory would have been updated at this time.

6. Finally, PM2 experiences a Write Miss and issues a Coherent Read and Invalidate and a Write transaction. The Coherent Read and Invalidate causes the memory to supply the new data to PM2 and causes PM1 to invalidate its entry. The Write causes the previous cache line to be written into memory. These two transactions occur automically. Processor 2 updates the new line with the data from the write miss and marks the line Exclusive Modified.

Mechanical Specifications

The MBus specifies a standard connector, pin out, and full mechanical specifications for the module printed circuit boards for easy future module upgrades. The 100-pin AMP "Microstrip" (part #121354-4) was selected to provide high-reliability, ease of installation, and a fool-proof keying scheme. Two sizes of modules have been defined for more flexibility. Figure 30.7 shows the approximate sizes of the modules. Please refer to the MBus specification for full mechanicals specifications. The connector placement and width of the modules are constant between the two and can, therefore, be used within the same system.

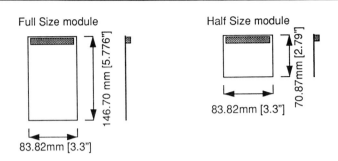

FIGURE 30.7. *MBus modules.*

Conclusion

SPARC MBus provides an easy, low-cost solution to designing modular, upgradable systems by providing a standard interface between processor and physcial memory. It also allows the development of a high-performance shared memory multiprocessing system by providing the protocol and HW support. Designing a SPARC MBus-based system allows a designer to develop a new revolutionary system architecture capable of quick, inexpensive and evolutionary performance upgrades.

SPARC Strategy

Licensing Strategy at Sun Microsystems

31

Sᴜɴ Cᴏʀᴘᴏʀᴀᴛᴇ Mᴀʀᴋᴇᴛɪɴɢ Wʜɪᴛᴇ Pᴀᴘᴇʀ

Overview

"Companies that have risen to global leadership over the past 20 years invariably began with ambitions that were out of all proportion to their resources . . ." stated Gary Hamel and C.K. Prahalad in the Harvard Business Review (May–June 1989). By using what the authors call "strategic intent," companies can "leverage resources to reach seemingly unattainable goals," they asserted. Such companies don't hesitate to take risks if there are possible gains. Indeed, "a quest for new rules . . . can devalue the incumbent's advantages," wrote the authors. "For smart competitors, the goal is not competitive imitation but competitive innovation, the art of containing competitive risks within manageable proportions."

The authors pointed out several tactics that have enabled companies to win against much larger competitors. To preempt leader Xerox in the personal copier business, Canon not only looked at ways of getting costs way down, the Japanese firm also literally "reinvented the copier" by designing a disposable cartridge. Creating new distribution channels, novel approaches to service, pioneering products—these are winning tactics. Companies that excel at strategic intent also use devices such as licensing, wrote the authors.

Technology licensing is a fundamental strategy of Sun Microsystems. It is an outgrowth of Sun's commitment to open systems, defined as standard—yet compatible—products that can be made in different versions by various vendors.

Open systems, licensing, partnerships and the promotion of next-generation technologies are some of the ways Sun is changing the rules to achieve strategic intent.

Historical Background

Strategic intent has been very visible in the computer industry, helping fuel innovation. From the first generation of mainframes, to time-shared minicomputers, to personal computers and now to distributed computing systems, the goal of computer companies has been finding larger markets and greater market share by pushing technology to meet user needs. A parallel trend that served users' needs in earlier days was proprietary products. Standardizing on one vendor's products offered a simpler solution, particularly since interoperability between manufacturers' systems wasn't possible.

This tradition of "closed" systems also offered benefits to computer companies, assuring them of continued sales from customers that had already made large investments in these computers. Few corporations that had spent millions of dollars on proprietary hardware and software would abandon these products and switch to another vendor without good reason. In today's market, however, proprietary systems not only limit a customer's choices of product and price. They also keep products behind the technology curve, since in a market without competition, there is little reason to innovate. As TIME Magazine pointed out in its October 30, 1989 issue, sales growth in the overall computer industry has slowed from 15–20% in the early 80s to an estimated 6–8% during the next few years. "Many established companies are repackaging old technology rather than developing daring new products," noted TIME.

Since healthy competition stimulates innovation and gives customers value (better products at lower prices), the solution is to open up markets to more vendors.

The Benefits of Competition

In a free market, customers seek value. There are many instances in the history of the computer industry in which the search for value has spurred competition, even in a world dominated by proprietary systems. Years ago, seven mainframe manufacturers that included Amdahl, Fujitsu, Hitachi and NEC braved legal suits to challenge IBM's control of the market. This competition—an example of companies practicing strategic intent—helped spur greater efforts to offer customers value, which quickly enlarges markets.

Years after the seven firms threw down the gauntlet to IBM's 370, IBM faced competition again in the PC market. Uncharacteristically, the Armonk computer giant had based its PC line on hardware and software from outside companies in order to get to market quickly and build up a large market share against Apple Computer. But this opened the door to a legion of PC clone makers, who could not copy Apple's patented, proprietary machines but could easily produce PCs by purchasing the operating system and CPU from Microsoft and Intel, respectively.

Ultimately, the PC clone market better served customer needs by promoting competition and thereby improving the choices of product and price. According to some industry observers, the PC market grew to become at least five times larger than it would have if only IBM had participated. While IBM now has a 13.9% share of an overall market of $64 billion (1989 worldwide estimates from Dataquest), IBM has still earned more money than it would have in a much smaller, single-vendor market. Underscoring the market benefits of open competition is the fact that IBM's share fell significantly as soon as it abandoned the open AT bus in favor of its originally-proprietary Micro Channel, noted Dataquest.

IBM is now reluctantly licensing Micro Channel after intense pressure from chip companies who had begun reverse-engineering this bus architecture. However, Joseph Farrell and Nancy Gallini pointed out in the November 1988 issue of Quarterly Journal of Economics that encouraging competition rather than trying to prevent it can be a successful business strategy. Since a monopolistic market works against customers, wrote the authors, "voluntarily inviting competitors into the market, usually by licensing a product . . . or by using an 'open architecture'," can be profitable.

This is because customers will always pick value—if they are given a choice.

Farrell and Bellini cited the example of Ethernet, which developer Xerox licensed at a nominal charge in order to encourage wide adoption—another example of strategic intent. The authors stated that Ethernet succeeded because Xerox had removed any customer fears that it would monopolistically price-gouge, since Ethernet chips were available from many vendors. Second-sourcing in the semiconductor industry—a traditional practice—works in similar fashion. Buyers (system vendors) want more than one source so they will not be affected if a manufacturing line goes down, a company goes out of business or other calamities occur. However, Farrell and Gallini argue that there is an even stronger motive—to avoid "the monopoly incentive to raise prices."

Anyone who buys a product—an end user or an OEM—resists being the hostage of a monopoly. Consider the recent case of Adobe, "the only source for a technology for which it thought there was no substitute," wrote analyst Richard Shaffer (Technologic Computer Letter, September 25, 1989). Charging what the market would bear for its graphics language, PostScript, made Adobe very successful—until Microsoft and Apple announced they would collaborate on their own, competing graphics language. So Adobe was forced into saying it will license its proprietary technology, which will surely mean less money for the company in the long run. Using the argument of Farrell and Gallini, might Adobe have fared better if it had begun with a carefully crafted open strategy rather than assuming it could forever lock out all competitors? According to Shaffer, the real irony is that Apple and Microsoft go to great lengths to protect their own products from any competition. By the maxims of strategic intent, this behavior substitutes for innovation and ultimately can cause economic defeat.

Licensing As a Way to Reduce Costs

Licensing can serve to lower the cost of developing and distributing a new product that is designed to become a standard. Early in the history of Sun Microsystems, the company developed a technology for sharing files among heterogeneous systems, called the Network File System (NFS™). As a young company, Sun did not have the resources to develop versions of this product for every platform in the industry, so it licensed the technology to many different computer and software firms, who did their own development. There are now more than 260 companies that license NFS, making it a de facto industry standard.

Competing through collaboration is an important method for achieving strategic intent. For example, a major semiconductor manufacturer noted that the cost of developing a new computer architecture alone can be $100 million, with millions more required to develop system and application software. Only the few largest companies can afford such an expense. However, leveraging resources through cooperative efforts makes development affordable for smaller firms.

There are many advantages in licensing a next-generation base technology that is flexible enough to be turned into a range of products. It encourages parallel innovation, as various companies concurrently design their own version of this technology. It opens the market to more companies, giving them opportunities they couldn't have afforded as single vendors. With more competition, customers have greater choices in terms of price and performance, which stimulates sales.

Licensing technology also helps establish new standards, reducing the risk for companies—by assuring them of a broad market—and for customers—by making sure they aren't captives of a single vendor.

A New Microprocessor Standard

As the 90s dawn, the promise of the 32-bit computer market is causing a revolution in the computer industry. With so much potential revenue at stake, the companies that practice strategic intent are beginning to battle with those that have long dominated markets by reducing competition. At the heart of this skirmish is the question of who will be a leader in the RISC market. Analysts predict that RISC processors could represent up to 41% of the office market in the next five years, "making RISC CPUs a $250 million to $1.3 billion-plus business," reported ELECTRONIC BUSINESS in the July 10, 1989 issue.

"This is the once-in-a-decade chance to establish a processor as a standard in the huge, $100 billion office computing market," stated ELECTRONIC BUSINESS. "The first time this opportunity came along was in 1980, and Intel seized it by getting its 8086/88 line designed into the IBM PC, whose products lie at the heart of the 36 million IBM PCs and clones that sit on desks from

Boston to Beijing. That made Intel a wealthy company, catapulting it from $789 million to $2.9 billion in the past eight years with a microprocessor monopoly that industrialist J.P. Morgan would have loved."

The rise of RISC amply demonstrates the dilemma of a company that has been forced by market evolution to offer a new product line that competes with one it already has. Both Intel and Motorola are in this position, wrote ELECTRONIC BUSINESS. While both companies have designed RISC products, these can potentially eat into their profitable CISC sales. Meanwhile, the RISC market has chosen two new leading architectures: SPARC and MIPS. According to market analysts Summit Strategies, "SPARC . . . is likely to become the dominant binary-compatible workstation platform in the industry by 1993 and even has a shot at becoming the leading workstation processor."

SPARC is a clear example of strategic intent, using licensing as a way of quickly building market share and establishing a standard. The initial goal was to rapidly increase the volume of SPARC machines being offered. "If enough manufacturers build Sun clones, the software companies will have to take notice," said BUSINESS WEEK in its July 24, 1989 issue. "In the end, everyone will prosper. And Sun's SPARC workstations . . . will become a desktop standard alongside 35 million IBM-style PCs and nearly three million Macintoshes . . ."

Why Licensing is Necessary

Encouraging competition is a new, daring strategy in the computer industry. But quickly building SPARC market share at this juncture is so crucial that "Sun has little choice but to gamble," noted BUSINESS WEEK. "To compete with the likes of IBM, it must coax software developers to write programs for SPARC machines . . . but developers demand a high-volume market and Sun can't produce that alone." By licensing technology to other companies, Sun has, in effect, made itself into a much larger company that can attract ISVs and—therefore—customers in great numbers.

One way to produce volume quickly is to encourage the participation of Asian manufacturers. According to BUSINESS

WEEK, "It may be worth losing some sales to Toshiba's SPARC PCs rather than risk seeing the influential Japanese computer maker choose a rival chip. Without such a partner to crank up the volume, Sun's strategy may never pay off."

This strategy takes into account both SPARC clones and SPARC compatibles. A clone is a duplicate of an existing system while a compatible—which has the same ABI (application binary interface) as the original—is a different machine that runs the same software. Both can exist as a result of SPARC licensing. Currently, SPARC compatibles are either available or under development, ranging from the low end (low-cost PC-class systems) to the high end (SPARC supercomputers). In a market growing as quickly as the SPARC market, clones are inevitable.

The proliferation of SPARC—both in compatibles and clones—creates a broader market for everyone.

SPARC As a Route to Strategic Intent

The origins of SPARC underscore Farrell and Bellini's assertion that companies prefer to have multiple sources of critical components. In the all-important 32-bit microprocessor market, the top semiconductor manufacturers (Intel, Motorola) had managed to crowd out second-source suppliers—a reversal from the traditional practice in previous generations of products. Thus Sun found itself with a single source for its CPUs, making it dependent upon the rate of innovation of its suppliers.

Performance was another key impetus leading to the creation of SPARC, since existing architectures were not adequate for Sun's future product directions, as dictated by the customer demands of the 90s. Since the top microprocessor vendors were not then interested in designing a flexible RISC architecture to meet Sun's needs, the idea for SPARC was born. However, Sun realized that as a company that had long promoted open standards, its new hardware architecture could not be proprietary. This was not just because of corporate tradition but also due to a belief in the principles of strategic intent.

Optimized for UNIX, SPARC delivers the performance and low price the customer of the 90s will expect. As a scalable architecture being implemented by various semiconductor vendors,

SPARC promotes another key goal in Sun's licensing strategy: the existence of many different compatible systems, from desktops to supercomputers. In addition, Sun has assured itself of multiple sources (and a range of implementations) by licensing the SPARC architecture to several semiconductor manufacturers.

While technology licensing and partnerships are a clear departure from the traditional computer market, these strategies will become a hallmark of the 90s. Already, other manufacturers are beginning to emulate these concepts.

Competitive RISCs

From the beginning, Sun designed SPARC as a multi-vendor standard that could be implemented using various semiconductor technologies (CMOS, ECL, GaAs) and put into a range of systems. This is in contrast to competing RISC designs, which perpetuate the single-vendor thinking of the past.

While the world's two leading microprocessor vendors, Intel and Motorola, have added RISC solutions to their product lines, it is doubtful either company will license their architectures for other vendors to implement, thereby reducing the value to customers. Nor will these two companies likely search for second source partners to fabricate their RISC chips. However, two other RISC vendors—MIPS and Hewlett-Packard—have recently adopted some version of the strategies of Sun.

MIPS implementations are fabricated by five outside vendors. While these firms are allowed to resell the CMOS MIPS chips they make, the new, high-performance MIPS ECL chip goes back to MIPS alone. No company but MIPS is *designing* these chips. Some observers have an explanation for this. The highly complex design of the MIPS RISC architecture (designed so to optimize performance) has made it very difficult to fabricate—and possibly, to implement by other vendors. Low yields are one result, which makes this architecture potentially less profitable for second sources and implementors.

It is unlikely MIPS will license its architecture, thereby reducing competition and potential innovation. Perhaps to counter this single-vendor limitation, MIPS recently announced it will offer a new common interface. Until now, different systems based on the MIPS CPU have been incompatible. The new interface is designed to overcome this handicap, offering source code compatibility. While such a strategy is more attractive to software developers, source code compatibility is not the same as binary compatibility—a recompile is still necessary. This means the existence of "shrink-wrapped" software for systems based on the MIPS chip is still not possible.

HP has also recently broken away from its traditional strategies. Alliances with Hitachi and Samsung were forged in an attempt to head off the momentum of SPARC and its open licensing strategy. These agreements will help enlarge the geographic market for HP RISC systems, will help HP fill in its product lacks on the low end and will teach HP about new semiconductor processes.

One question that arises is what HP will do about its software. The company has several proprietary operating systems, which complicates the task for third-party developers (even though HP makes the lion's share of applications itself). These could be major handicaps impeding the creation of HP compatibles. An essential fact that will always limit HP's employment of strategic intent is that its product line is mainly proprietary—and likely to remain so.

What Sets SPARC Apart

A key element in the SPARC strategy is vendor participation in the control and evolution of SPARC. This takes place through SPARC International, an organization open to all component and system manufacturers and software developers who design—or want to design—SPARC products. SPARC International has an important charter. It ensures binary compatibility among all SPARC chip implementations; supports the migration of application software to SPARC platforms; and serves the technical and information needs of the entire SPARC community. By turning SPARC over to an industry body, Sun reinforces the fact that SPARC is an open standard not totally controlled by its designer. This further encourages "competitor-partners" to commit to SPARC.

SPARC's scalability, open licensing and participation by SPARC International promote the quick creation of an entire

SPARC industry based on innovation. Ultimately, this meets the most important need of offering real value to end users.

The Benefits of SPARC

SPARC's scalability creates the potential for true compatibility across a wide range of systems, which users want. (For example, IBM is just now addressing the incompatibility of its various computing platforms.) Besides facilitating interoperability and leveraging an investment in software, this greatly simplifies training within an organization that uses a variety of SPARC systems.

The binary compatibility of SPARC systems will be very attractive to many technical users, who often write their own applications. If they choose SPARC computers, no longer will they need to create new software for newly acquired systems that offer a different level of performance.

Developers of commercial applications can benefit significantly from SPARC. Rather than investing in costly, time-consuming porting activities for each different SPARC system, they can allocate resources to a more rewarding endeavor: new product development. By fueling innovation, this also benefits end users.

A large selection of compatible SPARC systems broadens the buying audience for software companies, just as a breadth of existing software helps build system sales. This synergy also exists between component and system vendors, all of whom save money by building upon an established, successful base architecture. Unlike developers of PC compatibles, SPARC system designers aren't captives of the product, prices and production schedules of a single vendor.

Ultimately, everyone can benefit in an open marketplace, since this fosters innovation, gives customers more choices and leads to greater sales.

SPARC Competitive Analysis

An Analysis of MIPS and SPARC Instruction Set Utilization on the SPEC Benchmarks

32

ROBERT F. CMELIK • SHING I. KONG •
DAVID R. DITZEL • EDMUND J. KELLY •

Abstract

The dynamic instruction counts of MIPS and SPARC are compared using the SPEC benchmarks. MIPS typically executes more user-level instructions than SPARC. This difference can be accounted for by architectural differences, compiler differences, and library differences. The most significant differences are that SPARC's double-precision floating-point load/store is an architectural advantage in the SPEC floating-point benchmarks, while MIPS's compare-and-branch instruction is an architectural advantage in the SPEC integer benchmarks. After the differences in the two architectures are isolated, it appears that although MIPS and SPARC each have strengths and weaknesses in their compilers and library routines, the combined effect of compilers and library routines does not give either MIPS or SPARC a clear advantage in these areas.

Introduction

We analyze the instruction set utilization of MIPS[1] and SPARC[2] on the SPEC benchmarks.[3] Although many studies have been published on the instruction set utilization of CISC processors, such as the Dorado,[4] VAX,[5] IBM 360,[6] and PDP-10,[7] very few studies have been published on the instruction set utilization of commercial RISC processors.

The differences in instructions set utilization between MIPS and SPARC can only come from three sources:

1. Differences in the instruction set architectures.

2. Differences in the compilers.

3. Differences in the library routines, which may have been hand-coded or use different algorithms.

This paper first presents the instruction set utilization data we collected. It then analyzes this data based on differences among the MIPS and SPARC architectures, compilers, and library routines. The results of the analysis are then used to make conclusions about the profitability of different architectural, compiler, and library trade-offs.

Background

This section gives a brief discussion of the SPEC benchmarks. It then lists the major architectural differences between MIPS and SPARC, so that we can analyze the instruction set utilization data in terms of these differences.

The Benchmarks

We selected the SPEC benchmarks for this experiment because they are large and well-known programs that are widely accepted for benchmarking. The SPEC Benchmark Release 1.0 consists of ten programs:

1. *gcc1.35*   This is an integer benchmark written in C. It measures the time that the GNU C Compiler Version 1.35 takes to compile 19 pre-processed source files into optimized Sun-3 assembly language files.

2. *espresso*   This is an integer benchmark written in C. It measures the time it takes the PLA optimizer espresso to optimize four different PLAs.

3. *spice2g6*   This is an FP (floating point) benchmark written in FORTRAN. It is an analog circuit simulator.

4. *doduc*   This is an FP benchmark written in FORT-RAN. It simulates the time evolution of a

thermohydraulic model for a nuclear reactor's component.

5. *nasa7*   This is an FP benchmark written in FORTRAN. It is a collection of seven synthetic kernels.

6. *li*   This is an integer benchmark written in C. It is a LISP interpreter that measures the time it takes to solve the nine-queens problem.

7. *eqntott*   This is an integer benchmark written in C. It translates Boolean equations into a truth table.

8. *matrix300*   This is an FP benchmark written in FORTRAN. It exercises the Linpack routine saxpy on matrices of order 300.

9. *fpppp*   This is an FP benchmark written in FORTRAN. It calculates a two-electron integral derivative (quantum chemistry).

10. *tomcatv*   This is an FP benchmark written in FORTRAN. It is a vectorized mesh generation program.

Benchmark Compilation

On MIPS, the benchmarks were compiled using RISC Compilers 2.10 with optimization −03 (−02 for *gcc1.35*, *spice2g6*, and fpppp) per the SPEC Makefiles, best −G numbers per the linker, and −0limit values per the compiler.

On SPARC, the benchmarks were compiled with SPARC Compilers 1.0 (beta) (Sun C 1.1 (beta) and Sun FORTRAN 1.4 (beta)) using the options −cg89 −04 −libmil −dalign.

Data Collection

On MIPS, we used pixie and pixstats[8] (and an in-house pixstats-like program) to collect dynamic instruction counts. On SPARC, we used the corresponding tools, spix and spixstats,[9] pixie and spix instrument programs to collect enough information to determine how often each user-level instruction is executed. pixstats and spixstats produce summary data based on these counts. Additional data on SPARC were obtained using shadow,[10] which allowed us to perform efficient (traceless) trace-driven analyses.

Two of the benchmarks create subprocesses, which are not automatically handled by the tools. *gcc1.35* consists of two programs, one of which (gcc) invokes the other (cc1) to compile each input file; we counted both gcc and cc1. Similarly, *eqntott* invokes the local C preprocessor on the input file; we did not count the C preprocessor.

Architecture vs. Implementation

This paper compares the instructions executed by MIPS and SPARC on an architectural basis. This is because implementations change more frequently than instruction set architectures. However, to provide a more complete understanding of the architectural differences, it is sometimes necessary to refer to implementation characteristics.

For example, quite often, a load instruction cannot return its data before the cycle immediately following the load. MIPS requires an intervening instruction between the load and any instruction that uses the load data. This is an architectural trade-off that will last through future compatible implementations. SPARC requires the hardware to impose an interlock if the data were not ready for the following instruction. All current implementations of SPARC have a one-cycle interlock, though future implementations may have more or less than one. For equivalent implementations, interlocks result in a lower instruction count for SPARC and a lower cycles per instruction ratio for MIPS, even though both would give equivalent performance.

Another example involves register windows. One may argue that instructions executed in register window overflow/underflow trap handlers should be counted. One may also argue that for an implementation-independent study, these instructions should not be counted because the number of register windows is an implementation issue. In order to better understand the trade-offs, we have included numbers on register window overhead for a SPARC implementation with eight windows.

Architectural Differences Between MIPS and SPARC

MIPS (MIPS I: R3000/R3010) and SPARC (Version 7) have far more architectural similarities than differences. A full description of these similarities and differences appears in Appendix E of *Computer Architecture: A Quantitative Approach.*[11] For review, the major differences between the MIPS and SPARC instruction set architectures are:

1. MIPS uses a 32-register, fixed-size integer register file. SPARC uses a register window scheme with eight global registers and a set of 24-register overlapping windows.† Only 32 register are accessible at any given time.

2. MIPS has instructions to move values between integer and FP (floating-point) registers. SPARC uses integer and FP load/store sequences to move operands between register sets.

3. MIPS only has single-precision FP loads and stores. SPARC has single-precision and double-precision FP loads and stores.

4. MIPS loads and stores have one addressing mode: register+immediate. SPARC loads and stores have two addressing modes: register+immediate and register+register.

5. MIPS can often perform compare-and-branch in one instruction. SPARC uses one instruction to set condition codes and another instruction to branch.

6. MIPS branches require an instruction to be executed in the delay slot. SPARC has annulling branches that can cancel the execution of the delay slot instruction depending on whether the branch is taken.

7. MIPS requires an intervening instruction between a load and the use of the data from that load to prevent load-use data conflict. SPARC allows a load to be immediately followed by an instruction using that data. If necessary, the hardware will cause a delay automatically.

† So far, all SPARC implementations have either seven or eight register windows.

8. MIPS has an instruction to move values between single-precision FP registers and an instruction to move values between double-precision FP registers. SPARC only has the former.

9. MIPS has integar multiply and divide/remainder instructions. SPARC does not.

10. MIPS does not have FP square-root instructions. SPARC does.

11. MIPS does not have conditional trap instructions. SPARC does.

12. MIPS traps to software to manage its TLB, SPARC implements its memory management in hardware.

13. The immediate constant field in MIPS instructions is 16-bits wide. In SPARC, it is 13-bits wide.

14. Both MIPS and SPARC have a 32-entry, 32-bit FP register file, and both can have up to 16 double-precision registers. Single-precision FP operations in MIPS, however, can only access 16 (the even half) of these registers. The SPARC FP register file, on the other hand, can hold a mixture of up to 32 single-precision numbers, 16 double-precision numbers, or 8 quad-precision numbers.

The impact of items 1 through 10 on instruction utilization is analyzed later. Item 11 is not included in this study because SPARC does not use any conditional trap (ticc) instructions in the SPEC benchmarks. Item 12 is not included because the MIPS TLB trap handler is in the kernel, which is inaccessible to our tools. Item 13 is not included because it is difficult to estimate its effects. Finally, Item 14 is not included because single-precision FP arithmetic is seldom used and quad-precision FP arithmetic is never used in the SPEC benchmarks.

Raw Instruction Count Summary

Table 32.1 shows some of the instruction set utilization data we collected. It is included here to give readers an overview of the raw data. In order to compare the number of user-level instructions executed on each processor, the ratio of the two (M/S) is also given.

Overall MIPS executes significantly more user-level instructions than SPARC. Most of this comes from the FP benchmarks where MIPS executes 30% more. The integer benchmarks are more balanced with MIPS executing only 3% more instructions than SPARC.

We will refer to the numbers in Table 32.1 as the ordinary instruction total (**total**). This total does not include events such as load-use pipeline interlocks in SPARC and instructions SPARC executes in its window overflow/underflow trap handlers. Although these events do not show up as user-level instruction execution, they do consume cycles in all current SPARC implementations. Therefore, any direct inferences on performance based on the ordinary instructions counts alone would be inappropriate. We will correct these deficiencies by calculating an adjusted total (**Total +**) to take these events into account.

In order to study the effect of compiler optimizations and library routines, we would like to factor out all differences in the instruction set architectures. To do this, we add hypothetical instructions to each architecture to balance out differences and produce architecture-neutral totals (**Total + ~**).

Benchmark	MIPS	SPARC	M/S
spice2g6	21,569,202,673	22,878,017,309	0.94
doduc	1,613,227,089	1,303,276,485	1.24
nasa7	9,256,812,144	6,614,656,686	1.40
matrix300	2,775,967,947	1,693,589,255	1.64
fpppp	2,316,200,144	1,443,008,199	1.61
tomcatv	1,812,691,974	1,626,342,454	1.11
FP G. Mean:			1.30
gcc1.35	1,110,816,041	1,155,986,011	0.96
espresso	2,828,804,443	2,930,860,108	0.97
li	6,022,855,076	4,661,320,853	1.29
eqntott	1,243,469,361	1,321,536,444	0.94
Int G. Mean:			1.03
All G. Mean:			1.18

TABLE 32.1. *Overall dynamic instruction counts.*

The Data

Most of our data appear in Tables A 1 and A2 (appendices). Conceptually, these are one table (split for space reasons) with columns for benchmarks (and architectures) and rows for instruction categories. Table A1 is for the FP benchmarks, and Table A2 is for the integer benchmarks. Appendix 3 gives a brief description of each instruction category.

For each benchmark, we present MIPS and SPARC (order was decided by coin toss) counts and their ratio (M/S). Three columns provide geometric means of these ratios: **FP** for the six **FP** benchmarks, **Int** for the four integer benchmarks, and **All** for all ten benchmarks.

All counts are in millions. Counts come in four flavors, which may be distinguished by a trailing tag character:

" " (No tag) Ordinary user-level instruction counts.

"+" Other potential contributions to run time (e.g. trap handler instruction counts, or load-use interlock counts).

"~" Counts that illustrate the impact of hypothetical instructions included to account for achitectural differences.

"<" Counts for reference only (not included in totals or subtotals).

The **Subtotal** rows show sums of ordinary instruction counts only; subtotal percentages are with respect to the total ordinary instruction count.

Total	Sum of ordinary instruction counts.
Total +	**Total** above, plus '+' tagged counts.
Total + ~	**Total +** above, plus '~' tagged counts.

Detailed Discussion of the Results

This section first discusses the overall effects of library routines on the numbers in Tables A1 and A2. It then discusses the numbers in Tables A1 and A2 that highlight the architectural, compiler, and library differences that can affect instruction utilization in each instruction category.

The Effects of Library Routines

Row O3 shows the number of instructions executed in the library routines. The numbers on this row are given a "<" tag because they are already included in other instruction categories. They are listed separately here to show the overall effects of the library routines.

Overall, library routines account for a significant fraction of the instructions executed in four of the six FP benchmarks (*matrix300* and *tomcatv* are the exceptions) and in three of the four integer benchmarks (*li* is the exception). Table 32.2 shows the percentage of instructions executed in library routines for these benchmarks.

Row O3 shows that SPARC executes significantly more instructions in library routines than MIPS for *espresso, gcc1.35,* and *spice2g6.*

The main source of differences in *gcc1.35* and *espresso* are the routines malloc and free. In MIPS, malloc and free are optimized for speed. In SPARC, these routines try to minimize allocated space.

The main source of differences in *spice2g6* is that MIPS uses the routines memset, mcopy, memcopy, where SPARC uses the less-efficient routines bzero and bcopy.

Benchmark	MIPS	SPARC
013.spice2g6	4%	8%
015.doduc	19%	17%
020.nasa7	7%	9%
042.fpppp	2%	3%
001.gcc1.35	8%	19%
008.espresso	3%	15%
023.eqntott	4%	4%
All G. Mean:	5%	9%

TABLE 32.2. *Library routines.*

Finally, another source of differences in *gcc1.35* and *spice2g6* is that SPARC calls multiply, divide, and remainder routines (Tables 5 and 6) for which MIPS has instructions.

Load and Store Usage

Overall, MIPS executes significantly more FP loads (M/S=1.92) and FP stores (M/S=2.49) than SPARC in the FP benchmarks. On the integer benchmarks, there were fewer stores (M/S=1.07) for SPARC and an equal number of loads (M/S=1.00).

Register windows are supposed to reduce integer loads and stores for programs that have significant procedure call overhead. Unfortunately for SPARC, the frequency of calls in the SPEC benchmarks is very low. *gcc1.35* and *li* have more calls than other SPEC benchmarks. Even for these two benchmarks, the frequency of calls is only 1.1% of the instructions in *gcc1.35* and 2.0% of the instructions in *li*. This represents a low frequency compared with data such as that presented by Clark.[12] Even so, on both *gcc1.35* and *li*, SPARC has fewer integer loads and stores than MIPS.

Rows L4 and S4 illustrate the following architectural difference between MIPS and SPARC:

- MIPS uses a 32-register, fixed-size integer register file. SPARC uses a register window scheme with eight global registers and a set of 24-register overlapping windows.

MIPS' numbers here represent loads and stores that save and restore registers between function calls and returns. SPARC's numbers here are loads and stores that SPARC executes in the window overflow/underflow trap handlers (we assume there are eight register windows). SPARC only executes a small number of loads and stores to handle window overflows and underflows in all benchmarks except in *li*, where SPARC executes 33 million loads and 44 million stores.

Besides these loads and stores, SPARC must execute additional instructions in the overflow/underflow trap handlers. These other instructions are counted in Row O1. In order to compare the number of instructions MIPS and SPARC need to execute to save and restore registers, one must compare the sum of Rows L4, S4, and O1. This sum reveals that SPARC needs to execute fewer instructions in all SPEC benchmarks except *li*.

Rows L5 and S5 illustrate the following architectural difference between MIPS and SPARC:

  • MIPS has instructions to move values between integer and FP registers. SPARC uses load/store sequences to move operands between register sets.

This architectural difference also explains why SPARC has more integer loads and stores (Rows L1 and S1) than MIPS in the FP benchmarks. The number of loads and stores SPARC executes to move values between integer and FP registers via memory are shown in Rows L5 and S5. We will discuss this more in Section 5.6.

Rows L2, L3, S2, and S3 illustrate the following architectural difference between MIPS and SPARC:

  • MIPS only has single-precision FP loads and stores. SPARC has single-precision and double-precision FP loads and stores.

Lack of double-precision loads and stores for MIPS has the most dominant architectural affect on the SPEC FP benchmarks. Due to this architectural difference, MIPS has many more single-precision loads (Row L3) and stores (Row S3) than SPARC.

In order to remove this architectural difference from our final comparison (the **Total +** ~ line), we estimate how many single-precision load (store) instructions executed by MIPS might be replaced by double-precision load (store) instructions if MIPS had such instructions. These numbers are shown in Rows L2 and S2. Since *doduc* is the only benchmark in which MIPS' number on Row L2 (191 million) is smaller than half of the value on Row L3 (423 million), it would be the only benchmark in which MIPS needed to execute any significant number of single-precision loads ($423 - 2 \times 191 = 41$ million) if MIPS had a double-precision load instruction. Similarly, if MIPS had a double-precision store instruction, *spice2g6* would be the only benchmark in which MIPS needed to execute any significant number of single-precision stores ($786 - 2 \times 389 = 8$ million).

It is also possible to estimate the number of single-precision loads (stores) SPARC would execute if it did not have double-precision loads (stores) by multiplying SPARC's Row L2 (S2) by two and adding it to Row L3 (S3). This shows that even if SPARC did not have double-precision FP load and store, it would still have about the same number of single-precision loads and stores as MIPS in most SPEC FP benchmarks. This is unexpected. After the adjustments, one might expect SPARC would have many more single-precision FP loads and stores because it uses loads and stores to move values between integer and FP registers via memory (see discussion of Rows L5 and S5 above). The explanation is that the SPARC compiler is doing a better job of reducing FP loads and stores than the MIPS compiler.

Rows L6 and S6 illustrate the following architectural difference between MIPS and SPARC:

- MIPS loads and stores have one addressing mode: register +immediate. SPARC loads and stores have two addressing modes: register+immediate and register+register.

Using the numbers on Row L6 (S6) and the Ld (St) Subtotal line, we find that in *gcc1.35*, 33/214 = 15% of the loads and 24/94 = 25% of the stores use two non-R0 registers to form their effective address. In *espresso*, the numbers are 23% for load and 23% for store. Finally, in *spice2g6*, the numbers are 6% for load and 13% for store. This turns out to be a significant architectural advantage for SPARC, since it saves an add instruction for these loads and stores.

Control Transfer Usage

Overall, the total number of control transfer instructions executed by SPARC and MIPS in the SPEC benchmarks are about the same (M/S=0.98).

Row C1 shows that MIPS executes fewer integer conditional branches than SPARC in FP benchmarks *spice2g6*, *doduc*, and *tomcatv* and integer benchmarks in *gcc1.35* and *espresso*. Most of these differences are due to the effect of library routines.

Table 32.3 lists those SPEC benchmarks that require MIPS and SPARC to execute a significant number of conditional

Benchmark	MIPS	SPARC	M/S
013.spice2g6	78.42	357.00	0.22
015.doduc	11.91	18.63	0.64
020.nasa7	20.09	55.68	0.36
042.fpppp	3.46	4.54	0.76
001.gcc1.35	16.24	43.35	0.37
008.espresso	11.36	98.28	0.12
023.eqntott	5.47	4.15	1.32

TABLE 32.3. *Cond. branches executed in library routines.*

branches in library routines. The numbers in Table 32.3 are in millions. Once we subtract the conditional branch instructions shown in Table 32.3 from Tables A1 and A2, the number of conditional branches executed by MIPS and SPARC outside of library routines turn out to be approximately the same for all benchmarks, except *nasa7* (M/S now becomes 262/165 = 1.58) and *tomcatv* (M/S = 21.45/24.73 = 0.87).

Row C2 shows that MIPS executes fewer unconditional branches than SPARC in most benchmarks (overall M/S = 0.71). Unlike conditional branches, this difference is not caused by library routines. This, however, should have very little impact on performance because unconditional branches are infrequent operations.

Row C3 shows SPARC executes considerably fewer FP branches than MIPS in *spice2g6*, *doduc*, and *nasa7*. Our data show that these differences are due to the differences in library routines. All the M/S ratios on this row approach one if we subtract all the FP branches executed in library routines from Table A1.

Rows C4 and C5 show that MIPS executes many more calls and returns than SPARC in *doduc*, *matrix300*, and *li*. The difference in *doduc* is due to library routines in which MIPS executes 6.25 million calls in its library routines, while SPARC only executes one million. The differences in *matrix300* and *li* are due to compiler differences. In *matrix 300*, the SPARC compiler expands the procedure saxpy in-line, while the MIPS compiler generates calls to it. Similarly in *li*, the SPARC compiler expands the procedure livecar in-line while the MIPS compiler does not.

Differences between call and return instruction counts for SPARC (e.g. *li*) are due to a compiler optimization.

Nop Usage

MIPS executes many more nops than SPARC (M/S = 23.7). Overall, 4.2% of the instructions executed by MIPS were nops, while only 0.1% of SPARC instructions were nops. This difference in nop usage, however, does not always imply a performance difference. SPARC sometimes has to pay a price similar to executing a nop (for example, a one-cycle pipeline interlock) at the place where MIPS executes a nop. This difference in nop usage is due to different architectural trade-offs between MIPS and SPARC.

One major architectural difference between MIPS and SPARC that causes MIPS to execute many more nops is:

- MIPS requires an intervening instruction between a load and the use of the data from that load to prevent load-use data conflict. SPARC allows a load to be immediately followed by an instruction using that data. If necessary, the hardware will cause a delay automatically.

Row N1 shows the number of nops following integer loads for MIPS and the number of integer load-use pipeline interlock counts for SPARC. They are placed on the same row here because load nop and load-use interlock are two ways to solve the same problem: load-use data conflict. A load nop is cheaper in hardware but it increases the static code size and, therefore, decreases cache performance. It can also be slightly more expensive in performance, because fetching the nop may cause a miss in the instruction cache and require more than a cycle.

In general, MIPS and SPARC do not execute the same number of integer loads. Therefore, instead of making a direct comparison between MIPS' integer load nop counts and SPARC's integer load-use interlock counts, we calculate the percentage of integer loads followed by nop for MIPS and the percentage of integer loads followed by load-use interlock for SPARC.

Table 32.4 shows that the MIPS compiler schedules an independent instruction (an instruction that does not use the data being

Benchmark	MIPS	SPARC	M/S
013.spice2g6	72.1%	69.2%	1.04
015.doduc	13.3%	36.8%	0.36
020.nasa7	1.3%	44.4%	0.03
030.matrix300	12.5%	25.0%	0.50
042.fpppp	17.7%	51.7%	0.34
047.tomcatv	0.6%	10.0%	0.06
FP G. Mean:	7.48%	33.7%	0.22
001.gcc1.35	32.2%	55.1%	0.58
008.espresso	27.6%	43.2%	0.64
022.li	48.0%	76.3%	0.63
023.eqntott	6.3%	7.1%	0.89
Integer G. Mean:	22.8%	33.7%	0.68
Overall B. Mean:	11.7%	33.7%	0.35

TABLE 32.4. *Integer load followed by nop or interlock.*

loaded) after a load more often than the SPARC compiler does in all benchmarks except *spice2g6*. One example in which the MIPS compiler does an excellent job in preventing load-use conflict is *tomcatv,* in which only 0.6% of its integer loads are followed by a nop. On average, MIPS needs to place a nop after an integer load only 7.4% of the time for the FP benchmarks and 22.7% of the time for the integer benchmarks. On average, SPARC has a load-use conflict 33.7% of the time after an integer load.

Row N2 shows MIPS' FP load nop count and SPARC's potential FP load-use interlocks. The latter are shown for reference only. One should not make a direct comparison between MIPS' and SPARC's numbers on this row, because in SPARC, implementations that have a float-point queue, SPARC's potential FP load-use interlocks may not cause any extra cycles (depending on the state of the queue). Since potential FP load-use interlocks do not always cause SPARC extra cycles, current SPARC compilers do not attempt to schedule an independent instruction in the FP load-use delay slot.

Another architectural difference between MIPS and SPARC that causes MIPS to execute many more nops is:

• MIPS branches require an instruction to be executed in the delay slot. SPARC has annulling branches that can cancel the execution of the delay slot instruction, depending on whether the branch is taken.

Row N3 shows the number of times MIPS and SPARC executed a nop instruction in a branch delay slot. Row N4 shows the number of times that SPARC annulled an instruction in a branch delay slot. Annulled instructions are added to the **Total +** counts because they have the same performance effects as a MIPS nop in most SPARC implementations.

The potential advantage of the annulling branch is that it provides conditional execution of the delay slot instruction. This makes it easier for the compiler to fill the delay slot, because it can use an instruction from the target basic block. This potential advantage, however, is realized only if the delay instruction following an annulling branch is executed.

For *li* and *eqntott*, in which MIPS and SPARC execute about the same (and large) number of conditional branches, one can get an idea of how often this potential advantage is realized. This can be done by calculating SPARC's number of effective branch nops (Row N3 + Row N4) and then comparing it with MIPS' branch nops (Row N3). For example, in *li*, SPARC has 38 + 299 = 337 million effective branch nops, which is (534 − 337)/534 = 37% less than MIPS' number of branch nops. In *eqntott*, SPARC has 0.677 + 122 = 123 million effective branch nops, which is (165 − 123)/165 = 25% less than MIPS' number of branch nops.

We conclude that SPARC executes fewer nops than MIPS because it has annulling branches and it uses load-use interlocks instead of load nops. Furthermore, the annulling branches provide SPARC with the architectural advantage of conditional execution of the delay instruction.

Integer ALU Operations Usage

Overall, SPARC executes more integer ALU instructions in both SPEC integer benchmarks (M/S = 0.77) and SPEC FP benchmarks (M/S = 0.85). In general, MIPS executes more integer arithmetic instructions than SPARC, while SPARC executes more logical instructions than MIPS.

Rows I1 and I2 show the number of integer arithmetic and logical instructions executed by MIPS and SPARC. For SPARC, they do not include any operations that set condition codes. Operations that set condition codes are counted as compares in Rows I6 and I7.

We can think of two reasons why the numbers on Row I1 show that MIPS needs to execute more integer arithmetic instruction than SPARC. First, those SPARC arithmetic operations that set the condition codes as a side effect are grouped into impure integer compare (Row I7). Second, MIPS' load and store do not have the register + register addressing mode (Rows L6 and S6). This may require MIPS to do an extra add before a load or store in certain cases.

Row I3 shows the number of shift instructions executed by MIPS and SPARC. MIPS needs to execute many more shifts in *doduc, nasa7,* and *matrix300*. This is especially true for *matrix300* in which MIPS executes 400 million more shifts than SPARC. MIPS uses most of these shifts to perform multiplication by eight in *matrix300*.

The frequencies of SPARC's sethi and MIPS' lui are shown in Row I4 and I5. In general, SPARC has more sethis than MIPS has luis. This difference is caused by the following compiler difference:

- The MIPS compiler clusters smaller pieces of data so they may be addressed as offsets from a preinitialized base register (global pointer). The current SPARC compiler does not do this and needs to form a full 32-bit address using sethi.

MIPS' 16-bit immediate field is more useful for this optimization.

Rows I6 and I7 illustrate the following architectural difference between MIPS and SPARC:

- MIPS can often perform compare-and-branch in one instruction. SPARC must use one instruction to set condition codes and another instruction to branch.

The extra ALU instruction SPARC executes in order to set the condition codes is counted as a pure integer compare (Row I6) if it does not modify a register; otherwise, it is counted as an impure integer compare (Row I7).

Since SPARC does not have a compare-and-branch instruction, it is not surprising to see that SPARC has many more pure (Row I6) and impure integer compares (Row I7) than MIPS. It is interesting to note that SPARC has a large number of impure integer compares (Row I7) in all FP benchmrks. As a matter of fact, in *nasa7*, *matrix300*, and *tomcatv*, SPARC executes many more impure integer compares than pure integer compares. The condition code can be set as a side effect in most cases for these benchmarks as an induction variable update.

Rows I6 and I8 together show that in the best case, *spice2g6*, SPARC could eliminate up to 1315/1728 = 76% of its pure compares if it could perform compare-and-branch in one instruction. In the worst case, *matrix300*, most of the pure compares cannot be eliminated. Most SPEC benchmarks show that about 30% of their pure compares could be eliminated.

Tables 32.5 and 32.6 illustrate the following architectural difference between MIPS and SPARC:

- MIPS has integer multiply and divide/remainder instructions. SPARC does not.

The instruction counts in Tables 32.5 and 32.6 are in millions. Although MIPS has multiply and divide/remainder instructions, these instructions are seldom used in the SPEC benchmarks. For example, MIPS' highest integer multiply usage is only 0.21% in *matrix 300*, and its highest integer divide/remainder usage is only 0.02% in *gcc1.35* and *doduc*. The performance impact on SPARC due to the lack of these instructions is small. In the worst case, only 1.47% of the total instructions in *spice2g6* are executed in the multiply routine, and only 2.20% of the total instructions in *gcc1.35* are executed in the divide/remainder routine. Another interesting observation is the relatively small number of instructions SPARC needs to execute per call to the multiply routine. It never needs more than 25 instructions per call and, on average, only needs 20 instructions to perform a 32-bit multiply. This shows software multiply is an acceptable solution because the multiply instruction

Benchmark	MIPS		SPARC			
	#instr	%Total	#instr	%Total	#call	i/c
gcc1.35	0.521	0.05%	11.134	0.96%	0.620	18.0
espresso	0.364	0.01%	6.853	0.23%	0.364	18.8
spice2g6	19.063	0.09%	336.189	1.47%	19.060	17.6
doduc	0.000	0.00%	0.004	0.00%	0.000	19.0
nasa7	8.182	0.09%	36.592	0.55%	1.484	24.7
li	0.000	0.00%	0.000	0.00%	0.000	24.9
eqntott	0.014	0.00%	0.237	0.02%	0.014	17.2
matrix300	5.771	0.21%	0.000	0.00%	0.000	19.6
fpppp	0.608	0.03%	11.261	0.78%	0.518	21.8
tomcatv	0.002	0.00%	0.020	0.00%	0.001	18.2
G.mean						19.8

TABLE 32.5. *Multiply statistics.*

Benchmark	MIPS		SPARC			
	#instr	%Total	#instr	%Total	#call	i/c
gcc1.35	0.246	0.02%	25.465	2.20%	0.457	55.7
espresso	0.020	0.00%	0.809	0.03%	0.014	59.3
spice2g6	0.365	0.00%	28.614	0.13%	0.390	73.3
doduc	0.357	0.02%	2.784	0.21%	0.214	13.0
nasa7	0.080	0.00%	0.377	0.01%	0.014	26.4
li	0.000	0.00%	0.177	0.00%	0.013	13.6
eqntott	0.013	0.00%	0.753	0.06%	0.013	56.8
matrix300	0.000	0.00%	0.006	0.00%	0.000	35.8
fpppp	0.009	0.00%	0.410	0.03%	0.009	43.6
tomcatv	0.003	0.00%	0.042	0.00%	0.002	27.3
G.mean						35.0

TABLE 32.6. *Divide/remainder statistics.*

typically takes multiple cycles even if it is implemented in hardware.

Floating Point Operations Usage

In general, neither SPARC nor MIPS executes a significant number of single-precision FP operations in the SPEC FP benchmarks. Furthermore, only about 5% of the instructions executed in *spice2g6* are FP operations, although it is classified as an FP benchmark. The FP subtotal shows that overall, MIPS executes slightly more FP operations than SPARC in *spice2g6*, *douc* and *nasa7*. The biggest difference is found in *doduc*, in which MIPS executes 28% more FP operations.

One interesting observation is that MIPS executes many more other double-precision arithmetic operations than SPARC (Row F5). SPARC executes many more single-precision arithmetic operations than MIPS (Row F6). The reason is that SPARC can take the absolute value or negate the value of a double-precision register pair using a "single-precision" operation (fabss or fnegs, which are counted in Row F6). MIPS, on the other hand, accomplishes the same function using a double-precision operation (abs.d or neg.d, which are counted in Row F5). Since the single- and double-precision versions of these operations probably take the same number of cycles, this architectural difference should not affect the overall performance.

Row F8 illustrates the following architectural difference between MIPS and SPARC:

- MIPS has an instruction to move values between single-precision FP registers and an instruction to move values between double-precision FP registers. SPARC only has the former.

The MIPS numbers on Row F8 are actual instruction counts. The SPARC numbers here are our estimates of how many pairs of FP single-precision moves (fmovs, Row F9) could be replaced by a hypothetical FP double-precision move (fmovd) instruction if one were available. The SPARC numbers on Row F8 show that a significant number of fmovs pairs can be replaced by the hypothetical fmovd in all FP benchmarks execpt *tomcatv*. In *tomcatv*, all the fmovss (6.5 million, 0.4% of total) that cannot be replaced by the hypothetical fmovd are the fmovs half of a fmovs/fnegs pair. These could all be replaced by a double-precision negate (fnegd) if SPARC had such an instruction, but the overall effect is small.

Rows F10 and F11 illustrate the following architectural difference between MIPS and SPARC:

> • MIPS has instructions to move values between integer and FP registers. SPARC uses integer and FP load/store sequences to move operands between register sets.

The MIPS numbers on Rows F10 and F11 are actual instruction counts. The SPARC numbers are our estimate of how often SPARC could use the hypothetical int->fp and fp->int move instructions were available. The numbers on Rows F10 and F11, together with numbers on Rows L5 and S5, show that SPARC could reduce the dynamic instruction count in all but one SPEC FP benchmark (*matrix300* is the exception) if int->fp and fp->int move instructions were available.

For example, the number of loads and stores in *nasa7* can be reduced by 38.1 + 35.2 = 73.3 million (sum of Rows L5 and S5) while only increasing the number of FP operations by 24.39 + 13.73 = 38.12 million (sum of Rows F10 and F11), which is a net reduction of 73.3 − 38.12 = 35.2 million instructions (0.53% reduction of **Total**).

Row F10 also shows that MIPS requires fewer int->fp move instructions than SPARC (the geometric mean on this row is misleading due to *matrix300*'s large M/S). This is because of the following compiler difference:

> • The SPARC compiler passes FP parameters in integer registers, while the MIPS compiler passes them in FP registers.

The SPARC compiler designers chose this strategy to support C's ability to sequence through a variable-length list of variable type parameters (varargs or stdarg). SPARC compilers accomplish this by placing both the integer and FP parameters in integer registers, copying these integer registers onto the stack, and then using a pointer to sequence through the parameter list on the stack. Once this mechanism was selected for C, it was adopted for

FORTRAN so that one could easily link procedures written in different languages (such as libraries). This mechanism will not work if some of the parameters are passed in the FP registers, because then it is not clear where to place the FP and integer registers on the stack.

Table 32.7 illustrates the following architectural difference between MIPS and SPARC:

- MIPS does not have FP square-root instructions. SPARC does.

The instruction counts in Table 32.7 are in millions. Notice that although SPARC seldom uses its FP square-root instruction in the SPEC benchmarks, the instruction count impact on MIPS due to the lack of this instruction is 2% in *doduc, nasa7*, and *fppp*. The reason is that MIPS, on average, takes about 62 instructions per call (i/c) to perform the square-root operation.

Benchmark	SPARC		MIPS			
	#instr	%Total	#instr	%Total	#call	i/c
spice2g6	1.132	0.01%	70.209	0.31%	1.132	62.0
doduc	0.507	0.03%	31.504	2.42%	0.508	62.0
nasa7	2.060	0.02%	127.732	1.93%	2.060	62.0
fpppp	0.378	0.02%	23.354	1.62%	0.378	61.8
G.mean						62.0

TABLE 32.7. *FP square-root statistics.*

Final Data Summary

The ordinary instruction total (**Total**) in Table A2 shows that, on average, MIPS executes 18% more user-level instructions in the SPEC benchmarks. If libraries are factored out, the difference is 22%. This total, however, only includes user-level instructions and not events such as SPARC's register window overflow/underflow. In order to take these events into account, the adjusted total (**Total+**) is also given. This adjusted total for SPARC includes all instructions associated with register window handling, annulled instructions, and a one instruction penalty for load-use interlocks. The adjusted total shows that, on average, MIPS still needs to execute 9% more instructions (or instruction-equivalents) in the SPEC benchmarks. This reduction (18% to 9%) is mainly due to load-use interlocks.

In order to factor out all architectural differences from the instruction count, we calculate a hypothetical architecture-neutral number (**Total + ~**) by adding hypothetical instructions to each architecture. Since this hypothetical architecture-neutral number (**Total + ~**) matched to within 3%, we conclude that although MIPS and SPARC each have strengths and weaknesses in their compliers and library routines, the combined effect of compilers and library routines does not give either MIPS or SPARC a clear advantage in these areas.

Architecture Summary

It appears that architectural differences have the biggest effect on instruction utilization. The following architectural differences are significant contributors (all percentages quoted are the geometric mean of the ratios across the stated benchmarks):

- MIPS only has single-precision FP loads and stores. If MIPS had double-precision loads and stores, it could reduce its instruction count by 19% in the SPEC FP benchmarks.

- MIPS can often perform compare-and-branch in one instruction. If SPARC could perform compare-and-branch in one instruction, it could reduce its instruction count by 6% in the SPEC integer benchmarks. Reductions in the SPEC FP benchmarks are small except in *spice2g6*, which shows a 6% improvement.

- MIPS requires an intervening instruction between a load and the use of the data from that load to prevent load-use data conflict. IF MIPS had load-use hardware interlocks, it could eliminate all its load nops and reduce its instruction count by 4% in the SPEC integer benchmarks. Reductions in the SPEC FP benchmarks are small except in *spice2g6*, which shows an 11% improvement.

- MIPS does not have annulling branches that can cancel the execution of the delay slot instruction. This feature reduces the branch nops SPARC executes in the integer benchmarks to less than 0.3% of instructions. By comparison, 8% of the instructions MIPS executes in the integer benchmarks are branch nops.

- MIPS has instructions to move values between integer and FP registers. If SPARC had similar instructions, it could reduce its instruction count by 1% in the SPEC FP benchmarks (excluding *matrix300*, which would show no improvement).

- MIPS loads and stores have one addressing mode: register + immediate. SPARC's extra addressing mode, register + register, enables it to execute fewer instructions. This reduces SPARC's instruction count by 6% in *espresso* and 5% in *gcc1.35*.

Compiler Summary

The compiler differences do not appear to affect instruction set utilization as much as the architectural differences do. It is also hard to estimate quantitatively how many instructions can be eliminated by changing the compiler strategy. Nevertheless, the following compiler differences were seen to affect instruction set utilization:

- The MIPS compiler clusters smaller pieces of data so they may be addressed as offsets from a preinitialized base register (global pointer). The current SPARC compiler does not do this and needs to form a full 32-bit address using sethi.

- At the optimization level specified in the SPEC Makefiles, the MIPS compiler does not expand procedure calls in-line, while the SPARC compiler does.

- The SPARC compiler passes FP parameters in integer registers, while the MIPS compiler passes them in FP registers.

- The MIPS compiler schedules an independent instruction after the load to prevent load-use data conflict more often than the SPARC compiler does.

Library Summary

In all but three SPEC benchmarks (*li, matrix 300,* and *tom-catv*), both MIPS and SPARC execute more than 3% of instructions in library routines. On average, only 5% of the instructions executed by MIPS and 9% of the instructions executed by SPARC are in library routines. In general, SPARC executes more instructions in library routines than MIPS. We observed three reasons for this difference:

- SPARC needs to execute more instructions in the routines malloc and free because these routines in SPARC are designed to allocate space efficiently at the expense of speed.
- MIPS sometimes uses the more efficient routines, memset, mcopy, memcopy, shere SPARC uses routines bzero and bcopy.
- SPARC has to call library routines to perform multiply, divide, and remainder.

Conclusion

We have measured and analyzed the instruction set utilization of the SPEC benchmarks on MIPS and SPARC. MIPS typically executes 18% more user-level instructions than SPARC. A fairer comparison, which takes into account register window overhead, load-use interlocks, and annulled instructions, still shows a 9% advantage for SPARC. The most significant architectural differences are that SPARC's double-precision floating-point load/store is an advantage in the SPEC floating-point benchmarks, while MIPS's compare-and-branch instruction is an advantage in the SPEC integer benchmarks. SPARC executes about 4% more instructions in library routines, mainly due to emphasis (in malloc and free) on saving space, rather than execution speed. When architectural issues were factored out, the differences due to combined compiler/ library effects were so small (3%) that neither MIPS nor SPARC has any significant advantage.

Performing this study in a completely implementation-independent fashion proved quite difficult. Many implementation issues, particularly how to treat load-use interlocks, can have a significant outcome on the final results. Rather than provide particular conclusions on all these issues, we have commented on the most significant and tried to provide sufficient raw data to allow future implementation techniques to be judged against the pure instruction frequency data.

Future implementations of each architecture are likely to incorporate instruction extensions. Though we provided data on the effect of new instructions, the large installed base of current machines and software is likely to limit the ability to take advantage of new instructions for many years to come. Therefore, we feel that the characteristics of the first generation instruction sets for MIPS and SPARC as presented in this paper will remain significant through several processor implementations. The biggest practical changes to instruction utilization are likely to come from new compiler optimizations or tuning of library routines.

Acknowledgments

We would like to thank Marianne Mueller for preparing many versions of both the MIPS and SPARC benchmark binaries for us. Dave Patterson provided us with valuable architectural insights. George Taylor's careful scrutiny of the numbers from an alternate perspective proved invaluable. Malcolm Wing provided us with interesting compiler insights. Kaivalya Dixit, Dave Weaver, and Susan Hathaway gave us critical comments to improve this paper.

References

1. Gerry Kane, *MIPS R2000 RISC Architecture*, Prentice Hall, Englewood Cliffs, NJ, 1987.

2. "The SPARC Architecture Manual, Version 7," Part No: 800-1399-08, Sun Microsystems, Inc., Mountain View, California, 1987.

3. *The SPEC Benchmark Report*, c/o Waterside Associates, Fremont, California, January, 1990.

4. Gene McDaniel, "An Analysis of a Mesa Instruction Set Using Dynamic Instruction Frequencies," *ASPLOS Proceedings, published as SIGARCH Computer Architecture News*, vol. 10, no. 2, pp. 167–176, Palo Alto, California, March 1982.

5. Cheryl A. Wiecek, "A Case Study of VAX-11 Instruction Set Usage For Compiler Execution," *ASPLOS Proceedings, published as SIGARCH Computer Architecture News*, vol. 10, no. 2, pp. 177–184, Palo Alto, California, March 1982.

6. L.J. Shustek, *Analysis and Performance of Instruction Sets*, Doctoral Dissertation, Stanford Linear Accelerator Center, Stanford University, Stanford, California, May, 1978.

7. A. Lunde, "Empirical Evaluation of Some Features of Instruction Set Processor Architectures," *Communication of the ACM*, vol. 20, no. 3, pp. 143–153, March, 1977.

8. *UMIPS-V Reference Manual* (pixie and pixstats), MIPS Computer Systems, Sunnyvale, California, 1990.

9. R.F. Cmelik, *Introduction to SpixTools*, Sun Microsystems Technical Memorandum, July, 1989.

10. P. Hsu, *Introduction to SHADOW*, Sun Microsystems Technical Memorandum, July 1989.

11. David A. Patterson and John L. Hennessy, *Computer Architecture: A Quantitative Approach*, Morgan Kaufmann Publishers Inc., 1990.

12. Douglas W. Clark and Henry M. Levy, "Measurement and Analysis of Instruction Use in the VAX-11/780," *Proceedings of the 9th Annual Symposium on Computer Architecture*, pp. 9–17, April, 1982.

TABLE A1. *Floating-point benchmarks (top).*

	013.spice2g6			015.doduc			020.nasa7		
	MIPS	SPARC	M/S	MIPS	SPARC	M/S	MIPS	SPARC	M/S
L1. int load	3365	3762	0.89	27.62	54.12	0.51	15.95	199	0.08
L2. fp dp load	−969~	985	0.98	−191~	171	1.11	−1698~	1680	1.01
L3. fp sp load	1938	52.98	36.6	423	73.32	5.77	3395	.2021	
L4. fun int reg load	5.81<	.0076+	759.	4.15<	.0005+	8105	1.04<	.0006+	1688
L5. int<−>fp load	—	−140~		—	−32.6~		—	−38.1~	
L6. load r1+r2	—	294<		—	20.26<		—	95.96<	
Ld Subtotal	5303	4800	**1.10**	450	299	**1.51**	3411	1879	**1.81**
	24.58%	20.98%		27.92%	22.93%		36.85%	28.41%	
S1. int store	306	594	0.52	13.91	34.97	0.40	8.49	136	0.06
S2. fp dp store	−389~	297	1.31	−64.6~	40.60	1.59	−632~	597	1.06
S3. fp sp store	786	24.07	32.7	130	8.80	14.8	1302	4.22	308.
S4. fun int reg store	5.81<	.0076+	759.	4.15<	.0005+	7981	1.04<	.0006+	1688
S5. int<−>fp store	—	−82.0~		—	−22.7~		—	+35.2~	
S6. store r1+r2	—	118<		—	2.12<		—	41.43<	
St Subtotal	1091	915	**1.19**	144	84.37	**1.71**	1310	738	**1.78**
	5.06%	4.00%		8.95%	6.47%		14.15%	11.15%	
C1. cond int br	1832	2104	0.87	48.14	55.69	0.86	282	221	1.28
C2. uncond int br	243	788	0.31	11.23	5.13	2.19	.5916	2.67	0.22
C3. fp br	86.84	71.12	1.22	46.13	35.56	1.30	11.00	.5252	20.9
C4. call	49.20	67.81	0.73	12.77	7.11	1.80	10.86	12.04	0.90
C5. return	49.20	67.47	0.73	12.77	6.65	1.92	10.86	11.37	0.95
C6. other jump	3.74	3.37	1.00	.7607	.1737	4.38	.0009	.1028	0.01
Ctl Subtotal	2264	3102	**0.73**	132	110	**1.19**	315	248	**1.27**
	10.50%	13.56%		8.17%	8.47%		3.41%	3.74%	
N1. int load nop	2427	2602+	0.93	3.68	19.90+	0.18	.2058	88.34+	0.00
N2. fp load nop	159	645<	0.25	26.24	110<	0.24	118	732<	0.16
N3. br nop	466	31.06	15.0	26.90	.7486	35.9	4.69	4.12	1.14
N4. annulled	—	1036+		—	11.50+		—	15.88+	
N5. call/jump nop	13.45	4.14	3.25	5.02	.4329	11.6	3.78	.2074	18.2
N6. fp cmp nop	61.12	69.79	0.88	38.43	32.51	1.18	1.33	.5232	2.54
N7. other nop	28.05	.0035	7992	16.94	.3619	46.8	11.14	.0062	1783
Nop Subtotal	3155	105	**30.1**	117	34.05	**3.44**	139	4.86	**28.6**
	14.63%	0.46%		7.27%	2.61%		1.50%	0.07%	
I1. int arith	4655	6432	0.72	212	124	1.72	1419	1133	1.25
I2. logical	28.97	462	0.06	9.73	85.68	0.11	24.20	112	0.22
I3. shift	3763	3089	1.22	53.53	24.43	2.19	282	25.42	11.1
I4. lui/sethi addr	49.33	589	0.08	39.05	121	0.32	15.55	29.92	0.52
I5. lui/sethi data	3.99	64.59	0.06	3.91	12.80	0.31	7.47	86.63	0.09
I6. pure int cmp	114	1728	0.07	6.77	30.55	0.22	1.50	56.03	0.03
I7. impure int cmp	.0097	496	0.00	.0009	26.57	0.00	.0018	202	0.00
I8. cmpbr cmp	—	−1315~		—	−6.04~		—	−1.11~	
Int Subtotal	8614	12860	**0.67**	325	425	**0.76**	1749	1646	**1.06**
	39.94%	56.21%		20.15%	32.06%		18.90%	24.88%	
F1. dp add/sub	429	392	1.09	120	108	1.11	1061	1033	1.03
F2. dp mul	313	289	1.08	127	120	1.07	1021	1016	1.00
F3. dp div	83.52	83.98	0.99	25.93	24.34	1.07	27.43	19.03	1.44
F4. dp cmp	87.83	71.12	1.23	19.01	11.87	1.60	11.02	.5252	21.0
F5. other dp arith	63.47	1.13	56.0	5.30	.5066	10.5	5.23	2.06	2.54
F6. sp arith	0	68.33	0.00	62.19	40.09	1.55	0	3.79	0.00
F7. cvt	18.59	5.06	3.67	22.08	19.35	1.14	7.63	.0507	150.
F8. dp fp->fp	16.09	−24.0~	0.67	15.20	−4.82~	3.15	103	−.508~	201.
F9. sp fp->fp	0	55.94	0.00	1.68	13.97	0.12	0	1.02	0.00

| 030.matrix300 | | | 042.fpppp | | | 047.tomcatv | | | FP |
MIPS	SPARC	M/S	MIPS	SPARC	M/S	MIPS	SPARC	M/S	M/S
5.82	2.93	1.98	20.38	47.02	0.43	13.47	131	0.10	0.38
−433~	433	1.00	−552~	538	1.03	−325~	351	0.93	1.01
865	.0000		1104	4.48	246.	651	.0029		4143
.0049<	.0001+	47.0	.1659<	.0003+	609.	.0467<	.0017+	27.8	450.
—	−.000~		—	−84.1~		—	−52.5~		
—	.0007<		—	5.94<		—	.0144<		
871	436	**2.00**	1124	590	**1.91**	664	482	**1.38**	**1.59**
31.39%	**25.72%**		**48.53%**	**40.87%**		**36.64%**	**29.65%**		
2.20	.0313	70.1	8.91	30.14	0.30	13.44	111	0.12	0.56
−217~	217	1.00	−149~	97.83	1.52	−111~	78.11	1.42	1.30
434	.0000		297	1.42	209.	221	.0006		2818
.0049<	.0001+	40.8	.1659<	.0003+	592.	.0467<	.0017+	27.7	435.
—	−.000~		—	−23.6~		—	−32.6~		
—	.0032<		—	.4371<		—	.0034<		
436	217	**2.01**	306	129	**2.37**	235	189	**1.24**	**1.67**
15.72%	**12.82%**		**13.22%**	**8.97%**		**12.96%**	**11.62%**		
57.14	57.86	0.99	14.94	15.00	1.00	21.64	24.86	0.87	0.97
.0061	.0032	1.92	1.80	1.66	1.08	.0268	.1187	0.23	0.64
.0000	.0000	0.27	2.76	2.20	1.26	13.01	13.01	1.00	1.49
.7236	.0040	180.	1.14	1.04	1.10	.0307	.0200	1.53	2.67
.7236	.0040	182.	1.14	1.01	1.13	.0303	.0186	1.63	2.77
.0002	.0001	1.47	.5075	.5074	1.00	.0114	.0068	1.67	0.67
58.59	57.88	**1.01**	22.29	21.41	**1.04**	34.75	38.04	**0.91**	**1.01**
2.11%	**3.42%**		**0.96%**	**1.48%**		**1.92%**	**2.34%**		
.7274	.7335+	0.99	3.60	24.30+	0.15	.0856	13.15+	0.01	0.09
0	270<	0.00	182	280<	0.65	9.80	166<	0.06	0.20
.0130	.0052	2.50	3.35	.0008	4315	.0724	.0048	15.2	21.6
—	.7276+		—	4.28+		—	.1687+		
.0031	.0010	3.18	1.22	.5079	2.40	.0243	.0094	2.59	4.88
.0000	.0000	0.23	1.48	2.19	0.68	6.50	13.01	0.50	0.77
.0001	.0000	1.43	3.02	.0001		.0014	.0004	3.21	218.
.7436	.0062	**119.**	194	2.70	**72.1**	16.49	13.02	**1.27**	**17.8**
0.03%	**0.00%**		**8.39%**	**0.19%**		**0.91%**	**0.80%**		
525	492	1.07	29.66	26.12	1.14	292	312	0.94	1.10
.7273	.7616	0.95	5.59	20.42	0.27	.9612	6.85	0.14	0.20
446	.7526	592.	7.32	8.55	0.86	2.07	39.34	0.05	3.04
.0004	.0085	0.05	2.40	29.15	0.08	.0228	19.70	0.00	0.06
.0008	.0007	1.13	1.13	2.33	0.49	59.78	.0146	4095	1.24
.0015	1.51	0.00	2.86	11.30	0.25	.0547	.4595	0.12	0.05
.0001	56.38	0.00	.0728	8.33	0.01	.0042	24.42	0.00	0.00
—	−.004~		—	−3.36~		—	−.035~		
971	551	**1.76**	49.04	106	**0.46**	355	403	**0.88**	**0.85**
34.99%	**32.53%**		**2.12%**	**7.36%**		**19.59%**	**24.79%**		
216	216	1.00	274	267	1.03	247	247	1.00	1.04
216	216	1.00	309	304	1.02	195	195	1.00	1.03
.0000	.0000	5.00	2.84	1.48	1.91	6.53	6.50	1.00	1.56
.0000	.0000	0.27	2.76	2.20	1.26	13.01	13.01	1.00	1.55
.0000	0		4.79	.3776	12.7	32.51	0		11.7
0	.0000	0.00	0	5.65	0.00	0	32.51	0.00	1.55
.0000	.0000	0.91	2.69	1.31	2.06	.0003	.0005	0.56	2.95
0	−.000~	0.00	8.12	−4.57~	1.78	.0467	−.001~	72.4	8.87
0	.0000	0.00	0	10.28	0.00	0	6.50	0.00	0.12

TABLE A1. *(Continued)*

	013.spice2g6			015.doduc			020.nasa7		
	MIPS	**SPARC**	**M/S**	**MIPS**	**SPARC**	**M/S**	**MIPS**	**SPARC**	**M/S**
F10. int->fp	57.55	115~	0.50	19.37	23.73~	0.82	25.27	24.93~	1.04
F11. fp->int	22.36	24.76~	0.90	12.26	8.88~	1.38	27.39	13.73~	1.99
FP Subtotal	1091 **5.06%**	967 **4.23%**	**1.13**	430 **26.69%**	338 **25.90%**	**1.28**	2289 **24.73%**	2075 **31.37%**	**1.10**
O1. fun reg other	—	.0554+		—	.0037+		—	.0045+	
O2. other	50.49	129	0.39	13.92	13.20	1.05	42.86	24.05	1.78
O3. library	925<	1944<	0.48	310<	218<	1.42	614<	583<	1.05
Total	21569	22878	**0.94**	1613	1303	**1.24**	9257	6615	**1.40**
Total +	21569	26516	**0.81**	1613	1335	**1.21**	9257	6719	**1.38**
Total + ~	20211	25095	**0.81**	1358	1301	**1.04**	6927	6682	**1.04**

030.matrix300			042.fpppp			047.tomcatv			FP
MIPS	**SPARC**	**M/S**	**MIPS**	**SPARC**	**M/S**	**MIPS**	**SPARC**	**M/S**	**M/S**
.0048	.0000~	218.	3.48	81.83~	0.04	13.01	52.53~	0.25	1.00
.0000	.0000~	0.35	4.44	2.31~	1.92	.0008	.0016~	0.50	0.97
432	432	**1.00**	612	592	**1.04**	507	501	**1.01**	**1.09**
15.56%	25.51%		26.44%	40.99%		27.99%	30.79%		
—	.0008+		—	.0020+		—	.0122+		
5.77	.0069	837.	7.80	2.05	3.80	.0064	.0361	0.18	2.73
.0568<	.0664<	0.86	54.58<	38.66<	1.41	1.53<	.9373<	1.63	1.06
2776	1694	**1.64**	2316	1443	**1.61**	1813	1626	**1.11**	**1.30**
2776	1695	**1.64**	2316	1472	**1.57**	1813	1640	**1.11**	**1.25**
2126	1695	**1.25**	1616	1440	**1.12**	1377	1607	**0.86**	**1.01**

TABLE A2. *Integer benchmarks.*

	001.gcc1.35			008.espresso			022.li			023.eqntott			Int	All
	MIPS	SPARC	M/S	MIPS	SPARC	M/S	MIPS	SPARC	M/S	MIPS	SPARC	M/S	M/S	M/S
L1. int load	220	214	1.03	521	681	0.76	1322	1068	1.24	205	203	1.01	1.00	0.56
L4. fun int reg load	24.41<	.4607+	53.0	4.22<	.5857+	7.20	149<	32.62+	4.58	3.64<	.0047+	778.	34.1	160.
L6. load r1+r2	—	32.99<		—	155<		—	26.09<		—	.9977<			
Ld Subtotal	220 **19.83%**	214 **18.52%**	**1.03**	521 **18.42%**	681 **23.25%**	**0.76**	1322 **21.96%**	1068 **22.90%**	**1.24**	205 **16.46%**	203 **15.39%**	**1.01**	**1.00**	**1.32**
S1. int store	129	94.06	1.37	124	144	0.86	709	482	1.47	11.38	15.14	0.75	1.07	0.73
S4. fun int reg store	24.41<	.4608+	53.0	4.22<	.5858+	7.20	149<	44.44+	3.36	3.64<	.0047+	777.	31.6	152.
S6. store r1+r2	—	23.89<		—	32.93<		—	13.84<		—	.0183<			
St Subtotal	129 **11.58%**	94.06 **8.14%**	**1.37**	124 **4.38%**	144 **4.92%**	**0.86**	709 **11.78%**	482 **10.33%**	**1.47**	11.38 **0.91%**	15.14 **1.15%**	**0.75**	**1.07**	**1.40**
C1. cond int br	163	188	0.86	411	521	0.79	775	791	0.98	340	340	1.00	0.90	0.94
C2. uncond int br	14.62	16.53	0.88	12.01	40.95	0.29	112	111	1.01	3.07	1.66	1.85	0.83	0.71
C4. call	12.13	12.83	0.95	12.25	17.50	0.70	161	93.20	1.73	4.01	4.36	0.92	1.01	1.81
C5. return	12.13	12.23	0.99	12.25	17.27	0.71	160	90.18	1.77	4.01	4.36	0.92	1.04	1.87
C6. other jump	3.82	4.38	0.87	.0048	.1586	0.03	21.88	22.58	0.97	.3185	.3185	1.00	0.40	0.55
Ctl Subtotal	205 **18.50%**	234 **20.26%**	**0.88**	448 **15.83%**	597 **20.35%**	**0.75**	1230 **20.42%**	1108 **23.78%**	**1.11**	351 **28.23%**	350 **26.51%**	**1.00**	**0.93**	**0.98**
N1. int load nop	70.78	118+	0.60	144	294+	0.49	635	815+	0.78	12.91	14.33+	0.90	0.67	0.19
N3. br nop	65.97	6.06	10.9	192	6.46	29.8	534	37.79	14.1	165	.6776	2.44	32.5	25.4
N4. annulled	—	39.01+		—	167+		—	299+		—	122+			
N5. call/jump nop	11.34	5.74	1.98	4.28	2.50	1.71	148	26.77	5.52	2.56	.3244	7.88	3.48	4.27
N7. other nop	.1276	.0001	1387	.0261	0		.000	0		.0131	0		1387	283.
Nop Subtotal	148 **13.34%**	11.79 **1.02%**	**12.6**	341 **12.04%**	8.69 **0.31%**	**38.0**	1316 **21.86%**	64.56 **1.38%**	**20.4**	181 **14.54%**	1.00 **0.08%**	**180.**	**36.4**	**23.7**

I1. int arith	268	135	1.99	667	364	1.83	1146	3.87	402	260	1.54	2.16	1.44
I2. logical	21.71	95.11	0.23	330	282	1.17	134	0.44	2.37	135	0.02	0.21	0.20
I3. shift	69.70	56.07	1.24	254	195	1.30	39.21	1.04	2.04	2.29	0.89	1.10	2.03
I4. lui/sethi addr	10.46	88.90	0.12	2.27	106	0.02	21.88	0.07	1.29	12.20	0.11	0.06	0.06
I5. lui/sethi data	4.56	6.97	0.65	8.42	5.20	1.62	.7921	0.04	.0147	.6758	0.02	0.17	0.56
I6. pure int cmp	32.50	167	0.19	113	482	0.23	86.13	0.12	88.27	332	0.27	0.19	0.08
I7. impure int cmp	.7274	31.81	0.02	19.82	36.17	0.55	0	0.00	0	7.88	0.00	0.11	0.00
I8. cmpbr cmp	—	−54.6~		—	−109~		—		—	−86.6~			
Int Subtotal	407	580	**0.70**	1395	1472	**0.95**	1429	**0.80**	496	750	**0.66**	**0.77**	**0.82**
	36.66%	**50.20%**		**49.31%**	**50.21%**		**23.72%**	**38.42%**	**39.85%**	**56.77%**			
Fa.fp	.1221	.2592	0.47	.0174	.0140	1.24	16.10	11.4	0	0	1.00	1.61	1.00
Fb. fp~	−.012~	0~		−.003~	−.000~	15.6	−6.56~		0~	0~	1.00	3.95	1.00
O1. fun reg other	—	3.34+		—	4.25+		—		—	.0339+			
O2. other	.8645	21.34	0.04	.3852	28.09	0.01	.1515	0.00	.0273	1.51	0.02	0.01	0.29
O3. library	90.53<	214<	0.42	73.60<	447<	0.16	5.78<	2.00	47.09<	51.20<	0.92	0.60	0.84
Total	1111	1156	**0.96**	2829	2931	**0.97**	6023	**1.29**	1243	1322	**0.94**	**1.03**	**1.18**
Total +	1111	1317	**0.84**	2829	3397	**0.83**	6023	**0.98**	1243	1458	**0.85**	**0.88**	**1.09**
Total +~	1111	1262	**0.88**	2829	3288	**0.86**	6016	**1.07**	1243	1371	**0.91**	**0.93**	**0.97**

Appendix 3—Instruction Categories

Load Instructions

L1.   int load   integer (general purpose) register loads, all sizes, signed or unsigned.

L2.   fp dp load   64-bit FP register loads.

L3.   fp sp load   32-bit FP register loads.

L4.   fun int reg load   MIPS: loads to restore integer registers prior to function or procedure return. SPARC: 8 64-bit integer register loads per window underflow trap (see also S4 and O1).

L5.   int<->fp load   SPARC: integer and FP register loads that could have been replaced by int <->fp move instructions (see also S5, F10 and F11).

L6.   load r1 + r2   SPARC: all integer and FP loads which use the double register addressing mode (memory address is sum of contents of two registers).

Store Instructions

S1.   int store   like L1, but for stores.

S2.   fp dp store   like L2, but for stores.

S3.   fp sp store   like L3, but for stores.

S4.   fun int reg store   MIPS: stores to save integer (not FP) registers after entering a function or procedure. SPARC: 8 64-bit integer register stores per window overflow trap (see also L4 and O1).

S5.   int<->fp store   like L5, but for stores.

S6.   store r1 + r2   like L6, but for stores.

Control Transfer Instructions

C1.   cond int br   MIPS: compare-and-branch instructions, except C2. SPARC: branch on integer condition codes, except C2.

C2.   uncond int br   unconditional integer branches. MIPS: compare-and-branch instructions for which the comparison must result in a taken branch. SPARC: ba and ba, a.

C3.   fp br   all branches on FP condition code(s).

C4.   call   MIPS: jal and jalr with nonzero rd. SPARC: call, and jmpl with nonzero rd.

C5.   return   MIPS: jr $ra. SPARC: jmpl with %i7 or %o7 as rs1.

C6.   other jump   jump instructions excluded from C4 and C5.

Nop Instructions

N1.   int load nop   MIPS: nops preceded by an integer register load. SPARC: integer register loads where result is used in next instruction.

N2.   fp load nop   MIPS: nops preceded by an FP register load. SPARC: FP register loads where result is used in next instruction.

N3.   br nop   nops executed (SPARC: excludes N4) in branch delay slots.

N4.   annulled   SPARC: annulled instructions.

N5.   call/jump nop   nops executed in call and jump delay slots.

N6.   fp cmp nop   nops preceded by an FP register compare instruction.

N7.   other nop   all other nops.

ALU Instructions

I1.   int arith   integer add, subtract, multiply, and divide instructions.

I2.   logical   bitwise logical and, or, etc. instructions.

I3.   shift   logical and arithmetic, left and right shifts.

I4.   lui/sethi addr   lui (MIPS) and sethi (SPARC) instructions for which the upper bits of the result are in the range of the corresponding upper bits of the various data or bss segments.

I5.   lui/sethi data   lui (MIPS) and sethi (SPARC) instructions not counted in I4.

I6.   pure int cmp   MIPS: set-less-than instructions for which the result is only used in a compare-and-branch instruction. SPARC: instructions which set the integer condition codes but do not generate any other result (rd = 0).

I7.   impure int cmp   integer compare instructions excluded from I6.

I8.   cmpbr cmp   SPARC: pure integer compare instructions that could have been eliminated given MIPS' compare-and-branch instructions.

Floating Point Instructions

F1.   dp add/sub   double precision FP add and subtract.

F2.   dp mul   double precision FP multiply.

F3.   dp div   double precision FP divide.

F4.   dp cmp   double precision FP register compare.

F5.   other dp arith   double precision FP operations excluded in F1–F4.

F6.   sp arith   all single precision FP operations.

F7.   cvt   all to/from FP convert operations.

F8.   dp fp->fp   MIPS: double precision FP move. SPARC: number of single precision FP move instructions that could be replaced by a hypothetical double precision FP move.

F9.   sp fp->fp   single precision FP move.

F10.   int->fp   MIPS: all int->fp register move instructions. SPARC: number of hypothetical int->fp register move instructions that might have been used instead of loads (L5) and stores (S5).

F11.   fp->int   like F10, but other direction.

Fa.   fp   the sum of all plain FP counts from rows in Table A1 but not in Table A2.

Fb.   fp~   like Fa, except the sum of hypothetical counts.

Other Instructions

O1.	fun reg other	SPARC: 29 instructions per window overflow or underflow trap (see also L4 and S4).
O2.	other	user-mode instructions not counted elsewhere.
O3.	library	user-mode instructions executed in library routines.

Index